DATE DUE

CONSTITUTIONS
IN CRISIS

CONSTITUTIONS IN CRISIS

Political Violence and the Rule of Law

John E. Finn

New York   Oxford
OXFORD UNIVERSITY PRESS
1991

Oxford University Press

Oxford   New York   Toronto
Delhi   Bombay   Calcutta   Madras   Karachi
Petaling Jaya   Singapore   Hong Kong   Tokyo
Nairobi   Dar es Salaam   Cape Town
Melbourne   Auckland

and associated companies in
Berlin   Ibadan

Permission for reprinting previously published materials is hereby acknowledged:

Lines from "His Confidence" and "Sixteen Dead Men" are reprinted with permission of Macmillan Publishing
Company from *The Poems of W. B. Yeats: A New Edition*, edited by Richard J. Finneran. Copyright 1924, 1933
by Macmillan Publishing Company; renewed 1952, 1961 by Bertha Georgie Yeats.

Lines from "Those who will not reason" by W. H. Auden, from *W. H. Auden: Collected Poems*, edited by
Edward Mendelson. Copyright © 1976 by Edward Mendelson, William Meredith, and Monroe K. Spears.
Reprinted by permission of Random House, Inc.

Tables and figures in chapter 3 are reprinted with permission of Taylor and Francis from "Public Support for
Emergency (Anti-Terrorist) Legislation in Northern Ireland: A Preliminary Analysis," in *Terrorism*, vol. 10,
no. 2 (1987).

Table 3–5 in chapter 3 is reprinted with permission of Manchester University Press from *The Prevention of
Terrorism in British Law*, by Clive Walker (Manchester University Press, 1986).

Lines from "seven years and twenty later" by Heinrich Böll, from the *University of Dayton Review*, vol. 17, no. 2
(1985), are reprinted with permission of Robert C. Conrad, translator of the material and editor of the *University
of Dayton Review*.

Lines from the Civil Servant Loyalty Case, from Donald P. Kommers, *The Constitutional Jurisprudence of the
Federal Republic of Germany* (Duke University Press, 1989), are reprinted with permission of Donald P.
Kommers.

The SouthWest Case, 1 BVerfGE 14 (1951); Socialist Reich Party Case, 2 BVerfGE 1 (1952); Communist Party
Case, 5 BVerfGE 85 (1956); and Privacy of Communications Case (Klass Case), 30 BVerfGE 1 (1970), from
Walter F. Murphy and Joseph Tanenhaus, *Comparative Constitutional Law* (New York: St. Martin's Press,
1977). (Translated by Mrs. Renate Chestnut.)

Library of Congress Cataloging-in-Publication Data
Finn, John E.
Constitutions in crisis : political violence and the rule of law / John E. Finn.
p. cm.   Includes bibliographical references.
ISBN 0-19-505738-4
1. Terrorism.   2. Constitutional law.   3. Terrorism—Northern Ireland.
4. Northern Ireland—Constitutional law.   5. Terrorism—Germany.
6. Germany—Constitutional law.   I. Title.
K5256.F56   1991   342'.02—dc20   [342.22]   90-31794

2 4 6 8 9 7 5 3 1

Printed in the United States of America
on acid-free paper

In memory of my parents,
September 1947.

A secret between you two,
Between the proud and the proud.

Yeats, "Against Unworthy Praise"

Acknowledgments

During the course of this work many people offered advice and encouragement. But only my wife, Linda (and the pets, as she so properly insists), had to suffer daily my moods and distractions: "What payment were enough/For undying love?"

Others suffered only slightly less often and with no less grace. One of the many pleasurable consequences of their company is the chance now to acknowledge their assistance and to record my gratitude. My teachers at Princeton, Walter F. Murphy, Sotirios Barber, and Nancy Bermeo, read earlier drafts of the work with care and compassion. I might still be working on a dissertation proposal but for Walter's exhortations to be done and be gone. Sue Hemberger, Brian Mirsky, and David Aladjem also read individual chapters and offered good-natured criticism.

My colleagues at Wesleyan have done much to ease the transition from thesis to book. I want especially to thank Nancy Schwartz and Russell Murphy, both of whom read much of the manuscript. Barbara Craig, Martha Crenshaw, Tony Daley, Bruce Masters, Don Moon, and David Morgan also offered assistance in various ways. Margaret Miniter, of the Wesleyan Class of 1987, Carol Conerly, Class of 1988, and Bruce Peabody, Class of 1991, provided patient and helpful research assistance.

In addition, Donald Kommers of the University of Notre Dame, Gerard Braunthal of the University of Massachusetts, and Peter Euben of the University of California at Santa Cruz all read parts of the work and offered advice. John Fairleigh of the Queen's University Belfast provided assistance in locating certain materials.

Whatever errors remain are my responsibility alone. I would, however, much prefer a system of joint (and not several) liability.

Contents

Chapter 5
Constitutional Reconstruction, Militant
Democracy, and Antiterrorism Legislation in the
Federal Republic of Germany   179

CONSTITUTIONS
IN CRISIS

Those who will not reason
Perish in the act.
Those who will not act
Perish for that reason.

    Auden, "Those who will not reason"

Introduction

In Book Twelve of *The Odyssey*, Lady Kirkê draws Odysseus aside from the celebration of his success at the houses of death to warn of the trials that still await him on his long journey home.[1] The loveliest and most perilous of these are the Sêirenes, whose soulful melodies bewitch and entrance mere men. Anxious to hear their serenade and yet keep his mind, Odysseus, with Kirkê's assistance, devises a plan: His crew must lash him to the mast of his ship and plug up their ears with beeswax so as to hear neither the Sêirenes nor his cries to release him. Odysseus must then remain there, back to the mast, lashed to the mast, until the Sêirenes' song is faint in the distance.

Implicit in this one of Odysseus's many travails are questions of enduring significance for students of constitutional theory.[2] Odysseus's decision to be bound to the mast is an admission of weakness: He knows that when the Sêirenes sing he will not be fully rational, that he will not wish to be restrained. If we respect his earlier desire, later pleas to the contrary aside, do we do so because the original statement is now morally or legally binding, or because we doubt the rationality of the second?[3] And who should make such a decision? Surely not Odysseus, for he has admitted weakness in the face of temptation. He cannot now make the judgment that his earlier decision to be bound is more (or less) rational than his current wish to be released. And what of his crew? Their judgment cannot be fully rational either, for they do not hear the call of the Sêirenes and so cannot judge whether the temptation is worth the cost. Consider also that the crew acts under orders directed precisely to this situation. What are they to do if yet another calamity, this time unanticipated, arises while Odysseus is still bound? What should they do, for example, if a sudden and severe squall besets the ship while Odysseus is lashed to the mast?

Like Odysseus, we as individuals seek to manipulate future experience in our own lives. In all manners of fashion we lash ourselves to the mast, aware that in a moment of weakness we may later wish to be free of our self-imposed restraints. The commitments we make to loved ones, the favors we promise to friends, the contracts we make with business associates—all are bonds we may later wish to break. When are we compelled to honor these self-commands, and when, if ever, should an unforeseen contingency release us from them? Does it matter that we assumed such commitments precisely to guard against

3

temptation, or that they contain stipulations meant to influence and determine the conditions in which we voice subsequent desires?

Communities also agree to bind themselves, and constitutions are the (more or less) written evidence both of the binding and of the rules that bind.[4] But in our efforts to interpret these rules, to apply the majestic generalities of constitutional language to the vagaries of everyday political disputes, we occasionally lose sight of the vanity that gives rise to constitution *making* as a political activity. Constitutional self-commands embody our confidence in our ability to overcome human weakness and the whims of fate, a point Alexander Hamilton emphasized when he observed that "it seems to have been reserved to the people of this country . . . to decide the important question, whether societies of men are really capable or not of establishing good government from reflection and choice, or whether they are forever destined to depend for their political constitutions on accident and force."[5] In this respect constitutions, much like promises, are nothing less than attempts to fashion the future—to forge the institutional patterns and cultural folkways of political and social experience.[6] Indeed, carried to a logical extreme, an extreme fairly implied by Article VI, the ratification provisions of Article VII, and the limitations, both substantive and procedural, of Article V, the U.S. Constitution implies a complete and *perpetual* structuring of political reality.

Some readers may find this last claim quite unusual. It is true, of course, that the constitutional text makes no explicit claim to perpetuity. The reasons for its omission are unclear.[7] The framers were surely familiar with the concept of perpetual constitutions—the formal title of the Articles of Confederation was the "Articles of Confederation and Perpetual Union." And Article XIII of the Confederation likewise provided explicitly that the "Union shall be perpetual." Moreover, the language of perpetuity was commonplace at the founding. Noah Webster wrote disparagingly of his countrymen's efforts "to fix a form of government in perpetuity," arguing that "the very attempt to make *perpetual* constitutions, is the assumption of a right to control the opinions of future generations; and to legislate for those over whom we have as little authority as we have over a nation in Asia."[8] Thomas Jefferson similarly conceded that "[t]he question whether one generation of men has a right to bind another, seems never to have been stated. . . . Yet it is a question of such consequence not only to merit discussion, but place also among the fundamental principles of every government."[9]

As Webster's criticism suggests, perhaps the most striking aspect of the concept of constitutional perpetuity is its sheer extravagance. Yet one of the things I shall argue here is that the concept of perpetuity is an essential feature of the Constitution's claim to order political reality and "to secure the Blessings of Liberty to ourselves and our posterity." My thesis is that whatever its status in the constitutional *text*, the claim to perpetuity is an essential element of constitutional *practice*. As the foregoing quotation from the Preamble suggests, the claim was at least implicit in the founding; in any event, it has been an explicit part of our constitutional order since the Civil War. In his First Inaugural Address, Lincoln argued that "[p]erpetuity is implied . . . in the fundamental law of all national governments. It is safe to assert that no government proper ever had a provision in its organic law for its own termination."[10]

The political context in which Lincoln voiced this claim is central to its meaning: The concept of perpetuity served as a constitutional justification for the North's position in the war. Hence Lincoln's reliance on the principle was dictated by political necessity and should be seen as a rejection of the doctrine of nullification. If the Union were perpetual, then the consent freely given by Southern states in the ratification process (if indeed the states and not their peoples consented) could not later be revoked. No intervening contingency could break the bond of political obligation established through the mechanism of consent. The issue was settled as a matter of constitutional doctrine in the post–Civil War case of *Texas v. White*, in which the Supreme Court, in considering whether Texas had remained a sovereign state during the tenure of the war, concluded: "When, therefore, Texas became one of the United States, she entered into an indissoluble relation. All the obligations of *perpetual* Union, and all the guarantees of republican government in the Union, attached at once to the state."[11]

Notwithstanding the North's success in the Civil War and the Supreme Court's subsequent ratification of Lincoln's position, there is a sense in which the Constitution's claim to perpetuity must even now be regarded as fanciful. If perpetual constitutions evidence belief in our capacity not only to foresee but also to exercise some control over the future, then crises betray the conceit that gives rise to such an excess of confidence. The limits of human foresight guarantee the eventual failure of any constitutional document as an ordering principle of political experience. And insofar as emergencies expose those limits, they demonstrate the ultimate contingency of all constitutional orders. Anyone familiar with the histories of constitutional states knows how often they appeal to the exigencies of crisis as a justification for release from the constitutional restraints they put upon themselves. In this respect, the claims of the U.S. Constitution, indeed of *all* constitutions, to govern, much less to govern in perpetuity, are deeply troublesome.

But should an authentic crisis release constitutional states from obligations they freely take up in less troublesome times? In considering this question, we should not forget that our predicament is in some ways analogous to that of Odysseus. As Senator John Potter Stockton remarked in debates over the Ku Klux Klan Act of 1871, "Constitutions are chains with which men bind themselves in their sane moments that they may not die by a suicidal hand in the day of their frenzy."[12] We bind ourselves with constitutional rules to guard against future temptation. When temptation does appear—typically in the guise of an "emergency"—we must ask whether our commitment to constitutional maintenance demands that we honor the self-command, expressed as limitations on governmental power in the constitutional text, or surrender to the wish to be free of it.

The resolution of this question largely depends upon how we define the project, or the ends, of constitutional maintenance. I will argue that the conception of constitutional maintenance inherent in the Odysseus example and in Stockton's eloquent reference to the chains that bind—of respect for textually specific limitations upon powers—is inappropriate in times of authentic crisis and should be replaced by a conception of constitutional maintenance that focuses less on limitations and more on the reasons why we initially thought such limitations desirable.

On a more particular level, my concern is with a specific type of constitutional emergency, those occasioned by regnant domestic political violence. I concentrate on political violence not simply because it is among the most frequent and severe of constitutional emergencies, but because it is best suited to exposing the limits of constitutionalism itself as a basis for political community, and thus for considering which understanding of constitutionalism ought to guide our efforts at constitutional maintenance. Political violence challenges the very presuppositions upon which our commitment to constitutional politics must be predicated—the belief that "good government" may be established upon the basis of reason and deliberation, upon "reflection and choice," as Hamilton wrote, or in the words of Edmond Cahn, upon the promise "that persuasion and free assent can triumph over brute force and build the foundations of a happier commonwealth."[13] Conceived in this way, a study of political violence in constitutional democracies allows us to examine the cases in which this most basic of assumptions is exposed as contingent or naive. Political violence therefore constitutes a type of constitutional emergency in a very specific sense and a challenge to the task of constitutional maintenance in a larger sense.

It is that challenge I address in this book. In some ways this is an old project in public law, one which, in the words of Carl Friedrich, has long "challenged the ingenuity of the best minds" in public law scholarship.[14] An earlier generation of public law scholars, including Clinton Rossiter, Carl J. Friedrich and his student Frederick Watkins, Edward Corwin, Hans Kelsen, and Carl Schmitt, wrote extensively on what Rossiter called the problem of constitutional dictatorship. The immediate impetus of their inquiry was the well-known failure of Weimar Germany and other constitutional democracies between the two world wars, but Rossiter, Friedrich, and Watkins knew also that a theory of constitutional maintenance in times of crisis must be a central part of any coherent account of constitutional authority more generally. At the very least, a theory of constitutional emergencies must address the problem of political obligation through time and the nature of the relationship between past and future generations, as Thomas Jefferson and Noah Webster recognized. Moreover, as James Madison conceded in Federalist 40 and as Carl Schmitt argued much later, a theory of maintenance and crises must also address the problem of constitutional change, especially with regard to constitutional institutions and their relationship to the larger constitutional order.

In chapter 1 I argue that although emergencies test the limits of constitutional documents as effective ordering principles of political experience, there are basic principles (not legal rules) of constitutionalism that both permit and restrict the exercise of emergency powers in all constitutional democracies. In other words, our understanding of constitutional maintenance must admit a distinction between our commitment to a particular constitutional document and our commitment to what I shall call constitutive, or preconstitutional principles, of which any constitutional text is but a specific and historically contingent articulation. These principles are constitutive of constitutionalism and of constitutional governments: They do not depend for their authority upon their inclusion in, or recognition by, particular constitutional documents. Instead, they make up part of a universe of meaning within which the practices of constitution making, constitutional maintenance, and constitutional dissolution are coherent and interdependent activities. As a result, even suspension of a constitutional document, an act whose legitimacy itself depends upon its conformity with those principles, does not authorize a departure from them. The inevitable failure of any particular constitutional text need not, on this understanding, signify a retreat from a commitment to constitutional principles and thereby defeat the project of constitutional maintenance.

As should be clear from the foregoing, my argument supposes that no understanding of constitutional authority during times of emergency can be complete absent an appreciation of the relationship between constitutional documents and the constitutive principles of constitutionalism. I therefore discuss in some detail in chapter 1 why the practice of constitution making commits a framer to preconstitutional principles. My argument also requires some examination of those basic principles, a defense of their status as constitutive norms of every constitutional system, and an extended discussion of how and from where they should be derived. Constitutive principles culled from political practice may not necessarily correspond to those derived from constitutional philosophy.

In the remaining chapters I integrate the principles articulated in the first chapter with a comparative study of constitutional maintenance and the legal control of political violence. In cases where the rejection or denial of constitutional authority is violent, governments typically react by adopting legislation of unusually wide scope or by suspending specific constitutional provisions or entire constitutional documents. Lincoln's suspension of the writ of habeas corpus and the emergency provisions of the Weimar Constitution are the two best known historical examples, but there are numerous contemporary cases. Every major Western democracy, for instance, has either proposed or enacted antiterrorism legislation to cope with the unusual problems that terrorism poses for ordinary criminal processes. In the Republic of Ireland and Northern Ireland, the police possess expansive powers of arrest and detention, and in both Irelands there exist special courts with jurisdiction over terrorist offenses.[15] These courts sit without juries and apply relaxed rules of evidence. The constitutions of Italy and West Germany prohibit special courts, but both have enacted legislation that grants authorities sweeping powers of arrest and detention. The Contact Ban Law in the Federal Republic, for example, permits the Länder (states) to forbid contact between suspected terrorists and their attorneys, and Section 90 (a) (1) of the West German Criminal Code makes it an offense if one "insults or maliciously maligns the Federal Republic of Germany . . . or its constitutional order." The United States (and a majority of the individual states), France, Canada, and Great Britain, as well as the Netherlands, Denmark, and Belgium, have all enacted antiterrorism legislation.

My first concern in these later chapters, then, is to consider the ways in which emergency legislation in two countries, Northern Ireland and the Federal Republic of Germany, has worked changes in the constitutional politics of those countries and the extent to which these changes comport with the principles identified in earlier chapters. I concentrate on Northern Ireland and Germany for a number of reasons.

Northern Ireland is a likely first choice if only because the extent and duration of the terrorism that plagues it exceed the situation of any other Western democracy. The Northern Irish case is also instructive because of Ulster's unique constitutional status. For some fifty years Northern Ireland functioned as a semiautonomous state under a written constitutional document within a larger political community, Great Britain, which does not possess a written constitution. By commenting on British policies, I can show how the constitutive constitutional principles apply to all constitutional democracies, regardless of specific written provisions or, in their absence, specific historical practices.

I therefore consider in some detail Great Britain's efforts to control political violence in Northern Ireland through antiterrorism laws that work extraordinary changes in the normal criminal processes. In chapter 2 I briefly examine the constitutional and political history of Northern Ireland. One cannot understand Irish terrorism without some appreciation of Irish history, for it is a history in which the distinction between political violence and constitutional politics has never been as clear as one might hope. Chapter 3 examines the two main statutes upon which British antiterrorism policies are based—the Northern Ireland (Emergency Provisions) Act (1978 and 1987) and the Prevention of Terrorism Act (1976 and 1984).

Chapters 4 and 5 explore the efforts of German constitutionalists to cope with political violence. Germany is useful as a comparison in part because, like Northern Ireland, successive German states have chosen to cope with political violence through extensive changes in their criminal processes. Chapter 4 reviews Weimar's failed efforts at constitutional maintenance and the sophisticated scholarly literature those efforts produced. I argue that our understanding of Article 48 and the Law for the Protection of the Republic Acts must be adjusted to account not only for Weimar's failure but also for its successes. Germany is interesting also because one can identify significantly different approaches to constitutional maintenance between the Weimar Republic and the Federal Republic. The provisions in the Federal Republic's Basic Law that concern extraordinary powers and states of emergency are unusually specific and detailed (in part because of Weimar); thus they offer an interesting contrast both with the Weimar Constitution and with the British case. Moreover, like its republican predecessor and Northern Ireland, West Germany has enacted an expansive series of antiterrorism laws, including the "Termination of Radicals" (Radikalen-Erlasse) and Contact Ban (Kontaktsperregesetz) provisions. I discuss these statutes in chapter 5.

In the conclusion to this study I consider more fully the relationship between constitutional maintenance and constitutional emergencies. How we define the former, or what we identify as the *end* and purpose of constitutional maintenance, largely determines the proper utilization of emergency powers in a constitutional democracy.

Some readers may dispute the claim that underlies my project, namely, that constitutional considerations are somehow relevant to the control of political violence. They may object that constitutions are quaint relics in the modern world of politics, or that their relevance to political violence is especially remote. In most Western democracies, however, constitutions *do* matter. They affect and condition political behavior, determining the parameters of public debate and public policy.[16] Even public officials who propose action that is arguably extraconstitutional typically seek to justify their action on constitutional grounds, as did the framers in rejecting the Articles of Confederation and Lincoln during the Civil War. We shall see the same tendency in our case studies of Weimar and Northern Ireland.

Nevertheless, I do not deny that the imperative of self-preservation will finally overcome whatever conditions constitutionalism imposes on governments in crisis. But it would be wrong to conclude that because they inevitably yield to political necessity, constitutional principles are unimportant. Situations in which our commitment to constitutionalism seems most implausible posit something of a critical case for the very possibility of constitutional government. Crises are especially important to the theory and practice of constitutional maintenance precisely because they *do* challenge the claim that constitutions can govern. As Søren Kierkegaard observed, "[The exception] reveals everything more clearly than does the general" and enables us to "think the general with intense passion."[17]

My emphasis on constitutional crises, then, is an effort to rethink the more general subject of constitutional maintenance with intense passion. I do not suppose, however, that I have fully or finally resolved all the problems inherent in constitutional emergencies, or that I have succeeded where Corwin, Rossiter, Friedrich, and Watkins failed. If, however, constitutionalism itself imposes conditions on the exercise of emergency powers, conditions that do not depend for their authority upon specific provisions in particular constitutions, then we may be able to restrain government while nonetheless recognizing the practical necessity for expansive powers that are inconsistent with our best ideal vision of constitutional government, a vision ordained by the text and to which we aspire as a community. My approach thus tries to accommodate our understanding of constitutional government with the limits of human foresight and "the broad range of contingency in all matters concerning the future course of events."[18] The gods may have graced Odysseus with their prescience, but only rarely do they warn us of the specific forms of peril the future surely holds.

I

CONSTITUTIONAL MAINTENANCE AND THE LEGAL CONTROL OF POLITICAL VIOLENCE

1

A Theory of Constitutional Maintenance and Constitutional Crises

INTRODUCTION

Crises pose two distinct challenges to any constitution's claim to perpetuity. In the first, narrower, instance, crises raise issues of *how* (and when) to interpret specific provisions in a constitutional document. Almost every modern constitution makes some explicit provision for crisis government. Article I, Section 9, of the U.S. Constitution authorizes suspension of the writ of habeas corpus "when in cases of Rebellion or Invasion the public Safety may require it." Section 8 also empowers Congress to declare war, raise armies, and provide militia to suppress insurrections. Among less explicit provisions for crisis government are Article II, which provides that executive power is vested in the president, and Section 3 of the same article, which requires that the president faithfully execute the laws. Article IV guarantees the states that the Union shall protect them against invasion and domestic violence. Elsewhere, the Preamble indicates that among the purposes of the Union are to secure a common defense and domestic tranquillity.

Students of U.S. constitutional history know the controversies these and other provisions have generated. Various crises have forced us to ask whether power to suspend the writ of habeas corpus inheres in Congress alone or whether it is concurrent with the executive, as Lincoln sometimes appeared to claim in the Civil War.[1] We have debated the inherent powers of the president, if any, to protect the Union and whether the constitutional document authorizes martial rule, under what circumstances, and if a president's decision to initiate it can be reviewed by another branch of government. There are no certain answers to these questions.

Some European constitutions try to diminish controversy through greater specificity in constitutional draftsmanship. The Irish Constitution of 1937, whose framers had actual experience with the difficulties of crisis, expressly authorizes special emergency laws and sanctions the creation of emergency courts. Moreover, Article 28(3)(3) states: "Nothing in this Constitution shall be invoked to invalidate any law enacted by [the legislature] which is expressed to

13

be for the purpose of securing the public safety and the preservation of the State in time of war or armed rebellion."[2] In contrast, the West German Basic Law, whose framers perhaps even better than the Irish knew the difficulties constitutional crises pose for the task of constitutional maintenance, sets forth in Article 115 and various other provisions a detailed catalogue of procedures the German state must respect in declaring and coping with states of emergency. Article 101 of the Basic Law, for example, prohibits extraordinary courts in all cases, as did a similar provision in the Weimar Constitution. An amendment to the Basic Law, Article 115g, further states that the "constitutional status and the exercise of the constitutional functions [of the court] must not be impaired." The French Constitution of the Fifth Republic offers considerably less guidance. Article 16 simply grants the president of the republic wide powers to cope with emergencies but also provides that the Parliament may convene of right and that the president may not dissolve the National Assembly during an emergency.

As should be obvious from this brief review of emergency provisions, the typical constitutional document forthrightly acknowledges the inevitability of crises and the need for expansive powers to cope with them. But these self-conscious attempts to foresee crises hardly eliminate controversy. We might ask, for example, whether provisions against the suspension of particular constitutional institutions, such as Article 115g of the Basic Law or Article 16 of the French Constitution, mean that the constitutional document in toto cannot be suspended. Does Article 28(3) of the Irish Constitution imply that principles outside "the Constitution" (however defined), perhaps principles of natural law, cannot be invoked to invalidate emergency statutes? Some American readers may find such an argument implausible or antiquated, but in *McGee v. Attorney General and Revenue Commissioners*, the Irish Supreme Court concluded that there *are* such principles antecedent to the Irish Constitution:

> Arts. 41, 42 and 43 emphatically reject the theory that there are no rights without laws, no rights contrary to the law and no rights anterior to the law. They indicate that justice is placed above the law and acknowledge that natural rights or human rights are not created by law but that the Constitution confirms their existence and gives them protection. The individual has natural and human rights over which the state has no authority.[3]

Similarly, the West German Federal Constitutional Court, in language whose significance can be appreciated only by those familiar with the constitutional history of the Weimar Republic, recognized in the *SouthWest* case that "[T]here are constitutional principles that are so fundamental . . . that they also bind the framers of the Constitution."[4]

Greater specificity of constitutional language is therefore unlikely to resolve all questions of interpretation. In part this is a function of the inherent imprecision of language. But it is also true that crises raise interpretive problems that differ in important ways from those we routinely encounter in trying to apply constitutional language to political practice. Assessments of constitutional meaning proceed in large measure through judgments of purpose.[5] Constitutional crises are especially troublesome precisely because they involve conflicts of purpose—between the need for survival, our most urgent of objectives, and our commitment to constitutional government, our highest of purposes.

But the problems that crises pose for constitutional authority involve more than puzzling issues of how properly to interpret imprecise language. Crises also raise questions whose resolution are a necessary part of a coherent account of constitutional maintenance in times of emergency, such as who should declare the existence and the termination of an emergency, as well as whether it is possible to resolve it in a manner consistent with a commitment to constitutional values. Implicit in this last question is yet another: When do constitutions no longer bind the communities that enact them? Any sophisticated understanding of constitutionalism must offer some answer to this question, for no account of constitutional authority can be complete absent an appreciation of the limits of constitutionalism as a basis for political community. Hence questions of whether and when the constitution governs are also questions of the limits (and perhaps of the different kinds) of constitutional authority, of when constitutions bind and when they do not.

Cincinnatus and the Roman Dictatorship

Few of us doubt that states will take whatever action they deem necessary to ensure their physical survival. As a matter of political prudence, democratic governments are seldom willing to risk their survival by respecting a generous conception of individual liberties in times of crisis. Whatever the logic of the political theories to which governments subscribe, the harsh realities of necessity typically trump individual liberties and rights.

Even Thomas Jefferson, the sometimes Whiggish opponent of expansive national power, conceded:

> The laws of necessity, of self-preservation, of saving our country when in danger, are of higher obligation. To lose our country by a scrupulous adherence to written law, would be to lose the law itself, with life, liberty, property and all those who are enjoying them with us; thus absurdly sacrificing the end to the means.[6]

Jefferson's comments make clear that there is far from universal agreement that any set of limitations, irrespective of origin, can or should restrain the exercise of powers of emergency in a constitutional state. Likewise, Kenneth Wheare once concluded that "crisis or emergency government can seldom be constitutional government."[7]

Nevertheless, there is also a long tradition of scholarship that does accept the possibility of restraints upon the exercise of emergency powers. That tradition dates at least from Livy's history of the Roman Republic, in which he recounted the story of Lucius Quinctius Cincinnatus (519–439 B.C.), the elderly

Roman farmer twice destined to save his crisis-stricken country.[8] The story of Cincinnatus, like that of the Sêirenes, has a recurrent and lasting significance for students of constitutional theory.

A poor farmer, Cincinnatus was approached on his farm in 458 B.C. by an envoy from the Roman Senate, who, following a more or less well-defined procedure for such cases, informed him that the Senate had appointed him commander-general of the Roman Army and absolute dictator of the Roman Republic. The army was then in a precarious position, trapped at Mount Algidus by the fierce Aequi, a tribe from Central Italy. Cincinnatus's reign lasted but two weeks and two days, long enough to defeat the Aequi and to save the republic, whereupon he willingly abandoned the dictatorship and returned to his plow.

The account of Cincinnatus is of relevance to contemporary constitutional practice not because it shows that a successful resolution of a crisis often requires expansive powers. Instead, what matters is that the inauguration and use of absolute power in the Roman Republic were governed by law, by "precise constitutional forms."[9] Moreover, Cincinnatus returned willingly to his farm, having wielded absolute power no longer than necessity demanded and only for the purpose of restoring the constitutional order.

The modern history of constitutionalism and its tension with the executive power characteristic of crisis government thus begins not with Germanic customary law, nor with the development of the prerogative power of the English Crown in the middle ages, as some have argued, but with the Roman Republic, as Hamilton recognized in Federalist 70:

> Every man the least conversant in Roman history knows how often that republic was obliged to take refuge in the absolute power of a single man, under the formidable title of dictator, as well against the intrigues of ambitious individuals who aspired to tyranny, and the seditions of whole classes of the community, whose conduct threatened the existence of all government, as against the invasions of external enemies who menaced the conquest and destruction of Rome.[10]

Carl J. Friedrich and Carl Schmitt similarly began their well-known studies of constitutional emergency powers with a review of the Roman dictatorship, and others have found in that institution "a theoretical standard . . . a sort of moral yardstick against which to measure modern institutions of constitutional dictatorship."[11]

There were four conditions to the Roman dictatorship, all of which, Friedrich argued, are of contemporary utility:

1. The appointment of the "dictator" must take place according to precise constitutional forms.
2. The dictator must not have the power to declare or to terminate the state of emergency.
3. Dictatorial, discretionary powers must obtain for only a (relatively) precise time, and the limit must not be subject to indefinite extension.

4. The ultimate objective of constitutional emergency powers must be the defense and restoration of the constitutional order.[12]

Unlike Schmitt, who considered such limitations a function of political and not legal necessity, Friedrich failed to address the question of whether these conditions could constitute *legal* requirements on constitutional governments, and if so who could or should enforce them. But he clearly saw them as touchstones against which to measure the "suitability" of emergency provisions in contemporary constitutional systems. Clinton Rossiter also turned to the Roman dictatorship to formulate a long list of conditions that the "peoples of modern democracies" should insist govern the exercise of emergency powers.[13] The lesson Schmitt, Friedrich, and Rossiter drew from Livy's account of Cincinnatus was that it was possible to preserve a constitutional state in the face of crisis while nonetheless requiring that it respond through measures consistent with its constitutional heritage.

Constitutional Dictatorship and the Prerogative

More recently, Arthur Schlesinger, Jr., devoted much of *The Imperial Presidency* to the problem of emergency government.[14] Schlesinger conceded, as have all who preceded and followed him, that there will be times when the president must act in extraordinary fashion to ensure national survival. "Crises threatening the life of the nation," he wrote, "have happily been rare. But, if such a crisis comes, a President must act."[15] The question is whether the Constitution authorizes these extraordinary actions.

Schlesinger concluded that emergency government should be recognized "for what it is: an extra-constitutional resort to raw political power, necessary but not lawful."[16] The alternative view, that the Constitution contemplates (if it does not authorize) extraordinary power, renders the document so meaningless that it fails to possess real authority even in normal conditions, a conclusion Corwin had reached earlier in his pointed analysis of the effects of World War II and the New Deal upon American constitutional law.[17]

The similarities between Schlesinger's argument and the Lockean defense of executive prerogative are, of course, substantial. In the *Second Treatise of Government*, Locke argued, as did Jefferson later, that "a strict and rigid observation of the laws [in some cases] may do harm."[18] The executive must have a power—the prerogative—to act "according to discretion, for the public good, without the prescription of law, and sometimes even against it."[19]

The prerogative of the Crown, or some institution like it, suggested for Schlesinger that the American presidency "must be conceded reserve powers to meet authentic emergencies."[20] Without clearly specifying the source of their authority, Schlesinger argued that the invocation and use of emergency powers must be subject to a number of restraints, most of which are directed toward establishing the authenticity of the emergency:

1. there must be a clear, present and incontestable danger to the life of the nation;
2. the President must define and explain to Congress and the people the nature of this threat;
3. the perception of the emergency, the judgment that the life of the nation is truly at stake, must be broadly shared by Congress and by the people;
4. time must be of the essence; waiting for normal legislative action must constitute an unacceptable risk;
5. existing statutory authorizations must be inadequate, and Congress must be unwilling or unable to prescribe a national course;
6. the problem must be one that can be met in no other way than by presidential action beyond the laws and the Constitution;
7. the President must report what he has done to Congress, which will serve as the judge of his action;
8. none of the presidential acts can be directed against the political process itself.[21]

Insofar as Schlesinger conceded that at times the Constitution must be suspended, these restraints cannot strictly trace their authority to the constitutional document. Schlesinger failed to provide any source at all for their origination; presumably they find authority in political necessity and their fidelity to the Roman principle that all exercises of emergency power must be directed to defense and restoration of the constitutional order. But we might well wonder why these extratextual principles should bind in the absence of an obligation to respect limitations set forth in the constitutional document itself. As Madison counseled, "The restrictions however strongly marked on paper will never be regarded when opposed to the decided sense of the public, and after repeated violations in extraordinary cases they will lose even their ordinary efficacy."[22] It is difficult to see why a crisis severe enough to overwhelm the constitutional document would not also overwhelm extratextual restraints.

There is yet another difficulty with Schlesinger's argument. The second principle—which requires that the president must define and explain to Congress and the people the nature of the crisis—implies the continued constitutional status of both Congress and the presidency. But once we suspend the Constitution, the status of the offices and institutions it creates are themselves problematic. An official who claims the Lockean prerogative, the power to suspend the Constitution, "risks the absurdity of saying: 'An officer who shall be recognized by criteria set forth in this Constitution shall have the power to act contrary to this Constitution.'"[23] Officers in the strict sense cannot have such a power because "we need rules they cannot lawfully change if we are to recognize those persons who lawfully claim the authority to act as officials."[24] Arguably, then, an individual who claims the Lockean prerogative is not the "president" but rather is an individual "strategically situated" to exercise emergency power. Consequently, the constitutional status of an officer who claims the Lockean prerogative is troublesome, as is the status of the "Congress" to which he must report his actions. Moreoever, as some critics have observed, the crucial issue must be the severity of the danger, not how "Congress" judges its severity. Surely a president should not fail to act simply because Congress does not share his or her sense of alarm.[25]

Whatever the internal difficulties in Schlesinger's argument, one might object to the entire enterprise. The very idea that one can promulgate legal restraints to govern the exercise of prerogative power, some argue, betrays a misunderstanding of what crises are.[26] Crises are crises just because they cannot be subsumed under a constitutional norm—a point Schmitt insisted upon in his famous debate with Hans Kelsen over who should be considered the "defender" of the Weimar Constitution. Arguing that the concept of crisis in constitutional theory was somewhat akin to the concept of miracle in theology, Schmitt concluded that there could be no constitutional or legal norm "which would be applicable to chaos," for every norm "presupposes its normal situation, and becomes meaningless when this normal situation ceases to exist."[27] "The necessity which justifies prerogative," others have concluded, "cannot support 'stringent conditions' controlling its exercise."[28] The conditions that give rise to extraordinary action in the first place will invariably force departures from Schlesinger's restraints as well as those proposed by anyone else.

The seeming paradox of limitations upon the exercise of emergency power once the Constitution is suspended, coupled with a fear that a "public attitude that the Constitution must be 'set aside' during emergencies [undermines] the claim of Congress and the courts to moderate presidential power,"[29] led Schmitt in Weimar and, more recently, Bessette and Tulis in reply to Schlesinger to conclude that the preferable course is to conceive of the Constitution as authorizing whatever means are necessary for its self-preservation. On this approach, the text authorizes whatever powers are essential to constitutional maintenance.

This formulation of the problem denies the possibility that the Constitution's military powers are sufficient to cope with all emergencies. Instead, Bessette and Tulis defend a liberal method of interpretation that compensates for the shortcomings of these powers.[30] Their argument indicates that one possible way to make sense of the claim to perpetuity is to treat it as a claim about how to interpret constitutional language: When faced with a crisis, constitutional maintenance demands that we interpret the document in such a way as to authorize whatever powers and measures are necessary to cope with the emergency. The argument complements Hamilton's, who argued in Federalist 23 that a properly framed constitution accounts for the inevitability of crisis, so that there can be "no limitation of that authority which is to provide for the defense and protection of the community in a matter essential to its efficacy."[31] Hamilton merely restated the position Machiavelli adopted in his discussion of the Roman Republic in the *Discourses*:

> Now in a well-ordered republic it should never be necessary to resort to extra-constitutional measures; for although they may for the time be beneficial, yet the precedent is pernicious, for if the practice is once established of disregarding the laws for good objects, they will in a little while be disregarded under that pretext for evil purposes. Thus no republic will ever be perfect if she has not by law provided for everything, having a remedy for every emergency, and fixed rules for applying it.[32]

Compare Machiavelli's language with the Supreme Court's opinion in *Ex parte Milligan*:

> No doctrine, involving more pernicious consequences, was ever invented by the wit of man that any of [the Constitution's] provisions can be suspended during any of the great exigencies of government. Such a doctrine leads directly to anarchy or despotism, but the theory of necessity on which it is based is false; for the government, within the Constitution, has all the powers granted to it which are necessary to preserve its existence.[33]

There are subtle and important differences between this position and the one advanced by Bessette and Tulis (Hamilton's requires framers with extraordinary prescience, whereas Bessette and Tulis defend a method of interpretation that makes up for their lack of it), but both have the signal benefit of not impairing the constitutional status of the other branches of the federal government. Other institutions thus have some constitutional basis for questioning a president's exercise of emergency power, a legitimacy they cannot claim once the Constitution is set aside. "The decisive fact is that under the United States Constitution the functioning of the coordinate institutions of American government is not suspended nor is their authority dissolved . . . when the president undertakes extraordinary actions."[34]

In some respects, the preceding debate is simply one of whether and how the proper use of emergency power, a power everyone concedes will be necessary, can be constitutionally guaranteed. Those who argue for the Constitution's continued application quickly run afoul of the powerful objection that expansive readings of constitutional power distort the Constitution's meaning and its claim to authority in ordinary times. Although constitutional language admits of a wide range of acceptable meanings, constitutions properly understood cannot quarter an infinite range of acceptable interpretations, and in arguing that they can, at least in emergencies, Bessette and Tulis adopt an account of constitutionalism at odds with itself, for it denies the possibility that language can limit politics.[35] In arguing for a liberal interpretation of emergency powers, they risk advancing a solution to the problem of constitutional crises that threatens the larger project of constitutional maintenance.

Sotirios A. Barber reaches a similar conclusion, based not on the nature of constitution making as a human and inherently imperfect enterprise but rather on the basis of the Constitution's supremacy clause. Barber reasons that we cannot conceive of a constitution "as law without presupposing that circumstances can defeat its claim to supremacy or that we can justly reject its authority."[36] Constitutions anticipate conditions hospitable to their claim to authority. When circumstances depart too greatly from these relatively ideal conditions, it may be better to admit as much and to take whatever action is politically necessary.* If we try to accommodate contingency through a doctrine

---

*An apparent assumption in the argument that constitutions should accommodate the powers necessary to cope with crises is that crises have beginnings and endings—that most crises are

of constitutional interpretation that would have the Constitution mean whatever it must, whenever it must, we can no longer conceive of situations that would justify our rejection of the Constitution. We thus defeat what we tried to save, for "we cannot perceive the Constitution as law in the absence of a disinclination to follow its provisions."[37]

On the other hand, those who concede the necessity of extraconstitutional action fail to guarantee that such powers will not amount to more than the arbitrary will of the executive. If they do provide restraints, like Schlesinger, Friedrich, and Rossiter, they typically fail to specify from where such restraints derive their authority or why they should apply when constitutional texts do not. In doing so, they also commit themselves to constitutions and constitutional orders that are ultimately unequal to the exigencies of crisis and the demands of constitutional maintenance.

In addition, those who counsel suspension of textual restraints have mistakenly supposed that constitutional maintenance ultimately requires restoration of the preexisting constitutional order. Barber concludes, for example, that the government should "seek to restore that state of affairs in which the government can return to the rules."[39] (Such a course cannot be a strict requirement, however, for we may well decide that the inability of the original constitution to prevent this particular crisis from arising in the first instance is an argument against its reaffirmation.) They have thus assumed that instrumental or teleological forms of authority can apply when legal authority does not. The advocates of liberal readings of constitutional powers have also taken for granted that the ultimate purpose of such powers must be defense of the existing constitutional order. As I shall indicate later, however, restoration of the preexisting constitution may not always be the constitutionally correct course of action: In certain types of crises, the continued authority of the constitutional document cannot simply be assumed.

THE LIMITS CONSTITUTIONALISM IMPOSES ON CRISIS GOVERNMENT

Our commitment to constitutional principle seems to make less than good sense if it requires of us a type of national suicide, as Jefferson recognized when he argued that "the laws of necessity, of self-preservation, of saving our country when in danger, are of higher obligation" than all others.[40] Jefferson's conclu-

---

capable of resolution and that, upon their termination, the conditions and forms of constitutional government more or less return to "normal." Yet few would be so foolhardy as to suggest that the workings of crisis government, particularly the flow of power to the executive, do not effect some permanent change in the ordinary patterns of constitutional governments. Corwin even argued that postcrisis government may so little resemble precrisis government that the difference might, as in the case of the United States following World War II, or after the New Deal, amount to a constitutional revolution.[38] Moreover, the inability of particular constitutions to cope with crises of seemingly endless duration is an argument in favor of frankly acknowledging the inadequacy of current constitutional arrangements.

sion is a sensible answer to the wrong question. Whether we should suspend a constitution in the interest of self-preservation is a different question than whether standards derived from the basic principles of constitutionalism restrain the exercise of powers of emergency. How one approaches the former requires some understanding and appreciation of the second inquiry and therefore of the relationship between constitutions and constitutionalism.

Constitutions and Their Relationship to Constitutional Government

In 1961, responding to a flurry of constitution making in Western Europe and in many Eastern European countries as well as in Asia and Africa, Giovanni Sartori remarked that "[e]very state [has] a constitution, but only *some* states [are] constitutional."[41] Sartori's comment suggests a number of important insights about the enterprise of constitution making. How are we to account for the proliferation of constitution making in this century, especially if the presence of a constitutional document is not definitive evidence of a commitment to constitutional government? And if the latter is true, then what, if not possession of a document, distinguishes constitutional governments from others? Sartori attributed the proliferation of constitution making in the late nineteenth and mid twentieth centuries to an "abuse of political terminology" and the "political exploitation and manipulation of language."[42] As a consequence, he argued, there developed some confusion over the very meaning of the word "constitution." Whereas "in the nineteenth century what was meant by 'constitution' [the concept of limited government] was reasonably precise, definite, and clear,"[43] it seemed in the mid twentieth century that constitutional government meant simply that there existed in any given country a document formally styled the "constitution."

Whatever its causes, lost in the change was the nineteenth century's insistence on the concept of *jurisdictio*, of *guarantiste*, of *limited* government.[44] Consequently, some of the new constitutions, such as the Soviet constitutions of 1937 and 1977, may set forth operative principles of government that have little relationship to the actual business of governing and which certainly do not limit or restrain governmental power. Sartori proposed that such constitutions should be called "facade constitutions,"[45] and Karl Loewenstein termed them "fictive" constitutions.[46] For reasons that will be clear as we proceed, I prefer Herbert J. Spiro's reference to such documents as mere "paper constitutions."[47] In such cases, the existence of a constitutional document hardly warrants our conclusion that such governments are *constitutional* governments except in the least interesting and least useful of ways.

Sartori and Loewenstein used phrases like "fictive" and "facade" constitutions to highlight the divergence between constitutional aspiration and political reality. We might, however, understand such language in another way. To speak of fictive or facade constitutions is to acknowledge that there are boundaries of meaning that circumscribe constitution making as a particular type of political behavior. It suggests that there are principles that can enable us to distinguish "true" constitutions from other artifacts of human production; it suggests, in other words, that there are principles so basic to constitutionalism that a constitution that fails to comport with them is not, properly speaking, a "constitution."

If this is so, then the enterprise of constitution making commits the framers not only to a document, or to a paper constitution, but also to those "background principles" that make intelligible the activity they are engaged in. These principles are constitutive of the activity of constitution making properly understood; they bind because, in the words of the Federal Constitutional Court of West Germany, there are "constitutional principles that are so fundamental . . . that they also bind the framers."[48]

An Example from Contract

Perhaps I can make this point clearer with an example from the law of contracts. Most students of constitutional theory should be comfortable with the terminology of contracts, if only because constitutional history is replete with analogies and references to contract, both social and otherwise. (Some people, Lincoln included, have claimed that constitutions are just contracts—a position I do not adopt.[49] I claim only that the law of contracts provides a helpful analogy for understanding certain aspects of constitution making and constitutional maintenance.) Like constitutions, contracts are usually, although not always or necessarily, written. And like constitutions, contracts structure the future by setting forth terms that regulate particular relationships: They are intended to endure through time. (Indeed, some contracts, and some specific contractual provisions, such as restrictive covenants, even claim to exist in perpetuity.) Finally, and most important for our purposes, not every agreement the parties call a contract in fact gives rise to a contractual relationship.

Any two parties who intend to enter into a contractual agreement are bound by the principles that provide the universe of meaning, that constitute part of the ordinary presuppositions, within which the act of contracting takes place and acquires meaning and identity.[50] These principles enable both the parties to the contract and noncontracting third parties to distinguish contracting from similar forms of behavior, such as making a promise. In other words, these constitutive principles are what make contracts contracts. Among them are requirements that both parties possess the mental capacity necessary to ensure that they understand the significance of the agreement (the capacity to understand the nature of the obligation they have assumed and to reason), a requirement of legal consideration, and a requirement that the terms of the agreement not violate public policy.

The background principles of contract law are not so much "in" the contract as they are constitutive of the activity of contract making. A legally enforceable contract is no less a contract, for example, because it fails expressly to recite that both parties are of sufficient mental capacity to understand the agreement. The parties must in some sense be aware that such principles exist insofar as they desire to contract and, more important, to have *others* recognize their commitments as contractually binding. Moreover, either of the parties may appeal to these principles when they are relevant to disputes over the meaning of specific contractual provisions. But the parties need not have any particular knowledge of the principles; indeed, they might even misunderstand them. The principles still apply to the terms of their agreement.

My thesis is that the activity of constitution making takes place within a similar set of presuppositions and understandings, without which it would be impossible to distinguish constitution making from other forms of political behavior. And in the same way that the constitutive principles of contract law allow us to distinguish between contracts and promises, the constitutive principles of constitutionalism enable us to distinguish between constitution making and other forms of political behavior. It follows that an interpreter may properly appeal to these principles in disputes over constitutional meaning.[51]

An Example from Chess

Let me offer yet another analogy. What I call the constitutive principles of constitutionalism partly resemble the rules of a game. The rules of chess, for instance, determine how the game begins, limit the range of permissible moves, and govern the game's end as well. Without these rules, there would be no game of chess or, better, no way to distinguish between the game of chess and a game of checkers or Monopoly, each of which has its own set of rules that gives it meaning and identity. The game of chess thus takes place within a set of constitutive principles that distinguish it from other games. The players need not follow the rules (there is no sanction if they choose to disregard them), but failure to respect them means that the game they play is not chess. "Of a person who does not play in accordance with the rules . . . we would say either that he plays *incorrectly* or that he does not play *chess*."[52]

In a similar fashion, suppose the parties wish to make a contract that contravenes one of the constitutive principles of contract law—say they wish to enter into a contract that requires of one person that she completely subordinate her moral autonomy to the other person. (I put aside the ethical implications of such an agreement, but I think it fair to assume that anyone who would agree to such an arrangement lacks rational or physical capacity.) The parties are free to enter into a compact of this sort, but the law will not recognize their agreement as legally enforceable. It is not, to put it another way, a *contract*, for it offends the constitutive principle of contract law that requires of *both* parties that they be of sufficient mental capacity to both understand and voluntarily assume the terms of the agreement. (It may also be void because it offends public policy.)

Assume instead that the contract is legally binding and that the submissive party no longer wishes to be bound, perhaps because she has been ordered by the other party to harm a friend. The constitutive principles of contract law govern not only the making but also the dissolution of contractual relationships. Some of these principles excuse contractual obligations by calling into question the original validity of the agreement. The submissive party may have been defrauded or, as in the preceding case, may have lacked the mental capacity necessary to understand the terms of the agreement. (Moreover, the continuing validity of the agreement depends upon a judge's ability to know this, something the judge cannot know if the submissive party has in fact surrendered intellectual autonomy, for then she cannot possibly satisfy the judge that she had engaged in an act of deliberative choice when she submitted.)

Other principles acknowledge the validity of the contract but look to subsequent developments to excuse obligations. The most prominent of these common law principles are unforeseeability and frustration of purpose, or impossibility.[53] In limited cases, those in which subsequent realities are far from what the contracting parties could have foreseen, both doctrines excuse contractual obligations by incorporating commonsense understandings of the limits of human prescience. They forthrightly acknowledge the ultimate contingency of all contractual relationships.[54]

One example of how the law of contracts accommodates the limits of human foresight stems from an illness suffered by King Edward VII. In the case of *Krell v. Henry*,[55] the plaintiff, Paul Krell, contracted with C. S. Henry to rent Henry's flat at 56A Pall Mall for two days. Nowhere in the contract did it state why Krell had rented the flat, but there was no dispute that the place would afford an excellent view of King Edward's coronation procession. When the king fell ill and the procession was postponed, Krell refused to pay the rent. The court held that Krell's duty of payment should be excused, for the purpose of the contract had been "frustrated" by an intervening contingency that the parties could not reasonably have been expected to foresee. Nor is the problem of contingency unique to the law of contracts, as Frederick Watkins noted: "The purpose of all law is to impose fixed patterns of behavior upon the life of society. No fixed pattern can ever hope to be comprehensive enough to make adequate provision for all contingencies. . . . Thus the need for temporary deviations from ordinary standards is common to law in all its phases."[56]

Constitutions, like contracts, also presuppose certain realities. Indeed, they are attempts to restructure those realities, and, insofar as they are products of human effort, we must admit, as did Hamilton, that they are imperfect. Like contracts, they can and eventually will fail. A principled and sympathetic understanding of constitution making and constitutional maintenance should therefore acknowledge the ultimate contingency of constitutional authority. In the same way that constitutive contractual principles govern contract making and contractual dissolution, there should be constitutional principles that govern constitution making and constitutional dissolution.

My discussion of contracts focused not on principles of contractual interpretation but rather on principles that help us to understand the foundations and limits of contractual authority. I have been interested, in other words, in when and why contracts bind the contracting parties and when and why they do not. In doing so, I sought to establish the basis for a proposition, namely, constitution making and constitutional dissolution *are* analogous to contract making and contractual dissolution, in the sense that there are constitutive principles in both cases. That there are or may be such principles is a common, though contested assumption in contemporary constitutional theory.[57] Although the ontological status of such principles remains a source of much controversy (I briefly explore the main features and assess the significance of that controversy in an afterword to this chapter), I accept their existence as a recurrent feature of constitutional discourse that merits serious consideration.

I begin, then, with a proposition: What is true of contracts is true also of constitutions. There are background principles of constitutionalism that bind those who wish to understand themselves as engaged in the activities of constitution making, constitutional maintenance, and constitutional dissolution. Consequently, a constitutional government is under an obligation in an emergency to abide by the limitations constitutionalism itself imposes upon emergency powers. Because these limitations are background principles of constitutional practice, they bind independent of their expression or inclusion in any particular constitutional text, though ideally they are so recognized, and whether or not that particular text has been overtaken by contingency.

It is far beyond my means here to undertake an exhaustive examination of the entire range of preconstitutional principles. My purpose is more modest: I mean to explicate the requirements of dealing with certain situations, crises, in which granted powers are inadequate to secure our end, survival, in a fashion consistent with the predicates of constitutionalism. I shall show how an understanding of the existence of such principles can enable us to make sense of the Constitution's claim to perpetual authority and to do so in a way that accommodates it, as does the law of contracts, with human imperfection and the inevitability of contingency. To this end, I shall propose a constitutional analogue to the contractual principles of impossibility and frustration of purpose. First, however, I should return to the example of contract to make it clear that there *are* differences between contractual and constitutional dissolution.

In the case of contract, the constitutive principles derive their authority both from the consent of the parties *and* from a source outside the contractual relationship. One reason why contracts are contracts, rather than promises, is because their enforcement is guaranteed by the state. The constitutive principles obtain their obligatory force by virtue of an outside institution, the judicial apparatus of the state, which has the authority to enforce them. (This argument recalls Durkheim's statement in *The Division of Labor in Society* that individual contracts depend for their authority upon the existence of the *institution* of contract more generally.)[58]

The obligatory character of preconstitutional principles is less clear. As we saw, once the Constitution has been suspended, there appears to be no outside authority that can guarantee their enforcement or application. The principles might have some heuristic value, as do the requirements suggested by Schlesinger, Rossiter, and others, but they cannot, on this analysis, be said to be *constitutionally* required. In this respect, the constitutive principles more nearly resemble the analogy to game playing. In what sense can we think of the rules of chess as obligatory on the players? Unlike the rules of contract, the rules of chess are not legally enforceable by an outside authority (unless, perhaps, one is enrolled in a tournament, a point I shall expand upon presently). One might argue, however, that in the same way that a person's intent to contract implies consent to the rules of contract, a player's decision to play the game implies consent to the rules of that game or, at least, to some set of rules. This latter point is critical, for it acknowledges that on occasion the rules may be vague and hence subject to interpretation and dispute. But vagueness and indeterminacy, and consequently disagreement by the players over their *meaning*, do not amount to an argument that rules do not *exist*.[59]

We might say, then, that players who wish to understand themselves and, more important, to have *others* understand them (here is the significance of participation in a tournament) as playing the game of chess obligate themselves to play by a set of rules that define the game they wish to play. It may well be the case that any two players can choose to modify the rules to accommodate their own preferences. Insofar as the rules are vague and require interpretation, some modification may be inevitable. Indeed, the players can play any game they like and call it chess. But they are *not* entitled to play checkers, to call it chess, and to then expect others to respect their decision.* Once the enterprise is public, the parties forfeit some of the power of definition.

The same is true of constitution making. Framers who wish to understand themselves, and who wish to have others, including their fellow citizens and future generations (recall the appeal to posterity in the Preamble to the U.S. Constitution), recognize them as engaged in constitution making, are bound by the constitutive principles that give the activity meaning and identity. Countries may call whatever they like constitutions—the mere existence of a document does not necessarily entitle them to recognition by others as *constitutional* governments.

I must reiterate that suspension of the document cannot authorize a departure from these principles, for they do not depend for their authority upon inclusion in the written text. On the contrary, the authenticity of any document as a constitution depends in large part upon its conformity with these principles. They constitute the ordinary presuppositions, the universe of meaning, within which constitution making, constitutional suspension, and constitutional maintenance are coherent and interdependent activities. They even indicate when the dissolution of constitutional government is permissible (as the Declaration of Independence assumed in its charges against George III), just as the constitutive principles of contract law govern the dissolution of contractual relationships.

For communities that *do* desire to reaffirm their commitment to constitutional values, the constitutive principles are obligatory. In the remainder of this

---

*At least, they cannot be so entitled without marshaling some set of reasons on behalf of their reformulation. This is an important qualification. I shall expand upon it in my discussion of constitutionalism later in this section.

chapter, I indicate what those principles are, at least in the context of crisis, and specify what they require of crisis governments. These principles should govern constitutional interpretation and inform the larger enterprises of constitutional design and constitutional maintenance. Thus the identification of such principles provides a framework against which to measure the suitability of individual constitutional documents as well as restraints upon the exercise of power even in constitutional emergencies, when our commitment to constitutional values is most troublesome.

Before I undertake that analysis, I wish finally to emphasize that the principles do not deny governments the means or powers necessary to cope with crises. Nor do they greatly constrict the scope and breadth of such powers. Indeed, insofar as they permit suspension of documentary restraints upon power, they allow governments a very broad measure of discretion and authority to respond to emergencies. But they do so in a manner that does not threaten our commitment to constitutionalism itself. The principles ensure that the assumption and utilization of emergency powers takes place in a constitutional manner and that such powers are not exercised in an arbitrary fashion or solely for the self-interest of the holder. The real problem posed by emergency powers for students of constitutionalism "is not so much to curtail the use as to limit the abuse of those powers."[60] It is for this reason that the legend of Cincinnatus retains contemporary significance, for it suggests that even in a crisis, there is a sense in which constitutionalism, government based on reason and limited by the rule of law rather than government by will or self-interest, can persist.

Constitutive Principles of Constitutionalism

Constitutionalism is a wonderfully complex and rich theory of political organization. In Lord Bolingbroke's classic statement of the doctrine, constitutionalism is a form of government conducted by "fixed principles of reason" directed to certain fixed objects of public good.[61] These fixed principles of reason bind because, in Bolingbroke's formulation, the "community hath agreed" to be bound by them.

In what follows I develop a more specific and limited account of constitutionalism, the purpose of which is to formulate a statement of preconstitutional principles. But I shall borrow heavily from Bolingbroke's description of constitutionalism as a government based upon and conducted in conformance with "right reason." My account is premised on that claim as well. It takes seriously Noah Webster's description of constitutionalism as the "empire of reason" and Plato's suggestion that governments may be adjudged by the degree of their conformity with the demands of reason. Of course, any attempt to discern the precise content of the fixed principles of right reason will engender dispute, and as my case studies of Northern Ireland and Germany will suggest, the sorts of constitutive principles that can be culled from constitutional practice may differ in important ways from those we can derive from constitutional philosophy.

It would be a mistake to dismiss appeals to constitutive principles because of their definitional imprecision. No less than other forms of political organization, such as liberalism and democratic theory, constitutionalism is a living tradition capable of change and capable also of supporting multiple understandings, all of which share certain elements but may differ in others. Constitutionalism is therefore a composite of different historical practices and philosophical traditions, some cultural, some ideational. Moreover, because constitutionalism "never stays put" but instead "continually evolves in response to . . . transformations occurring in society,"[62] it is possible to trace how some of those concepts have been dominant at certain times and in specific places yet recessive at other times and in other cultures, as Charles McIlwain and Carl Friedrich so clearly demonstrated. Indeed, McIlwain thought it necessary to reject efforts at "any strict definition of constitutionalism," noting instead that "constitutional history is usually the record of a series of oscillations."[63] We should recall also that the problem that prompted this observation was precisely that of constitutionalism and crises, which led McIlwain to discuss the distinction between *jurisdictio* and *gubernaculum*.[64]

Consequently, a sophisticated account of constitutionalism must be less a matter of strict definition and more a matter of interpretation. "A living tradition is an argument . . . [and] a tradition . . . connotes not consensus, but dissensus and consensus."[65] I therefore propose not a definition but a way of understanding constitutionalism, not because it is correct in a narrow, technical sense, whether historical or philosophical (no such account is possible), but rather because it best helps us to understand and reconcile the difficulties for constitutional maintenance that inhere in constitutional emergencies. In short, my understanding of constitutionalism is informed by a series of problems about constitutional maintenance and the limits of constitutional authority. Central to my account is the language of reason and the distinction between constitutionalism and constitutions; the latter help us to understand the former, as we have seen, but they are not the same thing.

Notwithstanding its imprecision, most students of constitutionalism will accept as one constitutive principle the notion of *garantiste*—of limitations upon governmental power that cannot be altered by the ordinary means of legislation. In a constitutional government, there are substantive objectives (the "fixed objects of public good"), structural limitations, and procedural guarantees that limit the exercise of state power. Indeed, the concept of limited power, of restraints upon not only the exercise but also the proper objects of power, is central to any understanding of constitutionalism.[66]

In many ways, however, a definition of constitutionalism as limited government is no more instructive than Bolingbroke's formulation. All governments are limited in some way, whether by custom, culture, or limited resources, but not every limitation is a constitutional restraint. Constitutionalists typically insist upon a set of *legal* limitations, but here too the number of unresolved questions is surprising. How limited must a limited government be to qualify as a constitutional government? Some version of this unresolved question was the impetus behind Sartori's and Loewenstein's fascination with fictive and facade constitutions, and constitutional theorists have yet to develop a coherent answer to it.[67] But I want to make a stronger claim, that an account of constitutionalism as limited government is especially unsuited to the demands of constitutional emergencies, for it is precisely in such cases that "limits" upon the exercise of power seem most implausible and unwelcome. Indeed, when Kenneth Wheare wrote that "crisis government can seldom be constitutional government,"[68] he could only have meant that crisis government can seldom be limited government. For an earlier generation of public law scholarship, Wheare's understanding of the problem of constitutional dictatorship, how to reconcile limitations upon power with the need for expansive emergency powers, was the predominant one. That understanding has confused more than it has illuminated discussions of constitutional maintenance.

For these and other reasons it is more useful to understand constitutionalism at a different level of abstraction, one that does not deny the necessity of limited government but rather asks why we value that necessity and how we hope to secure it. It is here that the classical formulations of constitutionalism as government based upon reason, "upon the twin principles of reflection and choice," become instructive. At least for questions of constitutional emergencies, constitutionalism should be understood not in terms of limited government but rather as a commitment to a public life premised upon the public articulation of reasons in support of particular actions taken for the public welfare. On this understanding, the production of reasons enables governments to exercise particular types of political authority and influence. A government's failure to produce reasons represents a failure to govern in a fashion consistent with the "deep structure" of a constitutionalist regime.[69]

Of course, this restatement of constitutionalism as "articulated reason" (to borrow a phrase from Karl Llewellyn)[70] is not inconsistent with the concept of limited government. It is simply a more useful way of understanding constitutionalism and constitutional maintenance. Limited government implies a government in which power is exercised by accepted means. Acquiring consent— "the community hath agreed to be bound"—to the use of power through those means suggests that the claim to power is predicated upon the activity of reasoning, for both the exchange of consent and the exercise of consented-to power are based on the production of reasons that possess general consent and which thereby justify the exercise of any particular power.[71] Moreover, the necessity of producing reasons limits the range of actions that can be undertaken, for not all behavior can be supported by reason. In this sense, articulated reason limits the class of permissible actions but does not necessarily limit the scope of any particular action. The difference is akin to the distinction, so common in the classical literature on constitutionalism and a critical part of Blackstone's analysis of the royal prerogative, between arbitrary and absolute power.[72] Descriptions of constitutionalism typically insist that constitutionalism is "a safeguard . . . against arbitrary government"[73] or "the antithesis of arbitrary rule,"[74] or that the rule of law "must be maintained against arbitrary will."[75] Arbitrary power is power whose exercise need not be justified by reason, and it is precisely in this respect that it differs from absolute power. As Locke wrote, "even absolute power, when it is necessary, is not arbitrary by being absolute."[76] And Bodin noted similarly that "absolute [power] does not imply the entire absence of legal limitations."[77]

One might respond that the necessity of producing reasons is less useful than I and other constitutionalists assume. There are two sorts of objections possible here. One is based on history. Whatever the theoretical merit of a reasons requirement, one might argue that no executive has thought it necessary, or is likely to think it necessary, to offer reasons in support of the exercise of emergency powers. This objection reduces to a claim that the leaders of regimes in crisis "are not much concerned with the niceties of constitutional theory."[78] Unlike some other objections, this one admits of a test, and I shall test it in the case studies that follow this chapter.

A second and more troublesome objection concerns the nature of reason. One might argue that "reasons" can always be marshaled in support of any policy and therefore do not limit because they cannot disqualify any use of emergency powers. I want to forestall detailed consideration of this problem until we discuss how we can know good reasons from bad, but the gist of my argument will be that even if one can imagine a reason in support of any exercise of power, it is not always possible to offer reasons that can persuade others. As James Boyd White wrote:

> [L]anguage has a remarkable flexibility, for it can be used to justify a very wide range of conduct. Such flexibility is essential to the continued existence of any language of this kind [language that constitutes and orders]. . . . But not everything can be justified: the language has some actual effect on conduct.[79]

Insofar as the objection is founded on a more general epistemological skepticism concerning the nature of knowledge, language, or reason, there is plainly no way to respond fully to the objection here, but I shall examine it at greater length in the afterword to this chapter. I should anticipate that discussion by noting that this sort of skepticism must ultimately become a skepticism about the very possibility of a political order premised upon reason and reflection in public affairs. In that respect, the skeptic has a problem not so much with my efforts to reconcile constitutionalism with contingency as with the very tenets of constitutionalism.[80]

I shall concede, however, that a "reasons requirement" does not provide a set of discrete, substantive limits upon emergency powers, such as those proposed by Friedrich, Rossiter, and Schlesinger. My aim is rather to establish boundaries, within which a number of different reasons may finally justify the exercise of emergency powers. Our concern with such powers must be less with their limitation than with their justification, with establishing the authenticity of the need that gives rise to their use. A conception of constitutionalism as articulated reason focuses upon the activity of justification and is therefore better suited to the character of crisis and the needs of constitutional maintenance.

Let me restate that claim. Constitutional maintenance demands not substantive legal limitations upon emergency power but rather the reasoned justification of the need for, and utilization of, such powers. A conception of constitutionalism as articulated reason therefore requires that the exercise of emergency powers—the scope of which may be absolute—must not be arbitrary (or without reason). This understanding of constitutionalism is far better suited to the demands of constitutional crises, for it permits the exercise of expansive powers of self-defense while nonetheless ensuring that those powers are not arbitrary and hence "unconstitutional" in a grand sense.

This conception of constitutionalism is also useful for understanding the structural arrangements associated with constitutional governments and their significance for the project of constitutional maintenance. Constitutionalism typically implies a particular set of institutional devices designed to limit power. The most common and the most important of these devices, or "the sacred maxim of free government," in the words of *The Federalist Papers*, is the separation of powers, or a system of checks and balances. Again, the concern is less with absolute than with arbitrary power, as Madison noted in Federalist 47. In arguing for the necessity of separate institutions sharing power, Madison observed, quoting from Montesquieu, "Were the power of judging joined with the legislative, the life and liberty of the subject would be exposed to *arbitrary* control."[81]

The separation of power is a concession to the organization of a government whose power is "directed to certain fixed objects of public good." We value this institutional arrangement for limiting power not only for its own sake, but rather because we think it instrumental to constructing a political community based on reflection and choice; it is "the institutional embodiment of a national aspiration to rise above accident and force by governing ourselves by the claim of reason."[82] The separation of powers is thus an instrumental mechanism through which constitutionalism's commitment to a public life conducted on the basis of articulated reason is secured. As Justice Brandeis wrote in his dissent in *Myers v. United States*,[83] we separate power "to preclude the exercise of arbitrary power." Hence the separation and enumeration of power "informs constitutional theory with a hierarchy of objectives that enables us to identify a whole way of life, complete with affirmative commitments as well as procedures and proscriptions—commitments that enable us to transform mere procedures and proscriptions into objects of aspiration and pride."[84]

Other, only slightly less common, methods of limiting power include the vertical separation of power (federalism), constitutional review, and promotion of geographic and cultural diversity. Of these, constitutional review has evolved as the most important. The precise manner and character of review varies widely across contemporary constitutional systems. In some, such as the United States, West Germany, Ireland, and Japan, constitutional review means judicial review, whether *erga omnes* or *inter partes*, centralized or decentralized.[85] In other systems, notably England and France, constitutional review is the province of other branches of government. Whatever the mechanism, however, some type of constitutional review is a constitutive element of constitutionalism, for the activity of review, the very possibility of review, is predicated upon the necessity to produce reasons in support of action taken. If reasons need not be adduced in support of action, there can be no independent review, as we shall see in our review of antiterrorism legislation in Northern Ireland. Consequently, a reasons requirement necessarily implies the giving of reasons to someone else competent or qualified to adjudge the reason. So McIlwain thought constitutional review, and judicial review in particular, "the one institution above all others essential to the preservation of the law," and "it is the law that must be maintained against arbitrary will."[86] As with the separation of powers, we value the institutional arrangement of constitutional review because it promotes a community and a politics based upon the exchange of reasons.

Constitutionalism's commitment to reason is also often (but not always or even necessarily) reflected in a written catalogue of rights that citizens can claim against the state. Most Western constitutions include provisions that are similar in content and purpose to the U.S. Constitution's Bill of Rights.[87] The precise character and extent of constitutionally protected liberties varies across systems (post–World War II constitutions are typically more detailed than their American predecessor), but each assumes that some version of these liberties promotes the development of a community based on articulated reason on both a systemic and individual level.[88]

This is a point I want to stress, especially since it is so easily ignored or forgotten. Whatever the similarity or dissimilarity of protected rights and liberties (an issue to which I shall return), most constitutional systems protect certain civil liberties.* They do so not only because constitutionally protected civil liberties have some intrinsic merit (I have deliberately left this point vague and shall return to it shortly) but also because we think them instrumentally necessary to promote the exercise of reason and to communities who seek to order their political affairs on that basis. "Their main worth consists in being

---

*Representative democracies also typically recognize a wide variety of rights and liberties. In a democracy these liberties depend for their authority upon the consent of the majority. It is important to recognize, as legal positivists do not, that in a constitutional state these rights do *not* depend for their legitimacy upon majority approval. Instead, they are rights that attach to personhood, and not to citizenship (a distinction clearly acknowledged, one might add, in the Fourteenth Amendment). There is another way to appreciate the distinction: Constitutionalists argue that the constitutional text recognizes rights. Democrats, in turn, argue that the text creates rights. In normal times the difference may seem semantic, but in truth it is a very real one, as crises often make clear. I shall return to the point in my discussion of Weimar Germany.

Moreover, the breadth and depth of constitutional liberties can vary considerably depending upon whether one justifies their existence upon constitutionalist or democratic grounds. For example, one can argue that constitutionalism's insistence upon conditions in which moral and intellectual development can proceed (the "Blessings of Liberty") necessitates the protection of a wide range of speech and conduct not strictly political.[89] On the other hand, a democratic defense of freedom of speech leads quite easily and logically (if not inevitably) to a claim that the First Amendment protects only political speech, as Judge Bork has often argued and as Justice Stewart claimed in *Moore v. City of East Cleveland.*[90]

necessary conditions for the development, maintenance, and exercise of authority."[91]

The point is best appreciated when one considers which liberties appear in all bills of rights, or which liberties reside, in the language of comparative public lawyers, in the common core of constitutional systems. To my knowledge, every register of constitutional liberties contains a provision substantially like the American due process clause. On a particular level, of course, what constitutes due process varies tremendously across political systems, and within particular systems over time. At a more general level of abstraction, however, due process clauses of every sort amount to a command that governments not act upon individual rights unless they can articulate publicly a "good reason" on behalf of the proposed action.[92]*

Due process clauses, then, are more particular instances of the general constitutional requirement that government function under prospective, publicly articulated rules that enable a citizen to evaluate the justification for "whatever laws and policies are directed to him."[93] Moreover, the reasons governments marshal in support of proposed policies must stand or fall on their own merit. They must possess a persuasiveness independent of the speaker's position, and the citizen "must have a reasonable opportunity to register objections and to argue for whatever changes he believes ought to be made."[94]

The claim that reasons must possess a persuasiveness independent of the speaker's position of authority again raises the issue of what constitutes a "good reason," an issue I put to one side earlier. I wish to return to it now. Recall that our concern is not with constitutional interpretation in hard cases but rather with situating the claim to perpetuity within the larger project of constitutional maintenance. Recall also that there is some textual support for the claim of perpetuity in the Preamble. The Preamble also informs the project of constitutional maintenance, for its sets forth in "majestic generalities" what we believe in as a political community and what we hope to secure for ourselves and our posterity. The Preamble tells us who we are—it defines our innermost self, and in so doing tells us what the ultimate ends of constitutional maintenance must be. Constitutional maintenance should not be understood simply in terms of physical survival. Instead, the aim must be to defend our "inner-most self as well as . . . the outer-most boundary."[95] Any reason proffered as a justification for the exercise of emergency power must therefore fall within the category of "good reasons" set forth in the Preamble, which include the establishment of justice, domestic tranquillity, the general welfare, the common defense, and promotion of the blessings of liberty. In this respect (although not in some others), I agree with Barber's conclusion that constitutionally defensible "good" reasons must serve the common good,[96] although in crises the common good cannot be understood simply in terms of physical self-preservation, as the Preamble makes clear.

---

*The necessity that government adduce reasons on behalf of action that implicates the due process clause applies to all constitutional liberties. In the United States, the "strength" that such reasons must possess varies depending upon whether the liberty in question is fundamental.

To this point my argument has succeeded only in identifying, in broad terms, what constitutes an acceptable class of good reasons.[97] If a reason is actually to *justify* and not merely rationalize or explain an exercise of power, it must be a reason that admits of and indeed invites a response from others. The concept of justification is central to my account of constitutionalism and to the activity of giving reasons. "And the requirement of justification is the essential idea of what we mean by the rule of law: we insist that a police officer explain in terms of his legitimate needs and goals the reason why he made a particular search."[98] Owen Fiss's discussion of what constitutes a "good reason" in judicial constitutional interpretation is also founded on the distinction between justification and explanation:

> The notion of justification, as opposed to explanation, implies that the reasons supporting a [judicial] decision be "good" reasons, and this in turn requires norms or rules for determining what counts as a "good" reason. . . . [Such a reason] cannot consist of a preference . . . [and] the reason must somehow transcend the personal, transient beliefs of the judge or the body politic. . . . The statement "I prefer" or "we prefer" . . . merely constitutes an explanation, not a justification.[99]

A reason that depends for its ability to persuade solely on the authority of the speaker falls outside the pale of good reasons, for in such cases the speaker's position amounts to a claim that no justification is necessary. One could respond to such an argument only by questioning the authority of the speaker to make it. A reason that fails to admit of a response is not properly a part of a political community, or of a public discourse, that premises political authority on persuasion and consent because, as Michael Perry noted in a somewhat different context, "A failure to explain frustrates political dialogue."[100] A reason offered in support of emergency powers therefore cannot be a good reason if it is purely hortatory, for such reasons lack the capacity rationally to persuade others. The same would be true of reasons that are literally incoherent or that deny the value of reason itself, for they would defeat our efforts at constitutional maintenance.

Good reasons must be reasons that can persuade another on their own merit and must admit of a response. A politics predicated on articulated reasons that admit of response—or a political community committed to the necessity of public dialogue—also requires what every version of democratic theory supplies: Public participation in the process of governance is an essential element of both constitutional and democratic states.[101] But constitutionalism also limits the parameters of public policy in ways that democratic theory does not. The propriety of public policy in a democracy is measured by the legitimacy of procedure. Constitutionalism, however, imposes value judgments concerning the value of reason, and hence of the individual, that transcend the propriety of procedure.[102] Consequently, the legitimacy of governmental action in a constitutional state must be measured by its conformity with those essential value judgments, all of which are centrally concerned with reason in public affairs.

Articulated Reason and the
Principle of Dignity

Constitutionalism assumes that no exercise of power is legitimate unless predicated upon consent, and that consent is not possible unless informed by reason. Behind those assumptions, indeed, behind any theory of political obligation, must be an irreducible normative position. The normative premise upon which Western constitutionalism's concern for limited power and public reason rests is the protection of human dignity. As Carl Friedrich noted some thirty years ago, ours is a government "which rests upon a moral belief." [103] A moral belief in human dignity is an essential part of a constitutionalism whose origins "must be understood as embedded in the belief system of Western Christianity and the political thought that expresses its implications for the secular order." [104] I will resist the temptation to belabor the point with extensive quotations and note only that all serious students of constitutionalism have conceded that constitutionalism's concern for reason and liberty rests upon a set of assumptions about why those concerns are worthwhile. It is this concern above all others which justifies the claim that government must function under prospective, publicly articulated rules that enable the citizen to evaluate the justification for "whatever laws and policies are directed to him; and he must have a reasonable opportunity to register objections and to argue for whatever changes he believes ought to be made." [105] Efforts to rule "by whatever means are expedient," instead of "trying to provide . . . rational demonstration," [106] deny the premise of individual dignity upon which constitutional values rest.

If, as I and others have argued, respect for human dignity is the touchstone of Western constitutionalism, then it provides the ultimate benchmark against which the project of constitutional maintenance and any exercise of emergency power in constitutional states must be measured. But exactly what does such a measure require? It is at this level of specificity that references to human dignity appear at best useless and at worst mischievous and misleading, for the concept of dignity has about it a teasing imprecision that promises comfort to all suitors and satisfies none. Legal positivists (and others) will surely claim that a first principle built on dignity provides little in the way of guidance for conscientious public officials challenged by the demands of constitutional emergencies; skeptics routinely deny that moral truths (if they exist) can help us to decide hard cases. What John Hart Ely said about appeals to natural law, therefore, seems no less true of appeals to dignity: "The only propositions with a prayer of passing themselves off as 'natural law' are those so uselessly vague that no one will notice." [107]

I do not wish to argue (at least not in this forum) that concerns about the imprecision of dignity as a source of meaning in constitutional *interpretation* are unfounded. It is indeed true that appeals to dignity are unlikely to simplify the task of constitutional interpretation, as Ely, Brest, and many others have argued, although one might observe that the standard of simplification cannot be the measure of interpretive validity, for it denies the Herculean character of the task that positivists often assume to be a mechanical application of either "rules" or "preferences."[108] Elucidating the concept of dignity, applying it in concrete cases, no doubt demands a "great imagination as well as huge measures of technical legal knowledge, historical lore, political wisdom, and skill in human relations."[109]

I do mean to argue, however, that these interpretive concerns are misplaced in a *political* study of constitutional maintenance. My aim is certainly not to simplify the enterprise of constitutional interpretation; questions of interpretation are of a second order compared to the larger enterprise of constitutional maintenance, of which constitutional interpretation is but a part. My claim is rather that a study of constitutional maintenance as a political practice (and not as a problem of constitutional interpretation) which fails to account for the principle of human dignity (specific cases aside) is inartful and incomplete and fails to comport with the basic presuppositions of constitutionalism.

I want to claim further that no study of constitutionalism and constitutional maintenance as a political (and not simply a legal) practice could ignore the frequency with which such appeals appear. Talk about dignity may muddy legal understandings of the problems that inhere in constitutional emergencies, but a politically sensitive and relevant understanding of these problems must account for the way we typically talk about them. And it will not do to dismiss such talk as frivolous or specious, for as my case studies of Northern Ireland and the Federal Republic of Germany shall make clear, the language of dignity frequently appears in efforts at constitutional maintenance. Hence despite their controversial character, appeals to human dignity are a common, legitimate, and integral form of constitutional discourse in times of crisis.

Nor am I certain that its imprecision renders the concept of dignity meaningless even as a legal standard except insofar as we hope to cabin emergency powers through substantive limitations. Once we abandon that effort in favor of the one proposed here, the principle of dignity *does* yield a number of concrete propositions about constitutional maintenance and the exercise of emergency powers in constitutional democracies. For example, insofar as respect for the dignity of persons requires that government publicly produce reasons in support of an exercise of power, as I have argued, authorities are obliged to conduct the business of governing in accordance with publicly articulated, prospective rules that enable citizens to assess the legitimacy and propriety of public policies. One of the central functions of constitutions is to make the business of governing publicly accountable. I have made another claim as well: Constitutionalism is predicated upon the premise (the sacred premise, to paraphrase Madison) that our commitment to reason in public affairs—a commitment whose justification is cast in terms of human dignity—requires a set of institutional and structural arrangements which promote reason by separating and limiting power. These constitutive structural arrangements are the expression of our commitment to reason and dignity and consequently are essential to the realization of dignity in constitutional communities.

The Principles of Necessity and Review

The basic principles of constitutionalism as articulated reason provide that resort to emergency power in a constitutional democracy is improper unless the crisis cannot be resolved through normal constitutional channels.[110] The presumption, in other words, must weigh in favor of the text. Emergencies invariably result in an increase in governmental power and a consequent relaxation of limitations on power. This relaxation can be squared with the demands of constitutionalism only if a strict observance of parchment barriers risks a greater affront by impairing the government's ability to protect its citizens. As a general rule, moreover, authorities must respect the broadest conception of individual rights compatible with their efforts at constitutional self-defense.

The principles of constitutionalism also require that emergency powers be exercised in a nonarbitrary fashion and not simply for the good of the holder.* An executive's powers must not, in Locke's words, be used for his or her own advantage, but rather "for the good of the Nation."[111] In a constitutional state political power must be utilized in the public interest. Following the distinction between absolute and arbitrary power, the principle of necessity seeks not to limit the scope of power but rather requires that all exercises of emergency power must be subject to review by someone other than the holder of the power. This review is satisfied in the first instance by the proper inauguration of emergency powers and in the second by review after their exercise.

Most prior efforts to constrain emergency powers have implicitly acknowledged this requirement. In the common law of martial rule, for example, the principle that necessity be genuine is supposedly satisfied by judicial review of emergency action once the crisis terminates.[112] In the civil law state of siege, the principle of necessity is satisfied by legislative control over the inauguration of crisis government.[113] Some combination of the two is preferable to either alone, for each is fraught with disabilities.[114] As we shall see in our study of Northern Ireland, courts infrequently question an executive's exercise of emergency power; our study of Weimar similarly will show that legislatures rarely curb the power of executives who are also party leaders.

There are also serious problems of logic in such requirements, as our discussion of Schlesinger suggested. A requirement that crisis government be inaugurated by someone other than the holder of the power would further the principle of necessity, but it suffers from grave defects. Successful resolution of a crisis that demands immediate action may not be able to suffer the delays such a condition entails.[115] Indeed, as we saw earlier, if the crisis requires suspension of the constitutional document, the constitutional status of the other branches of government is open to question. Consequently, requiring the

---

*Here again the institutional necessity of separated power becomes clear. As Federalist 51 indicates, one way to ensure that power is exercised not simply for personal advantage is to make "the interest of the man [coextensive] with the constitutional rights of the place."

executive to seek authorization for use of emergency powers beyond their initial duration is problematic. We must ask from whom he or she should seek authorization, and who is constitutionally entitled to give it. If suspension of the constitutional document subverts the constitutional status of the offices it creates, who can enforce the requirement that the exercise of emergency power must be subject to review by someone other than the executive? Who other than the holder of power is constitutionally authorized to determine that an emergency exists or when it is over?

In answer to this question, some constitutional documents seem to imply that certain structural provisions are immune from alteration or suspension during an emergency. Article 115g of the West German Constitution states: "The constitutional status and the exercise of the constitutional functions of the Federal Constitutional Court and its judges must not be impaired." Other provisions of the Federal Republic's emergency constitution seek to guarantee the institutional integrity of the Parliament. Similarly, Article 16 of the French Constitution provides that the National Assembly may not be dissolved during an emergency. The meaning of these and similar provisions in other constitutional texts is problematic. Insofar as they suggest that structural rules are immune from the exigencies of crisis when other constitutional provisions are not, we must ask (as we did with Schlesinger) whether and why the reasons that counsel disregard of nonstructural constitutional provisions do not also apply to structural rules.[116] If we cannot conceive of such a reason—and many theorists, including Barber, cannot—then the argument must be that the text notwithstanding, when structural provisions obstruct the project of the constitutional maintenance they too must fall.

The more persuasive argument, however (and one that better accounts for these textual provisions,)* is that any and all efforts at constitutional maintenance must respect the structural arrangements that constitutionalists think necessary to the achievement of reason in public affairs. On this argument, "survival of a constitutional order involves more than mere self-preservation, because of the rational, the spiritual content of this kind of order."[117] We should read these provisions in a way that suggests that the institutions of constitutional government receive their expression, their peculiar character and design, from constitutional documents but derive their legitimacy, their

---

*Some readers may question my claim of fidelity to the text, arguing, as does Barber, that in the American case at least, Article VI provides no warrant for the distinction between structural and nonstructural (substantive) constitutional provisions. Barber's ultimate claim is that "the logic of the Constitution" precludes a sharp distinction between the two. This position is difficult to square with the wording of the habeas corpus clause, which seems to authorize someone (who is another question) to suspend or violate one of the Constitution's substantive, nonstructural provisions, thus implying a distinction between structural and nonstructural provisions. Barber suggests, therefore, that we read the clause not as an authorization to suspend the writ but rather as a power to "furnish a substitute for the civil authority . . . overthrown by events." I think it easier to cull a distinction between structural and nonstructural provisions from the document than to read the habeas corpus clause in the way Barber proposes. In the arena of constitutional crises it is not the logic of the document but the logic of the enterprise that must be our guide.

authority, from a nation's commitment to constitutionalism itself. They are, in other words, constitutive of constitutionalism. Hence these institutions retain their constitutional authority to question an exercise of the Lockean prerogative even when contingency has overtaken the text.

Constitutional Maintenance
and Constitutional Reconstruction

Constitutional requirements like necessity and review are familiar components of efforts to reconcile constitutions with crises, even if, as we saw, the logic behind such requirements is not always clear. Even more common in the literature on constitutional crises is the claim that all exercises of emergency power must promote the ultimate aim of restoration of the "Constitution." Friedrich first derived the condition of restoration from the Roman dictatorship, and Schmitt made it the essential distinction between the commissarial dictatorship, the purpose of which was to maintain the constitution, and the sovereign dictatorship, which could abrogate the existing constitution and replace it with some other form of political organization. (Only the former, he argued, could be pursued in the Weimar Republic.) Schlesinger and Rossiter simply assumed that the objective of emergency powers must be the defense and restoration of the constitution.

Exactly what this requirement means in any particular case may be unclear. In certain types of crises, such as those that arise from severe economic depression or, as in the case of Cincinnatus, invasion by a foreign enemy, an argument for restoration of the constitution makes sense, although it often rests on dubious assumptions about the manageability and duration of crises. This formulation, however, leaves many questions unasked about the requirements of constitutional maintenance and constitutional reconstruction and once again obscures the distinction between constitutions and constitutionalism.

There are times when restoration of a suspended constitution, at least in its original form, makes less than good sense and is actually counterproductive to the larger task of constitutional maintenance. In crises that result from civil insurrection or domestic political terrorism, as in Northern Ireland, the legitimacy of the preexisting constitutional order is often the most salient and troublesome of questions. Widespread domestic violence can present constitutional governments with a situation in which part of the citizenry no longer consents to and indeed rejects the current constitutional order. In these circumstances, political prudence alone, as well as a commitment to constitutional maintenance, demands not the restoration of a constitution whose legitimacy is in dispute but rather establishment of conditions that allow better reasoning about the proper reconstruction of the constitutional order. The responsibility of constitutional governments is to make possible conditions in which constitutional principles can be affirmed. The task of constitutional maintenance and the commitment to these constitutional principles is better served through the admission that contingency will eventually overcome the specifics of any particular constitutional framework.

Constitutional maintenance in such cases requires not the restoration of a constitution in dispute but rather the restoration of conditions in which all parties can reason fairly and honestly about the proper reconstruction of the constitutional order. Not restoration but reconstruction is the ultimate constitutional necessity. An effort to construct a community on the basis of reason requires that government rationally *demonstrate* the desirability of current constitutional realities. A government which frustrates that goal or denies its necessity repudiates the assumptions upon which constitutionalism is predicated. Constitutional maintenance therefore requires that governmental authorities restore conditions in which reason replaces violence as the means of politics.

My earlier discussion of "good reasons" indicates that the principles of constitutionalism put some boundaries upon what count as good and what count as bad reasons in such a dialogue. Good reasons are those that depend for their persuasiveness not upon the authority of those who utter them but rather upon their fidelity to the constitutive principles. Reasons that reject the values of constitutionalism, or of reason itself as a necessary part of legitimate authority, therefore fall outside the pale.

This suggests that we may wish to distinguish between two different sorts of cases. Some readers may argue that it makes sense for governments to respect constitutional principles in the former cases, those (as is arguably the case in Northern Ireland) in which terrorists challenge specific constitutions but not the desirability of some set of constitutional forms. But what about the second sort, those in which terrorists reject constitutionalism and its commitment to reasoning and rational demonstration (as I shall argue was the case in Weimar Germany and is the case in the Federal Republic), perhaps because they believe its fascination with liberal individualism is destructive of community?[118] My argument goes to the obligations *governments* (and not citizens) must respect: Whatever the character and content of its opponents' aspirations, established authorities must continue to abide by the dictates of constitutionalism.* In short, government must continue to respect the rule of articulated reason and must continue to try to establish conditions in which reason replaces violence. Recall in this context that my project is to understand what a commitment to constitutional maintenance permits and prohibits in such cases, and that I undertake that project without supposing that it is always possible for governments to abide by that commitment. Recall also that the distinction between texts and principles, and between arbitrary and absolute power, has the signifi-

---

*Some may object that this approach ignores the importance of community boundaries in such disputes. To some extent this objection makes assumptions about who constitutes the relevant community. Constitutionalism's commitment to reason, as reflected in Federalist 1 (as well as Federalist 63 and the Declaration of Independence's appeal to "the opinions of mankind"), is that the relevant community consists of all rational human creatures. Constitutionalism assumes that respect for reason can *constitute* a community.

cant advantage of forestalling that choice by making the conflict between security and principle less immediate.

I hope it is clear, therefore, that I am *not* arguing that constitutional democracies must meekly suffer violence. "Feebleness is no guarantee of constitutionalism,"[119] and if those who reject constitutionalism refuse to reason, government may—indeed must—take steps to protect the community. Political violence offends the dignity and security of all citizens, and the project of constitutional maintenance requires that governments seek to prevent this affront. There is little point in reasoning with those who refuse to accept reasoned discourse as a method for settling political disputes. I *do* argue, however, that in formulating responses to political violence, states that aspire to constitutional status must not act in ways that deny or ignore constitutional values in the name of defending them.

Consequently, a constitutional regime's opponents do not forfeit their right to be treated as creatures *capable* of reason simply because they do not or cannot respect the same right in others.[120] In a constitutional state essential rights are a function of personhood, not citizenship. It is possible to argue that citizenship in a constitutional state imposes upon citizens a duty to pursue constitutional change through constitutional channels.[121] But individuals do not forfeit all rights upon misbehavior (although we might choose to say that by their failure to pursue remedies through constitutional channels they have failed to act in a reasoned fashion). To hold otherwise would be to fail to distinguish between the concept of equal worth and the capacity to reason. Inability or unwillingness to reason may well result in some cases of the *temporary* deprivation of the right to be treated as a reasoning creature (either through involuntary commitment or incarceration), but it can never lead to forfeiture of the right to be treated as a person of equal moral worth.

In formulating a *constitutional* response to political violence, then, governmental authorities may, in certain cases of the sort I have identified, properly suspend a wide variety of individual liberties. But they cannot act arbitrarily and they cannot unilaterally deprive citizens of their citizenship[122] or act in ways that foreclose the possibility of reasoned deliberations in the future with their opponents. Constitutionalism, the "empire of reason," assumes that in principle all of us have the capacity to be reasonable.[123] That assumption may be factually false, an intolerable inconvenience, or merely naive, but constitutional communities must embrace it.

At times, then, constitutional maintenance and reconstruction—restoration of conditions in which reasoned, nonviolent debate can proceed—may necessitate suspension of specific constitutional provisions or of entire constitutional documents. James Madison advanced a similar argument when he dismissed complaints that the Philadelphia Convention had exceeded its authority in reporting a new plan of government for the Union rather than revisions of the Articles of Confederation.[124] The charge of illegality was far from spurious. Article XIII of the Confederation plainly stated that amendments required the approval of all states. (The same article contained the claim to perpetuity.) The Convention's proposals were to take effect upon ratification by only nine.

(Although the new constitution bound only those states that chose to ratify it, once it took effect it dissolved the Articles.) Madison first argued that the charge of illegality was an "absurdity" for it would have given a veto over the new constitution to as little as "1/60th of the people of America."[125] Madison's second argument confronted the reproach more directly. The "end" of the Convention's charge, he argued, was "a firm national government," adequate to the exigencies of government and the preservation of the Union."[126] Insofar as this end was inconsistent with specific constitutional provisions in the Articles, "the means should be sacrificed to the end."[127] At times, then, our commitment to a union premised upon constitutional values may necessitate the "violation" of specific constitutional provisions and arrangements.

Nevertheless, the suspension of documentary restraints on the exercise of emergency power is not tantamount to suspension of all restraints on the exercise of power. Governmental authorities must in such cases continue to respect requirements dictated by constitutionalism's insistence upon reason. Madison acknowledged this in Federalist 40, when he responded to the charge that "the fundamental principles of the Confederation were not within the purview of convention, and ought not to have been varied"[128] by replying: "The truth is that the great principles of the Constitution proposed by the convention may be considered less as absolutely new than as the expansion of principles which are found in the Articles of Confederation."[129] Madison's response may be disingenuous, but the great principles he spoke of included limited government and separated power, and those structural provisions *did* appear in both texts, although their peculiar design and character differed in each. Moreover, the one principle Madison conceded the Convention had violated was the Confederation's process of amendment, an important structural rule, but one of an entirely different character than separation of powers and constitutional review, and one arguably incompatible with the claim to perpetuity included in the same article.

CONCLUSION

I referred earlier to President Lincoln's claim in his First Inaugural Address that "perpetuity is implied, if not expressed, in the fundamental law of all national governments."[130] Some readers may remember that Lincoln's claims were *not* about the constitutional text, but rather were claims about the nature of the Union. "[T]he Union," Lincoln observed, "is perpetual, confirmed by the history of the Union itself. [It] is much older than the Constitution."[131] As president, Lincoln thought it his constitutional obligation to save the Union, not the constitutional text, and if that responsibility for constitutional maintenance required what the text did not appear to authorize, so be it. Skeptics may argue that Lincoln's conception of constitutional maintenance was rather unlike the one proposed here, that his unilateral decision to suspend the writ of habeas corpus and peremptory treatment of Chief Justice Taney hardly amount to respect for structural rules and coordinate institutional actors.

Perhaps. But Merryman *was* eventually released. Moreover, Lincoln's concern for the Union surely included the federal bond (see *Texas v. White*), and, more important, his claim faithfully to execute the laws must mean that he thought his own institutional position was intact. And Lincoln *did* respond to Congress. In his address of July 4, 1861, he proffered a well-known set of constitutional arguments, or reasons, in support of his actions. Similarly, the efforts of the Philadelphia Convention, although in apparent violation of the Articles of Confederation, were necessary for "the preservation of the Union."[132]

This concern for preservation of the Union, and less for the particular constitutional text that is its expression, captures the essence of the principle of constitutional reconstruction that I have proposed and the conception of constitutional maintenance upon which it is premised. My account of constitutional maintenance includes the task of "defending the *inner-most self*."[133] In this way, we can understand the principle of perpetuity not as a claim about the constitutional text or of the specific political order it envisions but rather as a claim about our commitment to a constitutional politics writ large.

Afterword:
Constitutive Principles
and Right Answers

Although the manner of their derivation is an important question, it would be far beyond my means to establish the ontological status of background principles of the kind I assume here. In recent years, however, this question has received increasing attention. Much of the discussion has proceeded in the context of constitutional interpretation and whether there can be any principled defense of noninterpretive judicial review. The literature then quickly proceeded to a discussion of whether there are or could be "right answers" to political–moral problems. At the risk of caricature, I think it fair to conclude that most observers have denied such a possibility and that such denials have been thought to lead to a politically limited role for judicial review in a democratic society.[134]

There are some, however, who do argue that right answers *are* possible in hard cases. Michael Perry, for example, discussed the issue at some length in *The Constitution, the Courts, and Human Rights*,[135] where, for purposes of argument, he simply assumed that there can be right answers. Perry "put the assumption in question" in a subsequent work. In *Morality, Politics, and Law*, Perry concluded that there can be a conception of moral knowledge, that it should be a "naturalist" (or neo-Aristotelian) conception, and that such knowledge is not of single right answers but rather of a "naturalist perspective of moral reasoning" or moral discourse.[136]

Perry's account of moral knowledge as "knowledge of how particular human beings ought to live if as social entities they are to flourish"[137] leads him to reject foundationalism's insistence upon single right answers. He is also careful to distinguish between moral skepticism and moral relativism. The former, Perry argues, completely denies the possibility that moral claims can have truth value or that there can be moral knowledge. One can accept at least some versions of moral relativism, however, for while they are at odds with moral foundationalism, they are not necessarily incompatible with a naturalist account of moral discourse.[138]

Michael Moore, in contrast, has argued for a "realist theory of meaning" that rejects conventionalist theories of meaning. (The status of moral knowledge in Perry's argument is somewhat confusing. He clearly rejects the conventionalism associated with moral skepticism, but there could be a "deep" conventionalist account of knowledge that is arguably compatible with moral relativism.) Moore argues that "there are . . . true natures of natural kinds of things," as opposed to merely conventional or contingent things. Moore is therefore committed to a conception of reality that admits of right answers, and as a consequence moral questions are not to be answered by looking to conventions: "Rather, one can only rely on the best theory one can muster about what rightness or goodness is in particular contexts. As a realist and a naturalist, one *is* committed to there being right answers to moral questions— right answers framed exclusively with reference to natural facts."[139] The necessity of right answers, however, does not simplify the task of interpretation. "The realist's assertions—that there are right answers, that moral words need not be vague and that moral principles need not conflict—do not imply that one will be certain about what to do in many particular cases."[140] Thus the "vague clauses" of constitutional documents, such as the equal protection and due process clauses in the U.S. Constitution, "are vague only if one's theory of meaning is conventionalist; to the realist whose realism extends to moral language . . . such phrases have a very definite meaning that it is the business of a progressively better moral theory to reveal."[141] A conventionalist, by contrast, would argue that the only "true" kinds, or right answers, are those that are true with regard to the conventions of a particular society or culture.

Moore admits some uncertainty concerning whether a naturalist theory of meaning can apply to artifactual words, such as "sloop," or to functional words, such as "vehicle, pet, or carburetor."[142] Insofar as some such words refer to basic (or shared) human needs,[143] however, it may be possible to argue that there are "functional kinds" logically related to those needs. If contract making arises from and is functionally related to fundamental human needs, such as the need for security and predictability in certain types of social relationships, then what some cultures might call contracts may fall short of the least that any and all contracts must do to satisfy the need. The same could be true of constitution making, for all constitutional arrangements are elaborate and composite forms of simpler functions, such as planning, accepting/consenting, binding, and reaffirming. Of course, arguments based on these sorts of presuppositions are commonplace. For example, Hobbes and Locke derive their versions of the social contract from human needs, those of order and security, and hence premise political organization upon those needs.[144]

But to proceed on a different assumption, that constitutionalism and constitutional maintenance are wholly contingent or conventional activities, would not affect my argument. The initial decision to make a constitution (or a contract) may be contingent; once made, however, there are certain formal, internal requirements that must be satisfied if one is to truly understand one's self as engaging in that activity. Thus a decision that citizens ought to have public criteria for determining the legitimacy of governmental power may in the first place be contingent—it need not necessarily follow from some unalterable (or "natural") conception of human needs. Once the decision is made, what must be done to provide public criteria is not completely conventional but is instead partly formal or necessary, for what must be done to satisfy an end is at least in part a function of certain logical relationships *between* means (or powers) and ends. There is thus an internal necessity associated with the doing of certain tasks.[145]

The Declaration of Independence illustrates my point. The Declaration posits abstract principles concerning the ends and origins of proper government (that it shall rest on the consent of the governed) and sets as formal requirements the promulgation of policies that promote reason and preserve individual liberties. In other words, the Declaration posits the existence of certain abstract principles and identifies the formal mechanisms necessary for their attainment. Lon Fuller referred to the internal formal requirements of a legal system as the "inner morality of the law." Of a system that failed to comport with these formal requirements, Fuller argued that "[a] total failure in any one of these . . . directions does not simply result in a bad system of law; it results in something that is not properly called a legal system at all."[146] The internal, formal requirements, then, are necessary and constitutive in much the same way that the rules of chess, to borrow an earlier example, or of contract are constitutive of chess playing or contracting.

Again, I emphasize that I do not wish to undertake a full-scale defense of constitutional presuppositions, whether based on foundationalism, naturalism, or conventionalism, or upon arguments about the logic of means and ends. The literature on such issues is voluminous and I have neither the time nor the means to address it satisfactorily in this work. Moreover, my argument can proceed without fully resolving the question of origin. I refer to such questions only to support further my assumption that such background principles exist (an assumption I share with many others), to propose a theory of what some of them are, and to rely upon that theory in a constitutional argument that explores the internal or necessary requirements of dealing with circumstances in which granted powers are inadequate to secure our chosen ends in a manner consistent with the constitutive principles of constitutionalism.

II

CONSTITUTIONAL MAINTENANCE AND DISSOLUTION IN NORTHERN IRELAND

There is a Catholic history of Northern Ireland, romantic but tragic, and a Protestant history, equally romantic and no less tragic. Catholics begin their histories of brutal mistreatment by the British with the forcible settling of the Ulster plantation with Scottish colonists in 1607. Protestant histories begin with the savage Catholic uprising against the same plantation in 1641. When in 1689 King William's Protestant forces finally secured the plantation by defeating James's Catholic army, they inaugurated a conflict that has endured three centuries. Indeed, in 1922 William Churchill remarked: "The integrity of their quarrel is one of the few institutions that has been unaltered in the cataclysm which has swept the world."[1] Nearly seventy years and a second world war have not muted the force of Churchill's observation.

Neither history is completely wrong, which may partially explain their enduring appeal, but both are misleading and each is a religion unto itself. The continued existence of separate schools for Catholic and Protestant children, a separation encouraged by both communities, perpetuates these myths.[2] One Catholic, describing his own education, observed: "We came very early to our politics. One learned, quite literally at one's mother's knee, that Christ died for the human race and Patrick Pearse for the Irish section of it."[3]

As the foregoing quote suggests, more important than the formal instruction Ulster's children receive is the informal education they acquire from their family, friends, and neighbors. Frank Burton underscored the extent of this learning when he wrote of the practice of "telling," or "the pattern of signs and cues by which religious ascription is arrived at in the everyday interactions of Protestants and Catholics."[4] Even toddlers can tell: Once, while sitting alone in a Belfast coffee shop, I was scouted by a young boy, who was perhaps three or four years old; after he concluded his elaborate surveillance, he returned to his mother and asked in a loud whisper if I was Catholic. He could have only guessed by the newspaper I was reading. But had I spoken to him, he might have noticed my pronunciation of the letter "h." Or he might have guessed by

47

my choice of words, especially had I sworn or taken the Lord's name in vain. All of these are supposed signs of my religious affiliation, and they take on a special significance in a country always on the brink of a civil war. It is, of course, difficult for an outsider (and most of Ulster's citizens as well) to take all of this seriously, but I never saw anyone make a mistake.

There can be no single constitutional history of such a society. There are instead competing histories and often there is no sound way to choose between them. And yet the constitutional issues raised by political violence in Ireland cannot be understood without some appreciation of the historical context within which they are situated. As William Butler Yeats wrote in "Sixteen Dead Men,"

> But who can talk of give and take,
> What should be and what not,
> While those dead men are loitering there
> To stir the boiling pot?[5]

Ulster's history still stirs the boiling pot.

Before I undertake an analysis of Northern Ireland's efforts at constitutional maintenance, therefore, I first review in some detail the political and legal history that supplies the context for these efforts. To those unfamiliar with what is often called the politics of the last atrocity, the troubles in Northern Ireland must often seem anachronistic, an unwelcome remnant of a less happy period of religious strife in Western Europe. We can better appreciate the problems, both political and constitutional, that terrorism poses if we understand the history that makes such violence possible.

Chapter 2 begins with the partition of Ireland into two distinct legal entities in 1921 and then examines the development of the Northern Irish civil rights movement in the 1960s, a movement overtaken in later years by the proponents of violence and the rebirth of the Irish Republican Army. Unfortunately, this pattern, in which plodding moderation inevitably succumbs to the imagined romance and efficacy of violence, is no less a constant in Irish history than is the separation of Catholic and Protestant. The chapter concludes with the dissolution of Stormont and Britain's recent efforts at constitutional reconstruction.

Chapter 3 considers how Great Britain and Northern Ireland have altered their normal criminal processes to cope with the unusual strains political terrorism imposes on the criminal judicial process. This discussion examines the extent to which the major features of the antiterrorism legislation conform with requirements of constitutional maintenance formulated in chapter 1. I again stress that I am not much concerned with whether these acts pass muster under English constitutional standards (though such an analysis would be important in its own right), for I am interested in whether the principles of constitutionalism, rather than the particular principles of specific constitutional regimes, provide a standard against which to measure efforts at constitutional maintenance in any democracy.

Britain's emergency legislation, however, is but part of a larger policy of controlling terrorism by downplaying its political character and emphasizing its criminality. This policy, criminalization, attempts to deny the political character of the terrorist offense by prosecuting terrorists in criminal courts which are not normal but at least resemble ordinary courts as closely as possible.[6] Since March 1976, criminalization has resulted in the denial of "special category" status to convicted terrorists—in other words, the refusal to concede that convicted terrorists are political prisoners.[7]

The policy of criminalization, like the terrorism it tries to overcome, is designed to influence and shape public opinion. Implicit in the denial of special category status, for example, is an attempt to persuade Northern Irish Catholics that terrorists are not heroic Irish patriots but brutal criminals. Even so, the emergency legislation under which terrorists are arrested, detained, tried, and sentenced explicitly defines terrorism as the use of violence for *political* ends,[8] thus creating something of a contradiction in British policy—a contradiction not lost on some Irish Catholics.

As I argued earlier, the constitutive principles of constitutionalism, in particular the principle of constitutional reconstruction, require that government rationally demonstrate the desirability of a disputed constitutional order. Constitutionalism depends for its authority upon a community consent engendered by respect for reason and reasoned discourse, not upon raw power. A constitutional response to forms of political terrorism which dispute the legitimacy of the constitutional order (as in Northern Ireland) must therefore recognize the political character and motivation of such violence. British antiterrorism statutes satisfy this requirement in their definitional aspects: Section 31 of the Emergency Provisions Act defines terrorism as the use of violence for political ends. The larger policy of criminalization, however, denies that Irish terrorism is politically and constitutionally motivated. In this respect, as we shall see, the policy of criminalization in general, and specific statutory provisions in particular, fail to comport with the demands of constitutional maintenance.

2

Constitutional Dissolution and
Reconstruction in Northern Ireland

THE CONSTITUTIONAL ORIGINS
OF NORTHERN IRELAND

The state of Northern Ireland was formally created with the passage in 1920 of
the Government of Ireland Act (GoA), which partitioned Ireland into two
distinct legal states, each with its own parliament, executive, and judiciary, and
both subordinate to Westminster.[1] The act also created a Council of Ireland,
"with a view to the eventual establishment of a parliament for the whole of
Ireland."[2] The council was to include members from both the Northern and
Southern legislatures and was given jurisdiction over less contentious matters,
such as fisheries and railroad services between the provinces. The GoA also
created a High Court of Appeal with jurisdiction over both provinces. The act's
terms, particularly the provision for the council, suggest that it was a provisional step toward a reunited Ireland.

Whatever the act's original purpose, however, it functioned as the constitution for the state of Northern Ireland for fifty years. The GoA transferred
legislative power from Westminster to Stormont, the North's legislature, in
order to promote "peace, order, and good government" in the province. In
many areas, Stormont could act freely:

> Put positively, the Northern Ireland Parliament [could] legislate on matters
> relating to law and order, to the police, to courts other than the Supreme
> Court, to civil and criminal law, to local government, to health and social
> services, to education, to planning and development, to commerce and indus-
> trial development and internal trade, to agriculture and to finance.[3]

Despite this expansive grant of power, Westminster reserved to itself authority over such areas as foreign policy, defense, taxation, external trade, and
all matters relating to the Crown. In addition, Section 75 of the GoA explicitly
provided that "[n]otwithstanding the establishment of the parliament of . . .
Northern Ireland, or anything contained in this Act, the Supreme Authority of
the Parliament of the United Kingdom shall remain unaffected and undimin-
ished over all persons, matters and things in [Northern] Ireland and every part
thereof."[4] In sum, Westminster and Stormont possessed concurrent authority

over a wide range of subjects, but there was no subject over which Stormont had exclusive jurisdiction. Consequently, the GoA did not establish a federation between Northern Ireland and England but rather instituted in Northern Ireland a form of devolved government.[5]

The apparent clarity of Section 75 notwithstanding, the degree of independence Stormont really possessed was always a matter of some controversy. There soon developed a poorly defined convention in Westminster–Stormont relations that Westminster would not entertain questions relating to Northern Ireland's internal affairs, so long as Stormont had acted on the issue.[6] Some Unionists claimed that the convention meant that Westminster was *incompetent* to legislate on matters transferred to Stormont, but the provision itself belied that interpretation. The better view was merely that transferred powers, as a matter of legislative diplomacy, should not be discussed in the House of Commons. The first "relate[d] to the competence of Parliament to legislate: the second relate[d] only to the procedures of the House of Commons with regard to parliamentary questions and debate."[7]

The GoA did not contain a bill of rights, but it did limit Stormont's powers in various other ways. The most important of these limitations was set forth in Section 5: "[The Parliament of Northern Ireland] shall [not] make a law so as either directly or indirectly to establish or endow any religion, or prohibit or restrict the free exercise thereof, or give a preference, privilege, or advantage, or impose any disability or disadvantage, on account of religious belief."[8]

The wording of Section 5 indicates that it proscribed laws discriminatory in both appearance and effect.[9] Thus "[p]atterns of discrimination arising in the distribution of welfare, unemployment benefits, or aid to education would [have been] prohibited by this section."[10] A similar provision, Section 8(6), prohibited the executive from discriminating on the basis of religious belief.

Notwithstanding these constitutional guarantees against religious discrimination, sparse though they were, the Northern Irish statelet was, to paraphrase the words of its first prime minister, a Protestant state for a Protestant people. Blessed with a two-thirds majority in population, but tortured by fear of the Catholic minority, Protestants controlled Stormont, the city of Belfast, and the other industrial centers of Ulster. Restrictive franchise laws and gerrymandering ensured Protestant dominance even in those areas, such as Newry and Derry, where Catholics constituted a majority.

Political discrimination was so pervasive that the Roman Catholic Nationalist party, although committed to reform through constitutional channels, refused to sit in Stormont until 1927 and even then refused to adopt the title of "Loyal Opposition." Like the nationalist parties that had preceded them, Northern Irish nationalists were in a precarious position, committed to peaceful reforms in a state in which they constituted a permanent minority both feared and reviled by the Protestant majority. The Nationalists were thus always at risk of being preempted by the supporters of the Irish Republican Army and its political wing, Sinn Fein, who shared neither their patience nor their commitment to nonviolence. From the 1920s to the 1950s, the IRA repeatedly waged terrorist campaigns against the new government, and on

December 12, 1956, it issued a formal declaration of war against the Northern Irish state.

EMERGENCY POWERS IN NORTHERN IRELAND: 1921-1971

The IRA's 1956 campaign was ineffectual, but some of its earlier efforts met with greater success. Upon its creation in 1921, Northern Ireland was in a state of incipient civil war. Its boundaries and the loyalties of one-third of its population, perhaps half in the border counties, were uncertain. Indeed, Ulster's second city was predominantly Catholic. Even more troubling, the IRA, having spurned Eamon De Valera's proposal that Sinn Fein enter the Southern Dáil, began to carry out guerrilla operations against the fledgling state. Protestant leaders feared a Catholic uprising, and not without reason, for sectarian violence was so widespread that almost 300 people were killed between 1920 and 1922. In the latter year alone "232 people were killed (including two Unionist MPs), nearly 1,000 were wounded, 400 were interned, and more than £3 million worth of property was destroyed."[11]

It is hardly surprising that Northern authorities enacted emergency legislation in such circumstances. Given the sad history of violence in the thirty-two counties, it would have been more surprising had the state *not* resorted to emergency measures. One constitutional lawyer described the resulting legislation, the Special Powers Act (SPA), as "a desperate measure taken to deal with a desperate situation."[12]

Desperate the SPA might have been, but the decision to employ emergency legislation was hardly an innovation in Irish politics. As early as 1781, the Irish Parliament had passed the Habeas Corpus Act, which provided that the legislature could suspend the great writ in an emergency. More immediate predecessors to the Special Powers Act included the Defense of the Realm (Consolidation) Act (1914) and later the Restoration of Order in Ireland Act (1920). The second authorized civil and military authorities to make regulations for dealing with disorders and civil disturbances under the Defense of the Realm Act, which was legally effective only during World War I. Except for courts martial, the Special Powers Act was identical to its predecessor: "Indeed the original 30 regulations dealing with powers of arrest, detention, search and seizure . . . were all directly adopted from the Restoration of Order in Ireland regulations."[13] Among these regulations were provisions that permitted authorities to detain individuals without formally charging them and to try them in secret courts.

As an emergency statute, then, the SPA (and its hardly less benign successors, as we shall see in the next chapter) should be thought of as "not as a unique piece of legislation, but as taking its place in that long line of repressive statutes which the unsettled state of Ireland has called forth."[14] Any analysis of antiterrorism legislation in Northern Ireland must acknowledge that emergency legislation, in one form or another, has been a permanent feature of Northern Irish law since the state's creation.

The Special Powers Act created two categories of offenses—those specified in the act itself and others set forth in regulations promulgated under the act. Authority to promulgate such regulations rested with the Northern Ireland executive, the minister of home affairs, who could in turn delegate this power to any of his deputies, including any officer of the Royal Ulster Constabulary. The potential reach of such regulations was nearly unlimited: Section 1 of the act gave the minister authority to "take all such steps and issue all such orders as may be necessary for preserving the peace and maintaining order."[15] Subsection 1(4) set forth a procedure for parliamentary review of such regulations, thus initially satisfying the constitutive principle of constitutional review, but the terms delegating the minister's authority provided that Parliament, to exercise its review, had to ask the minister to withdraw the regulation within fourteen days of its submission to Parliament.[16] The legislature's authority was thus entirely reactive in character.

Under Section 2(4), an equally expansive provision, an individual could be guilty of a criminal offense even if the action was not proscribed by a specific regulation: "If any person does any act of such a nature as to be calculated to be prejudicial to the preservation of the peace or maintenance of order in Northern Ireland and not specifically provided for in the regulations, he shall be deemed to be guilty of an offence against the regulations."* Other sections of the Special Powers Act now seem barbaric. Section 5, for example, authorized whippings for certain offenses, including possession of explosives and firearms. Section 6 authorized the death penlty for attempting to cause or causing an explosion endangering human life *or* property.

The Special Powers Act and its regulations thus abrogated a number of civil liberties often associated with constitutional democracies. It also significantly compromised a number of liberties arguably not strictly necessary for democratic government but nonetheless recognized elsewhere in the United Kingdom, including freedom from self-incrimination, freedom from arbitrary arrest and detention, presumption of innocence, and trial by jury. Practically speaking, the result of the SPA and the numerous regulations it spawned: "taken in conjunction with the existence of the Special Constabulary [then 44,000 men,] was that apart from . . . military courts, the Government enjoyed powers similar to those current in time of martial law."[17]

Desperate measures have a way of enduring beyond the life of the situations that give rise to them. As originally drafted, the Special Powers Act was a temporary measure, its duration limited to one year. Stormont annually renewed the act through 1928, when its duration was extended to five years. In 1933 Stormont simply made the act permanent, thus institutionalizing measures adopted during an emergency that had long since expired.

---

*Compare the German Penal Code Amendment Law, published by the Nazi cabinet on June 26, 1935, which provided that courts shall punish offenses not punishable under the code when they are deserving of punishment "according to the underlying idea of a penal code or according to healthy public sentiment [Volksempfinden]."

CONSTITUTIONAL CHANGE
AND THE CIVIL RIGHTS MOVEMENT

Repeal of the Special Powers Act was a central goal of the Northern Irish civil rights movement, which began in earnest in the early 1960s. The movement was fueled by a younger generation of middle-class, university-educated Catholics who had no firsthand experience with the violence that had beset Northern Ireland in its first years. Unlike the challenges to the Northern Irish state pressed by radical republicans, the civil rights movement campaigned peacefully for reforms *within* Ulster that would enable Catholics to participate fully and equally in the political and economic life of the province and for the equal application of civil and criminal laws. In this respect, it was fundamentally different from previous Catholic challenges to the state. In the 1920s and through the 1950s the IRA violently challenged the legitimacy of Northern Ireland's constitutional union with the United Kingdom. In contrast, the civil rights movement sought not the destruction of the existing constitutional order but rather full inclusion within that order. The civil rights movement concentrated, in other words, upon the construction of a constitutional community *within* Ulster, a community that would be

> centred on a number of fundamental democratic claims: the right to participate in the election of central and local government through a scrupulously fair electoral system; the right to pursue legitimate political and social objectives without interference from government; the right to share equitably in the allocation of state resources; and the right to freedom from arbitrary arrest or detention.[18]

In 1969 the Cameron Commission, appointed by Prime Minister Terence O'Neill to investigate the civil disturbances that wrenched Ulster in 1968 and 1969, concluded that most of the complaints of the civil rights movement were well-founded. With regard to charges that local and parliamentary elections were biased against Roman Catholics because of gerrymandering and restrictive franchise laws, for example, the commission observed that "we show that the complaint is abundantly justified. In each of the areas with Unionist majorities on their council the majority was far greater than the adult population balance would justify."[19]

The reforms needed to correct discriminatory electoral practices did not, of course, threaten the integrity of the Northern Irish state, at least not in any immediate sense. Nor did they "in any sense endanger the stability of the Constitution."[20] They did, however, threaten the Protestant hegemony that had characterized Northern Irish politics since the state's creation. Many Loyalists understandably reacted to the civil rights movement with hostility and distrust.

One Unionist who recognized the underlying legitimacy of Catholic grievances was Terence O'Neill, from 1963 to 1969 leader of the Unionist party and prime minister of the province. A thoughtful moderate among extremists of all persuasions, O'Neill recognized the need for fundamental changes in Northern Ireland and pressed a campaign of economic development, modernization, improved relations with the Republic, and the political integration of Ulster's Catholics.[21] His moderation contrasted starkly with the attitudes of his three predecessors, whose policy toward reconciliation with Ulster's Catholics was exemplified in a popular Unionist phrase, "Not an inch."

The foibles and fortunes of O'Neill's reign as prime minister parallel those of the civil rights movement. They began together in the early 1960s, complementing one another, and the collapse of O'Neill's government in 1969 was accompanied by the inability of moderate Catholic leaders to control the disparate elements of the civil rights movement. Their interwoven histories reflect the uncertain rise and tragic fall of the moderate center in Ulster's politics.

The Birth of the Civil Rights Movement

Like its American counterpart, from which it borrowed freely, the Northern Irish civil rights movement was composed of several large national organizations and a welter of local groups, each with its own program of reform. Membership in any one civil rights group did not preclude membership in another. As a consequence, Ulster's various civil rights organizations campaigned for similar goals, but they often could not agree on a common strategy for achieving shared objectives.

Much of the history of the civil rights movement thus is marked by bickering within and among the various groups that comprised it. Britain and Stormont's inability to recognize the independence and autonomy of the sundry groups, and their mistaken impression that the cooperation of one, the Northern Ireland Civil Rights Association (NICRA), would ensure the cooperation of others, seriously handicapped their efforts at reform in the late 1960s and early 1970s, much as it continues to hamper the process of constitutional reconstruction, as we shall see later in this chapter.

Partly as a propaganda tool and partly out of genuine belief, many Unionists attempted to undermine the credibility of the civil rights movement and NICRA by charging that both were controlled by the IRA or its sympathizers. The Cameron Commission, appointed by O'Neill to investigate several disturbances in the province, concluded that most of NICRA's members had no ties to radical republican groups and that on the whole the movement sought to achieve its aim "within the framework of the Constitution."[22] Nevertheless, the commission did find that NICRA's membership included some IRA sympathizers and that "there is little doubt that left wing extremists . . . would be ready to take over, if they could, the real direction of the Civil Rights Association and direct its activities from a reformist policy to a much more radical course."[23]

The Cameron Commission proved itself an astute student of Anglo-Irish history: There is little in that record to suggest that the Irish possess much patience with parliamentary efforts at reform and much to suggest that violence might work when all else fails. Had they permitted the Roman Catholic community to express dissent through constitutional channels, British and Protestant leaders in Northern Ireland might have forestalled the decision by certain elements of the civil rights movement eventually to adopt extraconstitutional tactics.

Instead, Westminster and Stormont initially responded to the movement with indifference and hostility. Under the cover of constitutional custom, Westminster simply refused to entertain questions relating to the internal affairs of Northern Ireland. As we saw, under Section 75 of the Government of Ireland Act (1920), the United Kingdom retained ultimate authority over the six counties. Had Westminster chosen to do so, it could have initiated reforms even over Stormont's objections. Indeed, Westminster's intervention after the civil rights demonstrations turned violent in the late 1960s ultimately led to its decision in 1972 to prorogue the Northern Irish Parliament. Britain's refusal to entertain the movement's parliamentary efforts should be seen, then, not only as a result of constitutional convention but also as a statement of England's general unwillingness to consider the problems of Ulster's Catholics. This reluctance was all the greater given O'Neill's public commitment to reform in the province.

In contrast, Stormont actively pursued policies designed to limit Catholic opportunities to express dissent. The 1967 Republican Clubs legislation, for example, promulgated under the Special Powers Act, made unlawful "organizations declaring themselves as 'republican clubs' or any like organization howsoever described." The legislation encouraged republicans and republican sympathizers to channel their energies into NICRA and the People's Democracy by restricting other avenues of legitimate dissent. The reach of the legislation is best appreciated by examining a test case brought before local magistrates.[24] In March 1968, Mr. McEldowney was alleged to be a member of the Slaughtneil Republican Club. The case was dismissed because the lower court found that the club could not reasonably be said to constitute a threat to the public peace. The Northern Irish Court of Appeals reversed the decision, concluding that only the minister of home affairs could make such a judgment. In dissent, Lord Chief Justice MacDermott argued that the legislation was too vague to be sufficiently related to the purpose of maintaining the public order.[25] The decision was appealed to the House of Lords, where it was dismissed by a majority of three lords to two. The majority, much in line with prevailing British constitutional law, concluded that absent proof of ministerial bad faith (which had not been alleged), the minister's discretion could not be challenged. The minority, comprised of Lord Justices Diplock and Pearce, argued much as had Lord Chief Justice MacDermott in the lower court.[26] As a result of the decision, the minister of home affairs could ban republican clubs, even in the absence of evidence reasonably supporting a finding that such clubs constituted an actual threat to public order.

More important than specific legislation, however, was the general intransigence of many Loyalists, often inspired by the Reverend Ian Paisley. This obdurateness, which usually expressed itself in calls for law and order and "get-tough" policies, ultimately undermined O'Neill's efforts as well as the ability of moderate Catholic leaders to control the civil rights movement.

The Civil Rights Movement and Public Demonstrations

The leaders of the civil rights movement first pursued their goals through peaceful political and legal action, hoping that public pressure would force Stormont and Westminster to undertake political, economic, and social reforms. When those efforts failed, the more aggressive elements of the civil rights movement, confirming the wisdom of the Cameron Commission and inspired by a history in which violence often achieves what peaceful agitation cannot, began to organize marches and protests. In the politics of the last atrocity, "all History is Applied History."[27]

The first public march in Northern Ireland arose from a specific instance of discrimination. In June 1968 a Nationalist MP, Austin Currie, attempted to get public housing in Caledon, County Tyrone, for a poor Catholic family. Local Unionist leaders resisted, preferring instead to let the house to an unmarried nineteen-year-old Protestant woman, who was also a secretary to a prominent Unionist official. Under the pretense that housing decisions were local matters, Unionists in Stormont refused to intervene in the controversy.[28] On June 20, 1968, Currie organized a "squat-in" at the house. Its success led Currie and others associated with the Campaign for Social Justice (CSJ) to organize a public march on Saturday, August 24, which attracted over twenty-five hundred participants.[29]

Upon hearing of the march, the Reverend Ian Paisley's Ulster Volunteer Party announced that it would organize a counterdemonstration in Dungannon. Minister of Home Affairs William Craig subsequently used his powers under the Public Order Act to reroute the CSJ march through the Catholic sections of Dungannon.[30] NICRA considered not joining the march but reluctantly agreed to participate. Its hesitation, coupled with the leadership of the more moderate CSJ, reflects the increasing frustration that moderate Catholic leaders felt at trying to secure civil rights through the normal channels of political participation.

Given the publicity the first march generated, it was not long before the civil rights movement began to plan others. At the suggestion of local civil rights groups in Derry, NICRA organized a second march, to begin on October 5, 1968.[31] Derry was the logical choice for the march, for it holds tremendous political and religious significance to both communities in Northern Ireland. The city's very name evokes conflict.[32] Catholics prefer the original name of Derry, whereas Protestants prefer the name adopted in 1613—Londonderry (pronounced "Londundree"). Although Catholics constitute a majority in Derry, gerrymandering and restrictive franchise laws usually have given Protestants control of the city's government.

On October 1 the Apprentice Boys, a local organization dedicated to the memory of King William's historic victory over James at Derry in 1689, notified the Royal Ulster Constabulary (RUC), as required by the Public Order Act, that they would hold their "annual" parade through the heart of Derry on the same day and along the same route that NICRA had planned its march.[33] NICRA's route would have taken the Catholic marchers through the Protestant sections of the city. Self-styled protectors of the city's virtue, the Apprentice Boys could not quietly suffer this deliberate provocation. The Cameron Commission later found that the parade was a ruse designed to force Craig to ban NICRA's demonstration.[34] The ruse worked, at least in part, for Craig banned both demonstrations.

Incensed at what they saw as another Unionist attempt to foreclose all avenues of political dissent, local activists in Derry, with the assistance of members of the Young Socialists group in Belfast, persuaded an averse NICRA to defy Craig's ban. On October 5 over two thousand people, including MPs Austin Currie, Eddie McAteer, and Gerry Fitt, gathered in the Bogside, a Catholic ghetto, to begin the march. As it began to cross Craigavon Bridge, which leads into the heart of the city, the march was intercepted by the RUC and the B Specials, who used batons and water cannons to break up the demonstration. The RUC's brutal attack against a peaceful, albeit illegal march resulted in injuries to seventy-seven civilians and eleven policemen and attracted worldwide television coverage.[35]

This violence polarized the Catholic and Protestant communities. Protestants saw the episode as further proof of treasonous Catholic intentions. Catholics, on the other hand, saw the incident as conclusive evidence that the state would never grant them political and social equality. Moderate Catholic leaders were increasingly frustrated at their inability to make progress through peaceful, constitutional channels, and on October 15 the Nationalist party withdrew as the official opposition in Stormont.[36]

On November 22, in an attempt to appease Catholics, O'Neill suspended the local authority in Derry and replaced it with a "development commission,"[37] comprised of four Catholics and five Protestants. The government also appointed an independent ombudsman to investigate Catholic grievances and promised that "as soon as . . . this can be done without undue hazard, such of the Special Powers as are in conflict with international obligations will . . . be withdrawn from current use."[38] Protestant reaction to O'Neills efforts was typically hostile. On November 30 the Reverend Ian Paisley led a demonstration designed to obstruct a Catholic march in Armagh that had been approved by the RUC and the minister of home affairs. Paisley was later arrested and sentenced to three months in jail.

Four days after the Derry march, students and lecturers at Queen's University in Belfast, most of whom were members of the Young Socialists or similar organizations, began a march of their own. The plan was to parade from the university to Belfast City Hall, which would take approximately forty-five minutes to an hour. Ten minutes from the university, in Shaftsbury Square, the students met a counterdemonstration, again led by Ian Paisley. After the march, quickly rerouted by the RUC, ended, its organizers met at the Student Activities Center at the university and created the People's Democracy (PD).

Founding members included Michael Farrell, a passionately committed socialist, and Bernadette Devlin (now Bernadette Devlin McAllister), who later
attracted worldwide notice as a Nationalist MP at Westminster.

Unlike other civil rights groups, the People's Democracy had no particular
desire to seek change through normal constitutional channels, even had such a
course been possible. The PD sought much more than the political and social
integration of Catholics in Ulster: It hoped to replace both Stormont and the
Dublin Parliament with a United Irish Workers' Republic.[39] The PD's tactics
also differed from those of mainstream civil rights groups.

NICRA, for example, had only hesitantly agreed to organize and participate in the earlier marches. In contrast, the People's Democracy aggressively
planned demonstrations, organizing several small marches throughout late
October and November, normally without the approval or assistance of other
civil rights groups in the province. In the meantime, O'Neill continued to seek
means to defuse the protracted violence. On October 28 the prime minister
asked William Craig, minister of home affairs, and therefore responsible in
large measure for the violence in Derry, to resign.[40] In a television speech on
December 9, O'Neill pleaded for an end to the marches and countermarches,
assuring Catholics that their complaints would be heard and acted upon. He
also warned Unionists that their failure to accept reforms might well lead
Westminster to intervene, explaining that

> Mr. Wilson made it absolutely clear . . . that if we did not face up to our
> problems the Westminster Parliament might well decide to act over our
> heads. Where would our Constitution be then? What shred of self-respect
> would be left to us? If we allowed others to solve our problems because we
> had not the guts—let me use a plain word—guts to face up to them, we would
> be utterly shamed.[41]

O'Neill's government did adopt a sweeping program of reform, but it did
not endorse the principle of "one man, one vote" in local elections, which was
of central symbolic significance to Catholics. As a consequence, many Catholics believed that the reforms did not go far enough. NICRA's representatives
did agree to call a truce on further demonstrations, however, recognizing that
O'Neill was sympathetic to their demands.[42] In turn, most Protestants thought
O'Neill went too far in appeasing a disloyal minority.

NICRA's moderation was well-meaning, but its executive committee could
not speak for the civil rights movement as a whole. On January 1, 1969, the
People's Democracy and a group of Young Socialists, led by Michael Farrell,
Kevin Boyle, and Louden Seth, announced that they would break the truce by
holding a march from Belfast to Derry.[43] Paisley and other Protestant Ultras
announced that they would organize a series of counterdemonstrations, but the
RUC refused to ban either march. The PD's march attracted only about eighty
participants. It was hardly representative of the civil rights movement as a
whole, but its very occurrence was dramatic evidence of the inability of
moderate Catholic leaders to exercise effective control over the increasingly
disparate elements of the civil rights movement.

The first days of the march were relatively uneventful. On January 4, however, the demonstrators were attacked by Loyalists with rocks and batons at the picturesque Burntollet Bridge, just outside Derry. No one was killed, but several of the marchers were severely injured. People's Democracy leaders insisted that the RUC had known of the impending attack, even chatting with the Loyalist crowd while waiting for the marchers to arrive, but had refused to warn the marchers or restrain the attackers.[44] The Cameron Commission, appointed by O'Neill to investigate the disturbance, disagreed but did conclude that a number of B Specials had participated in the attacks.[45]

The march struggled on to Derry, where it was once again attacked. That same night, members of the RUC stationed in Derry, shouting "Come out you Fenian bastards and we'll give you one for the Pope," ransacked Catholic ghettos in the city. In defense, Catholics erected barricades in the Bogside, created "Free Derry," and claimed to have seceded from Northern Ireland.[46] The Cameron Commission reported that "a number of policemen were guilty of misconduct which involved assault and battery, malicious damage to property in streets in the Catholic Bogside area, giving reasonable cause for apprehension of personal injury among other innocent inhabitants, and the use of provocative sectarian and political slogans."[47] The commission also concluded that the organizers were "ineffective" and that the leaders of the Civil Rights Association had little control over the march.[48]

O'Neill's decision to appoint the Cameron Commission prompted several resignations in his cabinet, including that of Brian Faulkner, who would later become prime minister.[49] Faulkner and his supporters believed that O'Neill's efforts at reconciliation had gone too far. In cabinet meetings, Faulkner had opposed electoral reforms, yet in his resignation speech he accused the prime minister of having appointed the Cameron Commission solely as a political sop that would urge the government to adopt the principle of one man, one vote. Faulkner demanded instead that the government simply effect the reform itself. O'Neill angrily accused Faulkner of disloyalty to the party and reminded Faulkner of his own longstanding opposition to the principle of one man, one vote.[50]

O'Neill's efforts likewise won him little support among Catholics, for his condemnation of the People's Democracy, absent a similar censure of the RUC, struck many Catholics as overly partisan. In a blunt statement issued on January 5, Prime Minister O'Neill stated:

> The march . . . planned by the so-called Peoples Democracy, was, from the start, a foolhardy and irresponsible undertaking. At best those who planned it were careless of the effects which it would have; at worse they embraced with enthusiasm the prospect of adverse publicity causing further damage to the interests of Northern Ireland.[51]

O'Neill also condemned the Protestant extremists who attacked the march and concluded by scolding: "Enough is enough. We have heard sufficient for now about civil rights; let us hear a little about civic responsibility."[52]

In an attempt to forestall a crisis of confidence in his administration and to quiet extremists on both sides, O'Neill gambled by calling for an election on February 27, 1969. The following day, the Unionist party met in caucus and reelected O'Neill as leader, although ten prominent party members, including Faulkner, abstained.[53] O'Neill thus escaped with a narrow victory, but if the election was meant to silence hard-line critics, it failed miserably. The closeness of the vote only encouraged critics within and without the government to step up their attacks.

Renewed cries for law and order in the Unionist party, for example, led to the introduction in March of a new Public Order Bill, which gave the government additional powers to control and to ban demonstrations. The bill seemed to make no difference—violence continued to flare in the Catholic areas of Belfast and Derry. Moreover, elections for NICRA's executive committee awarded two seats to People's Democracy leaders, one of whom was Michael Farrell. On March 14, four of the committee's more moderate members resigned, protesting that the organization was becoming too militant.[54] The center in Northern Irish politics was collapsing under the weight of an Irish history in which moderates play little part.

On April 19 NICRA's new leadership announced that it would hold a march from the Burntollet Bridge to Derry. When O'Neill responded by banning the march, NICRA decided instead to hold a sit-in demonstration, which once again led to a confrontation with the RUC and Paisley's supporters. Two hundred and nine policemen and seventy-nine civilians were injured in the rioting.

On the day after the disorder in Derry, there were bomb explosions throughout the province, including explosions at the Silent Valley Reservoir in County Down and at a power station in Portadown. Most observers blamed the IRA, but the government later concluded that the Ulster Volunteer Force, a Protestant paramilitary group, had framed the IRA, hoping that the explosions would provoke a harsh response from Unionists.[55] The plan worked. Moderates in the O'Neill administration, distressed with the government's inability to maintain order, moved further to the right. Nearly a week later, on April 28, the beleaguered prime minister resigned, stating, on television, "I have tried to break the chains of ancient hatreds. I have been unable to realise during my period of office all that I had sought to achieve. Whether now it can be achieved in my life-time I do not know. But one day these things will be and must be achieved."[56]

On May 1, after O'Neill's dramatic resignation, the Unionist party elected his cousin, Major James Chichester-Clark, to replace him. Brian Faulkner rejoined the cabinet. Chichester-Clark immediately announced that the government would grant amnesty to everyone convicted of a political offense since October 5, 1968.[57] Catholics and Protestants alike benefited from the amnesty—one of those released was the Reverend Paisley. NICRA responded to Chichester-Clark's efforts by temporarily banning all demonstrations. On May 21, Chichester-Clark, Faulkner, and other Unionist officials met with Prime Minister Harold Wilson and Home Secretary James Callaghan in London, after which they announced that the next local elections would be held on the one man, one vote principle. The measures did little to resolve the fundamental problems still facing Ulster, but they did reduce the tension. Despite periodic outbreaks of violence, the province was generally quiet.

On August 12 the respite ended. The annual Apprentice Boys march in Derry, which attracts thousands of participants, erupted into the worst violence Northern Ireland had suffered since the early 1920s. Catholics in Derry had feared that the Apprentice Boys parade might turn violent and that the RUC might once again ransack their neighborhoods. Their apprehension intensified when it became clear that the government would not intervene. Chichester-Clark's position was precarious: He could not afford to antagonize right-wing supporters by banning the march. In late July, under the leadership of IRA official Sean Keenan, Roman Catholics in Derry formed the Bogside Defence Association to protect themselves from Loyalist rioters and the RUC.[58] The Defence Association set up barricades and prepared petrol bombs.

As the parade began, Catholics stoned the march. The RUC charged with batons, only to be attacked in return by Catholics armed with rocks and the petrol bombs. When rioting ensued in Derry, Belfast, and Dungannon, Prime Minister Chichester-Clark, rather than pulling the RUC out of the Bogside, complicated matters by calling up the B Specials. Catholic reaction was predictably hostile. The chief inspector of the RUC, David Cushley, described the rioting in Belfast, in which five Catholics and two Protestants were killed, as equivalent to "a state of war."[59] Among the casualties was a nine-year-old boy.

The chief inspector's description was no exaggeration. In the second and third weeks of August 1969, Northern Ireland was indeed in a state of civil war. The government of the Republic, which had reacted to the civil rights movement with passing interest but little else, finally issued a public statement. Fianna Fáil cabinet ministers Charles Haughey, Neil Blaney, and Kevin Boland argued that troops should be sent to the North, presumably to seize Derry and Newry, but the government never seriously entertained the suggestion.[60] Instead, on August 13, following a day-long cabinet meeting, the southern Taoiseach (head of government), Jack Lynch, issued a speech on Irish television in which he announced that the Irish Army would set up field hospitals and refugee camps along the border. Lynch also asked the British to request that a United Nations peacekeeping force be sent to Ulster.[61]

The South did establish the refugee camps, and in 1969 Catholic youths in the North received military training in the Republic. It is also clear that the Republic's Ministry of Defence began to draw up military contingency plans and moved five hundred rifles near to the border.[62] But how much further the South went to assist Catholics in Ulster is a matter of some dispute.

In early May 1970, arms worth £80,000 and addressed to Charles Haughey's brother were seized at the Dublin Airport.[63] Prime Minister Lynch promptly threw Haughey and Blaney out of his cabinet, whereupon Kevin Boland resigned in protest. The Southern government then indicted Haughey, Blaney, and several others for participating in arms-running to the North. The charges against Blaney were later withdrawn.[64]

At the much-celebrated trial, which began on September 22, 1970, Irish Army captain John Kelly testified that he had visited the North on several occasions and had reported his visits to the minister of defence, James Gibbons.[65] Kelly told the court that the IRA—organized as the Catholic Defence Committee—had requested that the South provide them with arms: "They did not ask for blankets or feeding bottles—they asked for guns and no one from the Premier, Mr. Lynch down, refused that request or told them that this was contrary to government policy."[66] The Republic instead donated £100,000 in "relief" monies through bogus bank accounts.

Haughey and his codefendants did not deny the allegations. Instead, the gist of their defense was that the government had sanctioned the affair. Whatever the merits of this defense, Haughey and the codefendants were acquitted in October 1970.[67] The episode further poisoned relations between the two states and heightened the siege mentality of Northern Unionists.

Lynch had also stated in his speech that he would request that the British enter into talks with the Republic to "review the present constitutional position of the Six Counties of Northern Ireland."[68] Given the reaction of Protestant Ultras to the diplomatic meetings between Sean Lemass, Taoiseach of the Irish Republic, and Prime Minister O'Neill just five years earlier, their response to Lynch's ill-considered request was easy to foretell. Protestants attacked the Catholic ghettos of the Falls and Ardoyne in Belfast and the Bogside in Derry. The RUC reacted by firing at will. After three days of extensive rioting, there were seven dead and over five hundred homes, most of them Catholic, gutted by fire. Lynch later issued a more considered statement, in which he carefully noted that the Republic was "not seeking to overthrow by violence the Stormont Parliament and Government, but rather to win the agreement of a sufficient number of people in the North to an acceptable form of re-unification."[69]

On the eve of August 14, at Chichester-Clark's request, British troops marched into Derry. In return for the troops, the prime minister agreed to place the B Specials under the control of the British army.[70] Britain also appointed two committees, one headed by Lord Hunt to consider the future of the Specials, and one chaired by Lord Justice Scarman, to investigate how the RUC had handled the civil rights disturbances.[71] In October Hunt recommended that the B Specials be disbanded and replaced by an Ulster Defence Regiment, a more professional reserve force that would be under the control of the British Army in Northern Ireland.[72] Stormont and Westminster hurriedly accepted the recommendation, but even this limited change provoked an intense reaction among Protestant Ultras. Riots erupted along the Shankill Road, a Protestant stronghold in Belfast.

After negotiations with the Bogside Defence Association, the troops agreed to remove the RUC and the Specials from the area.[73] In Belfast, however, rioting continued. Catholics in the Lower Falls area of the city set up barricades, similar to those erected in Derry, to protect themselves from Protestant gangs that had traveled from the Shankill Road to burn out and gut hundreds of Catholic homes. The burning of Catholic homes in Belfast was later glorified in the following song, reprinted in a handbook for a Protestant paramilitary organization:

> On the 14th August we took a little trip,
> Up along Bombay Street and burned out all the shit,
> We took a little petrol and we took a little gun,
> And we fought the bloody fenians, till we had them on the run.[74]

The government responded by interning twenty-four suspected terrorists. British troops entered Catholic areas in Belfast the next day and set up a "peace line" between Roman Catholic and Protestant neighborhoods in West Belfast.[75] Over the next four days the rioting in Belfast slowly subsided. In the rioting's wake seven civilians were killed, scores more injured, and thousands of Catholics were driven from their homes. Many of the refugees crossed the border into the Republic. The Catholic areas of Belfast and Derry, behind barricades and impenetrable to the RUC, had virtually seceded from Ulster.

Stormont's order interning suspected republicans was countermanded by British Home Secretary James Callaghan, who had arrived in the province with the troops.[76] Following a meeting betwen Prime Minister Chichester-Clark and Callaghan, the British and Stormont governments issued a joint communiqué on August 19, detailing the reforms they would pursue. These measures included new statutes banning discrimination in employment and establishing reforms in public housing.[77] Most important, following the recommendations of the Hunt Committee in October, Stormont agreed to abolish the B Specials.[78] Catholics hesitantly welcomed the changes, but many Protestants felt that the British had violated the constitutional convention of noninterference with Stormont's affairs. Given O'Neill's earlier warning, however, Britain's decision to intervene should not have come as a surprise.

Before the August rioting, the role of the British troops in Northern Ireland had been solely to support the RUC and B Specials in emergencies. After the Derry riots, the role of the army changed significantly. Instead of a force of last resort, the army became a security agency whose primary purpose was to maintain public order and to collect intelligence concerning the IRA. The change of purpose was reflected in the level of staffing. There were fewer than 3,000 soldiers in Ulster before the rioting. Four years later, 16,500 troops were in the province.[79]

Roman Catholics in Northern Ireland initially welcomed the British Army, seeing in it protection against Protestant extremists and a hostile police force. But with time Catholics would resent the military. Bernadette Devlin may have been the first to predict the change, asking in a speech in Derry: "You're giving them tea now. What will you be giving them in six months?"[80] Protestants also distrusted the troops. Both sides surmised, correctly, that the troops' presence in the province would lead Westminster to take a more active interest in Ulster's affairs.

In the meantime, conservative Unionists were pressing the prime minister to take action against the IRA. On July 1 Chichester-Clark introduced a new

Criminal Justice (Temporary Provisions) Bill, which imposed mandatory six-month prison sentences for rioting.[81] On July 3, after imposing a thirty-four-hour curfew in the predominantly Catholic Lower Falls area of Belfast, the Army and the RUC conducted a joint patrol, looking for arms and explosives. In a search of some three thousand homes, the army uncovered fifty pistols, twenty-six rifles, five submachine guns, and over twenty-five thousand rounds of ammunition.[82] Certain that the army would not have conducted a similar search in Protestant strongholds, Catholics in the Falls reacted by stoning the troops. The army brought in reinforcements and countered with tear gas. They later rebuffed the efforts of local priests to help negotiate an end to the confrontation, which ultimately led to five civilian deaths and seventy-five injuries. A year earlier, General Ian Freeland had scorned the idea of a curfew, asking, "What do you do if people disobey it? Shoot them?"[83]

Another reason for Britain's inability to capitalize on the initial positive Catholic reaction to the army's presence was its decision to leave control of the troops with Stormont. Unionist leaders inevitably utilized the troops much as they had used the RUC and the Specials, thus destroying the army's image of impartiality. When Northern Irish courts ruled that Stormont's control over the troops was unconstitutional, Westminster squandered an opportunity to appease Catholics by passing the Northern Ireland Act (1972),[84] which returned control of the armed forces to Stormont. To compound its mistake, Britain conferred retroactive immunity upon the military and Stormont.

The Rebirth of the IRA

Although individual members of the Irish Republican Army had participated in the civil rights demonstrations, there is little evidence that the IRA itself had engaged in systematic violence or controlled the agenda of the movement. After the failure of its 1956–62 bombing campaign against the North, the IRA had adopted, after much bickering, a policy that discouraged armed conflict and emphasized political activity.[85] The aim of the new, docile IRA was not merely, as is commonly thought, the withdrawal of the British from Northern Ireland. Rather, the IRA advocated (and the Official IRA continues to advocate) the overthrow of the governments in both Ulster and the Republic and their replacement with a single workers'/socialist state. (Until the early 1980s, however, following the Dirty Protest and the celebrated hunger strikes, Provisional Sinn Fein was not a prominent political force in Northern elections.)

Following the RUC and B Special attacks on the Bogside and in the Falls, the IRA considered taking direct defensive action to protect Catholics. Its failure to do so in the Derry riots prompted graffiti in Catholic ghettos that read "IRA—I Ran Away."[86] The inactivity led to a split in the IRA at a Sinn Fein policy conference in Dublin in 1970, with the Officials largely eschewing violence after 1972, and the Provisionals, or Provos, supporting it.[87] (A number of Officials, dissatisfied with the organization's policy of nonviolence, later formed the radical Irish National Liberation Army.) Both the Officials and the Provos opened offices in Dublin.

The two wings of the IRA differ not only in tactics but in objectives as well. The Officials are Marxists who seek a united workers' republic.[88] When they announced in 1972 that they would discontinue their military campaign, the Officials stated that "working class Protestants and Catholics should be united in a struggle against capitalists instead of fighting each other."[89] The Provisionals, on the other hand, seek a united, Roman Catholic Ireland.[90] The Provos were led by Sean MacStiofain, an Englishman living in the Republic. MacStiofain, like many IRA members, had changed his English name, John Stephenson, to its Gaelic equivalent.

One observer, commenting on the rise of the Provos, noted:

> The formidable thing about the new I.R.A.—the Provisionals—was its simple relevance to the situation. Any ordinary, patriotic Catholic, clinging to the duel pieties of his community, could identify with the Provisionals. There was no "taint of communism" about them, nothing puzzling or foreign at all. And there was no nonsense about them either.[91]

The Provos initially saw themselves, and in large measure were seen by Catholics in Northern Ireland's slums, as a force that could protect Catholics from Protestant Ultras and a partisan police force. It can be fairly said that the IRA's initial resurgence was in fact defensive and a predictable reaction to Stormont's "law and order" policies. In 1971, however, the Provos slowly changed their course from defensive posturing to that of urban guerrillas seeking to force the British out of the province.

FROM CIVIL RIGHTS TO CIVIL WAR

Regnant violence in Northern Ireland continued through the summer of 1971, helped along by the rebirth of the IRA and the subsequent rise of a number of Protestant paramilitary groups, such as the Ulster Volunteer Force (UVF) and the Ulster Defence Association (UDA). On February 6, 1971, the IRA murdered its first British soldier.[92] Just over a month later, on March 11, the IRA assassinated three off-duty soldiers, which prompted riots in Belfast by Protestants unhappy with the government's seeming unwillingness to engage the Provos by entering Catholic "no-go" areas—Catholic ghettos in which the RUC could not safely conduct patrols.

On March 16 Chichester-Clark met in London with Prime Minister Edward Heath, Home Secretary Reginald Maulding, and Defense Secretary Lord Carrington. Chichester-Clark asked the prime minister to send more troops to the province so he could put an end to the no-go areas. Heath refused.[93] Chichester-Clark finally resigned on March 20, 1971. His replacement, Brian Faulkner, attempted to initiate a number of reforms to appease the Catholic community. On June 22 he proposed the establishment of three new parliamentary committees, at least two of which would be chaired by members of the opposition party.[94] The opposition, the moderate Catholic Social Democratic Labour Party (SDLP), at first responded favorably, but continued skirmishes between the army and Catholics in Derry handicapped the SDLP's efforts at moderation. On July 16 SDLP leaders withdrew from Stormont and announced their intention to set up an alternative assembly.[95]

Unimpressed by Faulkner's efforts, the Provos continued their guerrilla campaign throughout the summer. In many respects, Chichester-Clark's replacement with the more conservative Faulkner pleased the Provos. Earlier, the Provos had begun a campaign of bombing local post offices, primarily to provoke a violent counterresponse by the government that presumably would elicit Catholic sympathies. In this respect the IRA was successful, much as the Protestant Ulster Volunteer Force had been successful in provoking O'Neill's resignation. Conservative Unionists reacted to the continuing instability with calls for "law and order."

On July 17 the IRA responded by blowing up the new *Daily Mirror* printing plant and causing £2 million worth of damage to the complex. Two days later, Faulkner spoke with Prime Minister Heath about the possibility of resorting to internment under the Special Powers Act. On Thursday, August 5, Faulkner again met Heath and Lord Carrington and again argued that internment was necessary. Faulkner reminded Heath that the annual Apprentice Boys' parade was only a week away, and that he could not risk banning the parade without causing widespread rioting in Protestant sections of Ulster. Heath agreed to let Faulkner begin an internment operation.[96] To his credit, General Harry Tuzo, Army GOC, opposed the decision, fearing it would trigger a new round of violence. Tuzo thought internment a "distasteful weapon."[97]

The Internment Operation

The Northern Irish government had successfully employed internment several times before. In 1922 Sir James Craig, the first prime minister of the province, had detained approximately 1,000 suspected terrorists on a prison ship, the *Argenta*, in Belfast harbor and at the Ballykinlar prison.[98] The government used the same tactic in 1938, when the RUC arrested and detained 827 suspected IRA members. World War II delayed the release of many of the internees until 1945.[99] Under the supervision of Brian Faulkner, then minister of home affairs, the government once again imposed internment in 1956 to counter an abortive IRA bombing campaign.[100] The IRA dropped the campaign in 1962, its ranks depleted by internment. In the summer of 1971, then, Faulkner in particular had some reason to hope that internment would help quell civil disturbances.

At 4:30 A.M. on August 9, army patrols swept through Catholic ghettos in Belfast, Newry, Derry, Armagh, and Strabane, arresting "dangerous gunmen and terrorists." From almost every possible perspective, the operation was an overwhelming disaster. In the initial sweep of arrests, the RUC charged 342 men under Regulation 11 of the Special Powers Act "as acting in a manner prejudicial to the peace and maintenance of order." Between August 9 and December 14, 1971, a total of 1,576 people were interned; 934 were later released without charge. The RUC arrested and interned 2,357 more suspects in the six-month period following the decision. Of those, 1,600 were released after questioning.[101] Part of the reason for the large number of subsequent releases was that the information upon which the military authorities relied, supplied by the RUC Special Intelligence Branch, was inaccurate and out of date. Indeed, according to the Diplock Report:

> [I]t was recognized by those responsible for collecting and collating this kind
> of information that when internment was reintroduced in August 1971 the
> scale of the operation led to the arrest and detention of a number of persons
> against whom suspicion was founded on inadequate and inaccurate informa-
> tion.[102]

Instead of IRA members, the RUC had arrested moderate civil rights activists, young socialists, and outspoken intellectuals. "Very few were the 'dangerous gunmen and terrorists' that the government had declared them to be."[103]

The Political and Legal Ramifications of Internment and "Deep Interrogation"

Most of the internees were detained in Nissen huts and wooden shacks at the Long Kesh prison camp outside Belfast. A lawyer visiting the camp reported:

> The inmates live in groups of approximately 120, divided amongst three or
> four Nissen Huts set in a compound of perhaps one-fourth of an acre. High
> wire mesh fences separate the compounds and access roads, and the men
> remain in the compounds . . . where they sleep, eat and organise their
> recreation and other activities.[104]

Most observers agree that the scale of the internment operation, which touched almost every family in the Catholic ghettos of Derry and Belfast, coupled with the arrest, questioning, and systematic mistreatment of prisoners, greatly increased the IRA's membership and further handicapped the efforts of moderate Catholic and Protestant leaders alike to keep the peace.[105] Through August 11, twenty-three people died, and hundreds of Roman Catholic families were driven from their homes by Protestant extremists. More than five thousand families fled to the South.[106]

The intensity of Catholic reaction to the internment operation caught Stormont by surprise. According to the *Sunday Times* "Insight Team":

> [Westminster and Stormont] had foreseen rioting, but not warfare. The bald
> arithmetic tells the story. In the four months before internment—April to
> July 1971—four soldiers were killed, no policemen and four civilians. In the
> four months after it—August to November—thirty soldiers were killed,

eleven members of the RUC and the Ulster Defence Regiment, and seventy-three civilians. Stormont stolidly maintained that without internment things would have been worse. It could only be a matter of assertion.[107]

On August 9, the first day of the operation, two British soldiers and ten civilians were killed. Four days later, there were twenty-two dead, nineteen of whom were civilians. By the end of the month, thirty-five deaths and over a hundred explosions had rocked the province.[108] The IRA was seemingly unaffected by the sweep, its ranks instead swelled by new recruits. The Catholic community began a rent and rates strike to demonstrate its outrage. The government responded with the Payment for Debts Act (1971), which permitted the government to deduct the amount of the withheld payments from wages and social security benefits.[109]

Of the internment operation's many ramifications, perhaps the most important were allegations, first expressed by released suspects, that the RUC and the army were torturing internees.[110] The following statement from an internee, describing how he was tortured, is representative of the allegations:

> The door of the adjoining guardroom was left open and we were allowed to hear remarks from the soldiers and policemen there, such as "O.K., we'll dig a grave now," and, "Go in and bring in the electric torture machine." Soldiers would creep in from time to time and scream into our ears from behind, "Shut up, you bastard!"
>
> Shortly afterwards, I had my first taste of terror tactics. A loud voice in the guard room said, "Are you going to use it on him now?" and a few minutes later a soldier crept in, and out of the corner of my eye I saw him raise a rifle to the back of the head of a young fellow sitting beside me. He was an 18-year-old youth, I think from Andersontown. There was the noise of a rifle being cocked, and the young fellow started shaking. Then, in the silence of the room, the click of the rifle trigger was heard, and the detainee fell terrified in a heap on the floor.[111]

Public outcry over the mistreatment of internees was so great that the home secretary appointed a committee, headed by Sir Edward Compton, to investigate "allegations against the security forces of physical brutality" at the Holywood Police Barracks.[112] The committee could only consider, however, arrests that occurred on August 9. Moreover, it conducted hearings in private, to protect soldiers from possible retaliation by the IRA. Protesting that the committee's jurisdiction was too narrow and the procedures too biased, internees refused to testify. Lacking the authority to compel them to testify, the committee could hold only the most perfunctory of proceedings.

In its report in November 1971, the Compton Committee found that the RUC had subjected some internees to "interrogation in depth," a euphemism for torture.[113] Interrogation in depth consisted of forcing prisoners to endure prolonged periods of standing against walls, in some cases for more than forty hours, supported only by their fingertips, depriving them of food and sleep, subjecting them to continuous background noise, "hooding" prisoners (placing hoods over the prisoners' head, often for as long as six days), and, of course, beating them.[114] Together, these methods were known as the "five techniques"; they "were designed, in plain terms, to send men out of their minds."[115] The British Army had developed the techniques in Malaya, Kenya, Cyprus, and Aden.

In short, the committee found that many of the allegations were sound, but semantic quibbling muted the force of its conclusions. Early in its report, the committee argued that "brutality is an inhuman or savage form of cruelty, and . . . cruelty implies a disposition to inflict suffering coupled with indifference to, or pleasure in, the victim's pain."[116] Consequently, some internees had been subjected to interrogation in depth, but none of the complainants had been subjected to physical brutality "as we understand the term."[117]

Lord Gardiner, who later chaired a committee that reviewed the operation of the Emergency Powers Act, responded:

> [U]nder this definition, which some of our witnesses thought came from the Inquisition, if an interrogator believed, to his great regret, that it was necessary for him to cut off the fingers of a detainee one by one to get the required information out of him for the sole purpose of saving life, this would not be cruel and, because not cruel, not brutal.[118]

In a letter to the *Times* (London), Graham Greene was even more critical:

> "Deep interrogation"—a bureaucratic phrase which takes the place of the simpler word "torture" and is worthy of Orwell's *1984*—is on a different level of immorality than hysterical sadism or the indiscriminate bomb of urban guerrillas. It is something organised with imagination and a knowledge of psychology, calculated and cold blooded, and it is only half condemned by the Compton investigation.[119]

The British might better have mitigated the damaging findings if, instead of playing games with words, they had taken immediate steps to condemn the five techniques and to discipline guilty parties. Instead, the government appointed yet another committee, the Parker Committee, to determine if use of the five techniques was appropriate in Northern Ireland.[120] The Parker Committee conceded that many, if not all, of the techniques were illegal. Nonetheless, the committee concluded that they were necessary and therefore recommended that Westminster authorize their use by passing appropriate legislation.[121] In his minority report, Lord Gardiner argued that use of the techniques was unproductive and immoral:

> I do not believe that, whether in peace time for the purpose of obtaining information . . . or in emergency terrorist conditions, or even in a war against a ruthless enemy, such procedures are morally justifiable against those suspected of having information of importance to the police or army, even in light of any marginal advantages which may therefore by obtained.[122]

Without admitting the illegality or immorality of "deep interrogation," the British government announced in 1972 that it would no longer permit the security forces to use the five techniques.

Part of the decision can no doubt be attributed to the international embarrassment the allegations had caused Britain. In 1968 NICRA and twelve individuals had filed an application before the European Commission on Human Rights, alleging that the United Kingdom's treatment of detainees violated the Convention on Human Rights. In particular, NICRA argued that Britain had violated Article 3, which provides that "[n]o one shall be subjected to torture or to inhuman or degrading treatment."[123] NICRA also charged that Northern Ireland's electoral laws and practices, as well as several provisions of the Special Powers Act, violated various other articles of the Convention.[124] A dispute with NICRA's American attorney over legal fees stalled the case, however, and the commission never heard argument on the merits. The suit was eventually forgotten.

A second case, brought by the Irish Republic in 1971, was more successful. After the internment operation in August, the Republic filed a petition arguing that the Special Powers Act violated Articles 5 and 6 of the Convention, that Britain had failed to protect the right to life of Northern Catholics, thus violating Article 2, and that Britain had permitted security forces at the Holywood Barracks to torture detainees, thus violating Article 3.[125] The commission held hearings concerning the admissibility of the Republic's application for sixteen months, taking evidence from 119 witnesses and producing a record in excess of 45,000 pages.[126] Seven individuals filed applications against Britain in May 1972, complaining that they had been subjected to torture and inhuman and degrading treatment in violation of Article 3.[127]

Britain's unwillingness to cooperate with the commission did little to help its international reputation and reinforced Catholic distrust of the security forces. Throughout the hearings, the British government complained that the commission's security measures were inadequate. Indeed, the United Kingdom threatened to withdraw after its security experts concluded that the commission's headquarters at Strasbourg were too great a security risk—the commission finally held hearings under guard at an isolated Norwegian military complex.[128] British witnesses, identified only by a special code number, testified behind opaque screens.[129]

Oral hearings on the Republic's complaints were held at Strasbourg in September 1972. In October the commission ruled that only parts of the application were admissible. In particular, the alleged violation of Article 2 was dismissed for lack of evidence.[130] Six years later the commission found that Britain had indeed violated the torture provisions of Article 3. In its final report, the European commission stated:

> Quite a large number of those held in custody at [the Holywood Barracks] were subjected to violence by members of the RUC. It also led to intense suffering and to physical injury which on occasions was substantial. . . . No member of the security forces . . . admitted that he had beaten the men or knew that they had been beaten up. . . . Those in command . . . at the relevant time could not have been ignorant of the acts involved.[131]

Following the Parker Committee report and the initiation of international proceedings, the number of complaints concerning mistreatment decreased substantially. Reports of brutality increased in 1977, however, after Britain opened two new detention and interrogation centers, one at Castlereagh, outside Belfast, and the other at the Gough Army Barracks. In 1975 there were 180 reported complaints of mistreatment. The number increased to 384 in 1976 and to 671 the following year.[132]

In 1978, following repeated allegations of mistreatment and a report by Amnesty International which concluded that mistreatment was common, the United Kingdom appointed yet another committee to review interrogation practices. The Bennett Committee issued its report on March 16, 1979. In brief, the committee found that there were undeniably cases in which injuries to internees had not been self-inflicted, as the security forces often charged. The committee issued over sixty recommendations to minimize the possibility of brutality, including closed-circuit television monitoring of interrogations. The committee also recommended that the RUC promulgate a formal code of interrogation practices. Lord Bennett offered the following additional recommendations:

1. medical officers should examine suspects every twenty-four hours;
2. suspects should have an unqualified right to see a solicitor after forty-eight hours in custody;
3. no more than two detectives should be present at any time in the interview room;
4. no more than six officers should interrogate a single suspect.[133]

Secretary of State Roy Mason disingenuously argued that the Bennett Report had not actually concluded that the security forces had mistreated detainees, but the government announced that it would accept Bennett's recommendations.

Complaints of mistreatment have since decreased in frequency. Some might argue that the decrease is a consequence of the government's insistence that it will not tolerate abuse. But although there had been over "1,600 formal complaints of assault and battery" filed by 1979 alone,[134] there has yet to be a single conviction of a security officer in such a case. "Whatever the explanation the result has been that the RUC has been seen to be a force above the law when arresting and interrogating paramilitary suspects."[135]

CONSTITUTIONAL DISSOLUTION AND THE IMPOSITION OF DIRECT RULE

In January 1972 Ulster was in the throes of a near civil war. Internment continued, despite the unforeseen intensity of Catholic opposition and despite evidence that internment had increased the level of violence instead of controlling it. There was little reason to hope that the new year would find Ulster peaceful, and good reason to fear that the worst lay ahead.

In early January NICRA began to plan a major anti-internment demonstration. The march would take place in Derry on January 30 and would be the first in the city since the internment operation the preceding August.[136] Local RUC authorities advised the government to let the march proceed without interruption and subsequently to arrest its leaders under either the Special Powers Act or the Public Order Act.[137] The government instead gave in to demands for a show of force by Protestant Ultras, led by the Reverend Ian Paisley and former minister of home affairs William Craig, and enlisted the aid of a squadron of British paramilitaries. Paisley had threatened to stop the march if the government did not take action.

The demonstration began as planned on January 30, starting in Creggan and ending in Guildhall Square. It never reached the square. How the riot that ensued actually started is not clear. The army claimed that someone in the crowd fired on them first, but governmental inquiries concluded none of the demonstrators was armed.[138] Of the fourteen civilians killed by the army, all were unarmed. Following "Bloody Sunday," the province erupted into a sectarian warfare that moderate Catholic and Protestant leaders were unable to control. Catholics in Dublin burned the English embassy and at Westminster, Bernadette Devlin punched and scratched the British home secretary, Reginald Maulding, in the face. Two MPs pulled Devlin off the minister and escorted her, kicking and screaming, out of the building. Asked later by reporters if she would apologize, Devlin replied, "I'm only sorry I didn't get him by the throat."[139]

By March 20, fifty-six soldiers had been killed in the aftermath of Bloody Sunday.[140] The IRA initiated a new bombing campaign, and right-wing Unionists, distressed by the government's seeming unwillingness to engage the Provos and to enter Catholic no-go areas, formed the Ulster Vanguard Movement in February. Led by William Craig, the Vanguard was an umbrella organization that included a number of Orange Order lodges, the Apprentice Boys, and the Loyalist Association of Workers.[141] Vanguard members were passionately committed to preserving the Union, as Craig made clear in a speech on February 9: "We are determined to preserve our British traditions and way of life. God help those who get in our way."[142] Under Craig's tutelage, the Vanguard held paramilitary demonstrations, similar to those held by Sir Edward Carson in 1912, complete with paramilitary uniforms and Fascist salutes to Craig.[143]

Protestants demonstrated throughout February and March. Protestant paramilitary groups were stirring as well, celebrating the horror of Bloody Sunday, as the following song, published in a UDA handbook, makes clear:

> Sunday morning went for a drive,
> Took along my Colt 45.
> Hey, Hey, Hey, what a beautiful day.
> Went to Derry not on a hunch,
> Knew I'd get a taig* before lunch,
> Hey, Hey, Hey, what a beautiful day.
>
> Taigs were marching like on the Falls,
> I opened up from Derry's Walls,
> Hey, Hey, Hey, what a beautiful day.

*a slur by Protestant extremists aimed at the Catholic minority

Taigs to army said it was you,
Didn't know I was there too,
Hey, Hey, Hey, what a beautiful day.

Chorus

Bang, Bang, Bang, Bloody Sunday,
This is my, my, my, beautiful day,
When I say, say, say, Bloody Sunday,
I mean my, oh my,
What a beautiful day.[144]

The British government's response to Bloody Sunday was to appoint yet another committee, chaired by Lord Chief Justice Widgery, to investigate "a . . . matter of urgent public importance, namely the events of Sunday 30 January which led to loss of life in connection with the procession in Londonderry on that day."[145] The Widgery Report was a whitewash.[146] It found no evidence that the army had acted improperly. Lord Widgery concluded that IRA gunmen had fired first. And although Widgery conceded that some of the troops' behavior "bordered on the reckless," he found no evidence that soldiers had fired into the crowd without provocation.[147] The report argued instead that "there would have been no deaths in Londonderry on 30 January if those who had organized the illegal march had not thereby created a highly dangerous situation in which a clash between demonstrators and the security forces was almost inevitable."[148] Widgery's conclusion was hardly surprising: The committee took no evidence from any party other than the army. It need hardly be added that the Widgery Report did nothing to mollify the Catholic community in Northern Ireland.

A second committee, chaired by Samuel Dash, an American professor of law at Georgetown University and later special counsel to the Senate Watergate Committee, concluded that although IRA snipers were present at the demonstration, "the weight of civilian testimony was that the soldiers first fired upon leaving their army vehicles."[149] The report went on to state: "The presence of some gunmen did not justify the paratroopers in firing aimed or reckless shots at unarmed civilians."[150]

Dash based his report on his review of the twenty volumes of evidence produced by the Widgery inquiry and on statements from hundreds of civilian witnesses. The British dismissed the study, commissioned by the National Council for Civil Liberties in London and published by the International League for the Rights of Man, as biased and inaccurate, but did authorize out-of-court payments to the victims' relatives.

On March 22 Prime Minister Heath summoned Faulkner and his advisers to Downing Street. At a meeting attended by Faulkner, Maulding, and others, Heath informed Faulkner that Westminster, acting under Section 75 of the GoA, was taking control over security in the province. Faulkner threatened to resign, whereupon Heath offered him an even less acceptable alternative: Westminster could resume direct rule of Northern Ireland. Faulkner returned to Belfast to meet with his cabinet and advisers. Just two days later Heath prorogued Stormont under Section 75 and imposed direct rule on the province. The United Kingdom Parliament appointed a secretary of state to oversee the matters previously handled by Stormont.

Upon hearing of Westminster's decision, Protestant Ultras, led by Ian Paisley and William Craig, reacted by holding a two-day strike and organizing large public demonstrations.[151] Unionists saw the imposition of direct rule as a betrayal of their British loyalties. The anger many Protestants felt is captured in the following letter, published by the *Belfast Telegraph*: "There is a heavy stench of treason in the air. Ulster has been betrayed and Stormont executed by the greatest liars the world has ever seen . . . the sell-out to the hobgoblins of the IRA has been completed."[152]

It is hardly a surprise that Protestant paramilitary groups flourished in such an atmosphere. The Ulster Defence Association (UDA), a loose coalition of Protestant defense groups formed during the internment riots, demanded that the army eliminate the no-go areas in the Catholic ghettos of Belfast and Derry. In early May the UDA set up similar barricades in the Protestant areas of Belfast.[153] The UDA also adopted Provo tactics and soon began a campaign of assassinating Catholics and Protestants friendly with Catholics. The IRA could not fail to respond in kind. In the politics of the last atrocity, each killing demanded retribution, which in turn justified still another killing.

On July 31 joint army–RUC patrols began to break down the barricades to the Catholic and Protestant no-go areas of Belfast and Derry. The patrols arrested a prominent UDA leader, for which the UDA promised retaliation. Tommy Herron, a high-ranking UDA official, swore that "[t]he British Army and the British government are now our enemies."[154] Britain could do nothing to appease one community without risking a riot by the other.

CONSTITUTIONAL RECONSTRUCTION
IN NORTHERN IRELAND

Unionist fears that Westminster would seek to appease Catholics by instituting reforms were well-founded. One of Westminster's first acts was to replace the Special Powers Act with emergency legislation more amenable to Catholics. On the day after Britain resumed direct rule, William Whitelaw, the new Northern Ireland secretary, announced that he would personally review the files of every internee still detained.[155] During the following two months Whitelaw released 377 internees. The government interned another 21 suspects, however, under Regulation 11(2) of the SPA.

Britain's resumption of direct rule also put the constitutional status of the six counties in doubt. The decision to prorogue Stormont worked a fundamental change in the internal constitutional framework of Northern Ireland. Direct rule necessitated suspension of the North's Constitution (the Government of Ireland Act) as well as the constitutional institutions, such as Stormont, created by it. The Northern Irish Parliament and executive ceased to exist.

Responsibility for the administration of justice and internal security reverted to Westminster. Hence the internal constitutional structure of Northern Ireland was in a state of considerable confusion. But the fact of union—Ulster's constitutional position within the United Kingdom—was not affected by the decision to dissolve Stormont, and the structure and organization of Northern Ireland's judiciary and police force remained essentially unchanged.

The Prerequisites
of Constitutional Reconstruction

Also not in doubt was Britain's professed commitment to restore some measure of constitutional self-governance in the province. But that commitment did not necessarily include a commitment to the particular constitutional structures associated with the Government of Ireland Act. Instead, Britain recognized that much of the crisis involved a dispute over the proper construction of a constitutional order in Northern Ireland.

Nevertheless, Ulster's uncertain constitutional status has remained essentially unchanged. The relevant parties—and identifying those that are and are not relevant is itself a major problem—have been unable to set upon a constitutional framework for self-governance that can win the support of both Nationalists and Unionists. The failure of the constitutional process in Northern Ireland should not be attributed to a lack of ingenuity in the design of new constitutional forms but instead results from an insufficient understanding of what the process of constitutional reconstruction requires and how it should proceed.

In the early 1970s civil violence and political terrorism in Ulster eventually overwhelmed the Northern Irish government and the constitution under which it functioned. Northern Ireland was literally in a state of constitutional crisis. In such cases, the first order of government must be resolution of the crisis, and this will often require the utilization of emergency powers that would be constitutionally unacceptable in less troubled times. Whatever the specific faults of emergency legislation in Northern Ireland (and, as we shall see, they are many), the need for and the legitimacy of emergency legislation as a general principle cannot be denied. Every community has a right of self-defense, often expressed in the common law phrase *salus populi suprema lex esto*—the welfare of the people is the supreme law. The effect of such a principle, at least in the common law, is to equate legality with necessity.

Most students of constitutional theory, however, have been unwilling to embrace the justification of necessity without qualification. They have instead insisted that emergency powers, although expansive, are subject to certain constitutional limits: The objective of emergency powers must be the defense and ultimate restoration of the constitutional order itself.[156] In this way they seek to distinguish between the exercise of emergency powers and the *ends* of such powers, which they take to be the protection and restoration of the preexisting constitutional order.[157]

In certain types of constitutional crises, such as those that arise from invasion by a foreign enemy or severe economic depression, the argument for constitutional restoration makes sense (although, like constitutions themselves, it rests upon contestable assumptions about the manageability of human affairs). But in crises brought about by nationalistic and ethnic disputes, restoration of the previous constitutional order cannot be the constitutionally proper course of action. In such cases, as in Northern Ireland, a significant part of the population does not consent to, and indeed rejects the current construction of constitutional forms. Conflict in Northern Ireland is concerned with questions that are central to the proper design and the very definition of the constitutional order, as the civil rights movement of the late 1960s clearly demonstrated. In Ulster, the legitimacy of the preexisting constitutional order is precisely the most salient and intractable of questions.

As a result, a commitment to constitutional self-governance in the North should not include restoration of the particular constitutional structures associated with the Government of Ireland Act. The process of constitutional reconstruction requires not the restoration of a constitution or a constitutional order in dispute but rather promotion of the conditions in which nonviolent, reasoned debate about the proper reconstruction of a constitutional community can proceed. In other words, Britain's constitutional obligation is to restore the possibility of some form of constitutional government, not necessarily the one that predated the imposition of direct rule. Such an obligation derives from the fundamental, liberal predicate of consent, upon which constitutions and constitutional governments must ultimately rely for their legitimacy.[158]

Of course, every effort at constitutional reconstruction in Northern Ireland evokes talk about the importance of consent. Since the imposition of direct rule, the British have proposed a number of different constitutional proposals for the North, and in all of these they have recognized the need for a new constitutional framework, one that can gain the consent of both Protestants and Catholics, in Ulster. In every case, the difficulty has been in devising an institutional framework that can garner cross-denominational support in a society that lacks political, social, and cultural consensus. In every case, IRA and Protestant extremists alike have successfully (if not unilaterally) undertaken to dismantle delicate and elaborately designed constitutional proposals. In every case, constitutional "solutions" to the Northern Irish problem have foundered precisely on the problem of consent withheld.

The failure of the constitutional framework developed under the Northern Ireland Constitution Act (1973) is just one example. Drawing upon its 1973 White Paper, entitled *Northern Ireland Constitutional Proposals*, [159] the Constitution Act set forth an elaborate proposal for a parliamentary form of devolved government. At the center of the proposal were a unicameral assembly and a power-sharing executive. Elections for the new assembly were held in June 1973, but the representatives were unable to come to an agreement to form an executive. Under increasing pressure from Britain, the parties held a conference at Sunningdale, Berkshire, in December, at which an agreement was finally secured. On January 1, 1974, Westminster transferred responsibility for Northern Irish affairs to the new government.

On January 4, however, the Ulster Unionist Council, an umbrella organization that included representatives from the Official Unionist party, the Democratic Unionist party, and the Vanguard Unionists, announced its opposition to the Sunningdale compromise. In May the Ulster Workers' Council (UWC), which included representatives from each of the preceding parties, as well as members from the Ulster Defence Association and the Ulster Volunteer Force, both paramilitary organizations, organized a general strike that paralyzed the province. After several abortive attempts at negotiations between the UWC and Secretary of State Merlyn Rees, the new government collapsed.

This and other efforts at constitutional reconstruction have foundered because a part of the population, sometimes Catholic, sometimes Protestant, has withheld its consent from increasingly complex constitutional schemes. In part this failure can be attributed to the elusive nature of consent as a political requirement. Initial agreement upon the necessity of consent tells us little about from whom consent must be acquired in order to legitimate new constitutional forms. A related question concerns what effect a protracted and durable terrorist campaign by the IRA has upon the process of constitutional reconstruction. Under what obligation, if any, is the British government to include the IRA in its efforts to devise new constitutional forms? The Anglo-Irish Agreement of 1985 implies an answer to this question by including in the process of constitutional reconstruction only those who "aspire to a sovereign united Ireland . . . by peaceful means and through agreement."

Constitutional conventions have therefore typically included representatives from the Official Unionists, the SDLP, the Alliance, the Northern Ireland Labour party, and a few other organizations. Other interests, notably those represented by Protestant Ultras and the IRA, were not invited to these conventions. But insofar as it rests upon the necessity of consent, the principle of constitutional reconstruction requires that *all* interested parties be given the opportunity to participate in constitutional debate. There is no question that the IRA disputes the legitimacy of existing constitutional arrangements in Northern Ireland; although violent, its program and aims are fundamentally political in nature.[160] Britain's antiterrorism legislation admits as much in its definition of terrorism, stating that "terrorism means the use of violence for *political* ends."[161] The principle of reconstruction therefore requires of Great Britain that it acknowledge the political motivation behind the IRA's terrorism and that it consider the possibility of negotiations with representatives of Sinn Fein. My argument, in other words, is that the principle of constitutional reconstruction necessitates a particular answer to the question of which parties are relevant to and must be included in constitutional negotiations. The Provisional IRA disputes the legitimacy of current constitutional arrangements in the North, and its dispute must be accounted for in the process of constitutional reconstruction.

There is, of course, little point in negotiating with those who refuse to accept reason and compromise as methods for resolving political disputes, and I should not be taken as arguing that the process of constitutional reconstruction cannot proceed or is illegitimate without the IRA's participation. The principle requires that parties be given the opportunity to participate. It does *not* mean that they have a veto over the process.

Nor should I be taken as saying that the government must recognize the legitimacy of political violence. The process of constitutional reconstruction requires that all interested parties be given the opportunity to participate in the design of new constitutional frameworks. It does not mean that governments must tolerate the use of political violence in place of constitutional negotiations. If terrorists refuse to enter into constitutional negotiations, governmental authorities are, as I noted earlier, constitutionally obligated to take steps to protect the community. It does mean, however, that in formulating responses to political terrorism, constitutional states must respond in ways that are consistent with the fundamental premises of constitutional theory. Hence the possible presence of representatives of the IRA in future negotiations is a constitutional prerequisite.

There are also reasons for including Sinn Fein in constitutional negotiations that are premised simply upon political expediency. The history of constitutional reconstruction in Northern Ireland makes it clear that the process cannot work if it fails to address the concerns of the entire community. Failure to include the IRA, or representatives of more hard-line Protestants, ensures their subsequent opposition to a negotiated settlement, as happened at Sunningdale. Moreover, a prudent government can make much of another party's obdurateness. Despite the British government's current unwillingness to negotiate with the IRA, there *is* precedent for including IRA representatives in constitutional negotiations. In June 1972 Prime Minister Heath stunned Protestant MPs by agreeing to meet in secret with leaders of the Provisional IRA in London. On June 22, after repeated calls for a cease fire by Catholics of all persuasions, the Provos announced that they would declare a cease fire, to begin on June 26, if Britain would respond in kind. Provo representatives met with Secretary Whitelaw in London shortly thereafter. Although the talks seemed promising, the Provos ultimately would settle for nothing less than the complete withdrawal of the British presence in Northern Ireland. In the face of the IRA's intransigence, the talks, as well as the cease fire that accompanied them, collapsed after thirteen days.[162] On July 13 the IRA murdered five British soldiers. On July 21, "Bloody Friday," the IRA exploded twenty-two bombs, most of them car bombs, within a mile of city center. The IRA insisted that they had given advance warning of the explosions to military authorities, but the explosions killed eighteen civilians and two soldiers and injured hundreds.[163] Perhaps the worst was at the Oxford Street Bus Station. The explosion there killed four civilians, one a fourteen-year-old boy and another an eighteen-year-old young man. Two soldiers in a jeep were literally blown to pieces.

The Anglo-Irish Agreement

It is in this context, a context that includes failed constitutional conventions in Darlington and later in Sunningdale, that we must approach the Anglo-Irish Agreement. Whatever the utility of the agreement in other areas, it will be of limited benefit unless the British can devise ways in which to give *institutional* expression to the desire for constitutional self-governance in the province. There are any number of institutional mechanisms available for the project; few, if any, have not already been proposed or tried without success.

But the biggest difficulty with the agreement is that its fundamental assumption about the character and makeup of Ulster's political landscape is dangerously simplistic. The agreement is cast in language that speaks of the necessity to accommodate two distinct political and cultural traditions. The two-traditions approach assumes that there *are* two coherent and culturally distinct traditions in Ulster. But there is no monolithic Protestant community. Nor is there a monolithic Catholic community. The failures of Darlington and Sunningdale demonstrate the folly of facile assumptions about what either the Protestant or Catholic community wants—there is no such community or unity of interest. The continued viability of Sinn Fein and the intensity of its competition with the SDLP should make that clear. Likewise, the longstanding and oftentimes heated disputes between the Democratic and Official Unionist parties, and the proliferation of Unionist paramilitary organizations, do not point to a single Protestant political tradition.[164] There is instead a welter of interests *within* both traditions, as well as fundamentally different conceptions about the nature and identity of each, and these must be accounted for in the development of consensual constitutional institutions in the North.

This diversity within each of the two traditions is reflected in the electoral successes of Sinn Fein, the Provisional IRA's political wing. I certainly do not wish to claim that Sinn Fein is the authentic voice of Ulster's Catholics. The precise extent to which the Provisional IRA can claim to speak as an authentic, or legitimate, voice of Catholics is uncertain and difficult to assess. Much of the initial difficulty lies in determining what "support" consists of and whether it can be measured. Ideally, for example, one would want to distinguish between active and passive support, as well as account for degrees in the breadth and depth of support.

One possible measure, however, even given its limitations, is the extent of Catholic electoral support for Sinn Fein's candidates for public office. In a 1978 public opinion survey, 46 percent of the Catholic respondents saw the IRA as "basically patriots and idealists. Approximately one-third of those people further believed that the IRA were a positive force in the Northern Ireland problem."[165]

The electoral fortunes of Sinn Fein are generally consistent with these figures. In regional elections in 1982 Sinn Fein won 35 percent of the Catholic vote. Their share increased to 43 percent in the 1983 Westminster elections, and 38 percent in the European Parliament elections in the next year. Similarly, Sinn Fein won 35.4 percent in the British parliamentary elections of 1986, and about the same in the 1987 general elections. [166] How one should interpret these figures is a matter of some dispute. They seem to indicate that Sinn Fein routinely pulls about one-third of the Catholic vote in Ulster, but the numbers change depending upon how one figures the size of the sample. One-third of the Catholic vote represents only approximately 12 percent of the entire Northern Irish electorate, and Sin Fein drew only 1.9 percent of the vote in the 1987 general elections in the Republic. As a consequence, the extent of Catholic support for Sinn Fein can vary greatly, depending upon how narrowly or broadly one draws community boundaries. Similarly, the numbers do not speak to the depth of support for Sinn Fein or enable us to distinguish between support for certain aspects of its political program, such as its advocacy of cultural autonomy, and disapproval of others, such as its advocacy of political violence. Thus I do not want to claim that these electoral statistics amount to an irrefutable argument in favor of substantial Catholic support for Provisional Sinn Fein (PSF). Nevertheless, they do indicate that the claim cannot easily be dismissed.

Moreover, Sinn Fein appears to draw its support from particular sections of the Catholic community. Moxon-Browne's data indicate that PSF attracts predominantly younger voters and those at the lower end of the socioeconomic scale. The moderate Social Democratic Labour Party (SDLP), on the other hand, successor to the Catholic Nationalist party, appears to appeal to a different constituency. It attracts more support from middle-class and professional Catholics.[167] The "gap between Sinn Fein and the SDLP reflects two largely different electorates—only to a limited extent are they fishing for votes in the same pond."[168] The biggest difference between the two parties, however, is in the attitudes their constituencies have toward political violence. Some 70 percent of PSF supporters agree that violence is sometimes justified to bring about political change; only 7 percent of SDLP supporters agreed.[169] It seems clear, then, that Sinn Fein and the SDLP speak for diverse elements in a heterogeneous Catholic community. Excluding Sinn Fein from constitutional negotiations in Ulster may disfranchise those subsections of the Catholic community from which Sinn Fein draws its political support, and "it is difficult to envisage any effective political settlement being negotiated that does not elicit the support of both parties."[170]

CONCLUSION

It is precisely this heterogeneity *within* each of the communities that the Anglo-Irish Agreement tends to obscure. And insofar as it does account for familial diversity, the agreement cannot help but ask who speaks authoritatively as representatives of the two traditions in the constitution-making process. A confusion of groups and organizations claim to speak on behalf of Northern

Catholics; these include the Dublin government, the SDLP, Sinn Fein, the IRA, the Irish National Liberation Army (INLA), and various civil rights groups. There are no fewer potential representatives of Northern Protestants, and in both cases determining which of these would-be representatives is "authentic" is an ill-conceived, not to say futile, task. Each of these groups has a constituency, and almost all of them have the capability to wreck any constitutional agreement to which they are not a party. As we saw, Sinn Fein's claim that it speaks for a substantial part of Ulster's Catholic community cannot be dismissed as patently frivolous. A politically sensitive approach to the process of constitutional reconstruction must account for this subtle political reality.

The process of constitutional reconstruction must also seek to establish the conditions in which the relevant parties can make affirmative commitments to constitutionalism as a basis for a political community. This requirement provides the justification for the antiterrorism legislation currently in place in Northern Ireland, which we shall examine in the next chapter.

3

Political Violence and
Antiterrorism Legislation in
Great Britain and Northern Ireland

INTRODUCTION

Constitutional maintenance has at least two dimensions. As we saw in the preceding chapter, one concerns the reconstruction of constitutional forms and structures in societies where particular constitutional orders have failed. Fidelity to constitutional values in such cases requires that the process of reconstruction take place in certain ways. If the process is to succeed, it must also take place in certain types of conditions, conditions in which constitutionalism's commitment to reason can flourish. That commitment cannot prosper in communities where reason has been supplanted by or must compete with violence as the primary means of politics. Constitutional states are therefore obligated to protect themselves and their citizens against political violence, not only because it constitutes a challenge to the current constitutional order, but also because its persistence handicaps the process of reconstruction. The emergency legislation that constitutional states typically enact as a means to cope with political violence is, then, an essential element of both constitutional maintenance and constitutional reconstruction.

I argued in chapter 1 that constitutional maintenance is at once both a legal and a political enterprise. Recent controversies surrounding British antiterrorism policy, such as new measures abolishing the common law right to silence and prohibiting media interviews with terrorists and terrorist organizations, confirm the inherently political nature of constitutional maintenance and reconstruction.

It is therefore important that any review of emergency legislation in the United Kingdom situate those statutes in the larger context of British security policy, which since 1975 has been dominated by the twin concepts of "Ulsterization" and "criminalization."[1] The former seeks to transfer responsibility for the maintenance of public order from British to Northern Irish authorities. Its most visible effect has been to increase the size of the RUC and to decrease the number of British military personnel in the province. Policing and security thus become the primary responsibility of the local police force, but the British

84

Army maintains a supportive role and continues to discharge a limited number of other functions, such as bomb disposal and intelligence operations.

Under the policy of criminalization, Britain has sought to downplay the political character of Irish terrorism by emphasizing its criminality. In this respect, the policy of criminalization represents an effort by the government to shape, or to construct, the public perception of terrorism. One consequence of this policy was the decision in the mid-1970s to discontinue extrajudicial detention and to rely instead upon modified versions of the criminal law to cope with terrorism. The same policy explains the proscription of certain organizations which promote terrorism, as we shall see in our analysis of the Prevention of Terrorism Act. And criminalization was the policy behind the government's decision not to award special category status for prisoners in Northern Ireland, which ultimately resulted in the celebrated hunger strikes in the late 1970s and early 1980s.

The policy of criminalization is not, however, a completely coherent and inclusive response to terrorism. Most forms of terrorist activity are offenses against the criminal law, and in this respect a policy that stresses the necessity of coping with terrorism through the legal process has much to commend it. But while it is a form of criminal behavior, Irish terrorism in the United Kingdom is also undeniably political, as the emergency legislation itself admits by defining terrorism as the "use of violence for political ends."[2] Moreover, as will be evident in our analyses of several of the arrest provisions in the emergency legislation, the criminal law approach to counterterrorism has had the unfortunate result of blurring the distinction between criminal prosecution and intelligence gathering.

The policies of criminalization and Ulsterization have therefore had an important impact upon the development of antiterrorism legislation in the United Kingdom. The legislation itself has also been the subject of great controversy. As indicated in chapter 2, for example, repeal of the Special Powers Act was one of the central goals of the Northern Irish civil rights movement. One of Westminster's first objectives upon resuming direct control of Ulster was to mollify the Catholic community by replacing the act with more "acceptable" emergency legislation. In 1973 the government appointed Lord Chief Justice Diplock to chair a committee to consider

> [w]hat arrangements for the administration of justice in Northern Ireland could be made in order to deal more effectively with terrorist organizations by bringing to book, otherwise than by internment by the Executive, individuals involved in terrorist activities, particularly those who plan and direct, but do not necessarily take part in, terrorist acts.[3]

As the committee's charter makes clear, Lord Diplock proceeded on the assumption that the Northern Irish judicial system had been unable to cope effectively with criminal offenses involving acts of terrorism. Lord Diplock's recommendations thus accepted the continuing need for some type of emergency legislation in the province. Most of his recommendations were incorporated in the Northern Ireland (Emergency Provisions) Act (1973), and the committee's report remains the most articulate statement of the need for such powers.

Antiterrorism legislation in Great Britain and Northern Ireland thus proceeds on the assumption that political terrorism, although a form of criminal activity, does impose highly unusual strains on the ordinary criminal processes, strains so severe that they warrant the existence of special legislation to govern terrorist offenses. Whatever their familial differences, and in places they are substantial, these special statutes share a common trait in that they significantly relax normal statutory safeguards for protection of individual liberties and rights in the criminal process. There are two such statutes in force in the United Kingdom—the Northern Ireland (Emergency Provisions) Act, amended in 1987 and applicable only in Northern Ireland, and the Prevention of Terrorism (Temporary Provisions) Act (1984 and 1989), which applies both in Northern Ireland and in Great Britain.

Like their predecessors, these acts work sweeping changes in ordinary criminal procedures. In this chapter I shall examine the operation of the acts as well as the findings of the many governmental committees that have reviewed them. I shall also consider recent well-publicized changes in the legislation, which include removal of the right to silence in criminal trials and prohibitions on media coverage of and interviews with suspected terrorists. My concern is the extent to which these and other changes comport with the demands of constitutional maintenance.[4]

During the course of my analysis, I shall also comment upon how the emergency legislation increases executive power by removing or severely circumscribing judicial independence in, and control over, the criminal processes. A thorough understanding of how the antiterrorism legislation functions, as well as a determination of whether it accomplishes its many and sometimes competing purposes, requires some discussion of the complex interplay between executive and judicial authorities. How Northern Irish judges have responded to the antiterrorism legislation should tell us something about the capacity of courts to review exercises of emergency power more generally.

THE NORTHERN IRELAND (EMERGENCY PROVISIONS) ACTS OF 1978 AND 1987

The Emergency Provisions Act has attracted the attention of scholars largely because of provisions that establish special, juryless tribunals for the trial of terrorist offenses, tribunals first proposed by Lord Chief Justice Diplock and for whom they are named. The Diplock courts, however, are only the most obvious of the EPA's provisions—they are not necessarily the most important or troublesome. Lord Diplock had identified a number of problems in how the criminal process dealt with terrorism. First, the committee concluded that the "technical" common law rules on arrest and detention, as well as those governing admission of inculpatory statements, had "resulted in a substantial number of cases based on confessions obtained during prolonged interrogation being lost or withdrawn."[5] A second concern was the possibility that various para-military organizations, such as the IRA or the UVF, would intimidate prospective witnesses and jurors. The committee also feared the possibility of bias on the part of jurors: The prosecution's power to "stand by" (or disqualify) potential Catholic jurors had led to allegations of "perverse acquittals" in a number of cases involving Loyalist defendants.

Reflecting these wide-ranging concerns, the Emergency Provisions Act does not merely work changes in the trial of suspected terrorists but instead restructures the *entire* criminal process, from arrest and detention to sentencing and appeal. MP Arthur Davidson noted the extent of the change during debates on the act: "We are not tinkering around with minor evidentiary points, we are not altering some minor points of detail or technical rules of evidence. We are altering the whole fundamental criminal process in Northern Ireland for a whole range of substantial offences which rightly carry heavy penalties."[6]

For purposes of discussion, and because there is now a substantial literature on the act,[7] we can limit our analysis of the Emergency Provisions Act to three areas—those of arrest and detention, pretrial procedures and bail, and trial in the special courts. My general course in each of these areas shall be to consider how the 1978 act operates, although we shall see that in some areas the 1987 act has introduced important changes. We can better appreciate the extent of these changes if we compare them with the earlier practice. In each of the three areas, the EPA frees the state from burdens imposed by the common law—and, as I have argued, by the demands of constitutionalism itself—which require that it publicly demonstrate the existence of reasons which support the exercise of its coercive power. This relaxation ws accomplished in the 1978 act through provisions relating to arrest and detention by the simple elimination of the common law requirement that a suspicion to arrest must be reasonable. The 1987 act has substantially reworked the arrest and detention provisions of its predecessor by incorporating a requirement of reasonableness, but flaws remain. In bail and voir dire proceedings, both versions of the act shift burdens of proof—the requirement of producing reasons—from the state to the accused.

The Emergency Provisions Act:
Powers of Arrest and Detention

The general rules of arrest in Northern Ireland are set forth in the Criminal Law Act (1967), Section 2 of which permits the RUC to arrest only with a warrant, unless a constable has an objectively "reasonable cause" to suspect a person has committed, is committing, or is about to commit an "arrestable offense." An arrestable offense is one for which the punishment equals or exceeds imprisonment for a period of five years. In contrast, the emergency legislation enacted in the 1970s contained four different provisions relating to the authority of security forces to question or arrest suspected terrorists. Some of those provisions, such as Section 18, permitted the security forces to stop and question citizens. Others, such as Section 14, related to the power of the police and the military to arrest and detain individuals for nearly any offense, and not necessarily offenses related to terrorism. Some limited detention to four hours; others authorized detention for as long as three days. All four provisions, however, allowed the security forces to question or arrest citizens under procedures considerably less protective of individual rights than the ordinary criminal law of Northern Ireland.

I shall not review each of these four sections here, in part because some have been replaced and others have been amended by the 1987 legislation. Instead, I shall focus on just two: Section 11, the most general and most frequently utilized of the arrest provisions, and Section 12, which authorized indefinite detention without trial of suspected terrorists. I shall then review the changes made in the 1987 act.

Section 11: The Power to Arrest and Detain for Seventy-two Hours

Section 11(1) of the Emergency Provisions Act (1978) permitted the police to arrest and detain a suspected terrorist for as long as seventy-two hours. The constable was required to inform the suspect that he had been arrested under Section 11 as a suspected terrorist, but the constable did not need to demonstrate that his suspicion was reasonable or verifiable. Consequently, no warrant was necessary; and, because the suspect was not charged with a specific offense, he had no right, as he would under the common law, to a preliminary hearing.[8]

The police were permitted to interrogate suspects throughout the three-day period of detention. Detainees had no right to silence, as they would under the common law: A suspect was required to answer questions concerning his identity and recent movements. Moreover, persons arrested under Section 11 were also required to divulge any information they possessed concerning recent life-threatening terrorist incidents. Furthermore, there was no formal right to a solicitor during the three-day period unless and until the suspect was charged with a specific offense. In accordance with the recommendations of the Bennett Committee, however, charged in 1978 with reviewing police interrogation procedures in Northern Ireland, the RUC later agreed to permit suspects to see their solicitors after forty-eight hours, so long as it was practical to do so.[9] In practice, the RUC cautioned its officers not to tell suspects that they could see their solicitors. The form attached to the front of each prisoner's file specifically instructed constables: "Under *no* circumstances must the Prisoner be asked 'Do you wish to have a Solicitor?'"[10] The RUC apparently believed that the presence of legal counsel would disrupt its efforts to create an environment conducive to intensive questioning. (I shall consider the interrogation process more fully when I discuss Section 8 of the act, which governs the admissibility of confessions at trial.) The Baker Committee's review of the Emergency Provisions Act, commissioned by the government and made public in 1984, likewise concluded that "an unqualified right of access to a solicitor would defeat the purpose of interrogation, the object of which is to discover the truth."[11]

Unlike the powers contained in Sections 14 and 18, which authorized the security forces to stop, question, and detain individuals suspected of offenses even against the ordinary criminal law, Section 11 specifically required that the offense be related to terrorism. In this respect, Section 11 was more solicitous of individual liberties, but in practice there was little difference between Section 11 and the other provisions. The offense was defined in exceptionally broad terms, for Section 31 provided that terrorism is "the use of violence for political ends." The breadth and vagueness of the offense substantially impeded the ability of suspects to challenge the legality of the arrest through habeas corpus proceedings.[12] A majority of the Northern Irish Court of Appeal conceded that the scope of the phrase "terrorist activities" was "very wide and general,"[13] and in the same case the House of Lords ruled that a simple instruction from a superior constable to a subordinate was cause enough to give the arresting officer a "reasonable" suspicion.[14] "The RUC, therefore, was in a position to block judicial review of this arrest power by using the simple expedient of a superior telling a subordinate that an individual was suspected of being a terrorist and instructing him to arrest him."[15]

According to the Bennett Committee, the RUC used its power under Section 11 in over 90 percent of arrests under the emergency legislation.[16] But fully two-thirds of those detained under Section 11 were subsequently released without charge, thus indicating that the security forces used the provision primarily to detain individuals for whom they lacked enough evidence to charge, much less to convict.[17] The Baker Report confirmed this finding, determining that the RUC's own figures indicated that 76 percent of those arrested were released without charge.[18] Indeed, the individual detained often was not the target of the investigation.

Instead, the RUC used Section 11 to detain and question suspects who could later be rearrested under other sections and then charged with a scheduled offense (scheduled offenses typically include the more serious common law offenses, including offenses against persons and property). Section 11 in effect authorized the security forces to detain individuals for the sole purpose of gathering information and intelligence, which they could then use to arrest the individual or other persons. Such a procedure plainly violated the common law and severely compromised an individual's common law right to silence and the right to be free from arbitrary arrests.[19]

Section 11: Conformity with the Constitutive Principles

The arrest and detention provisions of the Emergency Provisions Act (1978) permitted the security forces in Northern Ireland to arrest and detain citizens on the basis of extremely vague and ill-defined suspicions. The suspicion need not have been that an individual had committed any particular offense but only that he was involved "in the commission or attempted commission of any act of

terrorism or in directing, organising or training persons for the purpose of
terrorism." (Under other provisions, the offense need only have been against
the ordinary criminal law.) There was no express requirement that the suspicion be reasonable or even verifiable. Moreover, Northern Irish (and British)
judges proved reluctant to infer an objective requirement of reasonableness in
the absence of an express statutory requirement to that effect.

Although it originated under the Special Powers Act, the case of *In re
McElduff*[20] demonstrates the difficulties the lack of such a requirement causes
for the criminal process. At issue was the RUC's power to arrest and detain
individuals under the internment provisions of the Special Powers Act. The
government argued that since it was emergency legislation, it would be improper for the court to impose the common law's standard of reasonableness to
arrests and detentions under the Special Powers Act.

Recognizing first that "[t]he issue is . . . whether this court can inquire into
the manner in which [the powers] have been exercised and whether in fact they
have been validly exercised,"[21] the court rejected the government's argument
and held that arrests under the SPA must meet the common law requirement
of informing the suspect of the grounds for his arrest. In addition, the court
ruled that the RUC had to inform suspects of the charges for which they were
arrested and under which provision of the act charges would be preferred.[22] (A
suspect's ability to challenge an arrest under the SPA varied depending upon
the provision under which he was charged.) The RUC had told McElduff only
that he was arrested under the general authority of the Special Powers Act.

As a result of *McElduff*, many of those arrested in the internment operation of 1971, described in chapter 2, sued the government for false arrest.[23] But
the RUC simply rearrested those who were released. Indeed, the RUC rearrested McElduff even as he left prison, and "there were no cases in which the
effective release of a person detained or interned . . . was secured by legal
action."[24]

Also at issue in *McElduff* was whether Regulation 11(1) of the SPA
required that the arresting officer's suspicion be reasonable. The court admitted that a contrary interpretation would mean that "a person completely
innocent [of] any crime or offence could be arrested on the merest suspicion
and then, since no time factor is imposed and no right of appeal or resort to the
court provided for in the regulations, held for an indefinite duration of time."[25]
The court nevertheless ruled that absent an express requirement of reasonableness set forth in the provision itself, "what is required . . . is a suspicion existing
in the mind of the constable. That is a subjective test."[26]

The practical result of the lack of a requirement of objectively reasonable
suspicion—or, in other words, the absence of a requirement that a constable
publicly produce reasons that support his suspicion—was that individuals who
committed no offense could be detained without charge, solely for the purpose
of questioning, for three days. And, as indicated earlier, fully two-thirds of
those detained under Section 11 were subsequently released without charge.
Coupled with the army's power to stop and question citizens under Sections 14
and 18, the arrest provisions of the EPA granted the security forces in Ulster

almost unlimited authority to question and detain citizens for the sole purpose of gathering information. Commonly known as "screening," this type of intelligence gathering and harassment was employed most frequently in the Roman Catholic sections of Belfast.[27] It was the army's foremost weapon against terrorism prior to 1973. Large-scale screening of the sort common in the early 1970s no longer occurs, in part because under the policy of Ulsterization, the RUC has assumed from the army a larger responsibility for maintaining public order, and in part because Section 11 no longer includes a power of arrest.

Detention without charge for the sole purpose of gathering intelligence and interrogation represents a significant departure from the common law. The practice demonstrates the inadvisability of confusing the needs of the criminal law with the requirements of state security. As an intelligence-gathering practice, screening may make sense, and the large number of individuals released without charge would say nothing about the effectiveness of Section 11 if its purpose was justified on those grounds. Lord Diplock, however, justified dropping the requirement of reasonableness not as necessary to facilitate intelligence gathering but rather by arguing that the common law rules of arrest and detention were too confusing for young soldiers unschooled in the law to understand: "We think that it is justifiable to take the risk that occasionally a person who takes no part in terrorist activity and has no special knowledge about terrorist organizations should be detained for such a short time . . . rather than that guilty men should escape justice because of technical rules about arrest."[28]

It is difficult to know what to make of Lord Diplock's concern about the "technical" common law rules of arrest. The ordinary rules of arrest in the United Kingdom, an amalgam of common law practices and statutory requirements, may well be confusing. But in the overwhelming majority of cases, these "technical" rules serve only to ensure that a constable's suspicion is in fact reasonable, as is required in the ordinary criminal law by the Criminal Law Act (1967). An express requirement of reasonableness would absolve security forces of more particular knowledge of the common law rules of arrest and would satisfy the constitutional principle which requires of constitutional states that they publicly articulate a reason in support of their use of coercive power against the individual.

Another consequence of the absence of a reasonable suspicion requirement is to preclude review of an arrest through habeas corpus. Indeed, the absence of such a requirement precludes effective review by *any* independent body on any question other than the good faith of the officer. Moreover, Northern Irish judges (and their British counterparts) generally have proven unwilling to infer a standard of reasonableness, presumably upon grounds that the doctrine of *salus populi suproma lex esto* preempts ordinary rules of statutory construction during times of emergency and precludes independent review of an executive's actions.

Perhaps more surprising has been the temerity of Northern Irish judges even in those cases where the relevant statutory provision itself specifies that suspicion must be reasonable. As we shall see when we examine the capacity of courts to review internment orders, judges in at least two cases, *Liversidge v. Anderson*[29] and *R. (O'Hanlon) v. Governor of Belfast Prison*,[30] interpreted a statutory provision requiring "reasonable suspicion" to mean subjectively reasonable suspicion, thus once again rendering independent review impossible. (An exception is the case of *In re Mackey*,[31] in which, contrary to *McElduff*, the court ruled that suspicion under Regulation 11[1] of the Special Powers Act must be an objectively reasonable suspicion.)

The failure publicly to produce reasons to support a decision to arrest—a failure to base the coercive powers of the state on information that can be independently reviewed—repudiates constitutionalism's insistence on the value of reason and the necessity of review to ensure the accountability of state power. It permits state officials to exercise power on the basis of no reason or upon reasons that are arbitrary and capricious. In this respect, Section 11 of the EPA (1978) violated elemental constitutional principles.

Section 12: The Power to Detain Without Trial

Unlike Section 11, which permitted detention for three days and then required the release or rearrest of a suspect, Section 12 permitted the security forces in Northern Ireland to detain suspected terrorists indefinitely without charge or trial. Internment, as the Gardiner Report observed, was a "decision by government to deprive individuals of their liberty without trial and without the normal safeguards which the law provides for the protection of the accused. It is an executive and not a judicial process. It is not known to the common law."[32]

Although it is not "known to the common law," internment has been a more or less permanent feature of Northern Irish law since the state's creation in 1921. As we saw in the preceding chapter, the internment operation in August 1971 set off a wave of violence that ultimately led to direct rule.[33] The Gardiner Committee in 1975 recommended that Section 12 be removed.[34] In 1980 the Standing Committee on Human Rights in Northern Ireland also urged that the power be withdrawn, arguing that "the power to detain without trial persons suspected of being terrorists has always been anathema to the rule of law and a serious obstacle to claims that human rights in Northern Ireland were as fully protected as they ought to be."[35] Baker likewise counseled repeal of Section 12.[36] No detention order has been issued since February 1975, and in 1980 the secretary of state for Northern Ireland announced that the government would permit the provision to lapse. It can, however, be renewed by the secretary of state without parliamentary approval by virtue of Sections 33(3)(c) and 32(3)(b). Such an order would subsequently be subject to cancellation if not approved by both houses of Parliament within a specified period of time. Notwithstanding the recommendations of Gardiner, Baker, and the Standing Committee, the 1987 act includes Section 12, and in 1988 there were repeated calls by some Protestant officials in Ulster for the reintroduction of "selective internment."

What the phrase "selective internment" means is open to question, and the authorities have denied that internment is likely to be reinstituted. If the power is revived, however unlikely, the process will no doubt resemble the one in operation in the mid-1970s.[37] The first stage in the internment proceedings was the making of an "interim custody" order (ICO) by the secretary of state for Northern Ireland or one of his deputies. The order did not need to set forth in detail the allegations against an individual; and, since no criminal charges were required, it rarely did so. An interim order authorized detention for fourteen days, but if the secretary referred the case to an adviser, a process described more fully later, the suspect could be held until the adviser decided the case. One study found that "[m]any suspects were held on interim custody orders for periods of five or six months or longer pending the hearing of their cases."[38]

After the secretary issued an interim order, there was a hearing before a "judicially qualified" adviser, appointed by the secretary. (The term "judicially qualified" means that an individual has either held judicial office in the United Kingdom or has been a barrister or solicitor of ten years' standing.) The adviser could order the further detention of a suspect if he was satisfied that the suspect had been involved in terrorist activities and that his "detention was necessary for the protection of the public."[39]

The adviser was required to hold a formal, private hearing in the presence of the suspect and his counsel. (The adviser could, however, exclude the suspect or his counsel if, in his opinion, public safety required it.) At the hearing, the suspect was first provided with a formal statement of the allegations. But the utility of even this minimal requirement was questionable: The allegations were not formal charges, hence they were set forth in vague and cryptic language that suggested much but disclosed very little.

The hearings themselves were informal and unstructured, governed only by the requirement that there be a written record and by whatever additional procedures the commissioner thought necessary. A suspect did have the right to cross-examine witnesses, but most were informants who testified behind screens to guard their identity. There were no rules of evidence prohibiting the introduction of hearsay or of prejudicial or unreliable information. At the conclusion of the hearing, the adviser could order the release or continued detention of the suspect. Internees could then appeal to a tribunal of three "legally qualified" persons, again appointed by the secretary of state. No formal procedures were required in the appellate hearings.

The final stage in the internment process was review by the adviser not less than twelve months after the issuance of the detention order, and then every six months. Reviews differed little from the original hearings, except that they were limited to the question of whether continued detention was necessary for the public safety. In addition, the secretary of state, who issued the order and appointed the adviser, could order the release of an internee at any time.

Judicial Review of Internment Orders

The secretary's power to intervene at any point during the proceedings demonstrates the essentially nonjudicial nature of the internment process: An order to intern without trial is not a judicial decision (although it may well be an exercise of judicial power).[40] It is instead an executive order which is in all essential respects immune from judicial supervision. An internee can petition a court for a writ of habeas corpus, but courts seldom seriously consider habeas petitions that arise from the emergency legislation.[41]

Most of the cases that do address the legality of internment procedures arose under the internment provisions of the now repealed Special Powers Act. For most purposes, the differences between those internment procedures and Section 12 are insignificant. But proceedings under Section 12 were more formal and institutionalized, and there were requirements under Section 12 that seem to accommodate judicial criticisms of the Special Powers Act. In general, however, courts do not now, and have not in the past, exercised control over internment proceedings.

In the first important test of internment under the Special Powers Act, for example, the Northern Irish courts indicated that they would not review internment orders. *R. (O'Hanlon) v. Governor of Belfast Prison*[42] concerned the arrest in 1922 of a hotel owner in Portadown (a town on the Northern coast) who was allegedly involved in a conspiracy against the Northern Irish government. The High Court rejected O'Hanlon's application for a writ of habeas corpus "on the ground that under the Act it was within the power of the Minister . . . to make what detention and internment orders he thought fit and that it was not for the Court to express an opinion on the facts of the case."[43] Scholars and lawyers severely criticized *O'Hanlon*, for the regulation had explicitly provided that the minister give reasonable grounds for his decision.[44] Perhaps to preclude judicial reconsideration, Stormont subsequently amended the regulation to read that the minister could intern anyone "whom he suspects of acting or of having acted or is acting or is a threat to public order."

Other cases involved postarrest proceedings under the Special Powers Act. *In re Mackey* (1971),[45] for example, concerned an arrest under Regulation 12(1) of the SPA, which provided that an internee could make representations before an Advisory Committee to the Minister of Home Affairs stating why he should not be interned. The process very much resembled the one used under Section 12. The question in *Mackey* was whether internees should be given legal counsel and provided with a complete statement of the charges against them. The court concluded that "principles of natural justice" required that internees appearing before the Advisory Committee be given a written summary of the charges and evidence against them and legal counsel if they so requested. The court qualified its ruling by stating that the committee could withhold the information when its release might compromise the public safety.

Mackey also criticized the ruling in *McElduff* that internees could be detained on an officer's subjective suspicion. According to the court:

> [Regulation 11(1)] indicates that a man may not be interned unless he has
> been suspected of acting, or having acted, or being about to act in a manner
> prejudicial to the preservation of peace and the maintenance of order. I read
> that requirement as involving the existence of facts or information of such a
> character and cogency as are *reasonably* capable of arousing a suspicion.[46]

Mackey, as *O'Hanlon* and *McElduff* suggest, is something of an oddity in British and Northern Irish jurisprudence. More representative are the cases of *R. v. Halliday, ex parte Zadig*,[47] and *Liversidge v. Anderson*.[48] In *ex parte Zadig*, the British home secretary had issued an order interning Zadig, a naturalized British citizen of German birth. The secretary issued the order under Regulation 14B of the Defence of the Realm (Consolidation) Act (1914) (DORA). Section 1(1) of the act gave the executive power to issue whatever regulations were necessary "for securing the public safety and the defence of the realm."

After he was interned, Zadig applied for a writ of habeas corpus, arguing that Regulation 14B was ultra vires the DORA.[49] The Court of Appeals dismissed Zadig's appeal from the denial of the writ, whereupon he appealed to the House of Lords. Lord Chancellor Finlay upheld the appellate court's decision, ruling:

> The statute was passed at a time of supreme national danger, which still exists. The danger of espionage and of damage by secret agents . . . had to be guarded against. The restraint imposed may be a necessary measure of precaution, and in the interests of the whole nation it may be regarded as expedient that such an order should be made in suitable cases.[50]

The court concluded by ruling that only the executive could decide whether to issue an internment order under Regulation 14B. *Zadig* thus stands for the proposition that the exercise of executive discretion, at least in emergencies, is subjective and consequently not subject to judicial supervision.

A second case concerning the authority of the British home secretary to issue internment orders arose in 1939 under the Emergency Powers (Defence) Act (1939). Section 1(1) of the act authorized the secretary to issue "[r]egulations . . . for the detention of persons whose detention appears . . . expedient in the interests of the public safety or the defence of the realm." Acting on this authority, the secretary promulgated Regulation 18B, which authorized internment "[i]f the Secretary of State has *reasonable cause* to believe any person to be of hostile origins or associations."

In *Liversidge v. Anderson*,[51] the home secretary had issued an internment order against Liversidge (also known as Perlzweig), who subsequently petitioned for a writ of habeas corpus. The minister's sole response was to provide the court with a copy of the order under Regulation 18B. Lord Chancellor Maughan concluded that the phrase "reasonable cause to believe" did *not* provide an objective limitation upon the secretary's discretion but rather meant only that the secretary had personally to review each case and that he must have acted in good faith.[52] An order to intern was thus not subject to judicial review but was, Lord Maughan stressed, still subject to parliamentary oversight.

In a powerful dissent, Lord Atkin argued that the majority's interpretation of the phrase "reasonable cause to believe" was disingenuous. "I know of only one authority," Lord Atkin wrote, which might justify [the majority's interpretation]. . . : When I use a word, Humpty Dumpty said in a rather scornful tone, it means just what I choose it to mean, neither more nor less. The question is, said Alice, whether you can make words mean so many different things. The question is, said Humpty Dumpty, which is to be master—that's all. . . .

[T]he question is whether the words "If a man has" can mean "If a man thinks he has." I am of the opinion that they cannot, and that the case should be decided accordingly.[53]

Liversidge and *Zadig* thus stand for the proposition that the doctrine of *salus populi suprema lex esto*, at least during times of emergency, preempts ordinary principles of statutory construction. Courts in Northern Ireland have generally followed this rule.

Section 12: Conformity with Constitutive Principles

In some ways Section 12 does satisfy the constitutional requirements of reason and review. There are biannual reviews of internment orders, and insofar as internees receive legal counsel and copies of the charges against them, Section 12 incorporates the requirements set forth by *Mackey*, principles said to be required by the "principles of natural justice." But the government need proffer no specific charges of criminal activity, so the internee has no particular knowledge of the charges and evidence against him, and review is limited to the question of whether an internee continues to pose a threat to public safety.

More important, the ability of the secretary of state to intervene at any point in the proceedings underscores the essentially administrative and executive nature of both the initial decision and subsequent review of it. Hence there is no independent review of an internment order, and review cannot be undertaken through a habeas proceeding because the grounds necessary to support a charge can be so vague. Such cases underscore how the constitutional principles of reason and review work in tandem: The absence of the former makes the second a mere formality.

Changes in the Emergency Provisions Act of 1987

In his 1984 review of the Emergency Provisions Act, Baker recommended that subsections (1) and (3) of Section 11 should be repealed and replaced with a single power of arrest, which would require reasonableness of suspicion. (Baker also recommended that the period of detention should be forty-eight rather than seventy-two hours.)[54] The 1987 amendments largely incorporated those recommendations. As a consequence, Section 11 no longer contains a power to arrest. There is instead a single provision, Section 13, which states that a constable may arrest a person without warrant when "he has reasonable grounds to suspect" the person has committed, is committing, or is about to commit an offense. Detention is then permitted for a period of forty-eight hours, which is the normal period permitted under Article 131 of the Magistrates' Courts (Northern Ireland) Order (1981) for any offense. (As we shall see, however, Article 131 does not apply to arrests under the Prevention of Terrorism Act.)

The addition of a reasonableness of suspicion standard in Section 13 (and also in Section 14, concerning the powers of the army) is a substantial improvement over Section 11 of the 1978 act and comes closer to satisfying the constitutional principle which requires that an individual be apprised of the reason for his detention. It also improves the likelihood of compliance with the principle of review by providing a court with an objective standard against which it can measure the legality of any particular arrest. But difficulties persist as long as the offense remains drafted in language so vague that almost any suspicion will support a criminal charge. The 1987 legislation still permits charges based simply on "suspicion of terrorism." As we shall see in our review of similar offenses under the Prevention of Terrorism Act, it is difficult to secure an independent review even of "reasonable" suspicions of such offenses. In addition, courts may still choose to interpret a requirement of reasonableness in the way chosen by the court in *McElduff*: "[W]hat is required . . . is a suspicion existing in the mind of the constable. That is a subjective test." This interpretation substantially undermines the usefulness of a reasonableness of suspicion requirement.[55]

Pretrial Procedures and Bail

A suspect who has been formally charged with a specific offense must be brought before a magistrate for a preliminary, or remand, hearing. Under the ordinary criminal law, the magistrate may release the suspect, "remand" him back into custody, or grant bail. Under the emergency legislation, bail for scheduled offenses may be granted only by a High Court judge under a separate application.

Between August 1973 and September 1983, there were 13,244 applications for bail in cases involving scheduled offenses. Some 41 percent, or 5,398 of those applications, were granted.[56] Table 3-1 indicates that slightly under one-third of the applications were granted in a sample of cases taken from January to April 1979. (The figures do not reflect the tendency of solicitors not to request bail in cases involving more serious offenses.)[57]

Section 2(2) of the 1978 act limited the traditional discretion of judges to grant bail by providing that it should not be allowed unless the judge was satisfied that "the applicant"

(a) will comply with the conditions on which he is admitted to bail; and
(b) will not interfere with any witnesses; and
(c) will not commit any offense while he is on bail.

Until changes made in the 1987 act, therefore, Section 2(2) embodied a presumption against the granting of bail. (The 1987 legislation left the presumption intact but shifted the burden of proof to the prosecution.)[58] Section 2(3)

Table 3-1. Bail and Remand Decisions (January–April 1979)

	Remanded	Bail Granted	Other
Loyalists	63 (62%)	30 (29%)	9 (9%)
Republicans	165 (69%)	66 (27%)	10 (4%)
Total	230 (66%)	96 (27%)	20 (6%)

Source: Kevin Boyle, Tom Hadden, and Paddy Hillyard, *Ten Years On in Northern Ireland* (London: Cobden Trust, 1980), 65.

also permitted judges to condition bail upon such other factors "as appear . . . necessary in the interest of justice or for the prevention of crime."

Normally, the prosecution bears the burden of justifying (i.e., of producing reasons that support) a decision to remand a defendant into custody. Under the 1978 emergency legislation, however, that burden was shifted to the defendant, who was required to produce reasons why he should *not* be remanded into custody. As a consequence, even at the remand hearing the state need not have publicly advanced a creditable or verifiable reason to support either the arrest or the detention. In ordinary law, a magistrate can dismiss weak cases at the remand hearing. Under the emergency legislation in place until 1987, a magistrate could not so much as compel the state to show probable cause, even though judicial approval is necessary to keep the suspect in custody. Again, this failure plainly offended the constitutional principle of independent review. Requiring the defendant to demonstrate why he should not be remanded puts the burden of proof upon a person who has yet to see what evidence, if any, the prosecution has to support the charge. It should also be clear that such a shift casts considerable doubt on the presumption of innocence.

One of the original justifications for the new bail requirements was that they were necessary to secure equality of treatment between Roman Catholic and Protestant defendants. In a 1973 study of the pre-Diplock courts, Boyle, Hadden, and Hillyard found that in cases involving political offenses, magistrates denied bail to 79 percent of Catholic defendants but to only 54 percent of Protestants.[59] In ordinary criminal trials, the rates were 50 and 53 percent, respectively. In a post-Diplock study, Boyle, Hadden, and Hillyard found no evidence that high court judges discriminated on the basis of religion, despite findings in earlier studies that sectarian bias among lower magistrates was routine. They thus recommended that Section 2 be allowed to lapse.[60] But given the terms of the provision itself and the additional requirement that an application for bail be made under separate cover, the better interpretation of Section 2 is not that its purpose was to reduce sectarian bias but rather that it limits judicial discretion in order to restrict the number of defendants who will qualify for bail.

Baker similarly found no factual support for Boyle's argument. For this and other reasons, Baker recommended that Section 2(1), which provides that only a judge of the high court may grant bail, be retained. With regard to the burden of proof, however, Baker recommended that Section 2(2) be redrafted to put the initial burden on the prosecution but leave the court with wide discretion in such cases, a discretion based on subsections (a), (b), and (c) of Section 2 and the Bail Act (1976).[61] This change, effected in the 1987 act and coupled with arrests under the new Section 13, more nearly accords with the principles of reason—the state must now at least bring forth some reason in support of detention—and therefore with the presumption of innocence.

Trial in the Diplock Courts

Section 7(1) of the Emergency Provisions Act (1987) establishes a system of special courts to hear cases involving terrorist offenses. In these tribunals, known as Diplock courts, a single high court judge, sitting without a jury, hears cases under relaxed rules of evidence. Thus the judge performs the traditional function of finding law, as well as assuming the jury's fact-finding role. (Less serious offenses may be heard by a county court judge, and the director of public prosecutions may "certify" a case out to a juried court if he concludes that it does not actually involve terrorism.)

The most striking element in Diplock cases is, of course, the suspension of trial by jury, a suspension the British government justified by warning of the possibility that terrorists would intimidate witnesses and jurors. The Diplock Committee also feared the possibility of "perverse" verdicts that might result from a jury's sectarian bias, although Lord Diplock conceded: "It is fair to say that we have not had our attention drawn to complaints of *convictions* that were plainly perverse and complaints of acquittals which were plainly perverse are rare."[62] Nonetheless, my interviews with solicitors and barristers in Northern Ireland suggest that the fear of perverse verdicts, at least in 1973, was well-founded.

As the preceding quote indicates, the committee's fear was in part one of perverse convictions: Authorities worried that Protestants would unfairly convict Catholics or (less likely, given the mechanics of jury selection in Ulster) that Catholics would unfairly convict Protestants. Prior to 1973 juries were composed almost exclusively of Protestants, partly because prosecutors could excuse, or "stand by," Catholic jurors on grounds that they were more likely than Protestants to be biased or subject to intimidation.[63]

Put in this way, the government could justify the suspension of trial by jury as a measure designed not only to protect witnesses and jurors but also to safeguard the rights of the accused, most of whom were Catholic. But magistrates always have the discretion to set aside improper verdicts, or verdicts in which the weight of the evidence is insufficient to support the conviction. The constitutional principle of mitigation does not necessarily prohibit suspension of trial by jury but rather requires that the state first explore less radical solutions to the problem. One possibility is to restrict the prosecution's right to stand by jurors to those cases in which it can show cause—to cases, in other words, where the prosecution can articulate a reason, other than a juror's religious affiliation, to show a danger of bias.

All of this at least suggests that concern over perverse convictions was not really what lay behind the decision to suspend juries. More probable was the fear of perverse *acquittals*, of cases in which Protestant juries would unfairly acquit Loyalists. After jury trials were suspended, the percentage of Protestant defendants who pled guilty rose considerably, "presumably because they could no longer count on a friendly jury."[64]

Unlike the problems of perverse convictions, there is little (other than suspending trial by jury) that the state can do to overcome the problem of perverse acquittals. Double jeopardy rules usually prohibit retrial of a defendant for the same offense. Hence it is always the case that some defendants who are no doubt guilty will be acquitted by biased or uninformed juries. And even with modifications in the prosecution's right to stand by jurors, some terrorists may still win acquittals from sympathetic juries. The risk of unjust acquittals is one that all common law systems suffer in ordinary times, but the risk takes on an added urgency when the defendant is a suspected terrorist. Coupled with well-founded fears of intimidation of jurors and witnesses, the risk of sectarian bias *may* necessitate suspension of jury trials for scheduled offenses.

One might argue that jury trials are constitutionally required because they promote the exchange of reasons and review in the criminal process, particularly with regard to admission of inculpatory statements. But a jury's review is essentially cumulative in nature. In the common law, the judge decides at the voir dire hearings whether a confession is admissible. A jury subsequently decides whether the statement is reliable, but that decision will almost always be based upon the same evidence the judge relied upon in the voir dire hearing. Juries do, of course, provide a measure of representation and public participation in the criminal process. But jury trials are hardly the only institutional means of securing participation or consent, and it is far from clear that they are a necessary condition of legitimacy in a society rent by political, cultural, and social division.

Thus the constitutive principles of constitutional maintenance permit suspension of trial by jury, so long as that suspension is itself justified by publicly stated reasons and is not based on pretext. A legitimate fear of intimidation, or of bias in cases where cause can be shown, would therefore be sufficient to justify suspension. But continued suspension of trial by jury must be periodically rejustified as the emergency continues. My interviews with attorneys suggest the fear was well-founded in the early years of direct rule. Its continued necessity is a matter of great dispute, but a report by the Association of the Bar of the City of New York in 1988 concluded that "an immediate, complete return to normal institutional life in Northern Ireland is [not] a realistic possibility."[65]

Moreover, only a few years ago the Baker Report found that "[t]he overwhelming weight of opinion from those best qualified to judge is that members of juries in serious cases would be in more danger today than ever before."[66] Baker therefore concluded that the present system of trial for scheduled offenses, one judge and no jury, should remain intact. In reaching this conclusion, he rejected numerous other proposals for reform, all of which are predicated on the assumption that full jury trials are not now feasible or desirable.[67] These proposals have included calls for anonymous juries, or for a presumptive (or contingent) jury trial system, but the most popular and frequent proposals have typically involved some sort of collegial court. Collegial court systems might include additional judges who participate only on matters of fact, or others in which the full court decides on matters of both law and fact, as well as systems that include lay assessors. All have engendered support in some quarters and disagreement in others.[68] The constitutional principle of mitigation requires that the government explore the feasibility of these alternatives. In the course of that examination, the government will be forced to periodically and publicly set forth the specific reasons, if any, that justify the continued suspension of trial by jury.

Trial by jury is important symbolically because it is among the most treasured of common law rights and one that most citizens can identify. A 1974 study, for example, found that 63 percent of the Protestants and 79 percent of the Catholics in Ulster knew that jury trials had been suspended in cases involving terrorist offenses.[69] But the symbolic importance of the juryless Diplock courts exceeds their real significance in the emergency criminal process: The legislation that creates the courts and defines their jurisdiction substantially limits the degree of discretion judges otherwise possess in the criminal process. We saw this strategy reflected in provisions that limit judicial discretion in bail decisions and other pretrial proceedings, and the arrest provisions limit judicial discretion in cases involving challenges to arrests and detentions. Other sections cabin judicial discretion by shifting the burden of proof in cases involving possession of firearms and explosives and by tightening the standards governing the admissibility of confessions.

Section 8: Admission of Confessions

In 1972 the Diplock Committee expressed concern that "the current technical rules, practices and *judicial discretions* as to the admissibility of confessions"[70] were "hampering the course of justice in the case of terrorist crimes."[71] (Compare the argument by the Baker Report: "The so-called right of silence . . . made it impossible to obtain admissible *evidence* against known terrorists, some of whom had even been named in open court.")[72] Section 8 of the Emergency Provisions Act accounts for this concern by arguably requiring admission of any and every confession obtained without "torture, inhuman or degrading treatment." The purpose of Section 8 "was clearly to authorize the admission of statements obtained in breach of the common law rules. It is rather less clear how far beyond those rules it was intended that interrogators might go."[73] Uncertainty under Section 8 has centered upon two distinct questions: What constitutes torture or inhuman or degrading treatment? Does Section 8 leave Diplock judges with any residual discretion to refuse to admit confessions that otherwise comply with its terms? How Diplock judges have tried to answer these questions illustrates the complex interplay between statutory law and judicial discretion in dealing with terrorism as a criminal offense. The process is of tremendous importance, for in most cases—perhaps 80 percent, as estimated by the Bennett Committee—the only significant evidence of a defendant's guilt is the confession.[74] (The director of public prosecutions has also reported that he relies on confessions in 75 percent of the cases.)[75] In only 30 percent of those cases was the confession supported by additional forensic or identification evidence. In over half the cases, then, the only significant evidence was the defendant's confession.[76]

Torture or Inhuman or Degrading Treatment

Section 8 permits, and arguably requires, the admission of all confessions obtained without "torture, inhuman or degrading treatment," as those terms are used in Article 3 of the European Convention on Human Rights. (The Diplock Committee deliberately used this terminology to comply with the convention's standard.) Diplock neglected, however, to consider an important procedural difference between Section 8 and the convention's standard: Under Section 8, and in keeping with the general strategy of the emergency legislation to shift burdens of proof, the defendant must first establish a prima facie case of mistreatment, whereas under the European standard, as in British common law, the prosecution bears the initial burden of establishing that a confession was made voluntarily.

The convention's standard is, moreover, considerably less stringent than British common law rules, which, as the court ruled in *D.P.P. v. Ping Lin* (1976),[77] require that a confession cannot be obtained by "hope of advantage, fear of prejudice . . . or oppression." In contrast, Section 8 permits the sort of psychological pressure condemned in *Ping Lin* and also by *R. v. Corr* (1968).[78]

Of particular interest to the Diplock Committee was the well-known case of *R. v. Flynn and Leonard* (1972).[79] The confession in doubt had been obtained at the Holywood Detention Center, which the court described as a "set-up officially organised and operated to obtain information." The court concluded that confessions obtained under such conditions "will often fail to qualify as voluntary statements." Between July 1976 and June 1978, fifteen confessions were not admitted.[80]

Responding to cases like *Flynn and Leonard*, Diplock argued that Section 8 would not prohibit admission of statements "obtained as a result of building up a psychological atmosphere in which the natural desire of the person being questioned to remain silent is replaced by an urge to confide in the questioner."[81] Nor would Section 8, in contrast to the rule in *Ping Lin*, prohibit statements "preceded by promises of favours or indications of the consequences which might follow if the person questioned persisted in refusing to answer."

Section 8 accomplishes this largely through changes in the procedure by which statements are admitted or denied admission at trial. In the common law, for example, the prosecution bears the initial burden of proving that a confession was voluntary before it can be introduced as evidence. Diplock recommended that the defendant should bear the burden of proving, "on a balance of probabilities," that he was subjected to torture or inhuman or degrading treatment.[82] The act, however, requires instead that the defendant present a prima facie case of such treatment, after which the prosecution must demonstrate that the confession was indeed voluntary.

In practice, Northern Irish judges have interpreted Section 8 so that only rarely will a defendant's allegation be dismissed for failure to establish a prima facie case. In *R. v. Milne* (1978),[83] for example, Lord Justice McGonigal noted that "although the accused has taken no point on the admissibility of the statement it is still for me to be satisfied that it is . . . admissible." The prosecution's burden in response is the ordinary standard of proof beyond a reasonable doubt.[84] The state must establish, then, that the accused made the statement and was not subjected to torture or inhuman treatment, or that such treatment was not calculated to induce the defendant to make a statement.

The terms of Section 8 go to the judge's initial decision to admit or exclude inculpatory statements. Even at the common law, the judge makes an initial decision on admissibility at the voir dire proceedings. At trial, the jury may then refuse to credit the statement as reliable. The jury's decision will normally be based on much the same evidence presented at the voir dire proceedings. In Diplock cases, however, the judge finds both law and fact. Hence he must make both the initial decision to admit or exclude (a question of law) and the second decision concerning credibility and reliability (a question of fact). (Walker has argued that if a statement is excluded, a judge will often step down, as provided by Section 8[2][b],[85] but other observers have argued that this provision "receives little use.")[86] Perhaps because of this added responsibility, Diplock judges have jealously guarded their discretion to determine admissibility.

Supplementing the common law rules of admissibility are the Judges' Rules and Administrative Directions to the Police (1976). These rules provide that the police must stop questioning a suspect once it is clear they will charge the suspect with a specific offense. There are several additional rules that govern the taking of such statements, including a *Miranda*-like rule requiring the RUC explicitly to caution suspects that their statements may be used against them in court.[87]

Under Section 11 of the 1978 act, detention and questioning were authorized for seventy-two hours without having to charge a suspect with a specific offense (and under Section 12 of the Prevention of Terrorism Act (1984), suspects can be held without specific charge for up to seven days). This effectively permitted the RUC to sidestep the Judges' Rules in most cases. Moreover, it is not clear that a confession obtained in breach of the Judges' Rules is a sufficient reason to exclude it at trial. Such a violation is almost certainly sufficient to establish the defendant's prima facie case, but at least one court has ruled that the confession can still be admitted.[88] In 1979, for example, a Diplock judge admitted a confession by a fifteen-year-old boy who was a student at a school for the mentally disabled and who "was assessed as having the mental age of a child of eight."[89] The Judges' Rules required the presence of a parent or relative during the questioning, a requirement the RUC had ignored.

Residual Discretion to Admit or Exclude Statements

As we saw, the Diplock Report concluded that "the current rules, practices, and *judicial discretions* as to the admissibility of confessions ought to be suspended . . . [and] should be replaced by a simple legislative provision."[90] Section 8 responds to this concern by arguably requiring admission of any statement that complies with its terms. The Gardiner Committee, however, thought this conclusion unwarranted: "It is difficult to conclude that Parliament intended to withdraw from the judiciary a well-established discretion . . . without saying so in clear terms . . . the construction we favour, which leaves the judicial discretion unimpaired, should be stated expressly."[91] Lord Gardiner therefore recommended that the 1978 act be amended to provide explicitly that "it does not prevent a court from exercising discretion to refuse to admit a confession."[92] The government did not adopt Gardiner's recommendation.

Nevertheless, some Diplock judges have argued that they may still exclude prejudicial confessions, even if they otherwise satisfy the terms of Section 8. In *R. v. Corey* (1979),[93] the court held that "there is always a discretion, unless it is expressly removed, to exclude any admissible evidence on the ground that . . . its prejudicial effect outweighs its probative value and that to admit the evidence would not be in the interests of justice."[94] The basis for this discretion is unclear, and "in fact, few reported cases can be found where a discretion has actually been used to exclude an otherwise admissible confession."[95] In *Corey* exclusion was required because its admission "would not be in the interests of justice." Alternatively, the discretion has been justified on grounds that "in a civilized society it is vital that persons in custody or charged with offences should not be subjected to ill-treatment or improper pressure in order to extract confessions."[96]

Whatever the basis for the discretion (it is plainly required by the constitutional principles of reason and respect), its existence and repeated use could surely negate Section 8 altogether, as the court acknowledged in the leading case of *R. v. McCormick* (1977).[97] In *McCormick*, Lord Justice McGonigal ruled that Section 8 permits the RUC to use "a moderate degree of physical maltreatment for the purpose of inducing a person to make a statement."[98] Justice McGonigal nevertheless excluded the challenged statement, holding that even given the express terms of Section 8, courts need not tolerate physical mistreatment *purposely designed* to induce a person to make a statement. To do otherwise would "be an offense under the ordinary criminal law . . . [and] repugnant to all principles of justice."[99]

Of course, the very purpose of Section 8 was to alter the ordinary criminal law to which McGonigal referred. (The second claim, of repugnance to all principles of justice, is a different question.) Aware that his newly created exception might render Section 8 altogether null, McGonigal also suggested that "[the discretion] should only be exercised in such cases where failure to exercise it might create injustice by admitting a statement which though admissible under the section . . . was . . . suspect by reason of the method by which it was obtained."[100]

A more recent case, *R. v. O'Halloran* (1979), raised the obvious objection to this argument by observing that it is "difficult . . . to envisage any form of physical violence which is relevant to the interrogation of a suspect in custody and which, if it had occurred, could at the same time leave a court satisfied beyond a reasonable doubt [as to the confession's voluntariness]."[101] Baker thought *O'Halloran* correctly decided and therefore concluded that it would not be permissible to use even a "moderate" degree of physical mistreatment to induce a confession, the international standard notwithstanding. "I am convinced," he wrote, "that no physical violence of any degree would now be tolerated."[102]

Perhaps because they recognize the difficulty of reconciling residual discretion with the terms of Section 8, Diplock judges rarely exercise it. Between July 1976 and July 1982, Diplock judges heard almost four thousand cases.[103] In the overwhelming majority of these cases, a confession was the only significant evidence of guilt. Diplock judges ruled confessions inadmissible in just thirty-two, or less than 1 percent, of those cases. (During the same period, the director of public prosecutions declined to proceed with eleven cases for fear that the confessions in those cases would not be admitted.) Baker's figures confirm the trend, leading him to conclude: "In recent years few confessions have been excluded."[104] And in most of the cases where a confession was excluded, there was persuasive medical evidence of physical abuse. Nevertheless, the Gardiner Committee concluded that "so long as the judicial discretion remains, we think the chances of . . . an unjust trial or an unjust verdict are remote."[105] Baker agreed but like Gardiner recommended that Section 8 be redrafted explicitly to exclude violence and to authorize judicial discretion to exclude statements.[106]

The 1987 act incorporated these recommendations. A new provision, Section 5, now declares that statements are inadmissible if there is evidence that the defendant was mistreated or that a "threat of violence" existed. Subsection 3 of the act also states that judges possess a discretion to exclude statements "in the interest" of justice.

Section 8: Conformity with the Constitutive Principles

Insofar as it adopted the European Convention standard of torture and inhuman treatment, Section 8 of the 1978 act permitted the admission of confessions elicited through "moderate" physical and psychological abuse in interrogations. In the *Greek* case (1969),[107] the Report of the Commission indicated that inhuman or degrading treatment did not include slaps to the head or similar forms of rough treatment, for a distinction should be drawn "between acts prohibited . . . and a 'certain roughness of treatment' [which] . . . may . . . [include] slaps or blows of the hand on the head or face."[108] A majority decision in the case of *Ireland v. United Kingdom* (1978) reached the same conclusion.[109]

The constitutional principles of reason and respect for persons do not allow physical or psychological abuse of criminal defendants. The *Greek* case failed to recognize, as constitutional states must, that the mere threat of "moderate" violence toward prisoners, already deprived of their liberty and unable to defend themselves, can be abusive and cruel. Indeed, such threats alone deny constitutionalism's respect for reason and the premise that reason is preferable to violence in public affairs. The use of violence, or of threats of violence, therefore degrades the value of reason itself and in doing so undermines the ultimate purpose of the emergency legislation, which must be to replace violence with reason in public affairs. (The same disability attaches to the major procedural difference between the convention's standard and Section 8, concerning the burden of proof.)

Insofar as Section 8 required admission of inculpatory statements that satisfy the European standard, it offended the constitutional principle of review by denying judges the authority to review the integrity of such evidence. As we have seen, though, Northern Ireland's judges have responded in ingenious ways to protect their discretion to refuse to admit confessions. On occasion, Diplock judges have appealed to the "principles of natural justice" or to "the requirements of civilized society" to support such decisions. These appeals should be seen, and thus defended, as attempts to articulate an appeal to the authority of the constitutive principles of constitutionalism. Baker's conclusions, that judicial discretion ought to be authorized explicitly and that Section 8 ought to exclude violence, both included in the 1987 act, are more in conformity with the demands of constitutionalism. It would be preferable, however, as the National Council for Civil Liberties recommended, to have a statutory provision requiring exclusion of all statements obtained by "any threat, inducement or oppressive treatment."[110]

There is also a continuing procedural difficulty that the 1987 act has not touched. The absence of jury trials means judges must still make an initial decision on a confession's admissibility. A decision to exclude a statement never reaches a jury, of course, and as a consequence the statement cannot influence the jury's decision. But in the Diplock courts, a judge's decision not to admit evidence is more troublesome, for the judge now knows the evidence upon which he is not to premise his conclusion. The only safeguard that a judge will in fact disregard such evidence is the honor of the office. Some have responded to this criticism by noting that judges also possess a discretion to abandon the trial,[111] but this remedy must also rely for its effectiveness upon the integrity of the presiding judge.

Although their use of discretion has been relatively infrequent, the response by judges to executive encroachments in the admission of evidence has been considerably more aggressive than their response to extensive changes in the areas of arrest and detention. One explanation for this difference is that the police and security forces are initially responsible for the arrest and detention stages of the criminal process, whereas courts are responsible primarily for the conduct of the trial. Consequently, judges would be more likely to resist changes that directly impede on their institutional prerogatives.

The Right to Silence and the Criminal Evidence (N.I.) Order of 1988

On October 21, 1988, the British secretary of state for Northern Ireland announced that the government would introduce new measures that would permit Diplock judges to "attach whatever weight they considered proper to the fact that a suspect had remained silent under police questioning or had refused to give evidence in court."[112] The legislation effecting this change took effect in November. (The government also announced that it would seek a similar change in England and Wales for the ordinary criminal law.)

The right to silence is a long recognized part of the common law (and is included in the U.S. Constitution's Fifth Amendment), and its repeal represents a major change in the emergency law. But the change is not completely novel. As we have seen, various other provisions of the emergency law, such as Section 11 of the Prevention of Terrorism Act, had already made substantial inroads on this right. Indeed, the change was recommended by the Criminal Law Revision Committee for the entire criminal law in 1972, but it was rejected by the Royal Commission on Criminal Procedure in 1981.

The justification for abrogation of this right is said to be the increasing sophistication of members of the IRA and other paramilitary organizations in resisting questioning, which makes it more difficult to secure convictions. The secretary of state best voiced this concern, claiming that "anybody who has any experience of the recent operation of the criminal justice system in Northern Ireland . . . [must] recognize that the right was being systematically abused."[113] It is certainly true that the IRA coaches its members to resist interrogation. One of its pamphlets warns: "Interrogation is like walking a dangerous tightrope: the only safety net one has is to maintain absolute silence, from the moment of arrest until the moment of release."[114]

In some respects, the new rule is consistent with the recent revisions of Section 8, which ratify judicial discretion to admit or exclude inculpatory statements. But it also works a significant change in the burden of proof. Insofar as the defendant's silence can now be used as proof of guilt—in other words, as a "reason"—it becomes necessary for the defendant to testify in response in order to prove his or her innocence. The insufficiency of such a reason is a matter for great concern, especially in conjunction with the overwhelming tendency of convictions to be premised solely upon confessions unsupported by additional evidence. The problem is partially offset by a provision in the order which states that a person shall not be committed for trial, or convicted, solely upon an inference drawn from that person's silence. But even this qualification takes no account of the legitimate reasons why an accused might choose to remain silent.

Section 9: Possession Offenses

Like Sections 2(2) and 8, Section 9 significantly alters the ordinary common law rules of evidence. Normally, in cases concerning possession of firearms and other dangerous articles, the prosecution bears the burden of proving both the physical presence of the article and the defendant's knowledge of its presence. Under Section 9, however, the prosecutor need only show the first element. The burden then shifts to the defendant to show that he had no knowledge of the article or control over it.* If the defendant can satisfy this requirement, the court may then choose not to accept the evidence. As noted by the Diplock Committee, "The effect . . . would be to make it incumbent upon persons charged . . . to go into the witness box and give an explanation of their own conduct."[115]

Lord Diplock justified this change from the common law by citing pre-act cases like *R. v. Whelan* (1972).[116] In *Whelan*, the RUC found a gun in a bedroom shared by three brothers. All three men were present when the gun was found, but each denied knowledge of it. None of the defendants testified at trial; all were convicted. An appellate court reversed the convictions, ruling that the lower court should not have given the case to the jury because there was insufficient evidence that any of the men were in possession of the gun, or that they were in joint possession of it. Under Section 9, each of the men would have been compelled to give evidence concerning his knowledge of and control over the object.

Although Section 9 does work a significant change in the burden of proof (it requires, in effect, that defendants demonstrate the *nonexistence* of knowledge or control, a much more significant burden than the one shouldered by the prosecution under the ordinary law), it does not offend the demands of constitutionalism. Even under Section 9, the state must still first demonstrate the presence of the article. It has therefore articulated a reason, and one that can plausibly support a charge of criminal possession, and it is only after that initial demonstration that the burden shifts. In most cases, the defendant will simply deny knowledge or control, and the judge must then assess the credibility of his or her testimony.

Section 9, then, does represent a significant change from the common law, but it does not necessarily violate elemental constitutional principles. Both the Gardiner and Baker reports recommended the continuance of Section 9 with-

---

*There is some precedent for the shift. Under Section 24 of the Metropolitan Courts Act (1839, repealed in 1977), a person found in possession of stolen goods could be convicted unless he could account for his possession. Lord Gardiner found similar shifts in twenty-nine other acts in the United Kingdom, and Baker discovered a "surprisingly large number of similar provisions."[117]

out modification. Indeed, Baker thought its repeal "would be an affront to justice."[118]

"Supergrasses" and the Use of Accomplice Evidence

In 1981, six years after Gardiner completed his review of the emergency legislation and three years after the Emergency Provisions Act was reorganized and consolidated (the 1978 act), the prosecution began to seek convictions in the Diplock courts through the extensive use of informants ("supergrasses") and accomplice evidence. Its origin is a matter of some dispute, but most observers have concluded that the term "supergrass" derives from "snake in the grass" or from the slang phrase "grasshopper–copper."[119] In the Diplock courts, the term refers to an informant who has agreed to testify at trial in exchange for limited immunity, police protection, or, on occasion, a new identity.

According to Lord Baker's figures, between 1981 and 1983 the information provided by supergrasses led to approximately 1,000 arrests under the Emergency Powers Act.[120] In his exhaustive study of the supergrass system, Greer concluded that during the same period, testimony from 7 Unionist and 18 nationalist informants led to nearly 600 arrests.[121] Of these 25 witnesses, 15 later recanted their stories, but 217 defendants had their cases taken to trial; 120 pled guilty or were convicted. Five cases were appealed to higher courts, where 67 of 74 convictions were overturned.[122]

The law in Northern Ireland concerning admissibility of accomplice evidence provides that such evidence may be admitted or excluded upon the judge's discretion. In cases where the evidence is admitted, it must be accompanied by a warning to jurors telling them that although they may convict solely "upon uncorroborated accomplice evidence it [is] dangerous to do so." As Greer noted, the warning is based upon fear that such witnesses and the evidence they supply are likely to be unreliable.[123]

The operation of the accomplice evidence rule takes on a peculiar character in the juryless Diplock courts, for the judge must address the warning to himself. Greer concluded that the utility of the warning in such circumstances is doubtful because the whole point of the rule "is the assumption that there is a jury" to whom the warning should be issued.[124] Baker thought this criticism unwarranted, noting that unlike a jury, a judge must specify the reasoning behind a decision, reasoning which is subject to review in an appellate court.[125]

Some support for Baker's conclusion can be found in the significant number of reversals at the appellate level, but the need for those reversals indicates the dangers of large-scale supergrass trials. In any event, most observers agree that the system has been in decline since 1986. Greer attributes much of the decline to a decision by Northern Irish judges to become "more critical of this type of evidence" than they were in the initial supergrass trials.[126]

Results in Diplock Trials

Any statistical study of trial results in the Diplock courts is likely to be misleading, for "it is notoriously difficult to give a simple account of the results in any trial system. At each stage in the process there are a number of possible outcomes."[127] Even so, there are several questions we should ask concerning results in Diplock trials. First, in the absence of juries, have judges become more willing to convict? In other words, is there evidence of "case hardening" among Diplock judges? Second, is there any evidence of sectarian bias, either in rates of conviction or in sentencing? Both questions, and especially the first, have been the subject of much research and great controversy.

Rates of Conviction

Concerns about case hardening, about the eagerness of Diplock judges to convict in the absence of juries, have been raised over the emergency legislation. From 1973 to 1979 there was a progressive increase in the proportion of guilty pleas and a noticeable decline in the number of acquittals in contested cases. One possible reason for the trend is that "in the absence of juries, judges have become case-hardened and thus more ready to convict, and that defendants and their legal advisers have responded by pleading guilty in greater numbers in the hope of securing a more lenient sentence."[128] An alternative explanation is that the director of public prosecutions and RUC are preparing cases more carefully.[129]

The increase in the number of guilty pleas is also associated with a corresponding decline in the number of defendants who refuse to recognize the jurisdiction of the Diplock courts.[130] When the latter are treated as having pled guilty, the proportion of guilty pleas in earlier years increases, thereby increasing the corresponding rates of acquittal. The overall rate of acquittal in contested cases then approaches 40 percent. Given the large size of the samples, this figure compares unfavorably with acquittal rates of 47 percent in ordinary jury trials in England and Wales.[131] Moreover, acquittal rates in the Diplock courts themselves declined from 50 percent in 1973 and 1974 to 35 percent in 1979. This compares rather unfavorably with rate of acquittal in ordinary jury trials in Northern Ireland between 1974 and 1980, which was roughly 55 percent.[132] Boyle and his co-authors concluded that this evidence "provide[s] strong support for the view that the declining acquittal rates in Diplock trials is the result of judges becoming case-hardened. . . . [T]he risk of innocent persons being convicted in Diplock courts is substantially greater than in jury trials."[133]

Baker found that the acquittal rate in the Diplock courts was 38 percent in 1973, remained at 20 percent through 1980, but rose to 34 percent and 35 percent in 1981 and 1982. He therefore concluded that the figures do not prove "or even tend to prove anything."[134] Hogan and Walker report that the effective conviction rate was 65 percent in 1983, 47 percent in 1984, 50 percent in 1985, and 57 percent in 1986.[135] Overall, official statistics

> show that the average acquittal rate in contested Diplock cases is lower than that of contested non-scheduled cases tried by jury in Northern Ireland. In the 1974–86 period 55 per cent of Crown Court defendants who pleaded not guilty were acquitted by juries whereas only 33 per cent of Diplock defendants who pleaded not guilty were acquitted.[136]

Whatever the frequency of convictions in Diplock courts, the suspicion of case hardening persists, and that suspicion in itself brings disrepute to the emergency system, especially in the minority community. One way to counteract the possibility of case hardening, of course, would be to restore jury trials. But there remains a well-grounded fear of intimidation and perverse verdicts, as Baker and some independent observers recently concluded. Nevertheless, there are less radical alternatives to the restoration of jury trials, as we saw, and the constitutional principle of mitigation requires that the government explore the feasibility of these alternatives.

Sectarian Bias in the Diplock Courts

Systematic bias on the basis of religious preference was a persistent problem under the Special Powers Act. Differences in religious affiliation are rarely, if ever, a sufficient or legitimate reason in themselves to treat some persons differently from others. Religious preferences may coincide with other differences that *do* justify different treatment, but in such cases we must be careful to insure that we do not use religious affiliation as a substitute for demonstrating the existence of those other reasons. Thus it *may* indeed be the case that Catholic jurors are more susceptible in general to intimidation than are Protestants. Even so, the constitutive principles of constitutionalism require that the prosecution articulate a reason for fear of bias in *each* case, rather than relying on a person's religious preference as a general reason for disqualifying all Catholics or all Protestants, as was arguably the case under the Special Powers Act.

Fear of sectarian bias was a considerable factor in the government's decision to suspend jury trials in 1973. Much the same fear, of sectarian bias in *all* aspects of the pre-Diplock courts, led to the creation in 1972 of the Office of the Director of Public Prosecutions (DPP). The DPP's primary function is to ensure that public prosecutions do not manifest gross sectarian bias. The DPP prosecutes in all cases involving scheduled offenses. It is important to note, however, that the initial decision concerning what offense a suspect should be charged with is made by the police. The decision is subject to review by the DPP's office, but as a practical matter the DPP is almost certain to ratify it. Between 1973 and 1979 the DPP withdrew the charge preferred by the police in only 564 of 7,279 cases, or less than 8 percent of the cases.[137] (In most, the DPP elected to proceed on a lesser charge.)

To what extent have the suspension of jury trials and the Office of the DPP alleviated sectarian bias in the Diplock courts? There are two areas in which we might expect to see sectarian bias—in different rates of conviction and in sentencing proceedings. One review of the DPP's performance concluded that the office has done much to reduce bias in the prosecution of terrorist offenses. The same report observed, however, that the DPP largely depends upon information submitted by the RUC, and thus has little control over the possibility of sectarian bias in the initial decision to arrest and select charges.[138] Sectarian bias at this stage of the criminal process is most likely to manifest itself in sentencing decisions, and there is some evidence of bias in this area.

But there is little statistical evidence to support repeated claims by some attorneys and defendants that sectarian bias is common in the Diplock courts themselves. In the first six months in which the courts sat, 5 percent of Loyalist defendants were acquitted. Catholics, in contrast, were acquitted in 12 percent of the cases.[139] The proportion of Loyalists who pled guilty rose considerably, from 31 to 70 percent, presumably because "they could no longer count on a friendly jury."[140] These rates have changed little over the past few years.

There is likewise very little statistical evidence of bias in sentencing proceedings. Boyle's figures indicate, for example, that a much higher proportion of Catholic than Protestant offenders receive noncustodial sentences, but there is very little difference between Catholics and Protestants in the average length of custodial sentences.[141] A number of factors other than sectarian bias could explain the difference in noncustodial sentences. The most important of these is that Loyalists were most often guilty of murder, manslaughter, and other serious offenses.[142] Republicans were more likely to be guilty of possession offenses. Not surprisingly, the latter class of offenses is more likely to merit noncustodial sentences than the former. But a second explanation is also persuasive. As Boyle et al. suggest, "The main reason for the greater proportion of non-custodial sentences in respect of Republican offenders . . . would appear to be that the net of criminal justice is cast more widely in respect of Republicans than in respect of Loyalists."[143]

Although this is a form of sectarian discrimination, it is one practiced by the security forces in their initial decisions to arrest and select charges, a decision the DPP routinely ratifies.[144] The tendency of the Diplock courts to impose noncustodial sentences for lesser scheduled offenses works to some extent to correct that initial bias but does not eradicate it.

Appeals in the Diplock Courts

The constitutive principle of review demands some type of appeal in the criminal process, but it says little about the precise form or manner of the review required. There is no *constitutional* reason why it should be limited to a review of legal error or why it must instead be review de novo. And there would appear to be no particular constitutional reason for more than one level of review. But the constitutive principles *do* require that the possibility of review be a meaningful one. Hence, as my discussion of Sections 11 and 12 indicated, the principle imposes requirements in the earlier stages of the criminal process that make subsequent review possible.

For reasons that are not entirely clear, appeals are a relatively unimportant part of the Diplock system (except, as we saw, in the cases involving supergrasses). Section 7(6) provides for an unlimited right of appeal against convictions and sentencing decisions, and Section 7(5) explicitly provides that the judge must state the reasons in support of a conviction. In 1977, defendants filed appeals in only 13 percent of the cases, but the figure increased to 26 percent in 1979.[145] Walker reports that through 1984, there were 418 appeals to convictions, of which 201 (48 percent) were withdrawn, 156 (37 percent) dismissed, and 61 (15 percent) upheld. There were 1,026 appeals against sentencing decisions, however. Of these, 500 (48 percent) were withdrawn, 388 (39 percent) dismissed, and 138 (13 percent) upheld.[146] Most of these appeals are not vigorously pursued and, as Walker's figures and Table 3-2 indicate, most are of sentencing decisions, rather than convictions. Baker thought it "virtually impossible to draw any worthwhile conclusion" from such figures.[147]

It is difficult to explain why appeals are so unimportant in the emergency process. One possible explanation is that serious scheduled offenses cases are heard by more experienced high court judges, whereas lesser offenses are heard by county court judges who presumably do not share the expertise and experience that high court judges possess and are thus more likely to commit errors.[148]

A more plausible explanation involves the restrictive nature of the emergency legislation binding Diplock judges. In most cases the only significant evidence of an accused's guilt is a confession. Section 8 of the EPA (1978) limited the discretion normally afforded judges to determine the admissibility of confessions and authorized admission of confessions obtained through use of "moderate" violence. Consequently, these changes narrowed the grounds on which the defendant could appeal. Moreover, Northern Irish judges have

Table 3-2. Appeals in Diplock Courts (1977–79)

| Year | Number of Appeals | | | | |
	Entered	Withdrawn	Dismissed	Upheld	Success Rate
Appeals to Convictions					
1977	39 (3.3%)	6 (15%)	29	4	12%
1978	56 (6.1%)	29 (52%)	23	4	14%
1979	82 (9.6%)	65 (79%)	13	4	24%
Appeals Against Sentencing					
1977	107 (9.2%)	30 (28%)	54	23	31%
1978	102 (11.2%)	55 (54%)	38	9	19%
1979	137 (16.1%)	104 (76%)	25	8	24%

Source: Kevin Boyle, Tom Hadden, and Paddy Hillyard, *Ten Years On in Northern Ireland* (London: Cobden Trust, 1980), 85.

proven reluctant to exercise what little authority and independence they do possess.

Cases Against the Security Forces

The extent to which a state applies the laws equally, to terrorists and recalcitrant members of the security forces alike, is an important element of constitutional maintenance and of inculcating respect for reason. In 1977, the year Amnesty International began its investigation of interrogation practices in Northern Ireland and the same year in which the Police Surgeons Association reported their concern that detained suspects were being mistreated by constables,[149] Britain established the Police Complaints Board to hear complaints concerning mistreatment of suspects. The board's authority was limited, however, for it could consider disciplinary action only against accused officers. Its authority was further circumscribed by a double jeopardy rule, which prohibited the board from instituting both criminal and disciplinary hearings against an officer for a single course of action. In short, the Police Complaints Board was an ineffective safeguard against physical abuse of suspects.

The board was replaced by an Order in Council, the Police (Northern Ireland) Order (1987), which established in its place an "Independent Commission for Police Complaints." The commission's membership is comprised of a chairman, two deputy chairmen, and four other members. All are appointed by the secretary of state for Northern Ireland.

If there are criminal proceedings, they must be initiated by the director of public prosecutions. In 1978, of 826 cases considered, the DPP did not bring charges in 787, or 97 percent of the cases.[150] The DPP's efforts are hampered by the tendency of the RUC to utilize two and often more than two constables during interrogations of a single suspect. Consequently, even if he has determined that an assault has occurred, the DPP is often unable to determine who committed it. Moreover, the director has indicated that he is uncomfortable in prosecuting members of the security forces. On at least one occasion, the DPP informed the government: "It is not . . . my function to determine whether or not an individual was assaulted. My function is to determine whether or not the evidence is sufficient upon which to direct the initiation of criminal proceedings in respect of such alleged assault."[151] The DPP's ability to carry out even this latter function is severely limited. The office has no real power of investigation and no staff to conduct one even if it had the authority. As a result, the DPP must rely upon the assistance of the RUC, whose officers are the focus of the complaint, to conduct an investigation.

Given these restraints, the rate of conviction is predictably unimpressive: The Bennett Committee reported that through 1978 there was no final conviction against any member of the security forces.[152] More recent figures confirm earlier findings. In 1986 there were 2,785 complaints directed to the Police Complaints Board. Of these, 1,684 were transferred to the DPP, and in 5 cases the DPP sought prosecutions.[153] As a measure for controlling the RUC and the army in the security process, then, lawsuits against members of the security forces fail miserably, a conclusion also shared by the Bennett Committee and others.[154]

The reasons for the inability of the criminal process to convict members of the security forces are not difficult to discern, for they are the same ones that hampered suits against the security forces prior to passage of the 1973 act. In practice, "a very high standard of proof is required to justify a prosecution or conviction against a member of the security forces."[155] Coupled with the undoubted tendency of policemen and soldiers not to report abuses committed by fellow officers or to testify against each other, "the difficulty in securing convictions can be understood, if not justified."[156]

Some of the difficulty is also a function of the legal standards that govern the use of force in Northern Ireland. Under Section 3(1) of the Criminal Law Act (1967), the relevant standard is one of "reasonableness." There have been repeated complaints that this standard is far too vague. In the leading case, *A.G. for Northern Ireland's Reference* (1977),[157] the House of Lords ruled that a decision (a question of fact, to be decided by a jury) on what constituted "reasonableness" could include not only an assessment of the immediate threat but also what future acts of violence might be prohibited by this use of force. Lord Diplock defined the "imminent danger" and the future threat posed by the fleeing suspect in the case at hand as follows: "[I]f he got away, [he] was likely *sooner* or *later* to participate in acts of violence."[158] Likewise, in the case of *Farrell v. Secretary of State for Defence* (1980), the House of Lords held that a soldier's use of force was not unreasonable even if the overall operation was or might have been unreasonable.[159] (Farrell's case was heard by the European Commission on Human Rights but was settled before a decision was reached.)[160] As with internment orders (and exclusion orders under the Prevention of Terrorism Act), judges have been reluctant to undertake review in such cases or to impart an objective standard of reasonableness under Section 3(1).

Public Confidence in the Diplock Courts

In 1975 the Gardiner Committee concluded that "the new [emergency] system has worked fairly and well."[161] In certain respects, the Diplock courts have worked well. They have reduced, if not eliminated, the sectarian bias that troubled their predecessors in the areas of bail, rates of conviction, and sentencing. Certainly the incidence of violence has decreased since the courts were established in 1973, though whether the courts contributed to the decline is questionable.

As I have indicated elsewhere, however, the emergency legislation proceeds on the assumption that the existence of special criminal procedures for terrorists will not affect citizens' confidence in legal institutions more generally.[162] Do citizens in Northern Ireland support the special courts? Some commentators, such as Charles Carleton, have suggested that "Diplock Courts have gained a degree of acceptance among Ulster's minority community."[163] Carleton based his conclusion on the lack of assassination attempts against Diplock judges and the growing tendency of IRA defendants to plead guilty "and thus recognize the court's legitimacy."[164]

This reasoning is not persuasive. My interviews with barristers and solicitors in Belfast indicate that Republican defendants are more likely to plead guilty than to contest the court's jurisdiction, as they did in the early years of the courts' existence, because they hope to secure more lenient sentences in return for their pleas. Boyle et al. agree, suggesting that "the sharp decline in the number of refusals to recognize . . . appears to be due largely to the fact that defendants . . . are being instructed by their respective paramilitary organizations to recognize the court and to attempt to obtain either an acquittal or a less severe sentence."[165]

Moreover, Boyle et al. concluded that public dissatisfaction with the special courts and emergency legislation is considerable. In 1973 they interviewed 180 persons, selected on a quota basis to reflect class, sex, age, and religious divisions in Belfast.[166] As Table 3-3 indicates, the respondents demonstrated that they knew of the changes made in the province's criminal processes. For example, 63 percent of the Protestants and 79 percent of the Catholics knew that jury trials had been suspended in cases involving scheduled offenses. Catholics and Protestants differed considerably, however, in their support for these changes. As Table 3-3 also indicates, only 47 percent of the Protestants objected to internment without trial, whereas 95 percent of the Catholics objected to internment.

Perhaps the most striking finding was that changes in the administration of justice adversely affected the confidence of Protestants and Catholics alike in the ordinary courts. Table 3-4 discloses that 59 percent of the Protestant respondents and 93 percent of the Catholics reported that the practice of internment without trial decreased their faith that defendants received fair trials in Northern Ireland's ordinary courts. The implications of this finding are of tremendous significance, because it challenges the presuppositions—that the existence of special procedures for terrorist offenses will not decrease public confidence in the ordinary courts—upon which British attempts to control terrorism in the United Kingdom are predicated.

Table 3-3. Response to Changes

Protestant		Catholic	
No.	%	No.	%
Respondents Who Knew of Suspension of Jury Trials			
74	63	45	79
Respondents Opposed to Internment			
56	47	54	95

Source: Kevin Boyle, Tom Hadden, and Paddy Hillyard, *Law and State* (London: Martin Robertson, 1975), 145.

Table 3-4. Confidence in Ordinary Courts

	Protestant		Catholic	
	No.	%	No.	%
Increased confidence	17	14	1	2
Decreased confidence	70	59	53	93
No change	10	9	3	5
No opinion	21	18	—	—

Source: Kevin Boyle, Tom Hadden, and Paddy Hillyard, *Law and State* (London: Martin Robertson, 1975), 147.

Boyle et al. could not determine whether the government's decision to let Section 12 lapse affected public confidence in the criminal process. More recent studies suggest that the decision may have had some effect; they find that few respondents, whether Catholic or Protestant, reported a lack of confidence in the ordinary courts.[167]

One explanation for the change might be the mere passage of time: When Boyle undertook his survey, the emergency legislation was fresh and the contours of its eventual implementation and application were uncertain. But over the past decade, greater familiarity with the emergency legislation, although it apparently has done little to increase public confidence in the emergency courts themselves, may have reassured the public that the process does not affect the quality of British justice in ordinary courts.

This explanation, however, overlooks the importance of internment. A near majority of Protestants and almost all of the Catholics in the 1974 study reported that it was the practice of internment that had decreased their confidence in the ordinary courts. The British government has not used internment since 1975, and the statutory provisions that authorize it have been in abeyance since 1980. If internment is the key to the 1974 study, it should come as no surprise that public confidence in the ordinary courts would increase once internment had been phased out.

Although one cannot confidently generalize from such small samples and unsophisticated sampling techniques, one can rely upon them to suggest testable hypotheses. They might suggest, for example, that citizens in Northern Ireland can distinguish ordinary criminal procedures from emergency procedures and, more important, that their perceptions of one need not color their attitudes toward the other. This finding is important for societies which hope to control terrorism by relying upon modified versions of ordinary legal procedures, because it implies that it might be possible to segregate contentious legal matters from those less contentious.[168] Indeed, British antiterrorism legislation proceeds on precisely that assumption.

A related question concerns the extent to which, if any, the use of supergrasses has affected public confidence in the administration of justice. "Throughout its lifespan the supergrass system was the subject of intense public debate."[169] As we saw, in the supergrass system, large numbers of defendants are prosecuted in the Diplock courts, often solely on the strength of the informant's testimony. In the first three supergrass cases, 80 percent of those tried were ultimately found guilty, most without any corroborative evidence.[170]

A 1984 survey conducted by the Committee on the Administration of Justice found that 72 percent of Catholic respondents disapproved or strongly disapproved of the supergrass system, whereas only 21 percent of Protestant respondents expressed disapproval.[171] The precise extent to which the supergrass system may have eroded public confidence in the administration of criminal justice more generally is unclear. But the opinion of most observers is that it has had a negative effect. Jennings and Greer argue that the issuance of ritualistic warnings "has attracted much criticism from legal quarters and has exposed the legal process to public ridicule."[172] Similarly, Moxon-Browne concludes that "the system of supergrasses has tended to discredit the judicial system and is partly to blame for the alienation of the Catholic community from it."[173]

THE PREVENTION OF TERRORISM (TEMPORARY PROVISIONS) ACTS OF 1976 AND 1984

On November 21, 1974, a bomb hidden in a pub in Birmingham killed 21 people and injured more than 180 others. The alleged perpetrators were arrested the same day and subsequently convicted (a much publicized appeal was dismissed in 1988), but the IRA had demonstrated that terrorism in the United Kingdom was no longer a problem neatly confined to the isolated province of Ulster. Within a week of the bombing, Home Secretary Roy Jenkins introduced the Prevention of Terrorism (Temporary Provisions) Bill. Parliament enacted it just two days later. The act was amended in 1975 and again in 1983, following a review by Lord Jellicoe in 1982. Most of Jellicoe's recommendations were incorporated in the 1984 act, which was enacted for a period of five years.

Following yet another review of the act, this time by Lord Colville,[174] the government announced in February 1988 that it would seek a new bill, a permanent one, upon the act's expiration in March 1989. As with most other forms of emergency legislation, including the Special Powers Act, the Prevention of Terrorism Act is now certain to survive long after the emergency that gave rise to it has expired. The new act adopted most (but not all) of Colville's recommendations. It also had to account for a recent decision by the European Commission of Human Rights that a part of the 1984 act, permitting detention for a period of seven days, violated the European Convention on Human Rights.[175]

As amended in 1984 and 1989, the Prevention of Terrorism Act (PTA) consists of three main parts. The first proscribes membership in organizations related to terrorist activities. The second part permits the secretary of state to exclude suspected terrorists from Great Britain to Northern Ireland or from

Northern Ireland to Great Britain. The third part of the act extends the powers of the police to arrest and detain suspects for questioning. In contrast to the Emergency Provisions Act (EPA), the PTA does not relax common law rules of evidence or create special courts that sit without juries.

The Prevention of Terrorism Act differs from the EPA in other ways as well. Where the latter permits detention without trial, the PTA provides instead for the exclusion of British citizens from one section of the country to another. In addition, most of the PTA's provisions of arrest, unlike the 1978 Northern Irish legislation, provide that suspicion must be reasonable. As we saw, however, recent changes in the Emergency Provisions Act have incorporated the reasonableness of suspicion requirement. One effect of this change has been to make the arrest powers of the Prevention of Terrorism Act the statutory provision of choice in Northern Ireland.

Arrest and Detention Provisions Under the Prevention of Terrorism Act

Unlike the Emergency Provisions Act, which applies only in Ulster, the Prevention of Terrorism Act applies both in Northern Ireland and in Great Britain. The RUC may therefore arrest suspected terrorists in Northern Ireland under either act. British police may utilize either the special powers set forth in the PTA or their ordinary powers of arrest and detention. Until recently, the arrest provisions of the Prevention of Terrorism Act afforded more protection for the accused than did the Northern Irish legislation. For example, most of the PTA's arrest provisions require that an officer's suspicion must be reasonable. As a result, and in contrast to Section 11 of the 1978 legislation, a suspect arrested under the Prevention of Terrorism Act can challenge the lawfulness of the arrest on grounds that the constable's suspicion was not reasonable. But other obstacles, to be discussed later, make such a challenge unlikely.

Section 12: The Power to Detain for Forty-eight Hours

The most important power of arrest in the PTA is Section 12(1)(b), which provides that "a constable may arrest without warrant a person whom he has reasonable grounds for suspecting" of having committed an offense under Sections 1, 9, and 10 of the act, or whom he suspects of being "concerned in the commission, preparation or instigation of acts of terrorism." Section 12(1)(b) provides that the terrorist activities (or the preparation therefore) need not be related to Northern Ireland. Unlike the now repealed Section 11 of the Emergency Provisions Act 1978, Section 12 does include a requirement of reasonableness of suspicion. As we shall see later, however, the inclusion of such a requirement suffers from the same defects that accompanied the addition of a reasonableness requirement in the new Section 13 of the Emergency Provisions Act (1987).

120 Dissolution in Northern Ireland

In Northern Ireland, Article 131 of the Magistrate's Courts Order provides that the maximum length of detention prior to an appearance before a magistrate is forty-eight hours. Consequently, the length of detention under Section 13 of the Emergency Provisions Act cannot exceed two days. Individuals arrested under Section 12 of the Prevention of Terrorism Act may also be detained without charge for forty-eight hours. At the end of this period, however, the police may apply through New Scotland Yard to the secretary of state for permission to hold the suspect for an additional five days (but for no longer), thus extending the period of detention to seven days.* In September 1987, however, the European Commission of Human Rights found that seven-day detentions violated the European Convention on Human Rights and that detentions could not legally exceed five days.[176]

The purpose behind such extensions, as stated by the police and confirmed by the Bennett and Colville reports, is to make more effective the interrogation to which those arrested are subjected. As Lord Shackleton noted, the act "is not simply a question of arresting people."[177] Instead, it is about questioning individuals and gathering information and intelligence, for which the longer period of detention is invaluable. Indeed, at no point during the week-long detention need the police charge the suspect with a specific offense. He thus has no right to a preliminary hearing before a neutral magistrate, as he would under the common law.

As with the practice of screening under Section 11 of the 1978 Emergency Provisions Act, the purpose of Section 12 is not simply to generate criminal prosecutions. As a result, the relatively small number of prosecutions under Section 12 is not conclusive evidence concerning the provision's utility. Section 12's real benefit is in its usefulness as an intelligence tool, and the development of intelligence will often necessitate the gathering of information insufficient to support or irrelevant to a criminal charge. Even so, intelligence investigations do create the possibility that the information collected can be used to harass and intimidate citizens who (peacefully and lawfully) reject the current constitutional order. Combining both functions in the criminal law, a consequence of the policy of criminalization, ignores the very real differences between criminal investigations and intelligence investigations and greatly increases the possibility of abuse.[179] As one observer concluded, "The essence of the extended power of arrest is the gathering of information. As the statistics go some way to proving, there is no intention to charge the arrested person with any offence, merely to question them."[180]

Another difference between the Emergency Provisions Act and Section 12 is that under the latter the Judges' Rules and Administrative Directions to the Police clearly *do* apply. Following recommendations by the Bennett Report (reviewed in the preceding chapter), a suspect has an unconditional right to a

---

*There are no standards to govern what information such applications must contain, and the application is never subject to an independent review. Moreover, the secretary routinely grants such requests. Between August 1974 and September 1979, for example, the secretary granted approval for extended questioning in 582 of 711 cases and denied approval in only two. Nevertheless, only 327, or 46 percent of those arrested, were ultimately charged with criminal offenses.[178]

solicitor after forty-eight hours. A suspect should also be permitted access to his family, but Section 12 exempts such arrests from the normal rules concerning notification (which provide that notification must be within thirty-six hours of detention, but the period may be extended in limited circumstances). Under Section 12, notification may be withheld if it "will lead to interference with the gathering of information about . . . acts of terrorism." Many observers, including Clive Walker in his recent book-length study of the act, have concluded that most of the safeguards proposed by Bennett have been implemented.[181] But there are repeated complaints that the police often ignore the Judges' Rules, in part because the only consequence of their violation is the possible exclusion of statements at trial. Most individuals arrested under Section 12 are subsequently released without charge, thus negating the force of the remedy.

Since the original Prevention of Terrorism Act was passed in 1974, nearly eight thousand people have been arrested under Section 12. Walker found that extended detentions followed in approximately one-third of the arrests in Great Britain. Of the suspects who are not charged, 84 percent are released in the forty-eight hour period, and slightly over 90 percent of those arrested are released within three days. Walker estimated that the number of those ultimately charged with criminal offenses was 20 percent of those arrested.[182] Jellicoe concluded, partly as a result of such figures, that "[t]here can be no clear proof that the arrest powers . . . are, or are not, an essential weapon in the fight against terrorism."[183] But as we saw, given the multiple purposes of the act, which include not only criminal charges but also the gathering of intelligence, the utility of Section 12 cannot be measured solely by these statistics.

Section 13: Port Detention Arrests

Under Section 13(1)(a), which authorizes "port detention" arrests, anyone entering or leaving the United Kingdom can be detained at the port of entry. Most detentions are for an hour or less, but a detention may last for as long as twelve hours.[184] The "examining officer's" suspicions need not, at this initial stage, be reasonable. When the half-day period expires, the officer may then hold the suspect for an additional forty-eight hours, provided he now has reasonable grounds for suspicion, as he must under Section 12. The two-day period of detention is designed to give the secretary of state time to consider whether to exclude the person. As with Section 12, the secretary can authorize an additional five-day period of detention beyond the initial forty-eight hours. Section 13 also resembles Section 12 in that there is no requirement that the terrorism of which the individual is suspected be related to Northern Ireland. Unlike Section 12, however, Section 13 does *not* require that the constable's suspicions be reasonable. As my discussion of the 1978 Emergency Provisions Act made clear, the lack of a requirement of reasonableness severely limits the ability of a suspect to challenge the legality of the arrest. Baker noted that the replacement of Section 11 with Section 13 in the Emergency Provisions Act was a strong argument in

favor of amending Section 13 of the PTA to include a reasonableness requirement.[185] Colville, however, concluded that the initial detention allowed no room
for a reasonableness of suspicion requirement but recommended that the requirement be imposed for detentions exceeding one hour.[186]

The relative impotence of the courts in such cases is reflected in the following
quote from Lord Justice Donaldson in the case of *In re Boyle, O'Hare and
McAllister* (1980), in which the detainees sought a writ of habeas corpus:

> It follows that . . . an officer has to satisfy himself of the only matter upon
> which he must be satisfied, namely, that the person whom he seeks to
> examine is in the category of person where he can say to himself *bona fide* "I
> wish to find out whether this person has, for example, information which he
> or she should have disclosed under section 11."[187]

Therefore, a court will ask whether the officer "is acting *bona fide* and whether
. . . his conduct is *prima facie* such as no reasonable person could have
taken."[188]

The Jellicoe Report found that port detention controls have generated very
few detentions. On the mainland, less than 20 percent of the detentions were
extended, substantially less than the rate of extensions under Section 12.
Between January 1, 1979, and December 31, 1982, 11 percent of those arrested
under Section 13 were charged with criminal offenses and 6 percent were
excluded.[189] In the same period, 459 were detained for longer than forty-eight
hours. Of this group, 210, or 46 percent, were either charged with offenses or
excluded.[190] With regard to inland arrests (under Section 12), 30 percent of
those arrested were charged, but the figure was over 60 percent if the detention
period exceeded forty-eight hours.[191] Exclusion resulted from only 7 percent of
the inland arrests but in over 40 percent of port detention arrests exceeding
forty-eight hours. Jellicoe concluded that the port detention powers do deter
terrorism, although this cannot be "demonstrated by the numbers appre-
hended."[192] Another commentator noted in response: "The statistics do not
prove this . . . assertion [although it is] a view shared by Lord Shackleton's
Review. Nor can opponents of such powers establish their contention that
ordinary powers would suffice."[193] Walker also found Jellicoe's defense of the
power as a deterrent unconvincing. "In so far as terrorism is prevented in
Britain the unacceptable consequence will probably be its displacement to
Northern Ireland."[194] As with Section 12, however, another defense of Section
13 is that its primary justification is its utility in gathering information. For
that reason, Walker recommended a redrafted and more limited power, because some sort of port controls can "contribute significantly to the prevention
and control of terrorism."[195]

Arrests Under Sections 10 and 11
of the Prevention of Terrorism Act

Sections 10 and 11 of the PTA render illegal, in various ways, different types of
support for terrorism or for terrorist organizations. Section 10(1) makes it

an offense "If any person (a) solicits or invites any other person to give, lend or otherwise make available . . . any money or other property; or (b) receives or accepts [such] . . . from any other person" intending that it shall be used for or in connection with terrorism. The section also provides for forfeiture of such materials. In addition, Section 10(2) makes it illegal to contribute money to another person, if one "knows or suspects" it will be used to support terrorism.

As we shall see, Section 1 of the PTA also prohibits support for terrorism by proscribing certain organizations and by making membership in those organizations a criminal offense. Section 10 is the broader provision. Unlike Section 1, the support prohibited by Section 10 need *not* be directed to a proscribed organization. (This is an important difference, because certain Loyalist organizations are proscribed in Northern Ireland but not in Great Britain. Under Section 10, support for those organizations can be an offense, even though membership in them is not prohibited by Section 1. On the other hand, mere membership is not an offense under Section 10.)

Through 1984, there were only eleven charges in Great Britain under Section 10.[196] Baker found only eighteen prosecutions in Northern Ireland between 1977 and 1982,[197] and a more recent study found that through January 1, 1988, there were only fifty-six charges under Section 10.[198] Lord Colville also concluded that the provision was little used.[199] Nevertheless, Colville, like Baker and Jellicoe, recommended that the provision be left unchanged.[200] Walker also agreed that Section 10 was necessary, although he argued that it ought to include a defense of "reasonable excuse" to account for cases, especially in Belfast, where "contributions" by shopkeepers are not truly voluntary but are instead coerced.[201] A defense of reasonable excuse is incorporated under Section 11. Its omission in Section 10 might therefore be construed to disqualify the defense in a Section 10 prosecution.

Section 11(1) provides that any person who has information which he knows or believes might assist in the prevention of terrorism or in the apprehension or conviction of an individual involved in the preparation or instigation of terrorism must disclose the information to the specified authorities. In addition to the duty of positive disclosure, Section 11 makes it illegal to fail to answer a constable's questions.

In some ways, Section 11 is narrower than Section 10. The disclosure requirement under Section 11 follows if one "knows or believes" the information to be of "material assistance," whereas under Section 10, one need only "know or suspect." Moreover, Section 11, unlike Section 10, does acknowledge the defense of reasonable excuse, which means "a well-founded fear of personal injury falling outside the narrow bounds of a defence of duress." It appears that such a defense cannot be based on an individual's personal relationship with a suspect, either through marriage or family. On the other hand, it can be premised on the existence of a "privileged" relationship, such as those between a solicitor and a client, or between the clergy and individuals who confide in them.

Another problem with Section 11 concerns self-incrimination. Some observers have argued that because it fails to specify what sorts of information an individual must disclose, Section 11 may force a person to incriminate himself.[202] A Scottish case, however, suggests that the section should not be read so broadly. In *HM v. Von* (1979), Lord Ross held:

> In enacting . . . the Act of 1976, if Parliament had intended to make statements of suspects admissible against them in the event of their being subsequently charged I would have expected Parliament to have made that clear. I cannot believe that Parliament intended to alter the well established principle of our law that no man can be compelled to incriminate himself.[203]

As Clive Walker noted, an amendment in 1984 partly corrected this problem by indicating that the information must concern the activity of "any other person."[204] But since one may incriminate oneself, while giving information that primarily involves another, there may still be times when Section 11 directly implicates the common law right to silence.

In his review of the PTA, Lord Jellicoe admitted that he found the possibility of abuse under Section 11 "one of the most difficult issues with which I have had to deal."[205] He therefore recommended that the section should be used only in extreme cases. Lord Shackleton urged instead that the section be repealed, a position shared by Professor Boyle[206] (but not by Walker or by Baker in his review of the emergency legislation). In his review of the Prevention of Terrorism Act, Lord Colville also recommended that Section 11 be removed. In part, Colville's recommendation was a consequence of his finding that the provision was little used. Through January 1, 1988, there were but twenty-five arrests under Section 11, "and only one of these people had been charged since 1985."[207] Although the government has announced that it will accept most of Colville's recommendations, it has rejected his recommendation that Section 11 be repealed.

Another problem is the possible influence of Sections 10 and 11 upon media coverage of political terrorism. The BBC has declined to televise some documentaries on the conflict for fear that they might "encourage support" for the IRA or other banned organizations. In 1979 Pierre Salinger and members of his television crew were arrested with representatives of Sinn Fein whom Salinger had been interviewing. More recently, BBC broadcast journalists went on strike after the BBC's Board of Governors, under pressure from the home secretary, overruled management's decision to televise a documentary on Northern Ireland because it included interviews with Martin McGuinness of Sinn Fein and Gregory Campbell of the Democratic Unionist Party. Both men held elective office. In March 1988 the threat of Section 11 was used to seize film footage from television companies that had filmed attacks on two armed plainclothes policemen who had driven their car to a paramilitary funeral procession in Belfast.[208]

Both of these problems can be assessed only in light of recent announcements by the British government concerning the right to silence and new prohibitions on media coverage of terrorism. As we saw in our discussion of the Emergency Provisions Act, the government's decision to permit judges to draw "whatever inferences they think appropriate" from an accused's silence substantially erodes the common law principle of silence. That recommendation applies to the whole of the criminal law in England, Scotland, and Wales, as well as Northern Ireland. Concerns about Section 11 must therefore be subordinated to the larger governmental policy abrogating the right to silence in the criminal law more generally.

Similarly, concerns about the effects of Section 11 on media coverage of terrorism must be considered in light of the larger policy of limited coverage announced by the government on October 19, 1988. The new policy prohibits the media from conducting interviews with or covering speeches made by members of the IRA and Sinn Fein, but the ban will be lifted for speeches by Sinn Fein's candidates during election campaigns. Such regulations are permitted under the Official Secrets Act (1911), by the BBC's charter, and by the Broadcasting Act (1981).

The new policy followed repeated appeals to the media by Prime Minister Thatcher to deny terrorists the "oxygen of publicity," and it is generally consistent with the larger security policy of criminalization. But there can be no doubt that the issues involved are political in the most fundamental of ways, a point implied in the exception that will be made for campaign speeches. Efforts to limit certain types of political speech to identifiable and limited periods of time necessarily implicate fundamental constitutional values. Freedom of speech and association must hold a privileged constitutional position in democratic states. This does not mean that freedom of speech is inviolable or an absolute right. There may be cases—certain emergencies—when narrowly defined limits on speech may themselves be a necessary part of the activity of constitutional maintenance.

It does mean, however, that in a constitutional state, those who advocate restraints on speech bear the burden of showing—of producing reasons—why such restraints are necessary and indicating under what conditions they are constitutionally permissible. At the least, that burden would require of the state that it specify the relationship, if any, between media coverage of terrorism and the incidence of terrorism. Proponents of restraints have made this claim repeatedly, but merely repeating the claim does not prove it.

The Prevention of Terrorism Act in Northern Ireland

Northern Irish police may arrest suspected terrorists under either Section 13 of the Emergency Provisions Act or Section 12 of the Prevention of Terrorism Act. Both require that a constable's suspicion must be reasonable, but the latter allows the RUC to detain suspects for as long as seven days.[209] Under Section 11 of the 1978 act, suspects could be detained for three days, but a constable's suspicion need not have been reasonable and the detention did not have to be authorized by the secretary of state. The replacement of Section 11 with Section 13 in the 1987 act has dramatically affected how the Prevention of Terrorism Act is utilized in Northern Ireland.

While it had the opportunity, the RUC clearly preferred to bring charges under Section 11. Between September 1, 1977, and August 31, 1978, the police detained 2,814 persons under Section 11, whereas only 156 were detained under Section 12.[210] Interestingly, in Britain of those detained under Section 12 only 7 percent were charged with an offense. In Northern Ireland, the figure was 46 percent.[211] The RUC claimed that it used Section 12 only in preplanned cases where it had a strong suspicion that the person was involved in terrorist activities and where it thought questioning would be lengthy.[212] In the period 1974–84, before Section 11 was repealed, Walker found that extensions beyond the forty-eight-hour period were authorized in 71 percent of the cases.[213] And once again, very few applications for the extension were refused.

The difference in the number of suspects charged under Sections 11 and 12 reflected the different requirements the two sections imposed on the police. Since Section 12 requires that a constable's suspicion be reasonable, it is not surprising that more arrests under Section 12 lead to charges than those under Section 11, which did *not* require that the constable have a reasonable suspicion to arrest a suspect. Part of the RUC's preference for Section 11 may also have resulted from the relaxed rules of evidence that Diplock judges used when they tried cases under Section 11. In fact, Section 11 made "it . . . much easier for the police in Northern Ireland to secure a conviction for a terrorist offence than is the case in Britain."[214]

In the absence of Section 11, it seems clear that the RUC will prefer to bring charges under Section 12 of the PTA than under Section 13 of the 1987 Emergency Provisions Act. The reasons for this preference are not difficult to discern: Unlike Section 11, Section 13 offers no improvement over Section 12 in the standards authorizing arrest (indeed, as we saw, Section 13 differs not much from the ordinary power of arrest in Northern Ireland under the Criminal Law Act). Moreover, Section 13 authorizes detention for forty-eight hours, where Section 12 permits a longer period of detention. In part, this development was predicted by Baker, who found the standard of reasonable suspicion in Section 12 a welcome alternative to arrests under Section 11.[215] The standard of reasonableness in Section 12 is more in keeping with the constitutional requirement of articulated reason, but substantial difficulties remain, especially with the principle of constitutional review.

Habeas Corpus Petitions Under the Prevention of Terrorism Act

Under Section 11 of the 1978 act, it was common practice for the RUC to charge an individual under Section 11, question him throughout the three-day detention, release him, and then recharge him under Section 12 of the Prevention of Terrorism Act. Habeas petitions based on an arrest under Section 11 routinely failed because the section failed to require that suspicion be reasonable. As a consequence, judges possessed no independent standard against which they could assess the legality of the arrest.

One might expect a different result for habeas petitions filed under Section 12 of the Prevention of Terrorism Act (or Section 13 of the 1987 EPA), which *does* require reasonableness of suspicion. Moreover, a person charged under the section must be told that he is being arrested and must be informed of the grounds for the arrest. Even so, habeas petitions filed under Section 12 typically fare no better than those under Section 11 did. A well-known case demonstrates the difficulties that a typical petition faces. On May 27, 1980, the RUC arrested the defendant, Lynch, under Section 11.[216] Three days later they released him from custody without charge. On June 2 the police rearrested the defendant on suspicion of terrorism, this time under Section 12 of the PTA (1976). The secretary of state extended the period of detention until June 9.

Lynch applied *ex parte* the same day to a high court judge for a writ of habeas corpus. The court refused to issue the writ on grounds that what must be communicated to the suspect at the time of arrest is the "true ground" of the arrest, which means informing the suspect of the offense of which he is suspected. Moreover, the court concluded that Section 12(1)(b) is sufficiently broad that no *specific* offense need be suspected for a proper arrest.[217] Thus the officer's reasonable suspicion must only be a suspicion that the defendant is somehow involved with the "use of violence for political ends." Given the breadth of this offense, there is almost no way that the suspect can demonstrate that an officer's suspicion was unreasonable.

Slightly more in keeping with constitutional requirements is the case of *In re McElduff* (1972),[218] which we considered earlier in this chapter. McElduff was arrested under the Special Powers Act. When he challenged the arrest, the Northern Irish High Court ruled that an arrestee must be informed of the reasons for his arrest, since the "giving of reasons was 'a fundamental right.'" This meant that the officer was required to tell the suspect whether the suspicion was "directed to a past act, a present or a future intention, or even a combination of two or all three in the conjunctive." In contrast, *Lynch* held that the individual must be told only that he is being arrested for suspicion of involvement in "terrorist activities." But *McElduff* offers very little additional protection, for as we saw, the court's definitions of "reasonableness" and "suspicion" were expansive.

As the foregoing discussion indicates, the mere addition of a requirement of reasonableness is not in itself sufficient to ensure that the various provisions of arrest in the emergency statutes conform with the constitutive principle of review: Terrorist offenses must be defined with specificity sufficient to permit the possibility of meaningful review. Insofar as British antiterrorism legislation incorporates ordinary criminal offenses, such as kidnaping or possession of firearms, that are undertaken for political reasons, it satisfies the constitutive principles. But offenses of the sort in Section 12, such as "the use of violence for political ends," are so broad as to prohibit review even if suspicion is reasonable, as *Ex parte Lynch* illustrates. The constitutive principles therefore require that offenses like those in Section 12 be withdrawn or redefined with greater specificity.

Exclusion Orders

Sections 3 through 9 of the Prevention of Terrorism Act authorize the secretaries of state for Great Britain and Northern Ireland to exclude a person from entering any part of the United Kingdom, if it "appears expedient" to prevent acts of terrorism. The only substantial limitation on the power to order internal exile is contained in Section 3(4), which provides that exclusion orders expire after three years. Section 3(5), however, permits the secretary of state to reissue the order. (Section 3[6] also indicates that the acts must relate to Northern Ireland.) Noncitizens can be completely excluded from the United Kingdom. British citizens cannot be completely excluded, but the order can restrict the person to living in either Northern Ireland or Great Britain.*

There are actually three powers of exclusion. Under Section 4(1), the home secretary may exclude from Great Britain any individual whom he suspects of having been involved in terrorism or of planning to commit such an act. Under Section 5(1), the secretary of state for Northern Ireland has similar powers to exclude individuals from the province. Finally, Section 6(1) permits the exclusion of suspects from the Republic of Ireland throughout the United Kingdom.

In 1987 there were 23 orders in place excluding individuals from Ulster and 111 excluding people from Great Britain. Through December 1984 there were 246 persons removed from Great Britain to Northern Ireland and 40 from Great Britain to the Republic of Ireland.[219] Table 3-5 reveals that there were 310 exclusion orders between 1974 and 1984. The Northern Irish secretary has excluded 30 persons from Ulster; most of them went to the Republic of Ireland.[220] Most exclusions follow port detention arrests, which probably "reflects a change in the nature of the terrorist threat on the mainland. Reliance is no longer placed on supporters and activists among long-standing residents."[221] Rather, terrorist activity in recent years has probably been conducted by a group of persons who "operated as small, self-contained and independent units."[222]

How the Exclusion Orders Work

The first stage in the exclusion process is an "exclusion order." The most noticeable characteristic of the order is its failure to set forth the grounds that support it. Instead, the order states simply: "The Secretary of State . . . is satisfied that you (insert name) are concerned in the commission, preparation, or instigation of acts of terrorism." The secretary will base his decision on the reports submitted to the National Joint Unit at New Scotland Yard and the

---

*There are some qualifications to the power. Section 4(3) indicates that the secretary shall not make such an order against British citizens who are "ordinarily" resident at the time and have been so throughout the preceding three years, or who are already subject to an order under Section 5 (to do other would result in complete exclusion of citizens). Prior to the 1984 act, the "ordinarily resident" period was not three but twenty years. The change was recommended by the Jellicoe Committee.

Table 3-5. Exclusion Orders

Year	Applications	Orders made
1974	22	19
1975	61	50
1976	28	24
1977	18	18
1978	57	53
1979	58	53
1980	59	49
1981	17	11
1982	17	15
1983	16	15
1984	5	3
Total	358	310

Source: Clive Walker, *The Prevention of Terrorism in British Law* (Manchester, Eng.: Manchester University Press, 1986), 69.

notations that accompany them, which usually include information on an individual's prior convictions, his silence (which can be taken as evidence of training in anti-interrogation techniques), known associations, and political views. Most of this information, in Lord Shackleton's words, has "no evidential quality in the judicial sense."[223]

Section 7(1) provides that a person must be served notice once an order concerning him has been made, and must be notified of his rights. Section 7(2) requires that the person be given a copy of the order, and Section 7(3) provides that persons served with exclusion orders may make representations to the government. They may also request an oral hearing before an adviser nominated by the government. The secretary of state is *not* bound by the adviser's recommendations, but he usually accepts them. Under Section 7(4) the secretary may refuse to forward an excludee's representations to the adviser on grounds that they are frivolous, a procedure which underscores the essentially executive nature of the exclusion process. Lord Jellicoe recommended that Section 7(4) be withdrawn and that the time permitted for representations be extended from ninety-six hours to seven days.[224] The 1984 act adopted these recommendations and now provides that representations must be made within seven days after notice of the order is served. Most persons served with an exclusion order do not contest it—only 41 of 249 had done so through 1980.[225]

A detainee who wishes to contest an exclusion order soon learns that his or her ability to do so is severely limited. The notice itself does not set forth the reasons for the order. Hearings before the government's adviser are not regulated by any statutory procedures: The excludee has no legal right to cross-examine witnesses and no right to see or review the evidence upon which the adviser bases the decision. The excludee's solicitor must therefore guess at the evidence when making representations. The excludee has no legal right to have a solicitor when he or she meets with the adviser, although Walker notes that many persons have been permitted to bring counsel with them.[226] There is no right to a formal, public hearing or to know on what basis or in what degree representations to the adviser were successful or not. Moreover, the advisers need not have any particular knowledge of either Northern Ireland or the individual's case, as the following transcript indicates:

> This is not a court of law. This is not an interrogation by me. The object is to try and add to the background of the grounds for the representations that you have made against the exclusion order. . . . *I have not seen the police evidence.* I have not done so for two reasons. One is that I wanted to meet you . . . [and] . . . I do not want to be prejudiced in any way . . . by having read a record of whatever allegations are made against you by the police. . . . The second reason is that I do not want to be placed in a position whereby I might ask you questions which might be of an incriminating nature.[227]

Notwithstanding this quotation, the adviser will usually see all of the materials available to the secretary of state, including information submitted by the police to New Scotland Yard. Once again, however, the sort of information required to seek an order is substantially less detailed than what is required to support a charge under the ordinary criminal law.

One study concluded that excludees are successful in the hearings in approximately one-third of the cases.[228] (Walker's figures indicate that through 1984, fifteen orders were revoked after representations by forty-four persons in Great Britain, and through 1982, one out of two in Northern Ireland.)[229] In addition, the secretary refused to grant the order in approximately one-eighth of the cases.[230] As indicated, there is no right to an appeal to a judicial tribunal, but the secretary of state may, after three years, review an exclusion order upon the excludee's request. Section 3(3) authorizes the secretary to revoke an exclusion order at any time, which again emphasizes the fundamentally executive nature of the exclusion process.

Hence a decision to exclude is not a judicial proceeding, as Lord Shackleton, in his review of the act, acknowledged: "Exclusion is not a judicial proceeding and it involves no charges, trial or court."[231] Indeed, Shackleton went so far as to assert: "Nor is [exclusion] a punishment."[232] Likewise, with regard to hearings before the adviser, Lord Shackleton concluded: "The advisor system is not a judicial proceeding and is not intended as such. It is an independent review of the decision of the Secretary of State [and] a means of taking account of any points the subject of the order may wish to make."[233]

There can be no judicial or independent review of an exclusion order through habeas corpus proceedings. The statutory requirement is only that it "appear" expedient to the secretary to issue the order. A judicial challenge could be successful only upon a showing that the secretary acted in bad faith, as we saw in *Liversidge v. Anderson* (1941). On the other hand, the rule in *Anderson* may have been relaxed by subsequent cases, as Walker argued is the consequence of the case of *Secretary of State for Education and Science v. Tameside Metropolitan Borough Council* (1977).[234] In this case, the court ruled that if "a subjectively framed legal power involves an objectively determinable element,"[235] then the court "must enquire whether [the facts upon which he made his decision] exist, and have been taken into account, whether the judgment has not been made on other facts which ought not to have been taken into account."[236] Walker argued that exclusions must likewise be based on identifiable facts, and that British courts must therefore retain at least supervisory jurisdiction over the exclusion process. Review could include errors both of procedure and of substance, such as whether someone is or has been ordinarily resident, but is unlikely to extend to the question of whether the person involved is a "terrorist," as Walker conceded.[237] As recently as 1987, in the case of *R. v. Secretary of State for the Home Office, ex parte Stitt*, a court ruled that the home secretary need not produce the reasons supporting a decision to issue an order.[238]

In practice, then, judicial review will be available only in those cases where there has been an abuse of discretion, or "bad faith." (Walker distinguished between review on grounds of unreasonableness, failure to consider only relevant evidence, and bad faith.)[239] Review *is* possible in such cases, but in each there will be very difficult problems of proof and claims by the government that much of the information necessary for judicial resolution of the case is highly sensitive. For these reasons, Walker conceded that whatever may be possible in theory, judicial review will "be largely sacrificed to the totem of security interests."[240] The lack of review "thus allows a person to be plucked from society and banished without the right or ability to challenge as false the evidence and reasons."[241]

The Exclusion Process: Conformity with the Constitutive Principles

The similarities between the power to intern without trial and the power to exclude are substantial: Both permit the police and security forces to apply to the executive for an order that detains or restricts an individual, often because they lack enough evidence to charge that individual with an offense that is itself defined in exceptionally broad terms. In both cases, hearing procedures are largely arbitrary or nonexistent. And in both cases, there can be no meaningful, independent review of the executive's decision.

The government justifies the secrecy of exclusion orders on grounds that they must often be based, at least in part, on sensitive information that cannot be revealed in judicial proceedings. The Jellicoe Committee, in rejecting proposals for a system of binding judicial supervision of exclusion orders, argued that the orders are matters of public policy that are the proper province of the secretary, responsible only to Parliament.[242] Jellicoe recognized the severity of exclusion orders, conceding that the process is "in many ways the most extreme of the Act's powers: in its effect on civil liberties, it is . . . more severe than any other power in the Act; in its procedures and principles it departs more thoroughly from the normal criminal process than any other part of the Act."[243] Nevertheless, he concluded that "exclusion . . . has materially contributed to public safety in the United Kingdom and . . . this could not have been achieved through the normal criminal process."[244] He thus recommended that the power be retained, as did Shackleton before him.

The most recent report, by Colville, reached a rather different conclusion, recommending that the power to exclude be withdrawn when the government prepares the 1989 act. Colville repeated the claim that the process is not subject to independent review and that orders may be based on inaccurate information.[245] The government quickly announced, however, that it would not accept Colville's recommendation.

Colville noted also that the continued presence of the power has done little to help Britain's international reputation. The power also fails to satisfy the constitutional requirements of reason and review. As the process currently works, the state need never publicly advance a reason or produce evidence to support a decision to exclude a person. The defendant is given no opportunity to know what the charges are, no right to see or examine the evidence supporting those charges, and no right to challenge the evidence or cross-examine witnesses. The defendant may make representations protesting the decision (there is no right to counsel in the advisory hearings), but there are no formal avenues of appeal and no right to know the grounds upon which the protests are successful or unsuccessful. In addition, the failure to incorporate an objective standard to govern the secretary's decision effectively precludes independent review of the process, thus rendering compliance with the constitutional demand of review a practical impossibility. The power should therefore be withdrawn.

Proscription of Organizations

Both the Emergency Provisions Act and the Prevention of Terrorism Act permit the government to proscribe certain organizations (loosely defined in another subsection as "any association or combination of persons"). Consequently, Part I of the PTA, which concerns proscription, is the only part of the act that does not apply to Northern Ireland. (The relevant provision in the Emergency Provisions Act is Section 21. Offenses under that section "are the commonest of all in the Emergency Provisions Acts.")[246] Section 1(3) provides that any organization listed in a "schedule" appended to the act shall be proscribed; only two groups are included in the schedule, the IRA and the Irish National Liberation Army (INLA). Section 1(4) further provides that the secretary of state may add an organization to the schedule if it "appears to him to be concerned in terrorism occurring in the United Kingdom and connected with Northern Irish affairs, or in promoting or encouraging it."

In addition to proscribing certain organizations, this part of the act makes it an offense, under Section 1(1)(a), to belong to such an organization. A person charged under this section may offer a defense that he or she became a member before the organization was proscribed, or that since proscription he or she has not taken part in any of its activities. Section 1(1)(b) makes it an offense to solicit or invite "financial or other support" for a proscribed organization or to knowingly make or receive "any contribution in money or otherwise to the resources of a proscribed organization." As we saw, Section 1(1)(b) is closely related to Section 10, which prohibits aid to terrorism in general, and not simply to proscribed organizations. Section 1(1)(c) makes it illegal to arrange or address a meeting of three or more persons knowing that the meeting is to support or further the activities of a proscribed organization or that it will be addressed by a person who belongs to a proscribed organization. Finally, section 2(1) prohibits the wearing in any public place items of dress, or displaying in public items that might cause in others a reasonable apprehension that the person is a member or a supporter of a proscribed organization. (A similar provision is included in the Emergency Provisions Act.)

Lord Shackleton argued that the original purpose behind these provisions was that it was offensive to the public at large to see demonstrations of support for the IRA and other terrorist organizations.[247] (Similar justifications were adduced in support of proscription provisions in the Special Powers Act.) They were continued in the 1984 act to prevent the IRA's supporters from flaunting "themselves in public."[248] As this quote suggests, the provisions are also intricately related to the larger policy of criminalization. Indeed, the policy of criminalization is the only justification the provision can claim, as is implicitly acknowledged by both the Jellicoe and Colville reports.

More recently, Clive Walker concluded that these provisions have "had a marked effect in deterring displays of support for the I.R.A."[249] Even so, Walker found them flawed, merely "cosmetic," and urged that they be repealed.[250] The primary constitutional disadvantage to their use is that they have the effect of censoring even legitimate forms of support for republican causes. Jellicoe acknowledged this danger as well: "It is asking a lot of the police to apply these provisions fully . . . while not affecting the free expression of views about Northern Ireland."[251]

Proscription: Conformity with Constitutional Principles

The PTA's proscription provisions are in substantial conflict with the constitutional principles of mitigation, review, and reconstruction. As Walker concluded in his review of these provisions, it is not clear that their purpose could not be achieved through the ordinary criminal law.[252] Moreover, as with the powers of exclusion, Section 10, and Section 11 (since repealed) of Emergency Provisions Act (1978), there is no requirement of reasonableness in Section 1. Consequently, the secretary may proscribe an organization simply if it "appears" to him to be concerned with terrorism. It is very unlikely, therefore, that the secretary's decision could be subject to an independent review. Once again, such a review would be limited to questions of bad faith. As we saw in *McEldowney v. Forde*[253] in chapter 2, a case involving a proscription order under the Special Powers Act, the House of Lords was reluctant to impute an objective requirement of reasonableness to such decisions.

Insofar as proscription limits the expression of ideas and displays of support for republican causes, it conflicts with the constitutional requirements governing the process of constitutional reconstruction. Those requirements demand that all opinions, even those which reject the current constitutional order, are entitled to expression. They do *not* require the toleration of violence or threats of violence in public, but it is crucial to note that proscription is not limited to such cases. The same constitutional principles which require that the IRA and other paramilitary organizations be afforded an opportunity to participate in the constitutional reconstruction of Northern Ireland also demand that *nonviolent* expressions of support for their political position be protected. Consequently, the proscription process, if it is to be retained, must be redrafted to include an objective standard capable of independent review and must permit public displays of support for republican causes. The two requirements work in tandem: The lack of an objective standard and consequent futility of independent review make the abuses prohibited by the second requirement more likely and more difficult to rectify.

CONCLUSION

The constitutive principles of constitutionalism *do* permit the use of extraordinary powers in times of crisis. In this respect, they incorporate the common law principle of *salus populi suprema lex esto*. But the principles limit the exercise of that power in ways designed to reflect a commitment to constitutionalism. The extent to which antiterrorism legislation in the United Kingdom comports with the constitutive principles of constitutionalism is therefore a subtle and complex question. Certain provisions, such as those that suspend trial by jury, satisfy the principles, despite their symbolic importance to common law systems. But other provisions, such as those that permit arbitrary arrest and detention, or authorize the exclusion of citizens, violate elemental constitutional principles.

In most cases, those provisions can be made to comport with the demands of constitutionalism by incorporating changes that would permit independent review of emergency powers (a course partly adopted in the 1987 Emergency Provisions Act). In other cases, such as those that shift burdens of proof, the emergency legislation violates constitutional principles by permitting the government to exercise coercive powers without first providing reasons in support of those powers. There are also certain aspects of the emergency legislation, such as the power of proscription, which fail to satisfy the constitutional principles of mitigation and necessity.

Finally, recent controversies surrounding the right to silence and the government's decision to make the Prevention of Terrorism Act permanent underscore the most important danger with all forms of emergency legislation. The need that gives rise to emergency powers tends to expire long before the legislation passed to cope with it does. In this sense, effective emergency legislation threatens constitutional values even when it succeeds, for then the temptation to make such powers permanent increases.

III

CONSTITUTIONAL MAINTENANCE
AND RECONSTRUCTION IN GERMANY

Richard Wagner's *Die Meistersinger von Nürnberg*, begun in 1845, completed in 1867, and first performed a year later in Munich, has seemed to some audiences a prophetic account of German political development. Of special prescience is a well-known warning by Hans Sachs at the close of the opera, where he tells those gathered (and later generations, or so they thought, of völkisch German nationalists) that "an evil day . . . may dawn, when 'foreign mists before us rise to dupe and blind our German eyes.' When that happens, it will be the death of all that is good and true if the German race betrays its German art." It is not surprising that the chauvinistic tenor of Sachs's final lines later found use in nationalist causes, but this is only the most obvious and the clumsiest of lessons one might find in *Die Meistersinger*.

The opera is outwardly a story of love and artistic competition. A young Franconian knight, Walther von Stolzing, has fallen in love with Eva, the daughter of Veit Pogner. A goldsmith by trade, Pogner has offered Eva (and his fortune) as the main prize in a contest of song on Midsummer Day. Walther hopes to compete in the contest, but since he has none of the credentials of a Meistersinger, he must first perform in a trial, in which he must sing a song that offends none of the elaborate canons that govern the art of the guild of the Meistersinger. Of course, the untrained Walther knows nothing of the rules and indeed scoffs at such orthodoxy, claiming: "New is my heart, new my mind, new is everything I do."

David, an apprentice to Hans Sachs, a widowed cobbler and Nürnberg's greatest Meistersinger, tries to teach Walther the rules before the trial, but to no effect. The requirements are complex and Walther has no desire to learn them. Sensing certain failure, Sachs tries to exempt Walther from the rules altogether, arguing that "once a year I should find it wise to test the rules themselves, to see whether in the dull course of habit their strength and life don't get lost." His request is refused. Walther then sings a song of great beauty but poor technical expertise, especially as judged by Sixtus Beckmesser, the elderly town clerk and himself a Meistersinger and rival for Eva's heart. Beckmesser concludes that Walther's song fails all stylistic conventions. Sachs

135

defends Walther, pointing out that Beckmesser can hardly be considered an impartial judge. Nevertheless, Walther's song transcends their experience and the Meistersinger do not, indeed cannot, understand it.

In the third act, following a comic and confused second act highlighted by a botched attempt by the would-be lovers to elope, Hans convinces Walther that he must learn to sing in a manner consistent with the guild's artistic conventions. Walther, with Sachs's help, writes such a song. Beckmesser in turn steals it (thinking it the work of the great Meistersinger Sachs) and then performs the piece at the contest the following day. Sachs witnesses the theft but makes no effort to stop Beckmesser, for he knows that Beckmesser does not feel the song's beauty and hence cannot sing it with emotion or grace. When Beckmesser sings nonsense and the crowd jeers, he foolishly insists that Sachs wrote the song. Seeing his chance, Sachs denies authorship and again asks the guild to suspend the rules: Anyone—Meistersinger or not—who can sing the song beautifully must be its true author. "One weighs the value of rules by letting them occasionally suffer an exception," Sachs argues, and the other Meistersinger and the crowd soon agree. Walther sings beautifully and in so doing wins the contest, Pogner's fortune, and Eva's hand. The opera concludes with the old man's prophecy.

There is little doubt that *Die Meistersinger* is but a metaphor for much of Wagner's own struggle against suffocating artistic convention. In earlier drafts of the libretto, the character of Beckmesser was given the name Hans Lick, a parody of a prominent Viennese critic who often reviewed Wagner harshly. And it is important to remember that *Die Meistersinger* followed Wagner's *Tristan und Isolde*, in all respects an innovative and revolutionary opera. *Die Meistersinger*, in contrast, respects musical convention (at least to a point) even as it pokes fun at it. Surely the conflict between the unschooled beauty of Walther's song and the formalism that constrains the music of the Meistersinger represents the struggle between innovation and conservatism in art, so prominent in Wagner's own career.[1]

The political implications of *Die Meistersinger* are hardly less marked, though whether Wagner intended them is unclear. Walther's unsuccessful attempt to win Eva without regard to the rules of the contest, followed by success when he respects procedure, can be seen to foreshadow the varied strategies of National Socialists to gain power in the Weimar Republic, first through extraparliamentary violence, which failed miserably in the Beer Hall Putsch in 1923, and later (and more successfully) in accordance with the electoral rules of parliamentary democracy. Likewise, the conflict between the formalism of the Meistersinger and the experiential authenticity of Walther's song reappears as the conflict in Weimar between legality and legitimacy, between the rigid positive law of Hans Kelsen that dominated German legal thought—and the equal chance conception of electoral politics it supported— and Carl Schmitt's scientific jurisprudence of the exception and the distinction between the friend and foe it so obviously implied.[2]

The Schmitt–Kelsen debate over the nature of German legal theory and its implications for constitutional law in both Weimar and the Federal Republic— indeed the entire history of the Weimar Republic's failed efforts at constitutional maintenance—are a rich source for the study of constitutional crises. Weimar is now the classic case for such studies, and no student of "modern constitutional dictatorship could . . . possibly ignore the . . . German Republic."[3] Some of Weimar's appeal rests in the unusual specificity with which the Weimar Constitution dealt with emergency powers (unmatched among modern constitutions, except perhaps by the Federal Republic's Basic Law) and with the undoubted expansiveness of those powers. Still another part of Weimar's appeal must be the frequency and the variety of means through which emergency powers were utilized. As George Schwab observed, "Crises in Germany were the rule rather than the exception."[4] In its first five years the government relied upon the emergency provisions of the Weimar Constitution over 250 times,[5] and they were again the central means of politics in the republic's last years. "Thus in the case of the German Republic unusual need and unusual opportunity combined to produce a remarkably extensive series of experiments in emergency action."[6]

But the study of Weimar in terms of constitutional maintenance (and not simply constitutional crisis) is important not only because Weimar failed or because of the critical role its constitution played in that failure. We tend to forget that in some respects Weimar was a notable success. As a group the new democracies of the 1920s proved exceptionally fragile; of them, Weimar lasted nearly as long as any and longer than most. (Finland alone remained democratic until the onset of World War II.)[7] And Weimar fascinates too because of its extraordinary culture. The "spirit of Weimar," as Peter Gay noted, gave us Expressionism in art, the Bauhaus in architecture and design, and *The Cabinet of Dr. Caligari* in film. Weimar also produced a "dazzling array . . . of exiles— [including] Albert Einstein, Thomas Mann, Erwin Panofsky, Bertolt Brecht, Walter Gropius, George Grosz, Wassily Kandinsky, Max Reinhardt, Bruno Walter, Max Beckmann, Werner Jaeger, Wolfgang Kohler, Paul Tillich, [and] Ernst Cassirer."[8] Short-lived it may have been, but Weimer was a free and vigorous republic, Germany's first. "Few periods in history . . . have seen such lively debates on ideas and ideals or such spirited participation of all citizens in the battles over the common weal."[9] In chapter 4 I shall argue that the constitution that played such a prominent part in Weimar's ultimate failure, and was itself so much a part of those battles, also helped to secure the republic's early success.

Weimar's final failure was not a consequence of its constitutional text or of specific provisions in it. Instead, Weimar's ruin was the failure of a constitutional jurisprudence that could not respond to challenges to constitutionalism disguised in the language of democratic legality. As we shall see in chapter 5, however, the Basic Law of the Federal Republic of Germany expressly rejects Weimar's concept of constitutional neutrality in favor of a "militant democracy." A militant democracy seeks to protect not the state but democracy from its internal enemies, even those enemies who seek legally to turn "the arsenal of democracy" against itself. In the Federal Republic, the concept of militant democracy finds expression not only in specific constitutional provisions in the Basic Law but in internal security policy more generally and in the comprehensive antiterrorism legislation enacted in the 1970s and 1980s.

4

Constitutional Dissolution in the Weimar Republic

THE CONSTITUENT ASSEMBLY AND THE DRAFTING OF THE WEIMAR CONSTITUTION

The Weimar Republic, like Northern Ireland, was born in crisis. "At the close of the World War," wrote Frederick Watkins, "conditions [in Weimar] were not far removed from anarchy."[1] Both states were created in the immediate aftermath of World War I, and both faced an uncertain future. In its first two years of existence, for example, political violence in Northern Ireland was widespread. The same was true in Weimar: Between 1919 and 1922, the first years of the new republic, there were at least 376 political murders and several attempted coups.[2] And when social and political unrest presented a serious challenge to the physical integrity of both regimes, both responded with military force and protective emergency legislation.

Despite their common problems, however, there were some substantial differences between the two states. The political instability they shared found its causes in different sources. In Northern Ireland, oppositional violence was national separatist and sectarian in nature. It challenged not the constitutional nature or design of the state, but rather its very existence. The prominence of violence in the early years of Northern Ireland notwithstanding, the IRA at best represented a minority within a somewhat larger but still small Catholic minority. Nominally a parliamentary democracy, Northern Ireland was in fact a one-party state dominated by the Protestant Unionist party. Restrictive franchise laws, coupled with the decision to abandon proportional representation, effectively made Northern Ireland a protestant state for a protestant people. As a consequence, the regime's survival, although disputed by some and violently challenged by others, was secured by the active support of a significant majority of the population.

The Weimar National Assembly was the product of national elections held on January 19, 1919; the results of those elections vividly demonstrate how electoral politics differed in Weimar and Northern Ireland. Where Northern Ireland was for all relevant purposes a one-party state, in Weimar no single party gained an absolute majority in the Assembly elections. German democracy was a literal farrago of nine larger and smaller political parties, some of which openly sought the end of the republic, and literally dozens of splinter parties. The Social Democrats, perhaps hurt by the reaction against socialism following the Spartacist troubles in late 1918 (discussed later in this chapter), gained 187 seats, but 22 of these belonged to Independent Socialists. The Christian Peoples' Party (Center Catholics) won 91 seats, followed by the German Democratic Party with 75, German Nationalists with 44, and the People's Party with 19 seats. In February the Assembly elected Friedrich Ebert, to whom Prince Max had handed over the seals of office and governmental power the preceding November, first president of the republic. Ebert then asked the Social Democrats to form a new government, which they did in alliance with the Center and Democratic parties. Philipp Scheidemann was appointed chancellor, and his cabinet, reflecting the makeup of the so-called Weimar Coalition, was comprised of six Social Democrats, three Centrists, and three Democrats.

The multipartied character of the Assembly differed little from those of the prewar Reichstags; the factionalism that ultimately "paralyzed the Reichstag and undermined respect for the parliamentary principle"[3] in Weimar was possessed of a long tradition in German history. This lack of respect for parliamentary principle was, as I have suggested, a small part of what was a much larger problem for German democracy. Even before the Assembly began its deliberations, the republic's legitimacy was a matter of open and bitter dispute in electoral politics. It has often been said that the Weimar Republic was a republic without republicans. There *were* republicans in Weimar, but the supporters of the republic and its enemies were nearly equally divided. As a consequence, "The democratic concept of political order was in a precarious position,"[4] and much of the political disquietude in the republic consisted of "opposition to the Republic and democracy as such."[5]

It is critical that we understand the character of this opposition and how it differed from the opposition in Northern Ireland. Until the 1960s revealed a rift within the civil rights movement, as well as between the Official and Provisional IRAs, opposition in Ulster was split essentially over tactics—whether and when to use violence—rather than purposes. Opposition to the German republic, however, was split over both tactics and purposes. As Ellen Kennedy observed, Weimar's opponents fell into three main categories: "[T]raditional-authoritarian critics, who preferred the monarchical and bureaucratic system of the *Kaiserreich*; nationalists such as Hitler and the men around him, who hoped to combine social change with dictatorial government; and the radical left, for whom the Russian model and a dictatorship of the proletariat were the goal."[6] As a consequence, the Assembly began its deliberations unable even to agree on the nature of the state it was to charter. If Weimar "was an idea seeking to become a reality,"[7] there were as many conceptions of that idea as there were political parties to voice them.

The tasks incumbent upon the two new states also differed in important ways. In Northern Ireland the new government's outstanding issue was settling the terms of its borders with the Republic of Ireland and maintaining its internal security. As a devolved state within the United Kingdom, it did not have complete legal competence to conclude either of these issues. Nor had the new government to decide upon its institutional structure, which was largely set forth in the Government of Ireland Act (1920). In contrast, the Weimar Assembly was faced with three monumental tasks. Technically, Germany was still at war with the Allied powers, and the new government—its very existence owed in large measure to the unwillingness of Germany's military leaders to accept responsibility for peace negotiations—was shouldered with the burden of accepting peace terms it had not the physical power to reject. When published, these terms angered many Germans, both civilian and military, by their severity; ultimately the founders of the new democracy were branded "November traitors," a term that referred not simply to the treaty but to the armistice in general, which limited the republic's ability to consolidate its legitimacy just when it needed it most.

Widespread dissatisfaction with the Versailles Treaty, coupled with a large population of displaced soldiers who could not be easily integrated into German political and economic life, rendered Weimar an exceptionally fragile new republic.[8] The resources it could draw upon to cope with its economic difficulties were also severely depleted by the war, and shortages were further compounded by the terms of the Versailles Treaty. Under the treaty, Germany lost its colonies, its merchant marine, 75 percent of its iron ore production, and 15 percent of its agricultural production.[9]

In addition to wrestling with its international burdens, the Weimar Assembly, unlike the first legislature in Northern Ireland, was a constituent body. One of its first responsibilities was to construct a permanent charter for the new republic. That the act of constitution making took place in the small city of Weimar rather than in Berlin, the political and cultural center of Germany, was significant. In part, the Assembly's choice to proceed somewhere other than Berlin was a result of simple necessity. In 1919 Berlin was still very much unsettled—well over a thousand people had died there in early January—and it was doubtful whether the Assembly could meet in Berlin safely. The small city of Weimar was attractive not only because of its relative safety but also because of its distinguished history, which had produced Goethe's *Faust* and Schiller's *Wilhelm Tell*. Weimar seemed the perfect symbol "of . . . lyrical poetry, Humanist philosophy, and pacific cosmopolitanism."[10] The symbolism was not lost on the devotees of the new republic or on its many opponents.

The weakness of democratic sentiments following World War I and the absence of a dominant democratic tradition in pre-Weimar Germany left the new state with "a very narrow democratic potential."[11] Even so, the Assembly did not begin the constitution-making process without historical guidance. The abortive revolution of 1848 in Frankfurt had produced at least a paper constitution, and the 1871 constitution of the empire, clearly a poor guide in so many respects, was nonetheless instructive in some others. Moreover, in November 1918 and in anticipation of the republic, Ebert instructed Hugo Preuss, a professor of constitutional law in Berlin, member of the centrist German Democratic party, and later minister of the interior in the short-lived Scheidemann cabinet, to prepare a draft constitution.[12] Preuss presented his initial draft (composed with occasional assistance from Max Weber) to the Provisional Assembly in early January. The second draft of the Preuss constitution was published on January 20, and this version provided the basis for subsequent discussions in the Assembly that convened in February. Another draft was produced by committee and modified yet again; the fifth and final copy was adopted on July 31 by a vote of 262 to 75. Most of the changes concerned the federal structure of the new republic. Preuss's initial draft had been strongly centrist in nature. The Assembly tempered some of those centrist tendencies and strengthened Weimar's system of administrative federalism, which would later play an important role in the fate of the republic. Perhaps most important, the states retained control over the administration of justice within their territories. But the final draft also gave extensive powers to national government, including the powers to alter state boundaries (this power was, however, severely circumscribed) and to collect taxes, formerly a state function.

In its structural provisions, the Weimar Constitution was a mixture of elements borrowed from Switzerland, France, and the United States. Legislative power was concentrated in a bicameral parliament whose design borrowed freely from the English and U.S. models. The lower house, the Reichstag, was elected every four years on the basis of proportional representation.[13] The upper house, the Reichsrat, was composed of state representatives chosen by the Länder. Its powers were limited primarily to a modified veto over national legislation, which could later be overridden in the Reichstag or through a national referendum.

Weimar was a parliamentary democracy in general design, as indicated by Article 54, which provided that the federal cabinet ministers were to resign if they lost the confidence of the Reichstag. Nevertheless, the office of the Reichspresident was structured to permit it to be a strong figure in the government, and one of the defining characteristics of the republic's subsequent constitutional evolution was the tension between Weimar's parliamentary design and the expansion of presidential power. Throughout the 1920s and early 1930s the powers of the German executive, and in particular his "dictatorial" powers, became the "dominant themes of political discussion."[14] The independence of the executive was promoted by the manner of his appointment. The president was elected not by the Reichstag but rather by direct elections for a seven-year term. Moreover, Article 53 provided that the president appointed the chancellor and determined, through the powers of nomination and dismissal, the selection of the chancellor's cabinet. The firmest foundation for presidential independence, however, was Article 25, which gave the president authority to dissolve the Reichstag. The power was formally limited by a requirement that dissolution could be ordered only once for the same reason, but majority scholarly opinion held that the president could order dissolution at any time, and that a determination of what was "cause" for dissolution was essentially an executive decision.[15] In all other respects the power was left unrestrained, and in time Article 25, in conjunction with Article 48, became the instrument through which Weimar's parliamentary democracy was transformed into presidential government.

There were also strict limits to the president's powers. Every presidential action (including emergency actions taken under the authority of Article 48) required the countersignature of the chancellor or of a cabinet minister. In addition to the countersignature requirement, the Reichstag could remove the president with a two-thirds vote accompanied by a national referendum. Both limitations were designed to enforce presidential accountability to the Reichstag and followed from the parliamentary design of Weimar. Whatever the possibilities inherent in the office of Reichspresident, therefore, the Assembly delegates expected that the true locus of authority in the republic would remain with the Reichstag.

The administration of justice in the new state borrowed much from the 1871 constitution, which had specified that the Reich possessed a sovereign power of "general legislation" over civil and criminal law but shared it with the state governments. Hence Article 103 of the Weimar Constitution provided that "[t]he ordinary jurisdiction will be exercised through the Reichsgericht and through the courts of the states." Supplemental statutory laws provided for a judicial system centered upon four different types of courts. As suggested by the terms of Article 103, ordinary jurisdiction (over civil and criminal affairs) was concentrated in the Reichsgericht and a series of state courts, at the base of which were the district courts. The Reichsgericht functioned generally as a court of final decision over the state courts. In addition, the judicial system included a series of administrative courts and special courts, notably the labor courts and certain emergency courts established under the authority of Article 48. As we shall see, the Constitution was silent on the question of whether Weimar's courts had the power of judicial review, but Article 108 did provide for a Staatsgerichtshof, which possessed original and final jurisdiction over a number of constitutional conflicts, including those between two or more states or between a state and the Reich. The Staatsgerichtshof also adjudicated conflicts between the Reichstag and the president or the chancellor.

The second section of the Weimar Constitution was concerned with the liberties and duties of citizenship in the republic. Articles 109 through 165 included an impressive catalogue of individual liberties and rights. The inclusion of these rights owed little to Preuss, who (not unlike James Madison) first opposed such a course altogether, and when pressed to include a Bill of Rights, produced a sparse and stingy list. The Assembly drew its inspiration instead from the rights guaranteed in the abortive 1848 constitution (no rights appeared in the Imperial Constitution of 1871). Included were freedom of speech and assembly, freedom of religion, and the rights to property, education, equality, and due process. Weimar's Bill of Rights was substantially more detailed and expansive than its U.S. counterpart. But unlike the bills of rights contained in some other constitutional orders, including the U.S. and the Irish, the Weimar Constitution, in keeping with the legal positivism so dominant in German legal thought, "simply contain[ed] *positive* rights guaranteed by the

Constitution, which can be abrogated by the Constitution if not indeed by simple law."*[16] In addition, a number of the guarantees were less of the character of fundamental rights than general directions of social policy of doubtful legal utility, somewhat similar to the social directives in the Irish constitutional text of 1937. At times these social directives, as well as several of the fundamental rights, reflected considerably different social, political, and economic values.

Weimar's Bill of Rights thus was a cacophony of compromises between the competing claims of liberals, democrats, and socialists. Carl Schmitt emphasized this point: "The second part of the Weimar Constitution demonstrates its mixed character" as well as reflecting an uneasy compromise between its liberal and democratic elements.[17] That compromise, between its liberal and democratic elements, was also reproduced, argued Schmitt, in the overall constitutional structure of the republic. In *The Crisis of Parliamentary Democracy*, an examination of the intellectual poverty of parliamentary government, Schmitt ultimately came to identify the liberal element of Weimar with the institution of the Reichstag, its democratic tendencies with the office of the Reichspresident.[18] There was, Schmitt argued, an inherent structural tension between Weimar's presidential and parliamentary elements. That tension came to dominate the republic's politics in the early 1930s.

It is common now to argue that if the Weimar Constitution (or rather certain provisions of it, such as Articles 22, 25, and 48) did not actually cause the collapse of the Weimar Republic, they at least hastened along or facilitated its downfall. Historical treatments of Weimar are replete with claims that "Germany . . . was almost bound to have a dictatorship,"[19] or that Weimar was doomed,[20] or that fascism in Germany was inevitable.[21] This simple (and nearly deterministic) evaluation is untenable, however, for the Weimar Constitution won immediate praise in many other quarters. The compromise document finally settled upon by the Assembly was in many respects a "model constitution,"[22] "worthy of veneration,"[23] and hailed by many commentators as the finest modern example of constitutional draftsmanship, "the best textbook so far written on modern democratic ideas."[24]

Weimar's constitution *was* a remarkable piece of draftsmanship, but there were at least three substantial flaws in the text (Articles 22, 25, and 48), all of which were ultimately to play a significant part in (but not cause) the republic's collapse. The first of these was Article 22, which provided for proportional representation in the Reichstag. As already indicated, no single party won an absolute majority in the 1919 Assembly elections, and the same was true throughout the fourteen-year history of the republic. Likewise, the great Weimar coalition that had provided a working majority in the constitutional assembly proved unstable: The coalition lost its electoral majority in the 1920 elections. The republic had six chancellors in its first five years, and of the twelve governments between 1919 and 1924, the two longest lasted about a year each.[25]

---

*Irish constitutional law makes this point explicitly. The claim is, of course, much more problematic in the U.S. case. For a discussion of this issue, see chapter 1.

Article 22's guarantee of proportional representation exaggerated the multiplicity and divisiveness of German politics in the Reichstag, but "[i]t was essentially the diversified political composition of the German people rather than Proportional Representation which barred the way to strong democratic government."[26] Weimar in the twenties was beset with "the rise of dozens of small new parties, most of them conservative or middle class."[27] Again, part of the explanation for this explosion is the system of proportional representation, but its root cause was the "disintegration of the traditional parties of the Right and Middle."[28] The reasons for this disintegration lie in German history generally and in the particular international and domestic problems that bedeviled the new republic. Dissatisfaction with the Versailles "Diktat" and a general lack of confidence in the republic, demonstrated by the coalition's dramatic losses in the 1920 elections, facilitated the rise of new parties. Moreover, some of Weimar's parliamentary unrest was an unwelcome inheritance from its prewar ancestors. Indeed, "One of the major lines of continuity between the Empire and the Republic was the practice of 'blockbuilding' (*Blockbildungen*), the formation of militant 'blocks' . . . designed to mobilize mass support either in favor of or in opposition to the prevailing social and political order."[29] Those divisions predated Article 22, and indeed the discordant character of the Assembly and early Weimar parliaments very much resembled those that had existed immediately prior to World War I.[30]

The unfinished character of the 1918 "revolution" did little to end such practices or to integrate German society. Instead, the republic was faced with reconciling the demands of liberals left disappointed by the abortive 1848 revolution and the interests of the newly enfranchised labor classes. As we saw, the compromises necessitated by the fractious nature of German civil society were ultimately reflected in Weimar's Bill of Rights, which contained a number of guarantees premised upon conflicting political philosophies. Proportional representation guaranteed the further expression of those conflicts in the Reichstag.

Also crucial to Weimar's collapse was the inadequacy of constitutional provisions intended to limit presidential power. Most of these limitations, especially those concerning emergency powers, were designed to enforce presidential accountability to the Reichstag. When parliamentary politics functioned more or less normally, as in the early and middle years of Weimar, these limitations worked reasonably well. But when parliamentary democracy proved incapable of functioning in the late 1920s and early 1930s, legislative limits upon presidential authority were rendered useless. The problem was complicated by Article 25, which permitted the president to evade legislative control through the simple expedient of dissolving parliament. As written, nothing in Article 25 prevented a president from dismissing the chancellor even if he had the confidence of the Reichstag, as would arguably be the case when Hindenburg dismissed Brüning in 1932. The combined effects of Article 25 and Article 48 (discussed in the next section) were disturbing, for the power to issue emergency decrees could, and did, pass to a president uncontrolled and unaccountable to the cabinet or the Reichstag.

EMERGENCY POWERS AND ARTICLE 48
OF THE WEIMAR CONSTITUTION

Even casual students of German constitutional history know of Article 48 of the Weimar Constitution, commonly criticized as a major factor in the final collapse of the republic. Article 48 was critical in the fate of the republic, but the role it played is much more intricate than is generally perceived: Many of the problems encountered in Weimar involved contestable interpretations of Article 48 in conjunction with other critical constitutional provisions, such as Articles 22 and 25.

Notwithstanding its later importance, Article 48 attracted comparatively little attention in the Weimar Assembly. The delegates were widely agreed that the German president ought to have recourse, when necessary, to expansive emergency powers. The political instability so prominent in the early years of the republic seemed to justify their belief. Dr. Ablass, a co-sponsor of the article, defended it by admitting: "This power goes very far. But when we consider the events of these days, we shall find that this power is born out of the emergency of our time. It gives to the president a strong weapon which we cannot renounce under any circumstances."[31] Preuss later wrote: "If ever in history, dictatorial powers were indispensable to a public authority, they were so for the national government of the young German Republic."[32]

The inclusion of emergency provisions in the Weimar Constitution was hardly an innovation in German constitutional politics. Article 68 of the 1871 constitution had given the Kaiser authority to declare a state of war (Kriegszustand), somewhat akin to the common law of martial rule, whenever he determined that the public safety was in danger. Executive powers were then transferred to military authorities, which could institute special military courts and suspend various civil liberties, including freedom of speech. Similar provisions had existed in several of the state constitutions. Another consequence of the state of war, in conjunction with Article 19's provision that when individual states failed to perform constitutional duties they could be compelled to do so by the Reich, was that power transferred directly to centralized authorities, thus providing a strong counterweight to the centrifugal demands of German federalism. Hence, "If German constitutional history meant anything, it was not strange . . . that Article 48 should have been placed in the Weimar constitution."[33]

Only the Independent Socialists opposed inclusion of emergency powers. "We all have vivid recollections," Dr. Oskar Cohn stated, "of the extreme manner in which the military authorities during the war used [emergency powers] to abuse the freedom of the press. . . . We know how they annihilated the right of assembly, and deprived innumerable individuals of their personal freedom."[34] At another point, in a statement possessed of a considerable foresight his colleagues lacked, Cohn warned that Article 48 was premised upon the naive belief that those who used emergency powers would seek only to protect the republic. In response to some of these objections, Preuss noted that "in times when the private property of citizens included machine guns it would be desirable not to insist upon due process."[35]

Discussion in the Assembly therefore concentrated not on the necessity of such powers, but rather on how to limit them. Whether the powers the Assembly settled upon were more limited than the Kaiser's power under Article 68 remains something of a controversy. Rossiter argued that Article 48 was substantially more limited: "For the irresponsible Kaiser was substituted the president and his responsible cabinet, and indeed . . . the Reichstag. Moreover, in any action . . . the military authorities were to be subordinate to the ordinary civil officials of the Reich government."[36] Heneman, however, argued that at least "[i]n the use of [Article 19] the kaiser was not as free as the president now is under a somewhat similar provision. The Bundesrat was an effective check upon the use of Article 19." Heneman did concede, however, that "no countersignature was necessary for the use of Article 68, and the Kaiser was not responsible to the Reichstag for the acts committed in accordance with its provisions."[37]

As it appeared in final form, Article 48 in full provided:

> If a state does not fulfill the duties incumbent upon it according to the national Constitution or laws, the President of the Reich may compel it to do so with the aid of the armed forces.

> If the public safety and order in the German Reich are seriously disturbed or endangered, the President . . . may take the measures necessary to the restoration of public safety and order, and may if necessary, intervene with the assistance of the armed forces. To this end, he may temporarily suspend in whole or in part, the fundamental rights established in Articles 114, 115, 117, 118, 123, 124, and 153.*

> The President . . . must immediately inform the Reichstag of all measures taken in conformity with sections one or two of this Article. The measures are to be revoked upon the demand of the Reichstag.

> In cases where delay would be dangerous, the state government may take for its territory temporary measures of the nature described in section two.

> The measures are to be revoked upon the demand of the President or the Reichstag.

> A national law shall prescribe the details.[38]

The national law promised in the last sentence was never enacted. But even without supplemental legislation, it was clear that emergency powers were ultimately subject to civilian, and in particular legislative, control. Article 48 nevertheless also reinforced the president's constitutional position because his authority derived directly and independently from the text and not from the delegated authority of the legislature, as was later the case with executive ordinances issued under Weimar's many enabling acts. In this respect Article 48, like so much of the Weimar Constitution, reflected an uneasy compromise between parliamentary and presidential government.

---

*These included: personal freedom; freedom of speech, assembly, and association; and the right to own property.

The structure of Article 48 also reflected the special difficulties engendered by the republic's federal character, and for this reason we should be careful to distinguish among the four paragraphs contained in Article 48. Paragraph four, of course, authorized the individual states to initiate steps to protect the public safety within their own borders. The Reich's final authority in such cases was safeguarded by a qualification that state measures were to be revoked upon the demand of the national government; if a state refused, the president could rely upon other provisions in Article 48 to issue emergency ordinances that would supersede state ordinances.

Paragraphs one and two provided more directly for federal emergency action. Paragraph one, in some ways reminiscent of Article 19 in the 1871 constitution, authorized the president to compel a state to fulfill its constitutional duties (the qualification of an actual threat to public safety and order, which appears in paragraph two, is absent from this paragraph). Hence the first paragraph deals with the somewhat narrow but politically important question of federal execution. In contrast, paragraph two authorized the president to take emergency action throughout the Reich, provided there existed a danger to public order and safety. The precise definition of what constituted a "danger" was uncertain, but it was clear as a matter of formal constitutional law that the president alone had the authority to make the decision. Unlike the French system, in which the parliament declared both the beginning and the termination of the state of siege,[39] legislative authority in Weimar was limited to the power to demand revocation of emergency action.

Commentators disagreed whether the Reichstag's right to demand revocation of emergency decrees acted as an important check on the executive's power to initiate a state of emergency. In 1930 Carl Friedrich concluded that it did, especially when read in conjunction with Article 67's requirement that the National Council be kept informed of the conduct of national affairs. Friedrich's caution not "to belittle the Reichstag's power" was an explicit rejection of Lindsay Rogers's argument earlier that the Reichstag's power was more formal than real. Rogers's conclusion proved more accurate with time.[40]

The extent of the power granted in paragraph two was also a matter of some dispute. The first sentence, or the general grant of authority, permitted the president to take the "measures necessary" to protect the republic. The sentence following it was much more specific, authorizing suspension of a number of fundamental rights, including those of speech and assembly, search and seizure, and property. The interpretive question was whether the second sentence conditioned and limited the first or was entirely distinct. In other words, a question arose as to whether paragraph two's specification of rights constituted a limitation on the president's emergency powers. Most constitutional scholars held that it did and therefore only those rights specifically listed in the second sentence could be suspended (a loose constitutional analogue to the maxim of statutory interpretation, "espressio unis est exclusio alterius"). Other constitutional scholars, such as Carl Schmitt and Erwin Jacobi, urged that the general powers contained in the first sentence could be limited only by political necessity. Their position was premised upon the claim that the president's oath to protect the republic superseded all other constitutional guarantees, save those required to maintain an "institutional minimum" of the constitutional order,[41] which was required by the terms of Article 48 proper. We shall examine that debate later in this chapter, when we review the Prussian controversy of 1932; as a practical matter, emergency action under Article 48 routinely interfered with constitutional provisions not listed in Article 48. Article 105, for example, prohibited the creation of extraordinary courts, but as we shall see, emergency courts were a recurrent feature of the republic's antiterrorism legislation.

Also left undefined was the nature of crises that might constitute a serious threat to the Reich. Without supplementary statutory definition, Article 48 could be construed, and finally was, to support a broad variety of emergency actions, including some, such as emergency economic decrees, not strictly related to the preservation of security and order as traditionally understood. Again, some of this dispute might have been foreclosed with the passage of national legislation, as several students of Weimar have argued. Such critics typically forget that Article 48 was, by modern standards, admirably specific and is surpassed among contemporary constitutions, if at all, only by the Basic Law of the Federal Republic. As I argued in chapter 1, greater specificity of language cannot resolve all questions of interpretation. Weimar's problems ultimately inhered in the tension between constitutionalism and contingency, and not in incompetent draftsmanship.

Limitations on the Use of Article 48

Notwithstanding its breadth, "notable as being the most extreme adopted in recent time by any major constitutional state,"[42] there were limitations on the president's use of Article 48. The foremost limitations rested in the necessity of ministerial countersignatures. To this extent, if not in most others, Article 48 approximated typical civil law practice, which seeks to secure control over emergency powers through legislative mechanisms. As we saw, some analyses of Article 48 concluded that the limitation of "[c]ountersignature . . . [was] much more than a formality. It may and frequently does mean that the power nominally belonging to the President [was] actually exercised by the Cabinet."[43] The chancellor and the cabinet had sufficient influence to ensure that the "dictatorship" was not the exclusive province of the president, bur rather a "group" responsibility. Legislative control was furthered by the additional requirement that all emergency actions were to be revoked upon the demand of the Reichstag. Control by the cabinet, responsible to the Reichstag rather than the president, would ensure that the "group" aspects of the dictatorship would not be merely formal or legalistic.[44]

In addition to control by the Reichstag, other constitutional provisions were expected to provide some protection against the misuse of Article 48. The president, for example, could always be removed for an abuse of office under Article 43. Article 53 likewise provided for presidential impeachment by two-thirds of the Reichstag "for having culpably violated the Constitution or a law of the Reich." Finally, and implicit in Articles 43 and 53, the president was bound by his oath of fidelity to the republic and its constitution. As Dr. Muhr inferred from those provisions: "It is . . . clear that the establishment of a new political situation does not belong to the functions of the dictator. Above the individual personality there stands a higher legal entity, the state. The dictator is a component part of it; he cannot raise himself above it and can change nothing in it."[45]

The Weimar Constitution, then, in keeping with its parliamentary character, clearly anticipated legislative control over the executive's exercise of emergency powers. The possibility of judicial review of emergency action was considerably more complicated. The Weimar Constitution did not explicitly authorize judicial review, but neither did it prohibit it. Scholars disagreed about whether the power could be fairly inferred from the test or from German legal history, in part because the issue opened questions of the most basic sort about the nature of Weimar's constitutional order and German legal theory. One of the leading commentators on the Weimar Constitution, for example, concluded that Article 76's grant of the amending power to the legislature precluded judicial review because it denied the difference between the constitution-making power and ordinary legislative power.[46] Consequently, the Constitution as such could not be considered a higher or supreme law over any subsequent legislative enactment. There could be no room for constitutional review in such a system except insofar as constitutional considerations were an ordinary part of the legislative process under Article 76. Opponents argued that this interpretation reduced the second part of the Constitution—concerning liberties and duties—to mere rhetoric: How could such rights be termed fundamental if they did not act as limits upon the exercise of governmental power?

The first clear judicial pronouncement came in the *Revaluation* case heard by the civil senate of the Reichsgericht in November 1925.[47] The case concerned the controversial national currency revaluation law, occasioned by the run-away inflation that plagued Weimar's economy in the early 1920s. The plaintiff had loaned the defendant 50,000 marks at an interest rate of 5 percent; the loan was secured by a mortgage. When the loan came due on April 1, 1914, the defendant had repaid only 5,000 marks. In June the mortgaged real estate was forfeited to clear the debt. The sale satisfied all but 2,110.87 marks of the remaining obligation. The debtor repaid the remainder in 1922–23, but by then inflation had greatly reduced its value. In 1925, when the revaluation law revalued preinflation debts by 25 percent, the plaintiff sued to recover the cost. The defendant in turn challenged the constitutionality of the revaluation law.

The defendant's response raised the larger question of whether the Reichsgericht had the authority to review the constitutionality of federal statutes. In concluding that it possessed such authority, the Reichsgericht reasoned that "[s]ince the national constitution itself contains no provisions according to which the decision on the constitutionality of national statutes has been taken away from the courts . . . the right and the obligation of the judge to examine the constitutionality of statutes must be recognized."[48]

The same logic might have authorized judicial review of emergency decrees, especially if read in conjunction with the ban on special courts. Given the extraordinary nature of the power, however, judicial review of emergency decrees was a different matter. As is typical in civil law countries, "the framers of the Weimar Constitution relied upon the legislature as the primary safeguard against the abuse of emergency powers, and judicial review was not seriously considered in this connection."[49] As a consequence, and in contrast to most common law countries, there were no significant judicial controls upon the president's use of Article 48. Judicial review in such cases was limited to questions of fact. So long as the evidence plausibly supported the government's contention that the public order was threatened, its decision as to the necessity of emergency action, as well as its character, was beyond judicial competence. As one decision by the Reichsgericht made clear:

> [The judge] must confine himself to the question whether the bearer of the dictatorial power . . . has at least exhibited the purpose specified in Article 48. . . . Only so far as there can be established a manifest misconstruction of the legal requirements of procedure on the ground of Article 48 . . . or a sheer willful misuse of authorization to the prosecution of a completely alien end, will the ordinance lack legal validity.[50]

The question of judicial review of emergency decrees also influenced the debate between Hans Kelsen and Carl Schmitt over which institution was the proper "defender of the Constitution." We shall examine this controversy in some detail later in this chapter. In brief, Kelsen favored judicial review as a means of constitutional self-defense. Kelsen's view was directly influenced by his constitutional jurisprudence, which essentially made constitutional interpretation the application and interpretation of legal rules (or "norms")—it was a jurisprudence of "technik," as Ellen Kennedy suggested.[51] The interpretation and application of norms was, Kelsen argued, the special province of the judiciary. In contrast, Schmitt favored a "scientific" jurisprudence that accounted for politics as an empirical reality and denied that all of political experience could be subsumed under a legal norm—a jurisprudence of political science. Schmitt's position favored the Reichspresident as defender of the Constitution, for only the president was capable of the decisive *political* action necessary to protect the Constitution.

Article 48 as an Instrument of Governance

When examining how Article 48 was actually applied, it is useful to distinguish three periods in the fourteen-year history of the republic. In his classic study of executive power in Germany, Heneman divided these periods into 1919–24, 1925–29, and 1930–33.[52] The same division is a useful way for approaching the history of Article 48.

Article 48 in the Period of 1919–24

Given the terms of the Versailles Treaty, the unruly character of Weimar's parliamentary politics, and widespread economic distress, it should hardly be a surprise that social and political unrest was endemic in the republic's early years. Left- and right-wing groups alike, opposed to the republic as a matter of principle, attempted to revitalize the aborted revolution of 1918 or to initiate new ones. Much of this opposition was extralegal and violent. Indeed, domestic political violence was so common that there were at least two significant attempts to overthrow the republic between 1919 and 1923, and many other, less spectacular efforts. Also troublesome was the new government's inability to secure the support of various state apparatuses and the civil service, a problem that would plague the state throughout its existence. As James Diehl noted, "Vital institutions upon whose loyalty the fate of the Republic depended were not democratized. The bureaucracy, the military, and the judiciary all remained powerful enclaves of authoritarian anti-Republicanism."[53]

Threats from the Left: 1918–19
The earliest threats to the republic were from the left, which was particularly active in Berlin in early 1919. Founded in 1916 and led by Karl Liebknecht and Rosa Luxemburg, the Spartacists were the most prominent of a number of left-wing organizations. They bitterly repudiated the Independent Socialists for their decision to enter into the Assembly and hence into parliamentary politics. The Spartacists were instead more than willing to use violence to hasten along the communist revolution, and that decision "made the danger from the left the severest and most critical problem for the new revolutionary regime."[54] Political violence, practiced not only by the Spartacists but also by elements within or associated with the Independent Socialists, was especially prominent in December 1918 and the early weeks of January 1919. On December 6 right-wing demonstrations, followed by counterdemonstrations on the left, led to the deaths of sixteen civilians. In January left-wing insurgents went so far as to occupy a number of public buildings, to issue proclamations deposing Ebert's government, and to call a general strike.

The government's reaction to the so-called Spartacist uprising proved of lasting significance to the republic. Ebert decided that his government's ability to maintain public order in the face of such demonstrations depended on the existence of a skilled and professional armed force. Independent Socialists had urged earlier the formation of an armed militia composed of civilians. For whatever reason, whether because of distrust of the Independent Socialists or a conviction that such a course could not succeed, Ebert instead sought an alliance with General Wilhelm Groener, Chief of Staff of the Reichswehr.[55] In return for its support in quelling the insurgency, Ebert permitted the Reichswehr to retain its old command structure and officer corps. Ebert entered into a similar agreement a year later with Groener's successor, Prussian General Hans von Seeckt. General von Seeckt was under the nominal control of the minister of war, but the terms of the agreement with Ebert left him free, with assistance from industrial leaders, to transform the Reichswehr into a highly professional and well-armed military. Ebert similarly garnered the support of the well-known Freikorps, army units composed mostly of displaced soldiers under the control of Groener and later von Seeckt.

Paramilitary Threats from the Right: 1920–23

Ebert found the Reichswehr and the Freikorps of tremendous temporary advantage in coping with the Spartacist violence. The military responded with speed and ruthlessness. Over a thousand people were killed in January, including Luxemburg and Liebknecht, who were murdered after they were arrested by military officers. Nevertheless, the republic's relationship with the military was a marriage of convenience. Ebert's government could rely upon military assistance against communist or left-wing threats, but the officers corps was never fully democratized and most officers desired not democracy, bur rather a return to a conservative monarchy similar to the one that predated Weimar. The military's ambivalence to Weimar was especially evident when the republic attempted to cope with threats from the right. The government's inability to exercise any real control over the Reichswehr contributed greatly to the overall militarization of German politics, which was beset with numerous left- and right-wing paramilitary organizations.[56] As Diehl argues, "Paramilitary politics was one of the most virulent manifestations of the widespread antipathy to parliamentary democracy which eventually destroyed Germany's first democratic experiment."[57] Many of the right-wing groups drew recruits from the Freikorps, which were disbanded on the strength of Allied pressure and with Seeckt's approval in the summer of 1920.

Following the dissolution of the Freikorps, literally dozens of new paramilitary groups were founded, including the Orgesch, whose not untypical ideological program was "shot through with social resentment, fear, and nostalgia for the authoritarian social and political structures of the Empire."[58] The Orgesch and similar groups were comprised essentially of bourgeois, conservative elites from the aristocratic and middle classes. Like much of the military, they sought a monarchical Germany. Other nationalist organizations, or paramilitary groups, such as the Bavarian paramilitary associations, and two larger groups, the Stahlhelm and the Jungdeutscher Orden, represented the völkisch, "proto-fascist" elements prominent in the middle and later years of Weimar, particularly after the Orgesch began to decline. Additional paramilitary organizations included "Organization C," a covert successor to the Ehrhardt Brigade that marched on Berlin during the Kapp Putsch in March 1920.

The Kapp Putsch represented the early culmination of right-wing hostility to the new republic. Early in the year, in accordance with the terms of the Treaty of Versailles, Ebert's government moved to reduce the armed forces to a limit of 100,000 men. Freiherr Walther von Lüttwitz, a général in Berlin, and Wolfgang Kapp, a leader of the staunchly nationalist Vaterlandspartei, had already decided to overthrow the government; Ebert's order to Lüttwitz to disband the famous Ehrhardt Brigade to comply with the Diktat merely supplied the pretext they desired.[59] When Lüttwitz refused to disband the brigade, the national government ordered his arrest. Lüttwitz responded in turn by marching his men and the brigade through the Brandenburg Gate into Berlin. Ebert had little choice but to order regular army units (the Reichswehr) to defend the capital. The Reichswehr had performed eagerly in service of the republic against left-wing threats, but it proved more reluctant to act against right-wing violence. General von Seeckt pointedly informed Ebert that "troops do not fire upon troops."[60]

The instability of the republic was aptly symbolized by Ebert's subsequent decision to leave Berlin, with his cabinet, for Stuttgart. Without military support, Ebert and Chancellor Gustav Bauer appealed to workers and the Socialist party to paralyze Berlin and the rest of Germany with a general strike. In the meantime, Kapp had declared a dictatorship. He fled in defeat just a few days later. His fall was precipitated by the general strike and hurried when other elements in the army and the German bureaucracy refused to cooperate with the new regime. Perhaps most important, the Reichsbank refused to lend financial support to Kapp, who had requested a loan of 10,000,000 rentmarks. The government then let the incident abate, permitting Lüttwitz to retire his position. Kapp died in prison awaiting trial.

The Kapp Putsch was soon followed by left-wing uprisings in the Ruhr in mid-March. In some respects these uprisings were inspired by the government's apparently ineffective response to the earlier disorder. There were, however, some notable differences in the way the Reich responded to the new uprisings. Chief among these was the government's unhesitating decision to rely upon the Reichswehr, whose loyalty in suppressing left-wing violence, at least, was undoubted. The government's ability to use the Reichswehr against the left also meant that it could rely more directly upon the emergency powers anticipated by Article 48, powers that were ultimately of little benefit in the Kapp Putsch. Hence when the Communists refused to disband an irregular army of some fifty thousand men, the government ordered in the Reichswehr. Unlike the insurgents on the right, the left was quickly and brutally suppressed, and similar results followed April uprisings in Saxony and Thuringia.

Although Article 48 had been used effectively against left-wing uprisings, it was useless in the Kapp Putsch because the government lacked the military resources to utilize it. In the end, Kapp's pretensions were defeated by the general strike, not by the government's emergency powers. Immediately after the Kapp crisis began, however, Ebert issued an expansive emergency decree which substantially increased penalties for a roster of crimes committed by the insurgents. The decree mandated the death penalty, for example, for arson and bombings as well as sabotage. The decree also established, in apparent violation of Article 105 of the Weimar Constitution, a number of special courts. (There was much debate in the Reichstag regarding the doubtful constitutionality of these special courts. The government's position was to distinguish between special courts, created under constitutional authorization, and exceptional courts, created without such authorization and hence prohibited under Article 105. This position was subsequently ratified by the regular courts. The distinction, then, was between special courts [Sondergerichte], which functioned "as the ordinary courts for specific matters in a general way,"[61] and exceptional courts [Ausnahmegerichte], which were unconstitutional.)

Two types of special courts were established. The first, the extraordinary war courts, possessed jurisdiction over offenses such as sabotage, arson, and bombings, for which the court could impose capital punishment. These courts, like the Diplock courts in Northern Ireland, operated under relaxed rules of procedure but, unlike the Northern Irish courts, were staffed by three professional jurists. For more serious offenses, such as actual insurrection, the minister of war could establish courts martial. These courts were created and staffed by the military commander in the relevant district. Once again, there were to be three judges, but there was no requirement that they be professional jurists. As with the other emergency courts, procedure was streamlined and judgment rapid—a decision was required within twenty-four hours of the hearing. No appeal was possible, and only one sentence was authorized, death by shooting, whatever the offense. Authorities made ample use of both types of courts in suppressing the communist violence in central Germany. Nevertheless, the draconian nature of the special courts, coupled with the government's apparent toleration of right-wing violence (and in particular the lenient treatment of Lüttwitz and Kapp), led to much criticism, and the decree authorizing them was revoked on April 3, "after an effective life span of less than three months."[62]

Although the government used Article 48 to great effect against the communist uprisings, and despite the rapid collapse of the Kapp Putsch in early 1923, political violence escalated throughout 1922 and 1923. Political murders soon supplanted the armed putsch as the revolutionary method of choice. Karl Liebknecht and Rosa Luxemburg were among the first murdered, killed while in military custody. Philipp Scheidemann was attacked with prussic acid in an attempt to blind him on June 4, 1921, and in August members of the nationalist group Organization C murdered Matthias Erzberger, a prominent negotiator in the armistice agreement. Less than a year later, in June 1922, right-wing nationalists (again Organization C) murdered Foreign Minister Walther Rathenau, who had supported a good-faith policy of full repayment of war reparations as the only chance to reduce the burden of the payments. This policy aggravated much of the right, which failed to appreciate the nuances of foreign policy.

Law for the Protection of the Republic (1922)
Given the political unrest so prominent in Weimar's first years, which Chancellor Josef Wirth said reflected "the political morality of the jungle,"[63] it was incumbent that the government enact protective measures. In 1922 the Reich responded by adopting ordinances prohibiting paramilitary demonstrations and military regalia. These ordinances did little to stop the escalation of violence.

After the attack upon Scheidemann and the murder of Rathenau, the Reich government enacted additional statutes and ordinances considerably more restrictive than those that had preceded them. The first of these, passed to supplement Article 48, was the Law for the Protection of the Republic, known colloquially as the anti-putsch law.[64] Enacted on July 18, 1922, by a vote of 303 to 102, the act satisfied the two-thirds majority requirement under Article 76 and thus won the status of a constitutional amendment. In general the act was directed at the right-wing paramilitary organizations that sought to destroy Weimar. Passed for an initial five-year period, and then extended for two more years, the Protection of the Republic Law was in many respects similar to the Special Powers legislation enacted at the same time in Northern Ireland. Like the Northern Irish legislation, the German statute identified a number of specified acts that would be met with criminal penalties, such as belonging to or "supporting" a group or an organization if one of the known purposes of the organization was the murder of a Weimar Republic official.

Other provisions allowed authorities to ban parades and meetings and to forbid and dissolve organizations that promoted antirepublican activities aimed "at undermining the constitutionally established Republican form of the Reich or the Länder."[65] (Article 3 also provided for a very limited system of immunity for informants.) Imprisonment could also result if one publicly approved of or supported any act of violence against the republic or the Länder or if one slandered anyone who died as a result of such violence. Additional sections of the act provided for a system of internal exile within Germany, as does the current Prevention of Terrorism Act in the United Kingdom, by restricting individuals to certain parts of the country. In addition to the main act, the government passed five supplemental laws, the most important of which was the National Civil Service law, which required an oath of fidelity to the Weimar Constitution by anyone in the national civil service.

Article 118 of the republic's Constitution guaranteed freedom of speech and press in Weimar, but the second paragraph of Article 48 provided the constitutional authority needed for the Protection of the Republic Act to include press restrictions. Chapter four of the act contained provisions permitting the government to ban publication of newspapers for up to four weeks and other publications for as long as six months, as well as providing for seizure of some printed materials.[66]

The second article in the act, following the precedent set in earlier ordinances, established a system of special courts for offenses against the emergency legislation. Called the special court for the protection of the republic (Staatsgerichtshof zum Schutz der Republik), its seven members were appointed by the president. No appeal was possible from this court, but it could remove proceedings to ordinary courts, and unlike the courts utilized in the communist uprisings earlier, it functioned under normal rules of judicial procedure. (In 1926 the court transferred its criminal jurisdiction to the ordinary courts.) The general perception among critics was that these courts were largely ineffective, a point underscored by Karl Loewenstein in his review of antifascist legislation in European democracies in 1937, in which he concluded that Weimar's "almost tragi-comical" efforts against internal subversion were "secretly made blunt by hyper-legalistic, or even mutinous, courts from the beginning."[67]

The act was also hampered by open opposition from at least one of the state governments. On July 24, Bavaria, which had opposed the federal law in the Federal Council, issued its own ordinance "to replace the national law." Bavaria's objections in the Reichsrat centered on the claim that the federal legislation interfered with the legitimate prerogatives of the states. No doubt part of Bavaria's opposition was based on genuine if misdirected concern for its traditional independence and the role it was to play in the new federal structure of the German state. As a practical matter, the new national courts would replace the Bavarian people's courts (Volksgerichte) established immediately after the war. In addition, Bavaria argued that the special courts contained in the act violated Article 105 and that the supplemental laws, notably the Civil Service Law, unconstitutionally infringed on the freedom of speech of civil servants. Bavaria's argument failed to acknowledge, however, that the national law had the status of a constitutional amendment.[68] (Article 130 provided that freedom of political opinion and association were guaranteed to all public officials. Judicial decisions later indicated that these freedoms included not only freedom of conviction but the freedom to practice those beliefs. Under the emergency legislation, the Reich was still prohibited from regulating political beliefs, but it could restrict behavior antithetical to the republic. Hence, according to the Prussian Supreme Administrative Tribunal, public officials could express support for subversive organizations, but "any positive action in favor of such parties was . . . incompatible with the special position of public officials.")[69]

As the weakness of its constitutional arguments hints, Bavaria's opposition was designed primarily to impress various right-wing organizations whose support Bavarian officials cultivated, if indeed they did not require (a position complicated by the presence, also, of an active left).[70] The controversy over the protective legislation reached new heights in the summer of 1923, when uncontrollable monetary inflation strengthened the appeal of antirepublican forces, especially in conservative Bavaria. The mark was four hundred to one against the American dollar in July; by August it was at four million and in November it was at four trillion to the dollar. The violence in Bavaria grew worse when the national government called an end to passive economic resistance in the Ruhr against the French occupation some months earlier. (The occupation was a futile effort to secure German compliance with impossible reparation schedules set forth in the Versailles Treaty.) Germany's dire economic condition made the government's decision the only one possible, but the republic's opponents quickly seized upon it as further proof of the government's impotence. To cope with increasing unrest, the Bavarian government, acting under the authority of paragraph four of Article 48, suspended various provisions of the Bill of Rights in its territory. The Bavarian government also appointed a state commissioner, Baron Gustov von Kahr, to exercise full administrative powers within the state.

Distrustful of Bavaria and uncertain of Kahr's loyalty to the Reich, the federal government immediately invoked Article 48 throughout the republic and appointed its own commissioner, who did not at first interfere with the

Bavarian authorities. (The Reich's suspicions were heightened by its conflict with Bavaria in the preceding year over the new emergency legislation.) Kahr began his tenure by ordering a general ban upon mass demonstrations. Rigorous enforcement against left-wing opponents, coupled with relative laxity against the National Socialists and other right-wing groups, increased the federal government's suspicion of Kahr. Those suspicions intensified when the federal minister of war ordered General Otto von Lossow, the local military commander, to close down a leading National Socialist newspaper. Lossow refused and Commissioner Kahr supported his decision.

The Beer Hall Putsch began when Hitler, fearful that Kahr's support was wavering, had his Brown Shirts interrupt a speech by Kahr at a public demonstration and forced him at gunpoint to agree to march with Hitler on Berlin. Kahr of course agreed, whereupon Hitler formally declared the Bavarian and Reich governments dissolved. Hitler's hurried and amateurish putsch ended the next day, when police fired upon and dispersed what was to be a triumphant National Socialist parade in celebration of their victory. Hitler and his colleagues subsequently were tried and received a lenient sentence of five years' incarceration with probation possible after six months in prison. On December 20, 1924, acting upon the recommendation of its minister of justice, Bavaria pardoned Hitler for his role in the putsch.[71] A year later, when Hitler began a second campaign of demonstrations, both Bavaria and Prussia reacted by forbidding him to make public speeches. (Bavaria lifted its ban in 1927, as did Prussia shortly thereafter.)

Article 48 and Emergency Economic Legislation

In addition to its public security functions, plainly anticipated by the Constituent Assembly, Article 48 also was used in the government's efforts to cope with its economic difficulties. As early as 1922, President Ebert and Chancellor Wirth concluded that the republic's economic distress constituted a "threat to the public safety and order."[72] In October they issued an order under Article 48 forbidding foreign monetary speculation, the sort of subject matter that typically calls for legislation, rather than emergency action on the part of the executive. Shortly thereafter, the cabinet issued additional ordinances which, among other things, changed tax laws, lowered the price of fuels, and regulated the efforts of individual states to secure foreign loans. Although not explicitly contemplated by Weimar's framers, the use of Article 48 as a font for executive lawmaking was not actually precluded by its terms, and the Reichstag's failure to demand revocation of Ebert and Wirth's ordinance seemed to legitimize the innovation.[73] The practice was frequently repeated in the first five years of the republic, so that "Article 48 became an instrument of emergency legislation" for the executive.[74] Between October 1922, and 1925, sixty-seven emergency decrees were issued, of which forty-four involved economic and financial concerns.[75]

The government's use of Article 48 to restore economic stability and reduce inflation set an important precedent for late Weimar, but in practice these efforts to utilize Article 48 to cope with economic emergencies were relatively limited. Instead, Ebert and the various chancellors derived wide authority from a series of enabling acts passed by the Reichstag. These acts authorized the executive to issue ordinances possessing the force of ordinary law, thus rendering recourse to Article 48 for such authority unnecessary. Enabling acts were possible only with the approval of two-thirds of the Reichstag, which in effect gave them the status of constitutional amendments. The first act, passed on February 24, 1923, permitted the government to take measures necessary to continue the campaign of passive economic resistance against the French occupation of the Ruhr.

In October, Chancellor Gustav Stresemann requested a second enabling act with broader authority to cope with the Reich's collapsing economy. The first paragraph of the new act provided: "The government of the Reich is authorized to adopt those measures which it considers to be absolutely necessary in the financial, economic, and social realms. Fundamental rights guaranteed in the Weimar Constitution may be disregarded in the process."[76] Other provisions required that any such ordinances be revoked upon the demand of the Reichstag and provided for the act's expiration upon a change in the party composition of the current government. Despite these limitations, the Enabling Act was substantially more expansive than the terms of Article 48 and was ultimately of tremendous significance in speeding the collapse of the republic. As the last sentence of the first paragraph made clear, the limitations in Article 48 on the suspension of fundamental rights were not repeated in the enabling legislation.

The government as then composed lasted a mere three weeks, from October 13 to November 2, but in that time Stresemann issued thirty-six ordinances, including decrees creating a new national bank and a new currency.[77] After the act expired, Stresemann continued to issue similar ordinances under Article 48 until his cabinet was replaced at the end of November by that of Chancellor Wilhelm Marx. Marx also sought an enabling act, but the one he secured differed in important ways from its predecessor. The Reichstag's control was increased by a provision requiring that all ordinances were first to be discussed with committees chosen by the Reichstag. More important, the second act, in direct contrast to the earlier legislation, specifically provided that the fundamental rights contained in the Constitution could not be disregarded by emergency ordinances. Marx's government ultimately issued over seventy ordinances on the strength of the act.[78]

The frequency with which the first governments of Weimar relied upon extraordinary powers is difficult to appreciate. Approximately 150 emergency decrees were issued under the 1923–24 enabling acts,[79] and by one count Article 48 was used over 130 times in the first five years of the republic.[80] On the whole, the emergency powers authorized by the Weimar Constitution worked well and indeed were critical to the survival of the republic in its first five years.[81] Article 48 permitted the government to respond effectively to recurrent and very real threats to the physical integrity of the republic from both left- and right-wing paramilitaries. In addition, Article 48 and the enabling acts were used with great effect to pass economic ordinances and enabling legislation to cope with the republic's immense financial difficulties. This repeated and apparently successful use of constitutional emergency powers helped forestall efforts to pass the more specific legislation expressly contemplated in Article 48 itself, and as a consequence, supplemental legislation was never enacted.

The early contribution of Article 48 to the security of the republic was largely acknowledged in scholarly literature at the time, both in Germany and in the United States. Indeed, most of the scholars whose work we reviewed in the first chapter, including Watkins, Loewenstein, Rossiter, and Friedrich, initially looked upon Article 48 with great favor. In their massive study of Weimar, for example, Blachly and Oatman argued: "There can be little doubt . . . that its [Article 48's] frequent use was of material assistance to Germany in conquering its various disorders, political, social, and economic, and emerging from floods of disaster as a unified self-governing nation."[82] In 1930 Friedrich concluded that "Germany might well be congratulated for the wisdom of its constitution-makers";[83] and, some years after Weimar, Herbert Spiro still thought Article 48 "soundly conceived."[84] It was only after events in the late 1920s and early 1930s that scholarly enthusiasm began to wane. In part this change has to do with the inadequacy of the limitations built into Article 48, which were not fully exposed until the early 1930s. During the first five years of Weimar those limitations, which centered upon the role of the Reichstag, worked as Weimar's framers had envisioned. No chancellor tried to subvert the role of the Reichstag, and as a consequence almost all emergency decrees, whether issued under Article 48 or the enabling acts, had parliamentary support. In the 1930s those limitations were exposed and exploited in the face of crises more severe and different in kind than those encountered in the early 1920s.

Article 48 in the Middle Years of the Republic

From 1924 to 1929 Weimar enjoyed a period of relative political stability and financial prosperity. The reparations issue was diminished by the Dawes Plan for refinancing, and foreign investors contributed heavily to Germany's reconstruction. By the late 1920s Germany's economic recovery was so extensive that it was once again one of Europe's industrial leaders.[85] The successful use of Article 48 in the early years of Weimar helped contribute to this stability, and it was used in this period only to repeal earlier emergency provisions.

The 1928 elections seemed to reflect the republic's newfound stability. Weimar's moderates fared well in those elections. Indeed, when Hermann Müller assumed the chancellorship, he was the first Social Democrat to do so since 1920. He governed with the support of the earlier Weimar coalition, comprised for the most part of Social Democrats, Democrats, and the Catholic Center, but the coalition once again fell short of an absolute majority in the Reichstag. Conservative nationalists, on the other hand, steadily lost support in Weimar's middle years. In May 1924, for example, the National Socialists had won 32 seats, but their total had declined to 12 in 1928. Similarly, the German Nationalists declined from 103 to 73 seats. But even the apparent success of moderates in the 1928 elections could not hide the continuing fractiousness of German parliamentary politics. Successive German governments were short-lived political coalitions. The task of coalition building was greatly complicated by the continued refusal of extremist parties on both the right and the left to enter such agreements. Chancellor Müller's cabinet, comprised of representatives from five different political parties, reflected that failure. The socialists' victory, moreover, only further distressed nationalists, who found additional ground for despair with the Young Plan on the reparations issue, and then with Germany's renewed economic misfortunes.

Article 48 in the Period 1930–1933

The collapse of the New York Stock Exchange and subsequent worldwide economic depression revealed the highly superficial and transitory nature of Weimar's economic and political stability. Unemployment in Germany reached approximately 900,000 persons in the middle months of 1929, and the figure would more than triple by the winter of 1930.[86] By 1929 the Reich's deficit had ballooned to nearly 1,700 million marks, leading to the collapse of Müller's cabinet and to the final dissolution of the Weimar coalition. In particular, Müller's cabinet divided over the details of proposed limitations on additional expenditures and tax increases to reduce the deficit. President Hindenburg refused Müller's request to push the program through on the strength of Article 48, whereupon Müller resigned and was replaced as chancellor by Heinrich Brüning of the Catholic Center party on March 28, 1930. Brüning's cabinet was, like Brüning himself, fiscally conservative. Many of its members were drawn from Müller's cabinet, but it failed to include representatives from the Social Democrats, still the largest party in the Reichstag.

If Brüning inherited much of Müller's cabinet, he inherited all of the economic problems that had troubled it. Deteriorating economic conditions seemed to require substantial increases in state and federal taxes, but there appeared little likelihood that the Reichstag could muster a majority in favor of a common economic program, especially since the Social Democrats were no longer included in the cabinet. Moreover, the Nationalists and the National Socialists often failed to attend parliamentary sessions or openly obstructed the proceedings; on more than one occasion fights erupted between the Communists and the National Socialists. In the ensuing weeks, the Reichstag was unable to reach a conclusion on Brüning's proposals for increased taxation. On July 15, as he presented his economic proposals to the Reichstag for their second reading, Brüning warned that if the Reichstag failed to pass his legislative program he would "have to make use of *all* constitutional means necessary to cover the budgetary deficit."[87]

Brüning's threats were hardly novel. He had said much the same in early April, noting, "This cabinet has been formed for the purpose of solving as quickly as possible those problems which are generally comprehended to be vital to our nation's existence. This will be the *last* attempt to arrive at a solution with *this* Reichstag."[88] The Reichstag rejected Brüning's proposals on the next day by a vote of 256 to 193.[89] Brüning in turn sidestepped the Reichstag, issuing the tax increases through two decrees issued the same day under the authority of Article 48. Two days later, on July 16, and in complete accordance with the terms of Article 48, the Reichstag voted, 236 to 221, to demand revocation of the decrees.

Brüning did revoke the tax decrees, as he was constitutionally required, but there was nothing to keep him from reintroducing them after he dissolved the Reichstag under Article 25, which he did on July 18, stating: "Because the Reichstag today demanded that my decree of July 16 issued on the base of Article 48, should be revoked, I dissolve the Reichstag in virtue of Article 25 of the Constitution."[90] Historians disagree about whether Brüning did all he could to secure parliamentary approval for his legislative program,[91] but given the sorry history of parliamentary politics in Weimar, and a genuine concern for the fate of the republic, he should not be faulted for acting as he thought his oath and office required of him. Nevertheless, Brüning's action set an ominous precedent, as Arnold Brecht noted in his comparison of the incident with Cicero's decision in 63 B.C. to seek the death penalty for the Catilinians in Rome. Then a senator, Julius Caesar objected, observing:

> All bad precedents have originated in cases which were good; but when the control of the government falls into the hands of men who are incompetent or bad, your new precedent is transferred [to punish] the undeserved and blameless. . . . It is possible that, when someone else is consul, some falsehood may be believed to be true. When the consul with this precedent before him shall draw the sword . . . who shall limit or restrain him?[92]

Whatever its political merits, Brüning's response finally exposed one of the critical procedural flaws in Weimar's treatment of constitutional emergency powers. In the Constituent Assembly, Hugo Preuss had argued that the Reichstag's right of revocation would ensure that the president's use of emergency powers would always remain subject to review by the Reichstag. But so long as the president or the chancellor had the constitutional authority under Article 25 to dissolve the Reichstag and order new elections, there existed the possibility that the executive could govern through the use of Article 48's emergency power without corresponding legislative control.

Brüning's dissolution of the Reichstag, however, did more than simply demonstrate the procedural flaws in Weimar's emergency provisions. It also exposed the most serious substantive flaw in the Weimar constitution as a whole. The Weimar Republic was in design an uneasy and uncertain compromise between parliamentary democracy and presidential democracy. All of the important limitations upon the emergency powers rested on a viable, working parliamentary body capable of reviewing the president's use of those powers. The president's constitutional authority to dismiss and appoint chancellors at will, coupled with emergency powers insufficiently limited, facilitated the development of presidential government. After Brüning began to govern with President Hindenburg on the strength of Article 48, the issue was settled, as a matter of constitutional practice, if not constitutional theory, in favor of presidential government.

As was true with the Catilinian threat to the Roman Republic and in the first years of German democracy, economic distress in late Weimar was accompanied by political unrest. The form in which that unrest expressed itself, however, changed dramatically after the ignominy of the Kapp and Beer Hall putschs. Instead of directly challenging the state, antirepublican opposition to Weimar in the late 1920s and early 1930s took new and more subtle forms, later called the "new technique of revolution" by Frederick Watkins.[93] The new technique was to seek power through accepted democratic channels—to turn "the arsenal of democracy," in Goebbels's words, against itself.[94] Put simply, this new technique was required because rightist opposition to the republic became convinced that no armed insurrection was likely to succeed against the superior resources of even a relatively weak state, such as Weimar. In the mid-1920s, therefore, rightist opposition began to field candidates for the Reichstag. While their popularity was somewhat limited throughout the 1920s, proportional representation guaranteed at least a small parliamentary presence for these groups. As we saw, after the Beer Hall Putsch the National Socialist party won thirty-two seats in the Reichstag.[95] (These figures decreased at a small but steady pace throughout the rest of the 1920s, so that in the 1928 elections, the National Socialists held only twelve seats in the Reichstag.)

Their newfound desire to enter parliamentary politics did not mean that these groups had reconciled themselves to the republic or even to nonviolent political action. Rather, as Hitler was later to testify in his well-known "oath of legality" in the trial against three army officers for high treason in the Staatsgerichtshof on September 25, 1930:

> The Constitution gives us the ground on which to wage our battle, but not its aim. We shall become members of all constitutional bodies, and in this manner make the Party a decisive factor. Of course, when we possess all constitutional rights we shall then mould the state into that form which we consider to be the right one.[96]

Hitler's purpose, in other words, was to destroy the republic legally. Goebbels had made the same point two years earlier in much more graphic language:

> We are entering the Reichstag to supply ourselves, in that arsenal of democracy, with democracy's own weapons. We become Reichstag deputies in order to paralyze the spirit of Weimar with its own aid. If democracy is so stupid as to pay our transportation and daily expenses for these "services" of ours, that is its own affair. . . . We come as enemies! As the wolf breaks into the sheepfold, so we come.[97]

Although the new technique of revolution embraced electoral politics, it did not abandon the use of political violence. Instead, it redirected that violence away from the state as such, which it could not hope to defeat directly, toward other political actors. Right- and left-wing organizations alike mounted vast private armies, the most prominent of which were the National Socialist's Storm Troopers. The violence practiced by these private armies served several purposes, including the obvious ones of intimidating political opponents and attracting new recruits. Their primary purpose, however, was to destabilize and delegitimize Weimar by frightening the middle classes into support for whatever party could promise public order and security.

The rise in domestic political violence caused by these efforts was assisted by the government's decision in July 1929 to permit the Law for the Protection of the Republic Act (1922) to lapse. Over strong and vocal opposition from the right, a new act was passed in March 1930, just before the critical September elections. The new act was considerably less stringent than its predecessor, in part a consequence of the right's increased parliamentary importance. The act's weakness, however, also resulted from a particular conception of German liberalism and constitutionalism known as the "equal chance" theory, which provided that any party willing to abide by the procedural rules of electoral democracy must be afforded an opportunity to contest for power, notwithstanding their commitment to democracy as such. As we shall see, the prevailing majority interpretation of constitutional liberalism provided the intellectual support for the equal chance doctrine, but there were alternative interpretations of the Weimar Constitution that argued in favor of a more "militant" democracy.[98]

Interior Minister Carl Severing had been the primary proponent of the new bill. Soon after it was adopted, Severing began to argue with Wilhelm Frick, a leading Nazi and minister of the interior and education in Thuringia, over its implementation. In particular, Severing wanted Thuringia to move against a paramilitary organization called the Eagle and Falcon. Frick objected, and thus began a longstanding conflict between Thuringia and the Reich, settled only when the Reich discontinued police subsidies to the state. Other states, however, notably Prussia, had taken active and aggressive measures against political violence. Prussia passed ordinances providing that no member of the National Socialist party could hold a position in the civil service, and in June 1930 the Prussian cabinet issued a decree banning the National Socialists from wearing military and paramilitary uniforms. Prussia also acted against the left, ordering the dissolution of a group called the Communist Front Fighter's Organization. The ban's legality was cast into doubt when similar state bans were ruled by the courts to be an unconstitutional infringement upon Article 118's guarantee of freedom of speech.[99] In March of the next year, the national government authorized the states to issue such bans by virtue of Article 48, and in December another decree made the wearing of paramilitary uniforms and political symbols illegal throughout the Reich. Chancellor Brüning, however, rescinded the decree in January, and Chancellor Franz von Papen's cabinet later rescinded almost all of these emergency decrees. The act passed in 1930 expired in 1932, only six weeks before Adolf Hitler assumed the chancellorship.

The Critical Election of September 14, 1930

When he dissolved the Reichstag in July, Brüning had hoped that new elections in September would provide him with a firmer parliamentary basis for his economic program. Neither Brüning nor anyone else anticipated the extraordinary gains made by the National Socialists in those elections. Two years earlier the Nazis had won 810,000 votes in parliamentary elections. In 1930 they garnered almost 65 million votes and 107 seats, making them the second largest party in the new Reichstag, inferior only to the Social Democrat's 143 members.[100] Less often appreciated is the success of extremism on the left, as the Communists increased to 77 seats from 54 in the 1928 elections. The implications of these results for the republic's democratic legitimacy were ominous, for "two out of every five Germans voted for parties bitterly opposed to the principles on which the Republic rested."[101] Parliamentary cooperation under such circumstances, although not a mathematical impossibility, was a political impossibility. "The result from 1930 onward was a progressive strangulation of parliamentary life in Germany."[102]

The September elections left Brüning with even less parliamentary support than before, but he was able to maintain his position as chancellor through the support of President Hindenburg. In the following two years Brüning made repeated efforts to secure parliamentary approval for his economic proposals, occasionally succeeding with the tolerance, if not the active support, of the Social Democrats. In October, for example, the Reichstag passed a vote of confidence in Brüning, but a majority could not bring itself to support his legislative program. In both cases it was the support of the Social Democrats that was determinative: The party was prepared to support Brüning on a no-confidence motion, but it would not pass his legislative program. Between September 1930 and March 1931, therefore, Brüning was forced to rely on Article 48 at least eight times, and after March he relied on the Reich's emergency powers almost exclusively, using them to cut the salaries of government employees, to reduce rents, to regulate commodity prices and interest rates, to guarantee bank deposits, to ensure arbitration of industrial disputes, and to reform bankruptcy laws.[103] Brüning continued his appeals to the Reichstag for periodic votes of confidence, but there was little other legislative business.

Brüning also used his authority under Article 48 to issue five emergency decrees "to combat political excesses" in March, July, August, October, and December 1931 and again in April 1932. These decrees complemented, rather than replaced, the Protection of the Republic Act.[104] Many of them resembled the Special Powers Act then in force in Northern Ireland. In both cases the police required advance notice (forty-eight hours in Weimar) of public meetings, demonstrations, and parades, all of which the police could forbid if they posed a substantial threat to the public order. All political tracts, including posters, had first to be submitted to the police, and state police were authorized to forbid private paramilitary uniforms and badges. (Federal action was necessary on this last matter because some courts had declared state efforts to ban party uniforms in violation of Article 118.)[105] Other decrees provided that individuals suspected of illegal possession of arms could be arrested and detained, with an appeal to a judge permitted only on questions of fact. An individual who violated the law could be detained for a period of three months. As I mentioned earlier, acting in response to pressure from the right, Brüning tempered some of these decrees in January 1932, and almost all of them were later rescinded by Papen.

Brüning had relied almost exclusively upon President Hindenburg's authority under Article 48 to govern. In doing so, he had made the transition from parliamentary to presidential government nearly complete. In some ways it was also a limited success. Few doubted Brüning's devotion to constitutional government and President Hindenburg, although not a passionate supporter of Weimar, had respected his presidential oath to defend its constitution. The whole enterprise seemed at risk when Hindenburg's term expired in 1932. Convinced that no other candidate could defeat Hitler, Brüning persuaded the elderly Hindenburg to run for another term. (The extent of Brüning's fear was evidenced by his efforts to seek a constitutional amendment extending Hindenburg's term, which failed when he could not muster the votes necessary in the Reichstag.) Hindenburg won in a second election, and Brüning no doubt expected to continue to govern on the strength of presidential emergency powers. But shortly after the election, near the end of May, Hindenburg dismissed Brüning as chancellor and replaced him with Franz von Papen.

The Dismissal of Brüning and the Prussian Controversy

Why Hindenburg withdrew his support from Brüning is a matter of some dispute,[106] but the decision was a blow to the defense of constitutional government and ultimately led to Hitler's assumption of the chancellorship less than a year later, in January 1933. Strictly speaking, however, Hindenburg's actions did not appear to violate the letter of the Weimar Constitution, which clearly provided that the president had the authority to appoint and dismiss chancellors, so long as the chancellor had the confidence of the Reichstag. Brüning's ability to survive no-confidence motions in the Reichstag, even though he was unable to win parliamentary support for his economic proposals, suggested that he had the Reichstag's confidence, but this did not necessarily bar his dismissal. In contrast, Papen surely lacked the confidence of the Reichstag, but the Constitution could be interpreted in a way that permitted Hindenburg to see if Papen could win a parliamentary majority after appointment to the office.

Like Brüning, both Papen and his successor Kurt von Schleicher, chancellors to the two Junker cabinets, relied exclusively for their authority to govern on Hindenburg's use of Article 48. Parliamentary democracy had ceased to function in Weimar. The elections of July 1932, for example, resulted in a Reichstag that met only twice in that year. At its second meeting, in September, the Reichstag passed a vote of no confidence in Papen by the overwhelming vote of 513 to 32, whereupon Papen, following Brüning's precedent and confirming the wisdom of Caesar, ordered parliament's dissolution under Article 25.

As we saw, Papen, in an effort to appease the right, emasculated the emergency ordinances passed by his predecessor. Nevertheless, Papen exhibited little hesitancy in utilizing the republic's emergency powers for his own purposes. On July 20 (not quite a fortnight before the parliamentary elections) the cabinet issued two decrees under the first and second paragraphs of Article 48. The first suspended fundamental rights in Berlin and Brandenburg and removed executive and police powers from Minister-President Otto Braun (of the powerful state of Prussia) and other state officials to the federal minister of defense. (Another decree in August authorized the death penalty for anyone who, "enraged by partisan passion, kills a political opponent out of hatred or anger" and created special courts to hear political cases.)[107] The second decree went even further, transferring "all the powers of the Prussian government" to Papen, who had appointed himself minister for Prussia. Papen then replaced Prussia's delegation to the Reichsrat with representatives of his own choice. The implications of this move were even more startling than the removal of Braun, for if successful, it would have substantially furthered Papen's "reactionary plan to restore the previous balance of parliamentary forces in Germany. Clearly the groundwork was being laid for a definite move against the Weimar Constitution."[108]

In some respects, the factual predicate for the Reich's assumption of state authority—concern about widespread civil unrest in Prussia's urban centers—was plausible. Political violence in Prussia was regnant, as indeed it was throughout the whole of the Reich. In all other respects, however, Papen's action was a ruse. Its actual purpose was to replace Prussia's Social Democratic government, which, under the leadership of Braun and Police Minister Severing, had staunchly supported democratic ideals.[109] Unlike some of the other Länder, Prussia had taken a strong position against reactionary elements within its own territory; its efforts were substantially undermined when Papen, acting upon a request from Hitler, rescinded Brüning's emergency decrees concerning the National Socialist's Storm Troopers.[110] In fact, the move against Prussia, like the relaxation of the emergency decrees, was designed to bolster "the . . . [national] government's position on the right during the elections by showing that it was decisive and that it could act effectively against the left."[111]

Upon their dismissal, the Prussian ministers filed a complaint in the Staatsgerichtshof, which under Article 19 of the Constitution had jurisdiction over conflicts between the national and state governments. The Prussian controversy dominated German constitutional politics through October 1932, ending just before the November elections. The case raised issues of the highest theoretical order in German constitutional jurisprudence. Indeed, the contest ultimately turned upon the very constitutional definition of the republic and upon considerably different and competing visions of Weimar's constitutional order, as evidenced by the presence of Weimar's leading constitutional lawyers at the trial. Carl Schmitt, whose arguments in favor of presidential government had been realized by Brüning and Hindenburg, served as counsel for the Reich, along with Erwin Jacobi and Karl Bilfinger. Friedrich Giese, Arnold Brecht, and Gerhard Anschütz were among the counsel for Prussia. Prussia first requested a temporary injunction, which the court rejected on July 25. On the merits, Prussia argued that the July 20 decree was unconstitutional because it exceeded the president's authority. It argued additionally that Article 48 was an improper source for the decrees, and finally that the factual predicate for the Reich's action under both the first and second paragraphs, namely, that the Prussian government had failed to discharge its constitutional duties, was empirically false.

Also in contention was who bore responsibility for resolving such thorny questions of constitutional maintenance or, in the parlance of Weimar's constitutional theory, who could properly claim to be the "defender of the Constitution." Brecht's insistence that presidential actions taken under Article 48 were justiciable was a claim in favor of the judiciary as defender of the Weimar Constitution. Schmitt's arguments clearly amounted to a claim in favor of presidential authority. In his view, defense of the Constitution involved far more than the interpretation and application of legal norms. It was instead an elemental *political* act that the court was manifestly unsuited to discharge.

The Staatsgerichtshof rejected Prussia's invitation to define the extent of Article 48, finding instead that the factual conditional alleged to be the basis for federal intervention under paragraph two, although not under paragraph one, in fact existed. Consequently, the federal government was within its authority to replace the state government for the purpose of protecting the public safety, and the means it chose of doing so were beyond the legal competence of any court to judge. It held also, however, that Papen's temporary authority in Prussia could not encompass a permanent structural alteration of the state's role in the federal government. Papen's efforts to replace Prussia's delegation in the Reichsrat were therefore unconstitutional, for Article 17 guaranteed every Land its own independent government. (This last holding also indicated that the court had reasserted its own authority to review presidential acts for their constitutionality, even if its review was narrowly limited.)

The court's decision was a compromise, on the one hand upholding Papen's decision to appoint a federal minister in Prussia, but on the other hand clearly frustrating his efforts to remove permanently the state government and to alter its representation in the Reichsrat. A second case arose four months later, in February 1933, when Hitler, claiming that the court's earlier decision had caused "confusion to enter into the life of the state,"[112] issued an order under Article 48 removing all vestiges of authority from Prussian officials. Braun again challenged the Reich's intervention in the Staatsgerichtshof, but the suit expired when Braun fled Nazi Germany.

HITLER AND ARTICLE 48

After the collapse of the Beer Hall Putsch in 1923, Hitler and the National Socialists "officially annexed legality."[113] Hence, as Karl Dietrich Bracher observed, "The lasting significance of the abortive *Putsch* of 1923 is that it made Hitler realize that a direct assault on the existing order was doomed to failure."[114] Hitler's respect for democratic legality, however, implied no respect for the republic or the values expressed in its constitution. As we saw, he had testified in a court of law to his desire to obtain power legally and to his intent to use that power to destroy the republic.[115]

But when Hindenburg appointed him chancellor on January 30, 1933, Hitler swore immediately to the oath required of all chancellors to protect the republic and the constitution. In all critical respects, then, "the transition of power from the cabinet of von Schleicher to the cabinet of Hitler was in accordance with the actual requirements of the political situation and preserved . . . legal continuity."[116] The same could be said of the Third Reich, which was also effected with the appearance of constitutional legality. The details are of little more than historical signficance. In brief, a fire in the Reichstag building on the night of February 27, which Hitler blamed on the Communists, provided Hitler with the opportunity he sought to utilize Article 48. In the decree he issued on the next day, all fundamental rights were suspended throughout the Reich. Again, "All this involved no departure from the formal requirements of the Weimar Constitution."[117] Indeed, Ebert had used Article 48 in much the same way ten years earlier. What was novel was the absence in Hitler's decree of a requirement which had appeared in Ebert's decree, that a detained individual was entitled to a hearing before an ordinary court within twenty-four hours of his detention. As a consequence, executive authority under Hitler's decree was not subject to judicial review of any sort.

Hitler also used Article 48 to intimidate his opposition in the March elections, in which the National Socialists, coupled with the Nationalists, finally secured an absolute majority in the Reichstag. Again in accordance with constitutional precedent, Hitler then sought an enabling act in which the Reichstag would effectively yield its legislative competence to the executive. The Reichstag, over the objection of the Social Democrats, granted the authority (in the Law for the Relief of the People and the Reich) for a period of four years, but conditioned it with limitations designed to protect itself and the institutional structure of the republic. Paragraph two, sentence one provided: "The statutes decreed by the government may deviate from the constitution with the reservation that they should not affect the institutions of the Reichstag and of the Federal Council."[118] These qualifications did not, however, prevent Hitler from abolishing life tenure for civil servants or from compromising the independence of the judiciary. Nor did the act contain protections for individual liberties. In some ways the legislation was reminiscent of a similar act passed under Chancellor Stresemann—here again the formal bow to legality— but the earlier legislation had been limited to six months and required the presentation of all orders to the Reichstag. Hitler's assumption of power became complete when in July he issued a decree rendering all political parties except that of the National Socialists illegal. In a new act passed after the November elections, the Reichstag gave the cabinet the right to "determine new constitutional law."[119] The Reconstruction Act in January 1934 gave the cabinet unrestricted power and thereby rescinded the last of the limitations in the Enabling Act.[120] Through the constitutional devices of Article 48 and a series of enabling acts, Hitler dismantled German democracy. The republic's emergency powers, once so useful in defense of the republic, provided Hitler with the means he needed to end it.

ARTICLE 48 AND CONSTITUTIONAL SELF-DEFENSE FROM THREATS WITHIN: THE SCHMITT–KELSEN DEBATE OVER THE "DEFENDER OF THE CONSTITUTION"

The collapse of the Weimar Republic and the rise to power by the National Socialists, although intricately related, were two distinct events.[121] The collapse of Weimar represented the failure of parliamentary politics and its replacement with presidential government. Hitler's rise to power was facilitated by that collapse, but it was not the necessary result of Article 48 or the Weimar Constitution more generally. Instead, Hitler's utilization of Article 48 and the enabling acts were made possible because of how those mechanisms were interpreted in the context of German liberal legal thought, which provided no means of constitutional defense from internal threats to the republic's legitimacy other than insistence upon respect for procedure. Consequently, the republic could enact emergency legislation against political violence but was incapable of responding to threats couched in the language of legality.

The failure was not of resolve but of philosophy. German legal thought was dominated by a neo-Kantian legal positivism best represented by the work of Hans Kelsen, the most influential of the German legal positivists. Kelsen's juristic conception of the state and legal formalism sought to develop a "juristic norm" for every empirical reality. The study of jurisprudence thus became the study of norms (for this reason it was often termed a normativist jurisprudence, its positivism notwithstanding) and was emptied of, or "uncontaminated by politics, ethics, sociology, [and] history."[122] "Jurisprudence, then, was the comprehension of norms, not the explanation of a real world of politics."[123] It became "politically neutral."[124]

Kelsen's formalism rejected an inquiry into the "subjectivity" of value; its political neutrality was a result of that rejection and consequently provided the intellectual justification for the "equal chance" doctrine, which ultimately crippled Weimar. Put simply, the equal chance doctrine held that anyone willing to abide by the strict formality of electoral procedure should be permitted in the contest for political power, independent of his or her loyalty to the republic or intention to destroy it.

Carl Schmitt, Kelsen's major intellectual opponent and also a prominent professor of law, rejected Kelsen's positivism and the value neutrality that accompanied it.[125] (Indeed, Schmitt's consistently controversial definition of politics as the power to decide between who was friend and who was foe should be understood contextually as an explicit rejection of neo-Kantian legal positivism and legal formalism.) Early in Weimar's tenure, Schmitt concluded that the value-free perspective of German legal positivism, which separated the law from political and moral inquiry, was no longer capable of formulating questions about the legitimacy of the state and political power or a concept of justice that was relevant to the relationship of power and authority in the state.[126]

In contrast, Schmitt advocated a jurisprudence of the exception, which denied that formal *legal* norms could encompass all of *political* experience.[127] Not law but rather the state as an empirical sociological and historical fact had to be at the core of any politically relevant (and not rigidly normativist) jurisprudence. The very language Schmitt employed—of the exception, rather than crisis—indicates the nature and the depth of his objection to Kelsen's formalism. A state of exception could exist only in a constitutional order and implied a departure from the legal norm; crises, or emergencies, were a more general category which presupposed no particular type of preexisting political order or constitutional norm.[128] There could be no norm "which would be applicable to chaos,"[129] for every norm "presupposes its normal situation, and becomes meaningless when this normal situation ceases to exist."[130] (As an analytical construct, the political crisis was akin to the concept of the miracle in theology, which also implied a departure from the norm.)[131] "Crises," Schmitt therefore concluded, "are more interesting than the rule [because they] confirm not only the rule but also its existence, which derives only from the exception."[132] In *Political Theology*, Schmitt quoted Søren Kierkegaard:

> The exception explains the general and itself. And if one wants to study the general correctly, one only needs to look around for a true exception. It reveals everything more clearly than does the general. Endless talk about the general becomes boring; there are exceptions. If they cannot be explained, then the general also cannot be explained. The difficulty is usually not noticed because the general is not thought about with passion but with a comfortable superficiality. The exception, on the other hand, thinks the general with intense passion.[133]

Schmitt's insistence that jurisprudence account for politics also led him to reject efforts to constrain emergency powers through precise constitutional provisions. Crises were not susceptible of legal regulation because it "would be impossible to predict the nature of an *Ausnahmezustand*, or to prescribe beforehand in any precise detail the legally permissible procedures needed to deal with unique and varying situations."[134] The most guidance a constitution can provide "is to indicate who can act in such a case."[135] As a consequence, Schmitt was able to formulate questions Kelsen's formalism could not conceive, questions I addressed in some detail in the first chapter, such as who bears responsibility for determining when a crisis exists, how it should be resolved, and what limits, if any, constrain emergency powers. His ultimate project was, in the language of my first chapter, "to reconcile our understanding of constitutional government with the limits of human foresight."[136]

This abstract theoretical dispute was of considerable importance in the political life of the Weimar Republic. Kelsen's emphasis on what Loewenstein called "self-destroying legality" provided the foundation for the equal chance approach to electoral contests because it admitted no inquiry into the political agenda of the contestants. Schmitt's friend–foe conception of politics, on the other hand, might have provided the intellectual foundation necessary for a decision to outlaw political parties and organizations not committed to a democratic, constitutional political community, a decision not taken in Weimar but one that does influence the practice of constitutional maintenance in the Federal Republic of Germany, as we shall see in the next chapter.[137]

In Weimar, however, the presence of anticonstitutional parties could and did choke parliamentary procedure. The republic "foundered on its own concepts of constitutional legality," concepts whose definition was determined by Kelsen's formalism and German legal positivism.[138] Leading interpretations of various constitutional provisions (such as Articles 54, 68, and 76) and particular conceptions of German liberalism worked together to promote a theory of constitutional self-defense that would permit any qualified majority, whether republican or fascist, to effect fundamental constitutional amendments or to abrogate constitutional forms altogether.

Schmitt addressed this conception of liberalism in his work *Legalität und Legitimität*,[139] in which (in early 1932) he explicitly rejected the equal chance theory. Instead, Schmitt argued that in every constitutional order there are implicit principles—or constitutive principles, in the terminology of chapter 1—that cannot be compromised. One of these principles was of constitutional self-defense: No constitution could legitimately anticipate or authorize its own self-destruction; accordingly, "an equal chance should be accorded only to those parties committed to the preservation of the existing constitutional order."[140] As an example, Schmitt referred to Article 68, which provided simply that "Reich laws are enacted by the Reichstag." A purely formal interpretation of Article 68 led to a requirement that Reich laws must satisfy procedure only, so that "laws" enacted under Article 68 might "contradict the basic values" expressed in the text or in the legal order more generally.[141] Any party legally possessed of power, whatever its loyalty to the republic or the constitution, could then pass statutes designed to destroy the state from within. In a remarkably prescient passage, Schmitt warned that antirepublican parties could, under such an interpretation, declare their domestic competitors to be illegal,[142] a step Hitler took in July 1933.[143] "The majority is then suddenly no longer a party, it is the state itself."[144]

It is in this context that Schmitt's controversial distinction between the friend and foe should be understood: Schmitt wanted to elevate this most basic and existential of political decisions into a normative constitutional principle of self-defense. The making of such distinctions in domestic political practice, the essence of sovereignty, was entrusted to the state and in particular to the executive. The state alone was possessed of the authority to determine its enemy. It is again important to emphasize that for Schmitt the constitutional distinction between friend and foe was the ultimate expression of realpolitik and not simply a theoretical exercise. In practice, Schmitt strongly supported the state's enactment of emergency legislation (the Law for the Protection of the Republic), complaining only that it failed to go as far as was necessary.[145] Some twenty-five years later, in 1958, Schmitt wrote that his *Legalität und Legitimität* "was a desperate effort to save the presidial system . . . from a jurisprudence which refused" to adopt the friend–foe distinction.[146]

Schmitt's arguments were not completely consistent with Weimar's constitutional text, which, as we saw earlier, he thought was inconsistent internally. The first part of the Constitution, he argued, expressed the value neutrality characteristic of Kelsen's jurisprudence, whereas the second part, concerning fundamental liberties, spoke of inviolable principles. Schmitt tried to reconcile the inconsistency in the following manner. The two parts of the Weimar Constitution had to be interpreted as a structural whole. Respect for the second might ultimately preserve at least a part of the Constitution and its essential values. An interpretation favoring the first, however, risked the complete destruction of the constitutional order by antirepublican parties. Schmitt's general approach to constitutional interpretation, then, emphasized a structuralism that was highly sensitive to the demands of political necessity, in stark contrast to the "clause-bound" formalism of legal positivism.[147] There was no room for this kind of political sensitivity in Kelsen's jurisprudence. These differences led Schmitt to characterize his debate with Kelsen (and Richard Thoma) as equivalent to the distinction between formalism, of which Kelsen represented "the most radical attempt to carry out the pure formalism of law,"[148] and political experience, or between legality and legitimacy. In the imagery of Wagner's *Die Meistersinger*, Schmitt emphasized not slavish obedience to the rules of the guild, but rather Walther's authenticity of experience. "One weighs the values of rules by letting them occasionally suffer an exception," observed Meistersinger Sachs,[149] in words Schmitt might have written.

These basic jurisprudential differences also manifested themselves in the more particular dispute between Kelsen and Schmitt over who should properly be considered the "defender of the Weimar Constitution." Kelsen's formalism and insistence that there was a juristic norm for every occasion led him to support arguments that the ultimate defender of the Weimar Constitution was the Staatsgerichtshof, which alone could assess the constitutionality and the legality of political action through the mechanism of norm enforcement.[150] Kelsen's position was supported by Article 102 of the text, which guaranteed judicial independence, and by judicial interpretations (as in the *Revaluation* case), suggesting that the judiciary could refuse to apply laws in conflict with a constitutional provision. In Kelsen's formulation, the concept of crisis could be subsumed in the juristic conception of the state and hence could be subsumed under a juristic norm; the divination and application of norms was the business of courts, and "[n]o act remain[ed] outside the normative system of law."[151]

Kelsen's arguments constituted the core of Prussia's position before the Staatsgerichtshof in 1932. Arnold Brecht argued that only the court could act as defender of the Constitution, and that constitutional review was essentially a judicial function.[152] Indeed, in pressing the argument, Brecht had sought to turn Schmitt's arguments concerning the equal chance doctrine against him, noting that Prussia's efforts against the National Socialists were consistent with Schmitt's friend–foe thesis.

Schmitt's response, and his arguments on behalf of the Reich, demonstrate how closely connected his rejection of the equal chance doctrine was with his support for presidential government. In his reply to Brecht before the court, Schmitt argued that utilization of the friend–foe distinction could not rest with any political party or with a state government. The decision could be entrusted only to a neutral, "higher" party, represented in the office of the president acting under the joint authority of the first and second paragraphs of Article 48 (which must be read, Schmitt argued, as complementing one another).

Schmitt therefore rejected Kelsen's belief that the judiciary should be the defender of the Weimar Constitution, favoring instead the office of the Reichspresident as "defender of the Constitution." As Schmitt argued in the Staatsgerichtshof, its competence being limited to the application of norms, the judiciary was singularly ill-suited for action in cases where the contingency of the norm itself was exposed. Moreover, the institutional structure of courts worked against them as substantial defenders of the Constitution. "[A] judiciary, for as long as it remains a judiciary, arrives, politically speaking, always too late."[153] What was critical was the power to act to prevent or to resolve crises. Judging was by definition a post hoc activity, and in any event the nature and requirements of constitutional self-defense were political rather than legal. (Schmitt partly based this conclusion on the amending power in Article 76, which, he argued, would effectively refute judicial efforts to defend the Constitution.)[154] In an emergency, real power would rest as a matter of political and historical fact with the executive, which alone could act with the speed and determination required to resolve a crisis. In addition, the judiciary could only apply norms—an expertise and function of little use in the case of exception.[155] The Reichspresident, on the other hand, could play a "neutral third force," what Benjamin Constant referred to as the "pouvoir neutre," which could protect the constitutional order.[156]

In making his argument in favor of the Reichspresident as the authentic "defender of the Constitution," Schmitt relied heavily on his pathbreaking work and the first modern theory of dictatorship, *Die Diktatur*,[157] published in 1921, during the time when the fragile new republic's very existence depended upon the exercise of emergency powers. Article 48 and the structure of the Weimar Constitution, in particular the president's popular electoral base, which made him independent of the Reichstag,[158] supported Schmitt's arguments in favor of presidential emergency powers and provided the institutional support for presidential government, as Brüning's chancellorship demonstrated. Indeed, Schmitt became a powerful proponent of presidential government in Weimar and of Brüning's chancellorship.

Schmitt's Jurisprudence of the Exception and Article 48

The disagreement between Schmitt and Kelsen over who bore institutional responsibility for Weimar's constitutional self-defense heavily influenced Schmitt's approach to Article 48. Schmitt first presented his views on Article 48 at a conference in April 1924 at Jena and later in the same year at a conference on jurisprudence.[159] The predominant school of legal thought, most ably advanced by Hugo Preuss, Richard Grau, and perhaps the leading commentator on the Weimar Constitution, Gerhard Anschütz, argued that the express authorization of suspension of certain fundamental rights in Article 48 functioned as a set of limitations upon the emergency powers more generally; only those provisions clearly identified by Article 48 could be suspended under that article. It is important to set this opinion in the larger context of German legal positivism: Here was the juristic norm, carefully specifying which constitutional provisions might be set aside to cope with crises, and by implication leaving all others intact. Schmitt was the most vocal proponent of the minority position, that the president's dictatorial powers could not be limited in the way Article 48 seemed to require. In his view, the two sentences were contradictory if the second was read to limit the first. (Schmitt relied in part upon the history of Weimar's founding for his conclusion: Sentences one and two, he argued, had been written separately in different committees. Hence Schmitt's final reading of the two sentences: "For the purpose of reestablishing public security and order the Reichspresident can undertake measures and he may suspend certain basic rights.")[160]

The general grant in the first sentence provided that the president could take the measures necessary to restore public order. The second sentence specifically enumerated seven articles that could be suspended to protect the republic: Did those seven exhaust the means available to the Reichspresident? The argument that they did rested, thought Schmitt, upon the mistaken, positivist premise that an exception could be subsumed in an a priori norm and was capable of legal specification in advance. Again, Schmitt's concern was dictated by his fascination with and his recognition of the limits of the norm. Crises—the exception—were the antithesis of rule through norms and hence, to borrow the language of an earlier chapter, demonstrated the ultimate contingency of all constitutional norms. The president's efforts to secure public safety could not be limited in the way the majority's interpretation of Article 48 demanded, for those limits were premised upon the belief that crises could be subsumed within the norm and could therefore be the subject of strict legal regulation. German constitutional practice, if not constitutional theory, seemed to support Schmitt's arguments,[161] for the republic's emergency legislation routinely interfered with other constitutional guarantees.

Schmitt's reading of Article 48 was substantially broader than the majority interpretation. This did not mean, as some of his critics have mistakenly concluded, that Schmitt advocated a conception of presidential emergency powers without constitutional limitation. Schmitt's distinction between the commissarial and sovereign dictatorship, formulated in an earlier work, *Die Diktatur*, implied at least one set of limitations. The commissarial dictator, the historical precedent for which was the Roman dictatorship we examined in chapter 1, could exercise emergency powers only for the protection of the republic and only in the face of an actual threat. In addition, the commissarial dictator received his appointment from the sovereign power, and the terms of his power ceased at the conclusion of the emergency.[162]

Nevertheless, the commissarial dictator's powers were substantial and included the authority to suspend certain constitutional provisions or even the entire constitutional text, so long as the purpose was to restore the constitution once the emergency was resolved. In contrast, the use of such powers to abrogate a constitution or to institute a new political order was a sovereign dictatorship,[163] which could find no authorization in the Weimar Constitution. The differences between the two sorts of dictatorships were akin to the distinction between the "pouvoir constitué" and the "pouvoir constituant." In the former the purpose is to defend the constitution; in the latter the dictator "sees in the total existing order the situation which it seeks to do away with through its actions."[164] Hence "the final aim of a sovereign dictatorship is 'to create a condition whereby a constitution which it considers to be a true constitution will become possible.'"[165] Critical to this part of Schmitt's argument was his distinction between dictatorial power and sovereignty, the definition of which he borrowed from Jean Bodin. The sovereign power "is the absolute and *perpetual* power of a Republic which the Latins call *maiestatem*" and can be exercised only by a prince or the people, the constituent power.[166] In contrast, the dictatorial power is not and cannot be a constituent power, but is instead a limited power designed to secure a particular purpose. Schmitt advocated a president, in other words, who would be a "pouvior neutre."

Consequently, the president's use of Article 48 was always restricted by his oath to defend the republic. Nevertheless, in Schmitt's formulation, there could be no formal legal limitations on Weimar's commissarial power, for its essence was precisely the absence of such limits. The power was limited only by its purpose, the preservation of the constitutional order. "The justification of Dictatorship lies herein, that it ignores right, but only for the sake of its realization."[167]

In addition, Schmitt argued that Article 48 provided for "an untouchable minimum of organization," so that certain institutions, those of the president, the cabinet, and the Reichstag, could not be altered or abrogated even through the use of emergency powers. Schmitt derived these structural guarantees in the following manner. The second paragraph of Article 48 expressly authorized the president to take certain emergency measures; the Office of the President, however, was itself defined by other provisions in the Weimar Constitution. Article 50, moreover, provided that all orders required a countersignature by the Reichschancellor or a Reichsminister. Hence the government must be preserved, there being nothing in Article 50 that would exempt emergency decrees from the countersignature requirement and nothing in Article 48 that would create such an exception. The Reichstag's continuation was secured by Article 54 and by the terms of Article 48 itself. This position is reminiscent of the structural guarantees argument developed in chapter 1, in which I argued that our understanding of constitutional democracy must accept certain structural conditions as constitutive of constitutionalism, but Schmitt's requirement of an institutional minimum resulted for his reading of the text and not, as does mine, from a prior understanding of constitutionalism proper.

Schmitt and the Third Reich

In a popular article, "The Abuse of Legality,"[168] which appeared in several German newspapers just before the general elections in July 1932, Schmitt warned that "[w]hoever provides the National Socialists with the majority on July 31—even though he is not a National Socialist and regards this party only as the lesser evil—acts *foolishly*. He gives this . . . movement . . . the *possibility* to change the Constitution."[169] In light of this opinion, and given the power of his work on constitutional self-defense, Schmitt's subsequent apologetics for Hitler's assumption of power are truly shocking and have ensured him a place as the consummate "theorist for the Reich." Nevertheless, his moral failures and the compromises he made with the Third Reich should not obscure the utility of the constitutional jurisprudence he had developed earlier, a jurisprudence that might have forestalled Hitler's "legal revolution," and which would later find expression in the Basic Law's conception of a "fighting," or militant, democracy.[170]

There is no doubt that Schmitt quickly embraced the National Socialists when Hitler assumed the chancellorship. The frequent charge by his many critics, however, that Schmitt's scholarly work in support of a strong presidential government made the transition to the Third Reich possible, rests upon a very limited contextual understanding of Schmitt's scholarship and obscures the substantial and useful work Schmitt developed on the use of emergency powers to maintain and defend constitutional states. Unfortunately, the tendency to dismiss Schmitt began almost immediately after Hitler assumed power. Indeed, Carl Friedrich wrote favorably of Schmitt as late as 1930, calling *Die Diktatur* an "epoch-making work," only to conclude later in his own epic work, *Constitutional Government and Politics* (much of which was based upon Schmitt's work), that Schmitt's piece was little more than a "partisan tract."[171] More recently, there has been something of a renewed effort to look more dispassionately at Schmitt, but unlike the case of Weimar, which inspired Schmitt, his work remains largely unstudied among contemporary constitutional theorists.[172]

CONCLUSION

Few states have felt the necessity of constitutional self-defense on so frequent and troublesome a basis as did the Weimar Republic. Its efforts at constitutional maintenance opened the most basic sorts of questions about constitutional authority in times of emergency, including questions of constitutional interpretation, who bore responsibility for the nation's survival, and whether it was possible to defend the republic in a manner consistent with its constitutional ideals. Weimar's occasionally successful but ultimately futile efforts to cope with these problems have much to teach other constitutional democracies.

The history of those efforts is commonly thought to be a history only of failure. Indeed, the foremost study of the subject made Weimar's failures its central thesis.[173] The republic did fail, but its downfall should not continue to obscure its many early successes. Nor should the fault of its ruin be attributed solely to Article 48. The ultimate inadequacy in the republic was not with its constitution (though it surely had flaws) but rather with its constitutional jurisprudence, which finally proved incapable of an effective response to challenges dressed in the language of legality. The great enduring significance of Weimar, then, is that it demonstrates why a theory of constitutional maintenance (and not simply of constitutional crises) matters, and why such a theory cannot be one strictly of legal logic but must instead account for political practice.

5

Constitutional Reconstruction, Militant Democracy, and Antiterrorism Legislation in the Federal Republic of Germany

INTRODUCTION

In 1989 the Federal Republic of Germany celebrated the fortieth anniversary of its constitutional charter, the Basic Law. The remarkable success and continuing vitality of constitutional democracy in the Federal Republic—at four decades, it has proven Germany's most durable democratic state—has, of course, much to do with the country's economic renewal and the particular historical forces that conditioned its founding. Germany's second defeat in a world war, unlike its first, did not give rise to a stab in the back myth or to internal recriminations that prevented the new regime from consolidating legitimacy.

But economic success (or failure, as was finally the end in Weimar) and historical context do not ordain the result of constitutional reconstruction. As I argued in the Introduction and chapter 1, every effort at constitutional reconstruction is ultimately premised upon the conviction that the affairs of human societies can be deliberately and self-consciously designed to promote certain values, what the founders of the United States Constitution called the Blessings of Liberty, and to achieve specific ends, "free government" based on reflection and choice.[1] Economic station and historical legacy provide the context within which constitutional choices must be defined, debated, and implemented. Weimar failed, but it might have survived, not if history or the gods (whether of humanity or economics) had been kinder, but if different choices had been made at different times. That interplay—between context and choice, past and prospect—is the central focus of this chapter.

Weimar's influence trickles throughout the Federal Republic. The Basic Law reflects decisions to reject much of Weimar's constitutional structure and, more important, some of the central tenets of its constitutional philosophy. These choices include a decision to restrain the commitment to plebiscitary democracy with constitutional limitations and to temper the equal chance conception of electoral politics with a "militant democracy." The concept of a militant democracy—a democracy that seeks through unalterable structural arrangements and sempiternal constitutional norms to protect democracy

179

against its internal enemies—expresses most directly and succinctly how the Bonn Constitution differs from Weimar's. The concept finds expression not only in specific provisions in the republic's constitutional text but also in its internal security policy more generally and in the antiterrorism policies and legislation it enacted in the 1970s and 1980s.

CONSTITUTIONAL RECONSTRUCTION IN POSTWAR GERMANY

Following Germany's surrender in 1945, its territory was divided among the four occupying powers (the United States, Britain, France, and the Soviet Union), which together comprised the Allied Control Authority. The process of constitutional reconstruction in postwar Germany began, therefore, as soon as each of the powers assumed complete legal and political control over the territory, or zone, assigned to it. Many Länder boundaries were drawn afresh, leading to the combination of some states, reorganization of others, such as North Rhine–Westphalia, and the dissolution of Prussia. Earlier conferences in the preceding four years between the Allied powers had established general agreements on Germany's international borders, on refugee policies, on the issue of reparations, and on demilitarization. Moreover, in the Berlin Conference of 1945, the Allies had directed the Control Authority to "prepare for the eventual reconstruction of . . . political life on a democratic basis."[2]

As the Berlin statement makes clear, all four powers professed a desire for democracy, but the Soviet vision of democratic centralism differed greatly from the French preference for a confederation of German states or the American proposal for a federal state with enumerated powers. As a consequence of these and other differences, such as various and sometimes competing self-understandings on the part of each occupying power about how reconstruction would affect its own security, zonal administration differed greatly in the four regions, especially in matters directly concerning the reconstruction of German political life.[3] In a manner reminiscent of the principle of "cuius regio, eius religio," established in the Augsburg Peace of 1555, these differences first manifested themselves in the economic and political reconstruction of each of the four zones and finally in the partition between the Federal Republic and the German Democratic Republic in 1948.[4]

Hence the reconstruction of Germany began not in the Parliamentary Council that drafted the Basic Law in the summer of 1949 but rather in the individual zones established four years earlier by the four occupying powers. Constitutional democracy was first reestablished in towns and localities in the Western zones. In the American zone, for example, elections were held in several of the new Länder as early as 1946, and some of the Länder had written new state constitutions by 1947. Political parties organized themselves by zone and under the supervision of the relevant occupying power.

Reconstruction of the three Western zones as a single political entity formally began on July 1, 1948, when the military governors directed the minister-presidents of the Western Länder to call a constituent assembly to "draft a democratic constitution . . . of [a] federal type . . . which will protect the rights of the participating states, provide adequate central authority and contain guarantees of individual rights and freedoms."[5] On July 26 the minister-presidents accepted the task, with some qualifications, and arranged for an assembly to meet in the small city of Bonn on September 1. On that date they convened not a constituent assembly but a Parliamentary Council, which produced not a constitution but a Basic Law (Grundgesetz), which, given its transitional status, was submitted not to a plebiscite, as the Allies had first requested, but rather to the state legislatures. The terminology and means of ratification are important. The Länder's representatives were fearful of seeming to accept the permanent partition of Germany into two sovereign states and so adopted a "provisional" charter pending the complete constitutional reconstruction of all of Germany and until "[t]he entire German people are called upon to achieve in free self-determination the unity and freedom of Germany."[6]

In late July and early August the Länder elected sixty-five delegates to the council (an additional five nonvoting delegates were sent from West Berlin). Seven political parties sent delegates to the council. The largest single delegation was that of the Social Democratic party (SPD), which won twenty-seven seats, followed by the Christian Democrats (CDU) with nineteen, the Christian Socialists (CSU) with eight seats (together, the CDU–CSU delegation equaled the twenty-seven seats of the SPD), and the Free Democratic party (FDP), with five. Three other parties, including the Communist party, sent two delegates each. Included among the delegates were several noted constitutional scholars, such as Theodor Heuss, soon to be the first president of the new republic, and Professor Carlo Schmid of the SPD. A coalition of the CDU, CSU, and FDP elected Konrad Adenauer, of the CDU in the British zone and later the first chancellor of the new republic, president of the council.[7]

Debates in the Parliamentary Council

In some respects, the Parliamentary Council was a continuation of a process that had begun just over a year earlier. (Bavarian Minister-President Hans Ehard had sponsored a conference in Munich in May 1947, with representatives from each of the four zones.) And before the council actually convened in Bonn, the ministers created a working committee comprised of constitutional experts and representatives from the Länder. Meeting at Herrenchiemsee on an island in the Chiemsee from August 10 to 23, the committee ultimately produced a draft document of nearly 150 separate articles.[8] Upon its completion, the Herrenchiemsee draft was presented to the council for its consideration, but there were other proposals circulating about the council as well, including drafts prepared by the SPD and the Communist party.

The council formally convened on September 1, 1948. Shortly thereafter it organized itself into working committees, each with its own area of inquiry. Committee deliberations continued through September and October, and some of the individual committees held hearings on their reports as early as November. When the main committee, chaired by Carlo Schmid, finished its second reading of the complete draft in December, it established a "committee of five," whose membership consisted of two representatives each from the CDU–CSU and the SPD and one from the FDP. The committee of five was charged with responsibility for negotiating most of the major points of conflict—generally concerning the role of the Bundesrat (the upper house of Parliament) and the precise parameters of a proposed system of financial federalism—between the various subcommittees and political parties. This committee completed its first set of revisions in the first few days in February and returned it to the main committee, which completed the third reading of the draft the second week of February 1949.

On March 2, the military governors returned the draft to the council with a list of objections, of which the most important concerned the division of fiscal powers between the Federation and the Länder. The Allied objections found favor with the CDU–CSU and opposition from the SPD. Stalemate ensued until April 25, when the military governors and representatives from the council finally agreed upon a new set of compromises. The text was then returned to the council for final readings, was accepted by a vote in council of fifty-three to twelve, and was approved by the military governors on May 12. The Basic Law was formally promulgated by the council on May 23, 1949.[9]

The Constitutional Order of the Basic Law
Institutional Structure

The Basic Law was produced by the Parliamentary Council in just over eight months, at the behest and under the supervision of outside powers. Outside pressures were an integral part of the process of constitutional reconstruction, but Bonn's framers labored also in the aftermath of Weimar's ruin. Accordingly, the lessons of Weimar, whether real or imagined, could not but help to influence the constitutional order envisioned by the Basic Law. One delegate captured this sense of historical burden when he argued that "[a] democracy which allows a tyranny to emerge from its midst with so little resistance, does not deserve being recreated for a second time."[10] But not all of Bonn's framers rejected Weimar. Former Prussian Minister-President Otto Braun, forced to leave Weimar with the advent of Hitler, wanted to retain much of the Weimar Constitution, and Theodor Heuss argued in front of the Parliamentary Council:

> The Weimar constitutional order was not such a bad one. It has become fashionable today—there have been echoes of it here in this assembly—to speak disparagingly of the Weimar constitution. . . . It is unquestionable that the Weimar constitution fell a victim to a stupendous error: overconfidence in the "fairness" of the German people.[11]

The Parliamentary Council was thus characterized by "a strangely ambivalent relationship"[12] to Weimar. The document it produced reflects that ambivalence. Retained in general form were Weimar's commitment to parliamentary democracy, federalism, and separation of powers. Rejected were the requirements of pure proportional representation, thought by many of Bonn's framers to have encouraged factionalism in Weimar; Weimar's system of strong presidential leadership, abused by Papen, Hitler, and Hindenburg; and the equal chance conception of electoral democracy, manipulated by the enemies of democracy in much the way Goebbels had warned.[13] In their place were substituted limited plebiscitary democracy, limitations upon executive and especially presidential power, judicial review, and the concept of militant democracy.

The Legislature

In general terms, the Basic Law provides for a parliamentary democracy, as did the Weimar Constitution, but with little of the plebiscitary or presidential features that characterized its forerunner. The legislative branch of the federal government is the institutional centerpiece of the republic's parliamentary democracy. Unlike the Reichstag, the Bundestag can insist upon the accountability of the executive, and the chancellor's authority to dissolve the parliament is strictly limited. The institutional stability of the legislature is therefore far greater than was true in Weimar, where the president had constitutional authority to dismiss parliament in a great number of instances. The Bundestag, unlike the Reichstag, cannot be dissolved except in two limited cases, described later. The upper house cannot be dissolved in any circumstances.

Parliament is composed of two houses. The lower house, or Bundestag, is the locus of legislative authority and governmental responsibility in the Federal Republic. Its 496 members are elected every four years, and the Bundestag is the only branch of the national government directly chosen by the electorate. Elections are secret, direct, and governed by an organic election law that combines proportional representation with some of the principles of direct election. There are 248 seats elected in single-member districts, and the remaining 248 are elected from party lists on the basis of proportional representation. To guard against the fragmentation of parties that tormented Weimar, the election law also provides that a political party must win at least 5 percent of the vote, or three seats, to gain representation in parliament. (The 5 percent clause was a source of much controversy in the Parliamentary Council. Some delegates blamed the electoral system for the collapse of parliamentary government in Weimar. Others argued that any political party that represents a segment of the population has a right of coparticipation.)

Essentially, the Bundestag has two functions. First, Article 77 provides that the Bundestag passes laws. Second, the Bundestag is directly involved in forming the executive and the judiciary. Article 54, for example, gives it a partial role in the election of the president; Articles 63 and 67 outline its role in the selection and dismissal of the chancellor; and Article 94 provides that the Bundestag elects half of the membership of the Federal Constitutional Court, while the second half is chosen by the Bundesrat. Constitutional amendments require a two-thirds majority of both houses.

As the debates in the Parliamentary Council make clear, West Germany is a federal state with an elaborate structure of partitioned administrative and financial powers. The Basic Law lists in great detail those powers assigned exclusively either to the national or to the ten state governments, as well as those possessed concurrently. The influence of the Länder is institutionally reflected in the Bundesrat, the upper chamber of parliament. Members of the Bundesrat are indirectly chosen; seats are apportioned among the Länder (from three to five each) on the basis of population. (The influence of the Länder is further promoted by a requirement that state delegations vote as a block.) The Bundesrat is an exceptionally strong upper chamber in most respects. Under Article 76 the Bundesrat may, in certain cases, initiate legislation. Other forms of legislation require the Bundesrat's approval, either by giving the Bundesrat an absolute or a suspensive veto. Interhouse cooperation is promoted by the Mediation Committee, composed of members from both houses.

The Executive

The president of the Federal Republic possesses very little of the power of the Weimar presidency. Weimar's president was chosen by direct election for a period of seven years. Article 54 of the Basic Law provides, in contrast, that the president of the republic is elected to a five-year term by the Federal Assembly, an electoral college of some thousand delegates whose only important purpose is to elect the president. Weimar's president also possessed authority to appoint the chancellor and, by virtue of Article 48, expansive emergency powers. The Federal Republic's president's powers are largely symbolic, confined to cere-monial functions of state and to representing the republic in the arena of international law (in this respect, but only in this respect, the president ap-proaches the "pouvoir neutre" that Schmitt meant to find in the Weimar presidency).[14] Indeed, the president may not give public speeches or issue formal publications without the approval of the chancellor, who holds the greater part of executive power. Articles 63 and 68 do, however, give the president the power to dissolve the parliament when a chancellor loses a vote of confidence and thereafter (within twenty-one days) requests the president to dissolve the Bundestag.

The chancellor is elected not by the public but by the Bundestag. Normally, the chancellor is nominated by the president after legislative elections. A success-ful nominee must then win at least half the votes in the Bundestag. In what is the most important structural innovation in the Basic Law, Article 67 attempts to impart greater stability to the executive and the cabinet than was present in Weimar by requiring that no chancellor can be voted out of office in the absence of a "constructive vote of no confidence." The constructive vote of no confidence provides that no chancellor may be removed unless a majority can name a successor. (This innovation originated in Württemberg-Baden, which incorpo-rated it in its state constitution at the suggestion of Carl Friedrich.)[15]

The chancellor's constitutional powers are equal to the security and pri-macy of his position: As the chief executive officer, the chancellor is solely responsible for the selection and removal of cabinet ministers. Consequently, cabinet ministers are accountable to the chancellor, not to the president or the legislature, as was the practice in Weimar. The chancellor's public policy and legislative proposals typically require the approval of either the Bundestag or both the Bundestag and the Bundesrat, but he also possesses a power of veto.

The Judiciary

Article 108 of the Weimar Constitution entrusted certain limited powers of constitutional review to the Staatsgerichtshof, Weimar's highest court, but there was no explicit grant of judicial review, and constitutional scholars were divided over whether such a power could be fairly inferred from the text. There is no doubt, however, that certain of the republic's courts are constitutionally possessed of the power of constitutional and judicial review. (Constitutional review concerns disputes between the various branches and agencies and government; judicial review, in German law, pertains to a court's authority to declare a legislative act unconstitutional.)[16] Under Article 93, the Federal Constitutional Court has jurisdiction over all constitutional disputes between the federation and Länder and between the various branches of the national government (the power of constitutional review). The Constitutional Court may also entertain constitutional complaints filed directly by citizens (judicial review). Article 93(1) (4a) gives it jurisdiction to hear constitutional complaints filed by a citizen claiming that a public official has deprived him or her of rights guaranteed by the Basic Law. Unlike the U.S. Supreme Court, the Constitutional Court has exclusive jurisdiction over constitutional disputes.[17]

In addition to the Constitutional Court, there are ordinary courts, as there were in Weimar, whose jurisdiction is divided functionally. Unlike the system of judicial federalism that exists in the United States, however, there are no separate federal courts of the first instance in the Federal Republic. Instead, courts in the Länder function as trial courts and as first-level appellate courts for both federal and state law. Federal courts are courts of final appeal. The highest ordinary court is the Federal Supreme Court of Justice. There are also separate administrative, fiscal, social, and labor courts, and most of the Länder have established their own constitutional courts.

The independence of the judiciary is further guaranteed by Articles 101 and 115g of the Basic Law. The former article, like a similar provision in the Weimar Constitution, specifically prohibits extraordinary courts. The latter and more important provision states that the Federal Constitutional Court may not be suspended during an emergency. Like those provisions concerning dissolution of the Bundestag, Article 115g seeks to ensure the institutional integrity of the judiciary during times of crisis and is thus related to the constitutive principle of separated power included in the free democratic basic order.

The Constitutional Philosophy of the Basic Law

The Basic Law is an extraordinary and unique document. It has none of the formal pretensions of perpetuity that attach to most constitutional charters.

Unlike the organic laws of most societies, this is a text that *does* anticipate its own end: The Basic Law explicitly acknowledges its transitional character and in so doing fails to make a claim of perpetuity for itself. But in other places, such as Articles 1, 20, and 79(3), and in other ways, such as the concepts of the free democratic basic order and militant democracy, the Basic Law *does* make claims to perpetuity, claims not about the text itself but about certain of the principles—such as the democratic, federal character of the state and respect for human dignity—that infuse the text and its understanding of constitutional democracy. In the words of the Federal Constitutional Court, there are "constitutional principles that are so fundamental . . . that they also bind the framers of the constitution."[18]

This notion of perpetuity is related to the most important difference between the Weimar Constitution and the Basic Law, concerning the legal status of the two texts. Unlike the Weimar Constitution, the Bonn Constitution *can* claim the status of superior law. This change can be seen most easily in the process of amendment provided for in each text. Article 76 of the Weimar Constitution permitted amendment through ordinary legislation passed by a majority of the Reichstag. As a consequence, the Weimar Constitution could not be said to be superior in any legal or political sense to ordinary law. No part of the constitutional text, whether concerning civil liberties or the institutional structure of state authority, was shielded from the temporary passions of a single legislative majority, or from democracy itself, and both were finally sacrificed to democracy. This easy process of amendment was consistent with the legal positivism that dominated German legal theory.

Weimar's twin commitments to legal positivism and mass democracy were substantially tempered by the framers of the Federal Republic. Again, this rejection is most obvious in the arena of constitutional amendment. Amendments to the Grundgesetz require a two-thirds majority of both houses of parliament, thus confirming its superior legal status. But the Basic Law goes even further by providing that there are parts of the Basic Law beyond the power even of qualified or super-majorities to amend. Article 79 states that Articles 1 and 20 are immune from the process of constitutional amendment and are thus perpetual and constitutive (in both a definitional and an ideal sense, as discussed in chapter 1) features of German constitutional politics. Article 1 raises to such superior standing the normative principle of respect for human dignity:

> The dignity of man shall be inviolable. To respect and protect it shall be the duty of all state authority.
>
> The German people therefore acknowledge inviolable and inalienable human rights as the basis of every community, of peace and justice in the world.
>
> The following basic rights shall bind the legislature, the executive and the judiciary as directly enforceable law.

It is "appropriately . . . the cornerstone of the Basic Law."[19] Article 20 identifies those structural arrangements so central to constitutional democracy that they too are immune from constitutional amendment. In full, Article 20 provides:

1. The Federal Republic of Germany is a democratic and social federal state.
2. All state authority emanates from the people. It shall be exercised by the people by means of elections and voting and by specific legislative, executive, and judicial organs.
3. Legislation shall be subject to the constitutional order; the executive and the judiciary shall be bound by law and justice.
4. All Germans shall have the right to resist any person or persons seeking to abolish that constitutional order, should no other remedy be possible.

Article 79, the "perpetuity" clause, further provides that amendments "affecting the division of the Federation into Länder, the participation on principle of the Länder in legislation, or the basic principles laid down in Articles 1 and 20, shall be inadmissible."

Together, Articles 1, 20, and 79 designate the normative and structural features of German constitutional democracy that are constitutive and which must exist in perpetuity. These include a requirement that all state policies must conform to the overarching commitment to human dignity and a structural requirement that state power must be exercised through legislative, executive, and judicial organs, thereby elevating the separation of powers to constitutive status. Their constitutive authority derives not from the text but from the commitment to constitutionalism proper.[20] Consequently, they are superior to the text, as is indicated by their immunity from the process of amendment. In this sense, these basic principles are both definitional characteristics and ideal norms to which the state and all state policies must conform. Their definitional and ideal status is underscored and supplemented, as we shall see, by more specific provisions that guarantee their continued status and functioning even in times of emergency. (These core provisions do not, however, include the concept of militant democracy itself.)

The understanding of constitutionalism expressed in the Basic Law therefore represents conscious decisions made in the Parliamentary Council to reject much of the Weimar Constitution and its constitutional philosophy. The lessons drawn from the failures of Weimar included fears of mass democracy, strong presidential power, and legal positivism, all of which contributed to Weimar's collapse. When expressed in the Basic Law, these fears amounted to the insistence upon federalism, the rule of law, limited democracy, and a strong catalogue of individual liberties. Also included were the concepts of the Rechtsstaat, or the rule of law state, of the Parteienstaat, or the political party state, and of the streitbare Demokratie, or militant democracy.

The Rechtsstaat, Individual Liberties, and the Rejection of Legal Positivism

One of the central features of the Federal Republic's constitutional democracy is the concept of the Rechtsstaat (or state based on the rule of law). The Rechtsstaat has a long history in German jurisprudence, where it is traditionally identified with legal positivism and the superior legal, political, and moral standing of the state.[21] The Basic Law retains the concept, but now, as Donald Kommers notes, it "is linked primarily to those political institutions and procedures designed to ground positive law in majority rule limited only by the higher law of the Constitution."[22]

The first provision in the text underscores this change by providing that "[t]he dignity of man shall be inviolable. To respect and to protect it shall be the duty of all state authority." Article 1 also indicates that the rights contained in Articles 1 through 18 are "inalienable and inviolable," thus indicating that the basis for such rights rests not in the Basic Law proper, instead resting in preconstitutional values and principles that the Basic Law recognizes and acknowledges but does not itself create.[23] The Federal Constitutional Court has repeatedly asserted that the concept of human dignity is the core value in the Basic Law, and Article 79 entrenches it by providing that Article 1 may not be amended. Article 19 reinforces the anterior status of constitutional liberties by indicating that the "essential content" of any basic right may not be substantially affected by the state.

The effect of Articles 1, 19, 20, and 79 is to provide a preconstitutional foundation for certain individual liberties and to limit the authority of democratic majorities, acting even through constitutional forms, to abridge those liberties, especially that of human dignity. As a constitutional norm, human dignity admits of imprecision; it is not self-implementing. But whatever the term's inherent imprecision, the Federal Constitutional Court has been willing to use the concept of human dignity as an independent ground upon which state action may be declared unconstitutional.[24] In addition, the norm implies an affirmative obligation on the part of the state not only to respect human dignity but also to promote the conditions in which human dignity can be realized.

The Basic Law thus implements Arnold Brecht's postwar recommendation that the new constitution should "contain certain sancrosanct principles and standards that could not be abolished or suspended by emergency decrees or by any parliamentary or plebiscitarian majorities, either directly or indirectly. . . . These should include fundamental principles regarding respect for the dignity of man."[25] This is a forceful rejection of the legal positivism that grounded individual liberties in Weimar, where such rights found their source in the authority of the state. In the Basic Law, such rights are anterior to the state. As Kommers observed, "Contrary to the prevailing legal positivism of the Weimar period, fundamental rights are not the creations of law. Rather, they are natural rights grounded in the concept of 'human dignity.'"[26]

The significance of this change is reflected in the structure of the Basic Law. Unlike the Weimar Constitution, the Basic Law begins, rather than ends, with a comprehensive list of individual liberties. Carlo Schmid best expressed the significance of this structural change in the Parliamentary Council: "The basic rights must govern the Basic Law; they must not be a mere appendix, like the Weimar catalogue was an appendix of the Constitution."[27]

The first twenty articles of the Basic Law contain an elaborate and comprehensive list of individual liberties, including human dignity, freedom of speech and association, freedom of religion and conscience, equal protection, due process, freedom of movement and occupation, and privacy of mail and communications. In general, then, the Basic Law includes the traditional liberties, such as freedom of speech and religion, and what are sometimes called social rights, such as the right to choose an occupation, rights relating to trade unions and collective bargaining, and the right to refuse military conscription in certain cases. In addition, there are protections against capital punishment, provisions for habeas corpus, and protections against double jeopardy and ex post facto laws.

The liberties recognized in the Basic Law are typically accompanied by corresponding political obligations, obligations that often recall the concept of militant democracy. The right to free development of personality, for example, is guaranteed only so long as the individual "does not violate the rights of others or offend against the constitutional order or the moral code."[28] The freedom of speech protected in Article 5 may be limited by "the provisions of the general laws," and the freedom to teach, also guaranteed in Article 5, "does not absolve loyalty to the Constitution." Moreover, all of these rights are subject to forfeiture under Article 18 if an individual uses them to injure the "free democratic basic order."

Militant Democracy

Constitutional thought in Weimar was dominated by the concept of neutrality and the equal chance conception of electoral politics. The jurisprudence that supported this concept of political struggle was unable, in Carl Schmitt's words, to distinguish friend from foe. Schmitt wanted to elevate the friend–foe distinction to a constitutive constitutional principle and to entrust the decision, as a matter of constitutional politics and not a rule of law, to the president. Notwithstanding Schmitt's personal ruin and the controversy surrounding his conversion to fascism, Schmitt's advocacy of the friend–foe distinction finally won favor in the Basic Law in the concept of militant democracy, a phrase first coined by Karl Loewenstein and popularized by Thomas Mann.[29]

The concept of militant democracy, of a democratic state, unlike Weimar, that makes the maintenance of democracy itself (understood in both normative and structural terms) a constitutional norm, courses throughout the Basic Law. Carlo Schmid captured the essence of the doctrine:

[I]t is not part of the concept of democracy that it creates the preconditions of its own destruction. I would even like to go further. I would like to say: democracy is more than a product of utilitarian considerations only in those places where the courage exists to believe in it as something indispensable for the dignity of man. If this courage exists, we should also have the courage to be intolerant towards those who wish to use a democratic system in order to kill it off.[30]

Schmid's rejection of the utilitarian defense of democracy illustrates the superior moral and legal status that constitutional democracy commands in the Basic Law.

In fact, then, although not in name, the Basic Law incorporates one of the cardinal features of Schmitt's theory of constitutional self-defense, that a constitutional democracy must have the right to defend the constitutional order against internal enemies. The Basic Law effectuates this policy by providing that certain structural and normative elements of the state, defined in Articles 1 and 20—what the text and the Federal Constitutional Court call the "free democratic basic order"—cannot be altered. These elements exist beyond the amendatory power. They are, as I have argued, constitutive and perpetual features of West German constitutional democracy. The "free democratic basic order" is not, in other words, coextensive with the constitution but rather includes only the highest values and most important structural features of the constitution.

The "free democratic basic order" has been defined by the Federal Constitutional Court:

> as an order which excludes any form of tyranny or arbitrariness and represents a governmental system under a rule of law, based upon self-determination of the people as expressed by the will of the existing majority and upon freedom and equality. The fundamental principles of this order include at least: respect for the human rights given concrete form in the Basic Law, in particular for the right of a person to life and free development; popular sovereignty; separation of powers; responsibility of government; lawfulness of administration; independence of the judiciary; the multi-party principle; and equality of opportunities for all political parties.[31]

The "preconstitutional" nature of those requirements was acknowledged by the Federal Constitutional Court in its first decision. In the *SouthWest* case (1951), the court concluded that "[t]here are constitutional principles that are so fundamental . . . that they also bind the framers of the constitution."[32] The court's opinion clearly suggests the existence of an order, or hierarchy, of constitutional values, in which subordinate provisions must give way when in conflict with superordinate provisons. Given such a hierarchy, it is quite possible to imagine that a specific constitutional provision or constitutional amendment, notwithstanding its procedural propriety, could still be "unconstitutional," "since the legislator may have inadvertently inserted protections of less fundamental values that conflict with those that are more fundamental."[33] Such an argument closely resembles President Lincoln's claim in his First Inaugural Address about the priority of the Union to the constitutional text or James Madison's arguments in Federalist 40 about the relationship of the 1787 Constitution to the Articles of Confederation.[34]

This definition and understanding of the free democratic basic order closely resembles both the content of, and the justification for, the constitutive principles identified in chapter 1. Like those principles—which include respect for human dignity, separation of powers, and government based on articulated reason[35]—the concept of the free democratic order posits the attainment of certain abstract ends, such as human dignity and government based on law rather than tyranny or arbitrariness, as constitutive of constitutional democracy. It further postulates, as did my discussion in chapter 1, that certain structural arrangements, such as separation of powers and judicial independence, are necessary means to the achievement of those ends.

As the foregoing discussion intimates, the Basic Law assigns to the Federal Constitutional Court, not to the executive, the role of guardian of the constitution. Thus the Basic Law *does* acknowledge the legitimacy of constitutional self-defense against the enemies of democracy, as Schmitt counseled, but the Parliamentary Council rejected Schmitt's insistence that the president alone should be entrusted with guardianship of the constitution; the abuses of presidential power in Weimar were reason enough for their decision. The Basic Law assigns guardianship of the constitution to the Federal Constitutional Court, which alone has the constitutional authority to enforce the protections of militant democracy.[36] Article 18, for example, provides that certain basic rights may be forfeited if they are misused to undermine the democratic order. The rights forfeited under Article 18, however, can be lost only through a decision of the Federal Constitutional Court. And only the Constitutional Court can declare a political party unconstitutional under Article 21, which provides that "parties which, by reason of their aims or the behavior of their adherents, seek to impair or abolish the free democratic basic order" may be banned.* Failing even these protections, Article 20 seeks the same purpose by providing that citizens have the right to resist attacks on the constitutional order, "should no other remedy be possible."

These provisions, together with Article 20's definition of the state as a "democratic and social welfare state," Article 115g's protection of the Federal Constitutional Court in times of emergency, and those provisions that protect against the dissolution of the Bundestag, attempt to guarantee the institutional integrity of the system of separated powers and its structural expression in the Basic Law.

Constitutional Democracy and the Political Party State

The demands of militant democracy also infuse the Basic Law's concept of the "political party state" (Parteienstaat). The political party state anticipates a major role for (legitimate) political parties in forming and expressing the will of the people through elections to the Bundestag. Article 38 provides that federal elections shall be secret, direct, open, equal, and free. All other requirements are to be prescribed by law. The statutory law now in place rejects the pure system of proportional representation adopted in Weimar.[37] Instead, every voter has two votes. Half of the membership of the Bundestag is elected by a simple majority in single-member constituencies. The second half is elected from candidate lists submitted by parties in the Länder. To gain representation in this second system, however, a party must win at least three districts or poll at least 5 percent of the total (second) vote.

---

*Article 9(2) further states: "Associations, the purposes or activities of which conflict with criminal laws or which are directed against the constitutional order or the concept of international understanding, are prohibited."

The concept of the political party state represents a significant departure from party politics in Weimar. The fragmentation of parliamentary politics and the rise of splinter parties, facilitated (but not caused) by the system of proportional representation, contributed substantially to governmental instability in Weimar. Weimar's Constitution was largely silent on the role of political parties. In contrast, Article 21 of the Basic Law specifically provides that "political parties shall participate in the forming of the political will of the people," and party competition has been found by the Constitutional Court to be a constitutive feature of the free democratic basic order.[38] The multiparty basis of the state is further promoted by a system of state financing of the major political parties.

Article 21 also provides that political parties "which, by reason of their aims or the behavior of their adherents, seek to impair or abolish the free democratic basic order or to endanger the existence of the Federal Republic of Germany, shall be unconstitutional." Consequently, Article 21 integrates the concepts of the political party state and militant democracy. In so doing, it sets limitations upon the behavior of political parties by providing that parties antithetical to the free democratic order may be declared unconstitutional by the Federal Constitutional Court. Moreover, it makes demands upon their internal organization, which must also conform to democratic principles. In addition, Article 20 places indirect limits upon the programs of parties by requiring that all legislation must "conform" to the existing order, and Article 79 forbids outright any effort to alter or amend or abolish certain constitutional provisions, such as the division of the state into Länder (federalism in perpetuity), or the principle of human dignity, or Article 20 itself. Parties are also constitutionally required to disclose their sources of funding.

The Federal Constitutional Court has declared two parties unconstitutional. In *The Socialist Reich Party Case* (1952),[39] the court was asked by the government to declare the Socialist Reich party, a neo-Nazi organization, unconstitutional under Article 21. The party was founded three years earlier, and although it could not be considered a major political presence, it had won two seats in the parliament. In concluding that the Socialist Reich party promoted a political program antithetical to the principles of a free democratic order, the court reviewed the party's policy pronouncements, the statements of its individual leaders, and the internal organization of the party itself, noting that its hierarchical structure suggested no commitment to democratic principles. As a consequence of the ruling, the party's representatives in the state and federal legislatures were required to forfeit their seats.

The government filed a similar petition concerning the German Communist party (KPD) in 1951.[40] In finally reaching its conclusion to ban the party in 1956, the court repeatedly stressed the incompatibility of "the dictatorship of the proletariat" with liberal democracy as envisioned in the Basic Law. Insofar as "[t]he conduct of the KPD as a political party in the Federal Republic of Germany corresponds to the teachings of Marxism-Leninism . . . it rejects principles and institutions whose validity and existence are a prerequisite for the functioning of a liberal democratic order."[41] This decision was *not* accompanied by a separate conclusion by the court that the party's activities actually constituted an immediate threat to the security of the state, as would be necessary, for example, in the United States. The court instead observed that "[n]o action in the sense of the criminal code is needed for a party to be unconstitutional."[42] The court consequently ordered the dissolution of the party and its delegates removed from their elected positions.

In both cases, therefore, the court found the parties hostile to the free democratic order, noting that the "special importance of parties in a democratic state does not justify their elimination . . . if by legal means, they wish to change individual provisions or even entire constitutional institutions, but only if they seek to topple the supreme fundamental values of the free democratic order."[43] Likewise, the court concluded that the fundamental objective "of every political party in a free democratic state" must be "to recognize publicly, by the form and manner of its political activities, the paramount and binding values of the constitution."[44]

The court's decisions, together with Article 21, amount to a rejection of the equal chance conception of electoral politics in favor of militant democracy. (The equal chance doctrine does, however, continue to serve as a regulatory principle concerning internal competition between those parties that are permitted to contest for power.) They may also have provided the basis for additional state activity in the arena of internal security. For example, Kommers argues that following the *Communist Party* decision, preliminary inquisitions by prosecutors rose from a figure of 7,975 in 1956 to 12,600 in 1957 and to over 13,000 another year later.[45] Notwithstanding this activity, in both cases the parties eventually reappeared. After the dissolution of the Socialist Reich party, a successor organization called the German National Democratic party (NPD) was formed in 1964.[46] The Communist party also reorganized (it is now the DKP) and held a national congress in 1968. Both successor parties have been careful to moderate their rhetoric.

Partly as a result of Article 21, Article 67, and the election law, party politics in the Federal Republic have been considerably more stable than in Weimar. In the first elections to the Bundestag in 1949, eleven parties won representation. The number decreased systematically in subsequent elections, so that by 1961 only three parties—the CDU–CSU, the SPD, and the FDP—had seats in the Bundestag.[47] Nevertheless, most governments have required a coalition between two of the three major parties, the CDU–CSU, the SPD, and the FDP.

THE BASIC LAW AND EMERGENCY POWERS

The original text of the Basic Law contained very few emergency powers. Instead, such powers were "reserved" to the Allied High Commission by the terms of an Occupation Statute enacted at the same time the Basic Law was ratified. Subjects reserved included disarmament, foreign affairs, control over the Ruhr, reparations, and foreign claims against Germany. Perhaps most important, the statute authorized the stationing of Allied troops in Germany and provided for abrogation of the new government's actions if, in the opinion of the Allied powers, to do so was "essential to security or to preserve democratic government in Germany."[48] All other legislative, executive, and judicial powers were returned to the new government, subject to the foregoing qualifications and other reserved powers, "necessary to ensure the fulfillment of the basic purposes of the occupation,"[49] including approval of amendments to the Basic Law and state constitutions.

The occupation regime ended formally in 1955, following the Paris Accord of 1954. At the Paris meeting, full sovereignty was transferred from the Allies to the Federal Republic, excepting still reserved powers over the protection of armed forces stationed in the Federal Republic, and "including the ability to deal with a serious disturbance of public security and order."[50] These final reservations were withdrawn following the passage of extensive emergency legislation in 1968, which we shall examine later in this chapter.

Given the failure of emergency powers under the Weimar Constitution, the few emergency provisions included in the original text of the Grundgesetz were carefully limited. We have already seen that Article 68 authorizes, in a few carefully identified circumstances, the dissolution of the Bundestag. Before the chancellor can utilize the power of dissolution, however, he must request and be denied by the Bundestag a vote of confidence. If these conditions are met, the president must decide whether to accede to the chancellor's request.

Article 81, also included in the original text, provides for a state of "legislative emergency." Such a condition exists when, under Article 68, the Bundestag is not dissolved. If the Bundestag consents, the president may then declare a state of legislative emergency with respect to a particular bill. All legislation must still be submitted to the Bundestag. If, however, after the declaration of an emergency under Article 81, the Bundestag rejects legislative proposals the government has declared "urgent," the proposals will become law if approved by the Bundesrat alone. In the term of any single chancellor a declaration of legislative emergency can be used only once, and the declaration expires automatically six months after it is declared, or upon the resignation of the chancellor. Article 81 is also limited by a subsection that prohibits amendments to, repeals of, or suspensions of the Basic Law through this emergency process.

Emergency Statutes and Policies in the 1950s and 1960s

Notwithstanding the silence of the Basic Law, internal security laws were enacted in the Federal Republic as early as 1951, largely in response to the cold war. Many sought to protect the security of the state and the constitution by prohibiting the publication of materials attacking the principles of the Basic Law. As Kommers noted, "These laws [were] enforced with vigor, for the number of criminal proceedings under [them] is staggering."[51]

Internal security was also the primary justification for the establishment in 1950 of the Federal Office for the Protection of the Constitution (Verfassungsschutz) which operates under the Federal Interior Ministry. The Länder have similar agencies of their own. The Verfassungsschutz does not possess police or enforcement powers but rather acts as an intelligence agency that gathers, monitors, and publishes information on anticonstitutional and unconstitutional activities. Its powers include authority to conduct both covert and overt operations, to open mail and install wiretaps (under a written application to the federal minister and overseen by a special parliamentary committee), and to conduct surveillance of public demonstration and marches. The Verfassungsschutz does *not* limit its monitoring functions to behavior that is illegal—the activity need only be "anticonstitutional,"[52] or opposed to the principles of constitutional democracy. "Anticonstitutional" also includes groups that are illegal and that may, under Article 9 of the Basic Law, be prohibited without a ruling to that effect by the Federal Constitutional Court. "Unconstitutional" refers to parties declared unconstitutional by the Federal Constitutional Court under Article 21.

Statutory law requires that the Verfassungsschutz publish an annual report on the activities of anticonstitutional associations, and the Office has a separate division to monitor the activities of groups suspected of plotting or committing acts of political violence. The Verfassungsschutz has approximately five thousand investigators at its disposal, as well as an integrated computer system which includes information on over two million citizens.[53]

In addition to the Federal Office for the Protection of the Constitution, the national government established in 1951 the Federal Criminal Police Office (BKA), which was to organize and coordinate police work in the Länder by serving as a clearinghouse for certain kinds of information. Since 1973 the Federal Criminal Police Office has had authority to investigate acts of terrorism. Its greatest asset is a technologically advanced computer system with a highly detailed and comprehensive data base. Some security functions were also assumed by the Federal Border Guard (BGS), whose jurisdiction and powers were also expanded by the 1968 emergency legislation and by additional legislation in 1972, which authorized use of the BGS in the Länder in the event of a national emergency.

Prior to passage of the emergency amendments in 1968, the most serious internal security incident in the 1960s was the *Spiegel* affair six years earlier.[54] The lead story in the October 8, 1962 issue of *Der Spiegel*, a weekly newsmagazine, involved a highly critical analysis of the poor performance by West German forces in a recent NATO exercise. Partly on the advice and at the insistence of the defense minister, Franz Josef Strauss (whose relations with *Der Spiegel* were unfriendly), federal and state police raided the offices of *Der Spiegel* on the night of October 26, armed with warrants permitting both searches and arrests on grounds of treason. The raid was poorly planned and implemented. The publisher, Rudolph Augstein, was out of the office and could not be located. And unknown to the police, one of the other main targets, military affairs editor Konrad Ahlers, was on holiday in Spain. Upon learning of Ahlers's trip, an official in the Defense Ministry telephoned the military attaché in Madrid, who secured the cooperation of Spanish authorities. Ahlers was returned to Germany the same day.

The legal and political charges that followed provoked a cabinet crisis between the Christian Democrats and their partners, the smaller Free Democratic party: Five FDP ministers resigned their positions because the raid had been authorized without first seeking the approval of FDP Minister of Justice Wolfgang Stammberger. Strauss was ultimately forced to resign as a condition of the FDP's continued presence in the coalition government. Ahlers and Augstein were eventually brought to trial on charges of threatening national security through publication of sensitive military information. The Federal Supreme Court dismissed the charges in 1965 for lack of evidence.[55] *Der Spiegel* subsequently filed a constitutional complaint in the Federal Constitutional Court alleging that the warrants violated freedom of the press, as provided for in Article 5 of the Basic Law, as well as other constitutional guarantees. The Constitutional Court divided evenly on the merits of the question. Since a majority is necessary for a finding of unconstitutionality, the ruling was a technical victory but a political embarrassment for the government.[56]

The pressures of state security and the cold war were evident throughout the *Spiegel* affair. Although the charges were finally dismissed by the Supreme Court, Kommers observed that "[t]he Court was far from convinced of the defendants' innocence. There is good reason for believing that the judges were as concerned with a public trial's harmful effect upon the nation's security."[57] Likewise, those judges on the Federal Constitutional Court who found in favor of the government, according to Kommers, "tended to treat the matter as if it were an ordinary criminal case, virtually ignoring the competing demands of a free press."[58]

The Grand Coalition and the 1968 Emergency Amendments

Internal security was a frequent concern throughout the 1950s and early 1960s. The same concern was behind efforts to "complete" the Basic Law by enacting amendments to it that would cover domestic and international emergencies. These efforts, to enact the legislation necessary to terminate the last vestiges of the Occupation Statute, began in the 1950s, primarily under the sponsorship of Chancellor Adenauer and the Christian Democrats. Proposals made in 1958 encountered the opposition of the Social Democrats and other groups, such as students, some intellectuals, and trade unions, for fear that such powers, assigned to the executive in the government's draft, would be inadequately limited. Fears were intensified when Interior Minister Gerhard Schroeder, whose ministry was drafting the needed constitutional amendments, stated that an emergency must be "the hour of the executive."[59] The government's proposals were approved by the cabinet in 1960 and made public at the same time, where they attracted widespread opposition and criticism. Negotiations continued after the 1961 elections, when Adenauer appointed a new interior minister, Hermann Höcherl. In 1962 Höcherl's new draft was sent to the Bundestag, which in turn sent the proposal, with its own changes, to the Bundesrat.[60] It too stalled, once again the victim of concerted opposition by the SPD and numerous extraparliamentary groups.

Following the 1966 elections, the CDU–CSU and the SPD entered into a "Grand Coalition," in which CDU representative Kurt Georg Kiesinger was made chancellor and Willy Brandt of the SPD vice-chancellor and minister of foreign affairs. The coalition commanded 447 seats to the FDP's 49. Given such a dominant legislative majority, the advent of the Grand Coalition finally seemed the occasion for passage of new emergency legislation. Interior Minister Paul Lucke drafted amendments which he sent to the Bundesrat in June.[61] But the legislation encountered resistance from some members of the SPD and was the object in 1967 of an extensive public campaign by the Extraparliamentary Opposition, organized in large part by student leaders.

Notwithstanding the strength of the Extraparliamentary Opposition and the great public controversy surrounding the legislation, the Bundesrat and the Bundestag approved the emergency amendments in May 1968. The amendments were then inserted individually into the relevant sections of the Basic Law. The amendments (or the emergency constitution, as it is sometimes called) total seventeen articles and provide for three distinct types of emergencies. These are the "state of defense" (Verteidigungsfall), the "state of tension" (Spannungsfall), and the "internal state of emergency" (innerer Notstand). The first two states of emergency may not be initiated without declaration by a two-thirds majority of both the Bundestag and the Bundesrat, which must also amount, in the Bundestag, to at least an absolute majority of the total membership.

State of Defense

Article 115 of the Basic Law provides that a state of defense exists when the republic is under attack or threat of an imminent attack by an armed force. In such circumstances, the government may request the Bundestag to initiate the state of defense. The decision must then be promulgated by the federal president. Article 115 also provides for an expedited form of legislative process. Legislative proposals may be submitted simultaneously to both houses of Parliament for immediate debate and consideration. Subsection f of Article 115 increases the scope of national authority by providing that in a state of defense the federal government may commit the Federal Border Guard throughout federal territory and may issue instructions directly to the Länder in matters of administration and state finances. Article 115i provides that in cases when the federation is incapable of responding to an emergency, the individual Länder may act, subject to subsequent revocation of their measures by federal authorities.

In the event that the Bundestag cannot meet or cannot summon a quorum, Article 115e authorizes establishment of a joint committee, composed of twenty-two members of the Bundestag and eleven from the Bundesrat, to function in its place. The article makes clear that the joint committee "takes the place of the Bundestag and Bundesrat and carries out their constitutional prerogatives," thereby further guaranteeing "the principle of full accountability of the executive to this parliamentary body."[62]

Hence the principle of separation of powers and legislative accountability is ensured in the state of defense by providing for the continuing exercise of legislative authority. Article 115h further stipulates that the Bundestag cannot be dissolved in a state of defense. Together these provisions are evidence of "one of the principle aims of the drafters: the intent to safeguard, within a very elaborate system of legal provisions, the participation of Parliament, or parts thereof, in the decision-making process under all feasible and foreseeable conditions."[63]

Similarly, Article 115g preserves the institutional integrity of judicial power by ensuring the continued functioning of the Federal Constitutional Court in a state of defense by providing that "[t]he constitutional status and the exercise of the constitutional functions of the Federal Constitutional Court and its judges must not be impaired." In this way, the emergency constitution seeks to guard against tyranny and the abuses that are possible from the concentration of power in the executive by "maintaining a strict separation of powers whilst limiting some of the constitutional rights of the population in times of need."[64] The continued institutional integrity of the Bundestag ensures parliamentary responsibility and oversight at the initial stages of an emergency, and the institutional integrity of the judiciary ensures the possibility of post hoc review, thereby combining the safeguards of both the civil and common law systems, as Frederick Watkins recommended in his study of emergency powers in Weimar.[65]

State of Tension

The "state of tension" is not defined precisely by the constitutional text but appears to cover the conditions that precede a state of defense, such as a "situation approaching civil war or preparation for international war."[66] Like the state of defense, Article 80a provides that the state of tension exists only if it is initiated by a two-thirds majority of the Bundestag. (The concurrence of the Bundesrat is not necessary, however, as it is with the state of defense.) The Bundestag also has the power to terminate the state of tension. There is no provision, as there is in the state of defense, for an expedited form of legislative process.

Internal State of Emergency

An internal state of emergency covers both natural catastrophes and threats to the liberal democratic order in either the federation or the Länder. It differs from the other two states in that it may be initiated without a formal finding by the Bundestag. The extent of the internal state of emergency is potentially far-reaching, encompassing any "threat to the liberal democratic order," but as we have seen, the concept of the liberal democratic order permeates the entire Basic Law (see, for examples, Articles 18, 20, and 21) and has been defined judicially.

Individual Rights in a State of Emergency

Under Article 48 of the Weimar Constitution, the executive had expansive authority to interfere with individual liberties in a state of emergency. Those powers are severely circumscribed under the Basic Law. Article 1, which protects human dignity, cannot be amended, and Article 19 prohibits any state action that would directly affect the substance or core of any protected right. As we saw earlier, however, almost all of these rights are coupled with restrictions that embody the philosophy of militant democracy, such as Article 5, which guarantees freedom of teaching but does not absolve "loyalty to the constitution." There are more precise and particular restrictions as well. Article 9(3), for example, limits the ability of the federal security forces to interfere in cases of "industrial unrest carried on to safeguard and promote the working and industrial conditions of associations." Article 11 of the Basic Law guarantees freedom of movement. But the emergency constitution limits that right if "necessary to avert an imminent danger to the existence or the free democratic order of the Federation or a Land." Conscription into federal forces is also circumscribed by a right of refusal in favor of alternative service under Article 12. Article 115c(2) (1) provides that in a state of defense, individuals may be deprived of their liberty for a period not to exceed four days, "if no judge has been able to act within the period applying in normal times [one day]."

Perhaps the most serious effect of the emergency amendments on civil liberties pertains to Article 10 of the Basic Law. As written in 1949, Article 10 stated that the "[p]rivacy of posts and telecommunications shall be inviolable. This right may be restricted only pursuant to a law." The emergency amendments provide that persons affected "pursuant to a law" under Article 10 "shall not be informed" of the restriction if it is designed to protect the free democratic basic order or the security of the federation or Länder. The amendment also provides that instead of recourse to the courts, review shall be by bodies or agencies appointed by the Bundestag. This latter provision is arguably incompatible with Article 20(4), which states that individuals whose rights have been violated may seek redress in the courts. Article 20 was therefore amended to read that the guarantee of judicial recourse shall not apply to the second paragraph of Article 10, thereby eliminating the potential conflict between the two provisions.[67]

The amendment was challenged in the Federal Constitutional Court in 1970, when the Land of Hesse and the Free Hanseatic City of Bremen asked the court to declare the amendment (and the statute implementing it) unconstitutional.[68] The challenge was premised upon Article 79, which forbids amendments to Article 1's requirement of respect for human dignity, Article 19(4), and upon Article 20, which recognizes the "social and democratic" character of the Federal Republic. The majority rejected the challenge, arguing that surveillance without notification to the affected party is "not an expression of disrespect for a human being and his dignity, but a burden imposed upon a citizen . . . to protect the existence of his state and of the free democratic order."[69] (Nearly a decade later, in September 1978, the European Commission ruled that the amendment to Article 10 did not violate the European Convention on Human Rights.)[70] The court also concluded that review by a nonjudicial agency did not violate the principle of separation of powers inherent in Article 20:

> For this principle [separation of powers] does not demand a strict separation of powers, but in exceptional cases permits legislative functions to be exercised by governmental and administrative bodies. . . . The essential point is that the rationale for separation of powers, namely reciprocal restriction and control of state powers, is still fulfilled.[71]

The court's understanding of separation of powers requires respect for the *purposes* and *functions* the principle is intended to secure, rather than respect, necessarily, for any particular institutional expression of the principle. The constitutionality of the review procedure is thus a function of whether it fulfills the purposes promoted by the separation of powers doctrine, thought by the court to be "reciprocal restriction and control" of state power.

In dissent, three justices criticized the majority's use of the concept of militant democracy, arguing that "[r]eason of state is not an absolutely preeminent value. If the legislator misjudges the limits, 'militant democracy' turns against itself. . . . It is contradictory to abandon inalienable constitutional principles in order to protect the Constitution."[72] The dissents' position finds some support in the Basic Law, which does *not* include the principle of militant democracy as a part of the free democratic basic order or as a constitutive principle of constitutional democracy.

The majority's rejection of the argument that surveillance without notification to the individual offends human dignity, because constitutional rights imply constitutional duties, is not so much wrong as irresponsive to the demands of constitutionalism. A requirement of notification does not absolve from or deny the existence of individual duties, but instead ensures the accountability of state actors by establishing the conditions that are minimally necessary to challenge state action.[73] As I argued in chapter 1, the constitutive principles of dignity and articulated reason impose requirements in the earlier stages of state policies and actions which make subsequent review by other independent actors and institutions possible. By negating the possibility of such a challenge and review, Article 10 offends the constitutive constitutional principle of reason in much the same way that arrest in the absence of reasonable suspicion offends the principle in Northern Ireland.[74] In both cases, the exercise of state power against an individual need not be supported or justified and the citizen is afforded no means by which he or she can evaluate or challenge the action.

201-4 209,15,17

POLITICAL VIOLENCE IN THE FEDERAL REPUBLIC

Unlike the conflict that endures in Northern Ireland or in the Basque region of Spain, most of the political violence in the Federal Republic is neither ethnic nor nationalistic. It is instead predominantly a type of revolutionary violence promoted by a supposed intellectual avant-garde of students (Red Army Faction) or workers (2d June Movement) against the values and symbols of the West, especially capitalism and NATO. It represents a complete rejection of the values of constitutional democracy and cannot be understood, as parts of the Extraparliamentary Opposition should be, as promoting an alternative vision of a democratic or constitutional community. It is in this central respect that the ideological premises of left-wing terrorism differ from the oftentimes legitimate criticisms of German democracy made by the Extraparliamentary Opposition and the student movement.

Indeed, the rise of the student movement and the Extraparliamentary Opposition in the mid to late 1960s was, in large measure, a result of the advent of the Grand Coalition and the perceived lack of a genuine or effective opposition presence in the Bundestag.[75] Although certain of its precursors reach to the 1950s, the movement gained strength in the mid 1960s as a direct consequence of its opposition to the emergency amendments proposed by the Coalition. The Extraparliamentary Opposition also campaigned against the many structural limits on German democracy, the Vietnam War, and antiquated and restrictive university policies. It "saw itself as being 'undogmatic,' 'antiauthoritarian,' and 'radically democratic.'"[76] According to one observer, the student movement was composed of at least two elements—one moderate, prodemocratic, and in favor of parliamentary reforms that would expand the republic's commitment to plebiscitary democracy beyond what its founders had contemplated. The second element was more radical. It too professed a commitment to democracy but argued that "true" democracy cannot be realized "within the framework of bourgeois society in the age of 'late capitalism.'"[77]

The student movement grew in strength and expanded territorially, beyond its base in West Berlin, following the June 1967 death of Benno Ohnesorg, who was shot by the police during a student demonstration against a visit by the Shah of Iran. An attack in 1968 on another student leader, Rudi Dutschke, was the occasion for a further escalation of the movement's strength and the beginnings, within parts of the movement, of violence. One of the most prominent of the early acts of violence was the bombing in April 1968 of a large department store in Frankfurt am Main. Arrested as suspects in the incident were Andreas Baader and Gudrun Ensslin, two of the founders of the Federal Republic's most prominent terrorist organization, the Red Army Faction. Later that year both Baader and Ensslin, whose legal representatives included the prominent left-wing lawyer Horst Mahler, were convicted and imprisoned.[78]

These two incidents had the effect of heightening the sense of urgency and increasing the violence associated with certain elements of the opposition. In an article published in a May issue of *Konkret*, a left-wing periodical, Ulrike Meinhof captured that sense of change: "The boundary between verbal protest and physical resistance has been transgressed in the protests against the attack on Dutschke these Easter holidays for the first time in a massive way."[79] Meinhof wrote more about herself than the student movement, however. Just two years later, on May 14, 1970, Meinhof and Mahler participated in a raid on Tegel Prison in West Berlin that "liberated" Andreas Baader. The prison raid was the first organized action by what was now called in the German press the "Baader–Meinhof Gang."

The Turn to Violence

Student unrest in the mid to late 1960s and early 1970s did not cause terrorism and other forms of political violence to appear in West Germany—some forms of political violence had existed since the state was founded in 1949. But it did provide the context within which some elements of that movement ultimately turned to violence.[80]

German terrorism has been characterized by three distinct phases—the first was from the late 1960s to 1972, the second from 1972 to 1977, and the third from 1984 to the present.[81] Between 1967 and 1972, the first period, there were an estimated 90 terrorist incidents; approximately 649 occurred between 1970 and 1979, when terrorism in the Federal Republic was most prominent.[82] In the period between 1980 and 1985 there were 1,601 attacks, many of much smaller dimension and scale than those in the 1970s; total damage has been estimated by the government to be between 200 million and 250 million Deutsche marks.[83] These figures are quite small when compared to the level of violence that existed in Weimar, or in Northern Ireland during the same period. (A comparison on the basis of fatalities makes this clear: In 1922 alone there were over 300 deaths due to political violence in Northern Ireland, and between 1919 and 1922 there were over 400 fatalities in Weimar. In West Germany, in the decade following 1968, there were 28 assassinations and 93 persons injured.)[84] Nevertheless, this violence produced an extraordinary reaction in the German press and on the part of the German government.

The Red Army Faction

The Red Army Faction (RAF) has been the most prominent and most durable of the terrorist organizations in the Federal Republic since the 1970s. Its original founders, Meinhof, Baader, and Mahler, and current membership were and are committed to a revolutionary program of armed revolution through urban guerrilla violence. The revolution will, they argue, be led by the elite avant-garde (the RAF), who alone are able to distance themselves from the class struggle and hence are capable of abstract, objective analysis of the "revolutionary moment." Beginning in 1970, the RAF undertook a program of violent actions, consisting primarily of arson, bank robberies, and bombings, which lasted until 1972, when most of its original founders were captured by the security forces. Baader was arrested in Frankfurt on June 1, 1972. Not long afterward, on June 7 and June 15, respectively, Ensslin and Meinhof were arrested as well. Three years later, all three (and one other, Jan-Carl Raspe) were put on trial in a "secure" courthouse built (at the cost of five million dollars)[85] just for their trial, in the Land of Baden-Württemberg, on charges of murder, attempted murder, robbery, and criminal association. Ultimately the defendants were sentenced to life imprisonment.

The trial attracted widespread international attention, especially after charges of complicity between certain defendants and their lawyers led to the exclusion of some of the attorneys for the defense. In addition, some of the defendants, notably Baader and Ensslin, engaged in tactics and displays designed, with at least partial success, to disrupt the proceedings. These tactics, and the exclusion of their attorneys, later formed the basis for sweeping changes in the Code of Criminal Procedure, which we shall review shortly.*

After the arrest of its leaders, the RAF shifted from the practice of violence designed to hasten along the "revolutionary moment" to tactics calculated to secure its organizational survival. As a consequence, most of the RAF's actions after 1972, such as its raid on the German Embassy in Stockholm in 1975 and the hijacking of a Lufthansa plane to Mogadishu, Somalia, in 1977, were conducted to secure the release of imprisoned comrades. Most of these operations failed in this purpose, although a 1975 operation by another group, the 2d June Movement, did win the release of five imprisoned terrorists, all of whom were subsequently recaptured. In May 1976 Ulrike Meinhof hanged herself (the RAF claims she was murdered by the state) in her prison cell. Baader, Ensslin, and Raspe committed suicide in their cells in October 1977.

Notwithstanding the suicides of Meinhof and Baader, the RAF was especially active in 1977 (often called the "German Autumn"), when it was responsible for the kidnaping and murder of Hans-Martin Schleyer, head of the German Employers Association, the murder of Attorney-General Siegfried Buback, an attempted attack on the Federal Justice offices in Karlsruhe, and several other incidents. After 1977 the organization suffered an apparent delcine, notwithstanding its attack on General Alexander Haig, supreme commander of NATO, in 1979 and the 1981 attack on U.S. Air Force headquarters in Ramstein. The RAF has managed to survive by securing new generations of leaders and recruits, and in 1984 it underwent an apparent resurgence. In early 1985, for example, the RAF announced it had formed a "united front" with the French group Action Directe (AD) and the Belgian Communist Cells (CCC);

*The defendants later filed an application with the European Commission on Human Rights, alleging that the conditions of their detention and other actions by the government violated Articles 3 (prohibiting torture and inhuman treatment), 6 (concerning procedural due process), 8 (respect for privacy and correspondence), and 10 (freedom of expression) of the European Convention. Eventually the commission ruled against the defendants on all of the allegations.[86]

ten days later, on January 25, 1985, the AD assassinated General René Audrian, a high-ranking French defense official, and on February 1, the RAF killed Ernst Zimmermann, a German arms manufacturer. Most of the RAF's recent violent activities have also been directed against NATO targets. Moreover, since 1989, approximately thirty imprisoned members of the RAF have been engaged in a series of hunger strikes designed to mobilize outside support and to win certain privileges with regard to their imprisonment, a tactic practiced on a recurrent basis since the 1970s.

The 2d June Movement

The 2d June Movement was founded in July 1971 by former students at the Free University in West Berlin. Its name commemorates the shooting of Benno Ohnesorg by the police on June 2, 1967. Initially the 2d June Movement envisioned the onset of the revolution through means distinctly different from those contemplated by the RAF, and the two groups were, in turn, fairly different in both ideology and strategy. The 2d June Movement rejected the intellectual pretensions of the RAF and sought to integrate the working classes into the concept of the armed struggle. Organizationally, the 2nd June Movement was comprised of members of several smaller anarchist groups and consequently was less structured and rigid than the RAF.[87]

The movement's most important action was its kidnaping in 1975 of Peter Lorenz, chairman of the CDU in Berlin. In return for the release of Lorenz, the 2d June sought the release of six imprisoned terrorists, including Horst Mahler. The government exchanged five prisoners (Mahler, however, refused to leave the prison) for Lorenz. Most of the kidnapers were subsequently arrested, and by 1980 some of the imprisoned leaders of the 2d June announced the dissolution of the movement and its absorption by the RAF.[88]

The Revolutionary Cells

Like the 2d June Movement, the Revolutionary Cells (RZ) have sought as a matter of revolutionary theory to distance themselves from the RAF. Instead of revolution through the leadership of the intellectual avant-garde, the RZ has emphasized the relationship of armed struggle to society through the "contact theory." The RZ seek through their actions "to have a clear connection with some local protest issue and remain at a popular level; imagination and spontaneity is to replace the elaborate planning and technical application for which the RAF was famous."[89] Occasionally called "weekend terrorists," the RZ reject the RAF's penchant for spectacular incidents against prominent targets in favor of smaller but more frequent actions. These tactical choices are closely related to the RZ's internal organization, which, like that of the IRA in Northern Ireland, is cellular, and consequently less rigid than the RAF's. Since 1973 the RZ has conducted more operations than either the RAF or the 2d June Movement, predominantly against American targets.[90]

Right-Wing Terrorism

Political violence in the Federal Republic began and is still practiced predominantly on the left, but it also includes actions by certain smaller groups on the right, and since the early 1980s right-wing violence has comprised a significant part of the total political violence in West Germany. Much as the violence on the left escalated with the decline of the student movement in the 1960s, violence on the right has increased as membership in the country's largest legal right-wing organization, the National Democratic party (NPD), has declined. At one point in the late 1960s the NPD claimed twenty-five thousand members. In 1978 it claimed nine thousand members, [91] and by 1985 its membership had fallen to just four thousand.[92] The NPD still runs candidates for office, however, and occasionally wins seats in local elections. In 1989, for example, the NPD won 6.6 percent of the vote in Frankfurt.

But membership in right-wing organizations more generally (including legal organizations) has held more or less constant at approximately twenty-two thousand since 1984, and the number of crimes committed by the right steadily increased in the early 1980s before declining to sixty-nine incidents in 1985, from a high of eighty-three the year before.[93] In his authoritative study of right-wing violence in Germany, Peter Merkl concluded that "[t]here can be no doubt that right-wing terrorism . . . is increasing again at the same time that political right-wing activities, with an estimated 20,000 members in various organizations, have not really expanded as expected under a conservative administration."[94]

There are currently three major organizations, as well as several smaller groups, which serve as focal points for younger, more radical individuals who might otherwise have been attracted to the NPD. These are the German Action Group (Deutsche Aktionsgruppen), headed by Manfred Roeder, the Hoffman Military Sport Group (Hoffmann Wehrsportgruppe), led by Karl-Heinz Hoffman, and the Popular Socialist Movement of Germany–Party of Labor (VSBD–PdA).[95] Yet another group is the Action Front of National Socialists (ANS), "known for intensive military training, and . . . suspected of being a terrorist organization."[96] The founders of all three groups are imprisoned. (Hoffman was arrested in 1980 for having murdered Shlomo Levin, a Jewish publisher who had written of the group and its activities. In 1986 he was acquitted of that charge but convicted of possession of firearms.)

In general, right-wing violence has had as its purpose the destruction of the liberal democratic state. Its virulent anti-Americanism has meant that its targets, usually NATO facilities and personnel, have often coincided with those of the left. Much of the remaining violence of these groups has been against foreigners and guest workers. The most spectacular incident, for example, involved a bombing in 1980 at the Munich Oktoberfest, which killed thirteen persons and injured over two hundred others.[97] The bombing is thought by security officials to have been the work of an individual associated with the Hoffmann group.

MILITANT DEMOCRACY AND ANTITERRORISM
LEGISLATION IN THE FEDERAL REPUBLIC

Antiterrorism policies in the Federal Republic are greatly conditioned by the normative context of the Basic Law and its commitments to human dignity, the preservation of the free democratic basic order, and the principle of militant democracy. But these norms are not self-implementing. Accordingly, the development of antiterrorism legislation in West Germany has given rise to and has been influenced by debates over the continuing vitality of these concepts and in part over their precise meaning, over what they require, what they permit, and what, if anything, they prohibit.[98]

West Germany's antiterrorism legislation has been the subject of much domestic and international criticism. Some critics have said that together the individual statutory provisions "probably amount to the most repressive anti-terrorist legislation in existence in a liberal democracy."[99] Another critic called the new legislation a "Germanic version of McCarthyism."[100] But others have thought the legislation "relatively moderate"[101] and evidence of "admirable restraint."[102] It is true that the range of matters covered by emergency legislation is comprehensive. Moreover, some of these policies are overreactions, given the rather small numbers of acts of political violence actually committed in the Federal Republic. Some of the more controversial provisions, however, resemble steps taken by other constitutional democracies, a point some of Germany's critics often overlook, and others find their explanation, if not a justification, in German history.

As we saw, the 1968 emergency amendments changed the institutional context of emergency policy in general and antiterrorism policy in particular by authorizing the federal government to deploy the Federal Border Guard throughout the individual Länder and to issue instructions directly to the Land governments. Subsequent institutional changes included the professionalization and expansion of the Federal Criminal Police Office (BKA), which now maintains a technologically sophisticated computer system for intelligence work,[103] and additional resources for the Federal Office for the Protection of the Constitution. In 1973 the BKA was given authority to direct all national operations against terrorism and responsibility for collecting and centralizing all information concerning terrorism. The 1973 changes also gave the BKA jurisdiction over crimes against governmental officials and certain international offenses. (Most other aspects of police work remain with the Länder.) Within the BKA there are two units concerned with terrorism—the Suppression of Terrorism (TE) department is responsible for investigating political crimes; the Special Branch (ST), which collects information and oversees the computer operations of the BKA, possesses information on several million German citizens.[104]

This policy of increased resources and expanded roles for institutional actors responsible for counterterrorism policy was followed by substantial changes in German antiterrorism policy more generally. In 1971 the government increased the penalties for hijackings and hostage-takings, and early in 1973 it enacted a national ammunitions law, but these were largely "ad hoc legal adaptations."[105] Before 1975 the government's response in areas other than increasing resources for various state agencies was sporadic, ineffective, and often accommodating, as evidenced by its willingness to comply with demands made by the 2d June Movement following the kidnaping of Lorenz. By 1975 and 1976, however, the government began systematic efforts at introducing changes in the penal and criminal procedure codes.

The Public Servant Loyalty Decree*

The controversy surrounding these changes was at least equaled by that surrounding what is perhaps the best known and most controversial aspect of internal security policy in the Federal Republic, the Termination of Radicals policy, or what is sometimes called the Berufsverbot (job ban). As Gerard Braunthal noted, "few government actions have produced controversy as emotional, polemical, and long lasting as the [Loyalty Decree]."[106] The Berufsverbot seeks to guarantee the fidelity of the German civil service to the free democratic basic order by ensuring that all candidates for a tenured position in the civil service have not engaged in or promoted actions or ideas hostile to the constitutional state. In pertinent part, the policy states:

> Pursuant to the civil service laws of the Federation and the States, only those persons who can show that they are prepared at all times to uphold the free democratic basic order and actively to defend this basic order, both on and off duty, may be appointed to the public service. This requirement is obligatory.[107]

In brief, the policy provides that persons, including employees of and applicants for the civil service, who are engaged in "anticonstitutional" activities or members of an organization that pursues such activities are barred from the civil service.

Strictly speaking, the job ban is not a federal statute but is instead a resolution adopted in January 1972 by the prime ministers of the national government and the Länder.[108] The policy is a series of guidelines which specify the criteria that the national and state governments should employ in assessing the suitability of civil service candidates. In this respect, it sought to standardize existing practices, which varied considerably among the Länder. The effort proved unsuccessful: Länder governed by the CDU–CSU still follow the terms of the original 1972 resolution, but Länder controlled by the SPD or the FDP follow a more liberal interpretation of the policy based on certain sections of a Federal Constitutional Court decision of 1975.[109]

---

*What one calls the decree is often related to one's support for or opposition to it. Opponents typically refer to the decree as the Job Ban (Berufsverbot) or the Radicals Decree. Supporters refer to it as the Decree against Extremists. The decree is formally entitled "Basic Principles on the Question of Anticonstitutional Personnel in the Public Service."

The Berufsverbot has been an extraordinarily controversial aspect of internal security policy and an expansive consequence of the concept of militant democracy. Part of the controversy stems from its breadth. Nothing in the policy restricts its application to positions of importance or sensitivity in the civil service; consequently, the policy applies to approximately 3.5 million people.[110] Between 1972 and 1987 millions of applicants were subjected to "loyalty screening." Braunthal noted that since the decree was adopted, "intelligence agencies submitted the names of 35,000 suspect applicants to hiring authorities who barred approximately 2,250 applicants for political reasons. In addition, 2,000 to 2,100 public servants were subject to disciplinary proceedings and 256 were dismissed."[111] According to another estimate, between 1973 and 1980 some 1.3 million applicants were screened, "and about thirteen hundred, or less than 0.001 percent, were finally barred from public-sector employment."[112]

Any evaluation of the radicals provision must begin with an understanding of the special role of the civil service in German politics and history. The Reich Civil Service Code of 1873, for example, gave civil servants a privileged position through lifetime tenure and generous pensions. This tradition has also given rise to special obligations. The National Civil Service Law required an oath of fidelity by members of the civil service to the Weimar Republic, and a 1933 law prohibited Communists in the civil service in the Third Reich. In addition, the Adenauer Decree of 1950 identified thirteen organizations as "opponents" of the state; support for them led to dismissal from the civil service.[113]

Article 33(3) of the Basic Law provides that "[t]he exercise of state authority as a permanent function shall as a rule be entrusted to members of the public service whose status, service and loyalty are governed by public law." Subsection 4 of Article 33 further states that "[t]he law of the public service shall be regulated with due regard to the traditional principles of the professional civil service." Regulations for the civil service thus are both explicitly contemplated by Article 33 and a longstanding tradition in German law. Consequently, some policy not unlike the one set forth in the Berufsverbot is probably permitted by Article 33.

But there remain constitutional ambiguities specific to the policy adopted in 1972, such as whether membership in a party or an organization that professes anticonstitutional goals is itself a legally sufficient basis for rejecting an applicant. In a 1975 decision the Federal Constitutional Court acknowledged that civil servants are under an obligation of loyalty to the free democratic basic order, and that acts of disloyalty are properly grounds for rejection or dismissal.[114] Membership in an anticonstitutional organization can, according to the court, be an "admissible factor" in reaching a determination under the policy but cannot by itself be the basis of a decision. The ruling sustained the validity of the loyalty statutes of one Land, but the court cautioned that membership alone must normally be complemented by independent evidence of an applicant's unsuitability for the position.[115]

In October 1975, following the decision, a majority (comprised of the SPD and FDP) in the Bundestag passed, over CDU–CSU opposition, a resolution requesting the federal government and the states to follow the principles enunciated by the court. The CDU–CSU majority in the Bundesrat rejected it.[116] As a consequence, policy varies in the individual states on the question of membership, with those Länder governed by the CDU–CSU largely following the principle that membership in an organization pursuing anticonstitutional goals is sufficient reason to reject or dismiss an applicant or employee.

The influence of Weimar and the concept of militant democracy are evident in Termination of Radicals policy. As Chancellor Brandt, a co-sponsor of the resolution, later explained:

> Whether it [the policy] was right or wrong, you must look at this in the context of the way in which we believed ourselves called upon to prevent a repetition of Weimar. Weimar had been ground to pieces. . . . Those who reject its [a democracy's] basic elements must not be given power to dispose of it. They have the same rights and enjoy the same legal protection as everybody else. But if they reject the basic democratic order, as it corresponds to our albeit brief constitutional tradition, they cannot at the same time occupy any civil service positions they want.[117]

Brandt's comments on the constitutional justifications for the Berufsverbot show how expansive and elastic the concept of militant democracy can be.

Indeed, some international and domestic critics have called the ban a form of McCarthyism because it attempts to criminalize legitimate political and social criticism of the state.[118] Some of this criticism is based upon several well-known instances of abuse. One public employee, for example, was discharged because he lived with Christel Ensslin, the sister of Gudrun Ensslin of the RAF, and another woman "faced disciplinary action because her *husband* was an attorney for an accused terrorist."[119]

The concept of militant democracy as used here *is* in some tension with some of the constitutive principles proposed in chapter 1. The breadth and reach of the Berufsverbot have been among its most controversial aspects. The constitutive principle of mitigation, however, requires that inroads into individual liberties be justified by necessity and be as limited and as narrow as possible. As a consequence, the principle would require that the overall policy be justified on the basis of necessity. The reasons requirement discussed in chapter 1 likewise demands an assumption of loyalty in individual cases; investigations should be conducted only in those cases where there are reasonable grounds to suspect disloyalty. In this respect, the decision by the Constitutional Court strikes the correct balance, and the differences between CDU–CSU and SPD practice are constitutionally significant. Changes made in 1979 now provide, in greater conformity with the principles of constitutional maintenance, that candidates for a position with the federal government are assumed to be loyal; investigative attention is therefore directed only to cases in which there is a specific reason to conduct an investigation.[120]

Other changes have brought the policy in greater conformity with the reasons requirement proposed in the first chapter, which provides that state actors must inform persons of the reasons for action taken against them and must provide them with an opportunity to respond. Every Land provides that an applicant must be apprised of information prejudicial to his candidacy and must be given an opportunity to respond to that information. Candidates possess a further right of appeal to an administrative court.[121]

Insofar as the major criticism of the Berufsverbot, that it suppresses legitimate criticism of the state, is accurate, it underscores the greatest danger in the concept of militant democracy, that the defense of democracy in general will become the defense of *this* democracy and *this* regime.[122] I am not, however, suggesting that all loyalty requirements necessarily offend the constitutional principles that govern constitutional maintenance. Many constitutional democracies have similar policies, and each must be examined on its own to assess its conformity with the demands of constitutional maintenance. In the United States, for example, the U.S. Code (5 U.S.C., Section 7311) provides that

> an individual may not accept or hold a position in the government of the United States or in the District of Columbia if he (1) advocates the overthrow of our constitutional form of government; (2) is a member of an organization that he knows advocates the overthrow of our constitutional form of government.

The constitutionality of this statutory provision has been upheld by inferior federal courts, which have noted that dismissals of government employees on grounds of loyalty or security are not in themselves unconstitutional.[123] Nevertheless, there are procedural protections, some statutory, others constitutional, that apply in such cases.[124]

Changes in the Substantive Criminal Law

Between 1974 and 1978, at what seemed the height of the terrorist threat in West Germany, the government introduced a number of important changes in the substantive criminal law to respond to public pressure to react to terrorism. Like the Berufsverbot, these changes have engendered widespread international and domestic criticism. Some of the earliest provisions, and the most far-reaching, have since been repealed, but the majority remain in force and grant to the security forces extraordinary powers that approximate, if they do not exceed, those in place in Northern Ireland. As we have already seen, these extraordinary provisions include expansive authority to wiretap communications and to search mails without notification to or judicial recourse for the individual affected, as provided for under Article 10 of the Basic Law.

The changes introduced in the Penal Code in the 1970s have substantially changed the landscape of German criminal law. Prior to these amendments, security officials possessed no statutory authority to initiate criminal investigations absent very specific evidence of criminal activity.[125] There existed, moreover, no substantial set of criminal offenses against the state or the free democratic order.[126] As with the British security legislation, the West German amendments have greatly increased the number of offenses to include "terrorist" crimes (now covered are exhortations to commit crimes, resisting state officials in the performance of their duties, disruptions of the public order and peace, failure to inform authorities of crimes, and support for terrorist organizations, hijacking, and others) and have substantially increased the powers of the police and security forces. In contrast to the British legislation, however, the West German statutes have tended to increase rather than limit judicial discretion, thereby underscoring the judiciary's role as guardian of the German democracy. Furthermore, the Basic Law explicitly forbids establishment of emergency courts. Hence there is no German equivalent to the Diplock courts that operate in Northern Ireland.

Section 88a: The Anti-Constitutional Advocacy Act of 1976

Among the most controversial additions to the Penal Code was Section 88a, which provided that offenses "against the Constitution" could be punished with imprisonment for up to three years. Entitled the Anti-Constitutional Advocacy Act, Section 88a was premised upon the assumption that a democracy's commitment to freedom of speech and expression may also be tempered by the concept of militant democracy. Under the article "anyone who disseminates, publicly issues, displays, produces or otherwise makes available any written material advocating illegal acts listed in paragraph 1 of section 126 [generally concerning disturbing the peace by threatening to commit a crime]" is guilty of a criminal offense. The written material referred to in Section 88a must be "capable of encouraging the willingness of other persons to commit offences against the existence or safety of the Federal Republic of Germany."[127]

Section 88a evoked widespread criticisms of censorship and interference with freedom of speech, especially when used in conjunction with Sections 129 and 129a, concerning criminal and terrorist associations (discussed later). There are, for example, several well-known instances of police searches of book stores for "subversive materials."[128] But the provision probably did not violate the Basic Law.[129] As we saw, constitutional guarantees of freedom of speech in the Basic Law are coupled with restrictions that require fidelity to the free democratic basic order and the Basic Law. Partly in reaction to such criticism, however, the government repealed Section 88a in 1981. In explanation, other provisions under Title III of the Penal Code, entitled "Endangering the Democratic Rule of Law," were said to cover already the offenses identified in Section 88a.[130] Sections 90, 90a, and 90b, still in place, provide that defamation of the federation, its institutions, or the Länder constitutes a criminal offense. Section 90a, for example, provides that anyone who publicly "insults or maliciously maligns the Federal Republic of Germany or one of its Länder or its constitutional order" shall be punished by fine or by imprisonment for up to three years.

Sections 129 and 129a:
Criminal and Terrorist Associations

Two of the most important amendments to the Criminal Code are Sections 129 and 129a. Together, these provisions make criminal the formation of a terrorist organization. Section 129 permits imprisonment for a period of five years for individuals who form an association directed to the commission of a criminal offense or who participate in, recruit for, or aid a criminal association. Subsection 2 of Section 129 qualifies this offense by excepting from its coverage associations that are political parties not declared to be unconstitutional by the Federal Constitutional Court, activities of "minor importance," and activities that constitute an offense under Sections 84 through 87 of the Penal Code, which generally cover unconstitutional political activities.

Section 129a concerns the formation of a terrorist organization. The provision states that anyone who sets up or attempts to set up "an organization whose purpose or activity consists in the commission" of a list of specified crimes (including murder, manslaughter, and genocide), or who is a member of such an association, or who recruits for or aids such an association may be deprived of liberty for a period of six months to five years. In addition, the court may, at its discretion, forbid an individual convicted of an offense under Section 129a to hold a public or elected office for a period of two to five years.

In many respects Section 129a resembles provisions contained in the British Prevention of Terrorism Act (PTA). Section 1 of the Prevention of Terrorism Act prohibits membership in a "proscribed" organization and also penalizes individuals who "solicit or invite financial or other support" for such an organization. Section 10 of the PTA, which is broader than Section 1, states that it is an offense for any person "to solicit or invite" support for terrorism. Section 129a thus suffers from many of the defects that plague the British provisions. "Intent" becomes an element of the offense itself, and courts are left with the unpleasant business of determining what constitutes "support."[131] But the British statute requires reasonableness of suspicion in order to bring charges under either provision of the act, whereas under Section 129a no suspicion is required. In this respect, the German provisions offend the constitutional requirement of articulated reason, which requires in such cases that authorities have reasonable grounds for suspecting an individual of having committed an offense.

As might be expected, in the absence of a requirement of reasonableness of suspicion, conviction rates under Section 129a are low, as they are under the Prevention of Terrorism Act.[132] According to one study conducted by the government, only 1.4 percent of the preliminary investigations conducted by the federal prosecutor yielded convictions (30 convictions of 2,131).[133] Other studies have put the figure at 6 percent.[134]

Sections 138 and 139: Duties to Inform

Like certain provisions of the British emergency legislation, such as Section 11 of the Prevention of Terrorism Act, Section 138 of the German Penal Code provides that persons who have knowledge of certain specified crimes, including crimes under Section 129a, and who fail to make "an immediate report," when such a report might have prevented the crime, have committed an offense that may result in a fine or up to five years' imprisonment.

Section 139 qualifies Section 138 in a number of respects. For example, it provides that the duty of disclosure does not overcome a privilege claimed by the clergy not to divulge such information. Section 139 further provides that "a lawyer, defense attorney or physician" is under no legal duty to reveal confidential information, so long as the conditions specified in subsection 3 of Section 139 are satisfied. Subsection 3 states that there shall be no punishment under Section 138 if the person who fails to reveal the information is related to one of the participants (in this respect, Section 139 is narrower than Section 11 of the PTA, which does not excuse failures to disclose on the basis of relationship) or if he sought to prevent the crime or to avert the danger, so long as the crime is not one specifically excepted in Section 3. "Excepted" crimes include murder, manslaughter, genocide, extortionary kidnaping, hostage taking, or an attack on air traffic by a terrorist organization.

Changes in the Code of Criminal Procedure

In addition to changes in the Penal Code, the Federal Republic has introduced substantial changes to the Code of Criminal Procedure to cope with the special demands of terrorist-related investigations and trials. These revisions do not, as do the British changes, substantially alter the rules of evidence or shift burdens of proof; instead they are largely concerned with attorney–client relationships and courtroom proceedings. Under the new provisions, the government may, under judicial supervision, monitor the exchange of documentary and written materials between attorneys and their clients. In certain circumstances, the government may exclude defense counsel from trial and may conduct trials without the presence of the defendant when he or she has intentionally disrupted the proceedings. Related postconviction changes authorize solitary confinement of prisoners for a period of thirty days.[135]

Two provisions in particular have generated controversy. The first concerns Sections 231a, 231b, and 255 of the Criminal Procedure Code, which together authorize courts to conduct proceedings in the absence of the defendant when he or she "intentionally and willfully causes his own unfitness to stand trial."[136] This provision was thought necessary because some defendants, such as Baader and Ensslin, had attempted to obstruct the cases against them by conducting hunger strikes or by disrupting the proceedings in other ways.* The exclusion

---

*The contrast with the behavior of IRA defendants is striking. The IRA now typically recognizes the jurisdiction of the Diplock courts and only rarely disrupts judicial proceedings. Part of the explanation for this difference is a function of the common practice of plea and charge bargaining in Northern Ireland, which provides an incentive for defendants to cooperate, and its absence in West Germany.

provisions are qualified, however, by the "self-infliction   ovision and by a
requirement that a defendant may not be excluded unle   e or she has first
been interrogated on the charges pending against him   er. Section 231b
permits exclusion for reasons of the defendant's hostil   nduct during the
proceedings, provided the defendant has been afforded an   portunity to enter
a plea to the charges.[137]

Although the practice of exclusion has been criticized as extreme, it is not
unknown in other democratic states. Exclusions of unruly defendants are also
possible, for example, in the United States, although it is done on a case-by-
case basis. An accused does have a constitutional right to be present at his or
her trial, either as a condition of due process[138] or on the basis of   explicit
constitutional right to confront witnesses,[139] and a right to   ce at trial
may easily be inferred from the constitutive principles iden   in chapter 1.
But the right may be forfeited by the defendant's own disr   ve behavior or
misconduct.[140] Forfeiture would not offend the constitutive principles, for the
defendant has been informed of the charge and has been given an opportunity
to respond to it—he has, simply, refused to avail himself of that opportunity.

More troublesome are provisions that authorize, in certain cases, the exclusion of defense attorneys from the proceedings. These amendments to the
procedural code permit higher regional courts or the Federal Court of Justice
(not the court in which the proceedings are being conducted) to issue an
exclusion order if defense counsel is suspected of having committed or having
aided in the commission of an offense, of having abused the right to contact the
accused in order to commit an offense or endanger prison security, or of
endangering the state. The immediate impetus behind these changes concerned
a decision by a lower court to exclude three defense attorneys during the trial
of Baader, Meinhof, and Ensslin. The lower court had assumed that there was
an inherent judicial power to exclude counsel in certain cases. In its finding
that the decision to exclude Ensslin's attorney was unconst utional, the Federal Constitutional Court relied upon the absence of a sta tory or constitutional grant of such power.[141]

Under Section 138a, subsequently enacted in 1974, a def se lawyer may be
excluded for the reasons already specified, upon the requ   the police, the
prosecutor, or the court. Section 138a provides:

> A defense attorney must be excluded from participation in a proceeding if he
> is urgently suspected . . . of having participated in the act which is the object
> of investigation or of having engaged in an activity which, were the accused to
> be found guilty, would make him an accessory, or constitute obstructing or
> impeding justice.[142]

Either the attorney or the defendant may appeal the exclusion order, and
where exclusion interferes with a mandatory defense, the defendant must be
given new counsel.

Although the power to exclude defense counsel may be harsh, it does not
necessarily offend the constitutive principles, so long as the suspicion that gives
rise to an order of exclusion must itself be reasonable. In the current process

such a decision may be appealed, and there are qualifications designed to mitigate the prejudicial effects this decision might have upon a defendant's trial. Without these requirements, however, such a power is easily subject to abuse and could be used not only to delay proceedings but to intimidate or harass the defendant or defense counsel.

The Contact Ban Law: Surveillance of Communications Between the Accused and Counsel

The Contact Ban Law, enacted in September 1977, was a response to allegations that some attorneys were transmitting illegal information to and from imprisoned terrorists. In particular, the provision was thought necessary by some because of suspicion that there was collaboration between certain of the imprisoned members of the RAF and the kidnapers of Hans Martin Schleyer.[143] Under the new provisions, a Land or the federal minister of justice is empowered to forbid written and oral contact between prisoners and their counsel, provided there is an immediate threat to life and liberty of an individual and where the contact ban may counteract the danger. As Wardlaw noted, "The ban is valid for 30 days, but must be upheld by a state court after 15 days or it automatically expires."[144] Upon expiration of the thirty days, a new ban may be imposed. During the thirty-day period, the defendant may not be interrogated and all criminal proceedings must be stayed.

Section 148 of the Procedural Code also anticipates that where a complete contact ban may be unwarranted, control over written communications may be exercised by the court or magistrate. Visual supervision is still impermissible, however, as is supervision of oral contacts.

In addition to these restrictions on the attorney–client relationship, Article 137 of the Procedural Code provides that a single defendant is entitled to no more than three attorneys. And as we saw earlier, Section 139 provides for a strictly limited attorney–client privilege under Section 138's disclosure requirements.

As was the case with the removal provisions, the Contact Ban Law, although a harsh provision, does not necessarily violate the constitutive principles. Once again, satisfaction of those principles demands that the initial basis for such a decision must be reasonableness of suspicion and allow for the possibility of subsequent independent review.[145]

Additional Special Powers and Provisions

Several other amendments to the Procedural Code concern the powers of the police in special circumstances. Section 103(1) indicates that the police may search without warrant an entire building if they believe that within it is a suspect who has committed an offense under Section 129 of the Penal Code. Other provisions (Section 111) authorize the police to conduct identity checks at roadblocks, provided there is reason to think there has been an offense under Section 129a or 250 (concerning aggravated robbery) and that the roadblocks are necessary to obtain evidence or to apprehend the suspect. A judicial order is required in such cases, except in a case of "immediate danger," when the prosecutor may authorize the roadblock.[146]

Identity checks are also permitted in some circumstances by virtue of Sections 163b and c. Individuals suspected of having committed a criminal offense are subject to identity checks by "any necessary legal measures."[147] Individuals not suspected of having committed an offense are still subject to identity checks, "including fingerprinting and having their photographs taken, but only to the extent of verifying the facts and circumstances of the case in question"[148] pending verification from other sources. The deprivation of liberty occasioned by an identity check may be for a period no longer than is necessary and may not in any case exceed twelve hours. A judicial order is necessary unless the check can be completed before such an order can be won, and all individuals must be promptly informed of the charges of which they are suspected.

In 1986 a new set of antiterrorism initiatives increased the length of sentences for certain terrorist acts, and in 1989 new legislation was enacted which permits, through 1991, the use of plea bargaining so that some individuals will be more likely to testify as state's witnesses. As a general principle, German criminal law does not permit plea bargaining, as does the law in the United States and the United Kingdom. Hence "charge bargaining" and the use of informants—prominent in the United Kingdom's antiterrorism policy in Ulster (or the Cossiga Law in Italy)—have not taken place in Germany.[149] Other changes provide for longer prison sentences for certain crimes, such as attacks on trains and aircraft and public utilities, and still others expanded the powers of the federal prosecutor in cases involving terrorist offenses.[150]

CONCLUSION

Antiterrorism legislation in West Germany finds its justification, if it can be found, in the Basic Law's concept of militant democracy and defense of the free democratic basic order. But whatever its appeal in the period shortly after World War II, and notwithstanding broad popular and parliamentary support for many antiterrorism initiatives, the concept of militant democracy no longer commands widespread or uncritical support in West Germany. Some of this erosion of support can be attributed to doubts about the efficacy of the concept itself. Some critics have complained that Article 21, for example, actually makes the defense of constitutional democracy more difficult because it drives the enemies of democracy to clothe their unconstitutional aims in constitutionally acceptable language, thus making foes appear as friends.[151]

In larger part, however, the erosion of support for the concept of militant democracy is a consequence of its unsavory association with the emergency amendments of 1968 and some of the more controversial antiterrorism policies of the 1970s and 1980s. Some of those policies, such as the Berufsverbot, are predicated upon a misunderstanding of what the concept of militant democracy properly demands in the way of constitutional maintenance. As I argued in chapter 1, the defense of constitutional democracy requires not the preservation of the contemporary West German state or of any particular regime (not even a particular democratic regime), but rather a defense of certain of the normative commitments (and their structural counterparts) that define constitutional democracy. Likewise, constitutional maintenance does not demand defense of the constitutional text, the Basic Law, but rather defense of those features in the Basic Law (the free democratic basic order) that are constitutive of not just this but of any constitutional democracy.

Some of the antiterrorism policies adopted by the Federal Republic neglect this fundamental distinction. As Kenneth H. F. Dyson noted in a study of the job ban, "One wonders . . . whether the prime purpose of the *Berufsverbot* is to protect the constitution's 'free democratic basic order' or whether it seeks by restrictive constitutional interpretation to protect a particular economic and social system against criticism and reform."[152] Dyson's criticism is shared by Heinrich Böll, who wrote in the poem "seven years and twenty later":

> just don't
> forget
> forget
> the free
> democratic
> constitutional system
> of BILD
> for BILD . . .*[153]

The Berufsverbot is not unique to the Federal Republic. As we saw, the United States and other European democracies have similar policies. But the vigor of its enforcement as a means for ensuring political orthodoxy, especially before the SPD and the CDU–CSU began to follow different interpretations of the decree, is a matter for concern. Moreover, most of the changes in the Penal and Criminal Procedure codes are not unique to West Germany, but their application has been extensive. The difficulty with the concept of militant democracy, therefore, as with the defense of constitutional democracy more generally, has been with its potentially expansive reach: "Unfortunately, a 'militant democracy' can easily become an illiberal democracy, more concerned with its own stability than with political development."[154]

A proper understanding of constitutional maintenance requires that we know when we must be tolerant, and when we must, in the words of Carlo Schmid, have the courage to be intolerant. Important in this respect is the nature of the political violence in the Federal Republic. The terrorism practiced by the RAF, the Revolutionary Cells, or smaller groups on the right

---

*"BILD" is a reference to the *Bild-Zeitung*, a conservative newspaper with a large circulation published in the Federal Republic by Springer-Verlag.

cannot be understood as promoting, however awkwardly, wrongfully, or violently, a different or better understanding of constitutional community. Instead, it completely rejects the desirability of constitutional democracy. The concept of militant democracy is right to see in that violence something intolerable. But insofar as the measures adopted in defense of democracy have suppressed legitimate political criticism, the concept of militant democracy has been misused to promote a democratic puritanism.

Conclusion

Nathaniel Ward, writing in *The Simple Cobbler of Aggawam*, advised his puritan congregation to practice "toleration in things tolerable," but warned also that "he [who] is willing to tolerate any unsound Opinion, that his own may also be tolerated, though never so sound, will for a need hang God's Bible at the Devil's girdle."[1] Ward's counsel illustrates the difficult and sensitive political judgments involved in the defense of constitutional democracy: Of what must we be tolerant, and what is there that must we not tolerate, of others and of ourselves, in that effort? I have tried to answer this question by exploring the limits of the first assumption (or hope?) upon which any conception of constitutional maintenance must ultimately rest, that "reflection and choice," and not passion or will, can be the basis of political community.[2] Widespread political violence challenges this presupposition. It is therefore a constitutional emergency in a very specific sense and a challenge to the general enterprise of constitutional maintenance in a larger sense. The efforts of constitutional democracies, such as the United Kingdom and the Federal Republic of Germany, to respond to such violence through antiterrorism and other forms of emergency legislation are not simply permitted but are required by the conception of constitutional maintenance proposed in this work.

But a proper understanding of constitutional maintenance, as Carl Friedrich once observed, requires not simply the defense of the outermost boundary but also the preservation of our innermost selves.[3] Our task, in other words, *is* to preserve our physical integrity but also, and no less important, our constitutional integrity. We must maintain and nourish our identity as political communities founded upon constitutionalism's twin commitments to reason and deliberation in public affairs. These commitments mean that there are constitutional principles that must govern our efforts to cope with political violence through changes in the rule of law.

I have tried to establish the foundation and the character of these principles by distinguishing between the defense of constitutionalism and the defense of specific constitutions. In so doing, I have argued that an account of constitutional maintenance must be sympathetic to the limits of human foresight and must include an understanding of constitutional claims to perpetuity which acknowledges the final and ultimate contingency of all constitutional documents. Machiavelli's counsel in the *Discourses* notwithstanding, no document can anticipate every challenge to its authority: Every constitutional text can, and will, fail.[4]

As a consequence, our efforts should be directed to the defense not of constitutions but of constitutionalism, of which any particular constitution is but a specific and historically contingent articulation. This suggestion does *not*, however, "disfranchise" the constitutional document by immediately securing our release from the limitations contained within it every time the Sêirenes sing. Our commitment to constitutionalism requires first that our efforts at defense comport with the bonds we put upon ourselves in less troubled times. Any constitutional text will admit of a wide range of legitimate interpretations of powers and liberties, and in many, if not most cases, interpretation will resolve apparent tensions between the need for expansive powers and constitutional limitations. But efforts to defend the text by interpreting it to mean whatever it has to mean in order to "maintain" it preserve not constitutional principles but rather a mere paper constitution.[5] Such a constitution can no longer be understood properly as resting within the fundamental predicates of constitutionalism itself.

My argument, then, is addressed to the inevitable cases when resolution through interpretation will not be possible; it assumes, as have most students of constitutional crises, that there will be times when contingency requires what the text, interpretation notwithstanding, prohibits. In these cases constitutionalism authorizes the suspension of parchment barriers, while nonetheless requiring that we continue to respect elemental constitutional principles. As I argued in chapter 1, these principles, which can be derived from both a historical and a philosophical understanding of constitutionalism, include certain normative commitments, such as reason and deliberation, human dignity, mitigation (or proportionality), and limited government, and the structural mechanisms necessary to their achievement, such as separation of powers and constitutional review.

I wrote earlier that Ward's admonition of "toleration in things tolerable" illustrates the difficult *political* judgments involved in the defense of constitutional democracy. The constitutive principles proposed in chapter 1—of reason and deliberation, dignity, mitigation, and review—should not be understood as discrete legal or constitutional rules that admit of easy or mechanical application. Nor should their relevance for the enterprise of constitutional maintenance be dismissed or discounted as a consequence of their inherent imprecision. As I have tried to show in my studies of constitutional crises in Germany and Northern Ireland, constitutional maintenance is a preeminently political task. The acts of constituting, maintaining, and dissolving communities involve questions concerning the very construction and governance of political life. The constitutive principles and constitutional norms that govern and inform those acts are not self-implementing; they admit of, if they do not demand, interpretation and elaboration. Thus they do not function as strict legal limitations upon the exercise of emergency powers, as some students of constitutional emergencies have thought necessary. They are, however, far better suited to a conception of constitutional life and emergencies that sees in constitutionalism a commitment not just to limited government but to a form of political community based upon the necessity for and the exchange of reason as the constitutive activity of public life. Constitutional discourse in such cases becomes not the private province of those with specialized knowledge of legal logic but rather the public language of the civic community.

Finally, my estimation of what constitutional maintenance demands in constitutional emergencies, although a necessary component, is hardly a complete account of constitutional maintenance more generally. A comprehensive narrative of constitutional maintenance would have to address questions concerning the creation, perpetuation, and intergenerational transmission of constitutional norms, rules, institutions, and texts, even, and perhaps especially, when those rules and structures are not directly or violently challenged. Included in such an account must be an understanding not only of the basis of constitutional claims to perpetuity, of the relationship between norms and structures, between constitution making and constitutional ends, as well as of constitutional interpretation and political representation, but also of civic education and constitutional literacy. If, as I have argued, constitutional integrity requires the preservation not of constitutional texts but of constitutional norms, then the perpetuation of these values is best served by the creation and maintenance of a political community in which constitutional concerns infuse politics every day and not simply or only during times of crisis. Constitutional maintenance in times of crisis is more likely to succeed when constitutional values are deeply held, or when they are an irreducible part of the deep structure of political life. As Robert Dahl wrote, "To assume that this country has remained democratic because of its Constitution seems . . . an obvious reversal of the relation; it is much more plausible to suppose that the Constitution has remained because our society is essentially democratic."[6]

A constitutional document cannot make us a constitutional community. Nor will its "defense" ensure our fidelity to constitutional values in an emergency. It is for this reason that the maintenance of constitutional democracy in times of crisis should be understood not simply as the physical defense of the state, or of the "constitution," but as the defense of a conception of ourselves as communities committed to the promotion and realization of a constitutional way of life. The seeming inability of "reason" to constitute such communities in places like Weimar Germany and Northern Ireland may suggest to some readers that constitutionalism's commitments to reason and deliberation in public affairs may be an unwarranted and dangerous form of naivete or idealism. But even if "the illusions of constitutionalism have great staying power among those who have never to pay the costs of their own illusions,"[7] we should set aside our commitment to constitutionalism only with a firm understanding of the sanguine conception of human potential which inheres in that "illusion."

Notes

INTRODUCTION

1. I adapt my account from Homer, *The Odyssey*, trans. Robert Fitzgerald (Garden City, N.Y. Anchor Books, 1963).

2. See, for example, Jon Elster and Rune Slagstad, eds., *Constitutionalism and Democracy: Studes in Rationality and Social Change* (New York: Cambridge University Press, 1988); Jon Elster, *Ulysses and the Sirens: Studies in Rationality and Irrationality* (New York: Cambridge University Press, 1979), 36–37, 94–96.

3. See Elster, *Ulysses, supra* n. 2 at 94–96; see generally Arthur Kuflick, "The Inalienability of Autonomy," 13 Phil. & Pub. Aff. 271 (1984); Derek Parfit, *Reasons and Persons* (New York: Oxford University Press, 1986), 11–13; Jon Elster, ed., *The Multiple Self* (New York: Cambridge University Press, 1986). On the topic of self-commands in general, see Thomas C. Schelling, *Choice and Consequence* (Cambridge, Mass: Harvard University Press, 1984); idem, "Self-Command in Practice, in Policy, and in a Theory of Rational Choice," 74 Am. Econ. Rev. 1 (1984).

4. For a discussion of this point as it relates to questions of constitutional interpretation rather than constitution making more generally, see William F. Harris II, "Bonding Word and Polity: The Logic of American Constitutionalism," 76 Am. Pol. Sci. Rev. 34 (1982).

5. Clinton Rossiter, ed., *The Federalist Papers* (New York: New American Library, 1961), No. 1, 33.

6. I do not, however, wish to say that constitutions literally construct reality, for this implies an epistemological position about the nature of political and social reality that I do not wish to defend or support. See generally Peter L. Berger and Thomas Luckman, *The Social Construction of Reality* (New York: Doubleday, 1967).

7. See Kenneth M. Stampp, "The Concept of Perpetual Union," 55 J. Am. Hist. 5 (1978); see also Alpheus T. Mason, "The Nature of Our Federal Union Reconsidered," 55 Pol. Sci. Q. 502 (1950).

8. As quoted in Gordon S. Wood, *The Creation of the American Republic, 1776–1787* (New York: W. W. Norton, 1972), 379 (emphasis in original).

9. Letter of Thomas Jefferson to James Madison, September 6, 1789, reprinted in Alpheus T. Mason, *Free Government in the Making*, 3rd ed. (New York: Oxford University Press, 1965), 374.

10. The entire speech is reprinted in Roy P. Basler, ed., *The Collected Works of Abraham Lincoln*, 9 vols. (New Brunswick, N.J.: Rutgers University Press, 1953), 4:262–71. As we shall see, the Basic Law of the Federal Republic of Germany explicitly

acknowledges its transitional character, but there are implicit and explicit claims of perpetuity throughout the text.

11. 74 U.S. (7 Wall.) 700 (1869).

12. Congressional Globe, April 11, 1871, 574.

13. Edmond Cahn, "The Consumers of Injustice," reprinted in Ephraim London, ed., *The Law as Literature* (New York: Simon and Schuster, 1960), 590.

14. Carl J. Friedrich, *Constitutional Reason of State: The Survival of the Constitutional Order* (Providence, R.I.: Brown University Press, 1957), 108.

15. For a comparison of the Irish Republic with Northern Ireland, see Gerard Hogan and Clive Walker, *Political Violence and the Law in Ireland* (Manchester, Eng.: Manchester University Press, 1989).

16. See generally Carl J. Friedrich, "The Constitution as a Political Force," in *Constitutional Government and Democracy*, rev. ed. (Waltham, Mass.: Blaisdell, 1950), 156–72.

17. Søren Kierkegaard, *Repetition*, ed. and trans. Howard H. Hong and Edna H. Hong (Princeton, N.J.: Princeton University Press, 1983); and as quoted in Carl Schmitt, *Political Theology*, trans. George Schwab (Cambridge, Mass.: MIT Press, 1985), 15.

18. Friedrich, *Constitutional Reason*, supra n. 14 at 8.

CHAPTER 1

1. James D. Richardson, ed. *Messages and Papers of the Presidents*, 10 vols. (Washington, D.C.: Government Printing Office, 1896), 6: 24–25.

2. Article 28(3)(3), Eire Constitution of 1937. See John Kelly, *The Irish Constitution* (Dublin: Jurist Publishing Co., 1984), 132–41.

3. McGee v. Attorney General and Revenue Commissioners, 1974 I.R. 284, 109 I.L.T.R. 29.

4. The SouthWest Case, 1 BVerfGE 14 (1951).

5. Sotirios Barber, *On What the Constitution Means* (Baltimore, Md.: Johns Hopkins University Press, 1984), 117–18.

6. Thomas Jefferson, letter to John V. Colvin, September 10, 1810, in *The Writings of Thomas Jefferson*, ed. Paul Leicester Ford, 10 vols. (New York: G. P. Putnam's Sons, 1893), 9: 279–80.

7. Kenneth Wheare, *Modern Constitutions* (London: Oxford University Press, 1966), 138.

8. I base my account on Livy, *The Early History of Rome*, trans. Aubrey de Selincourt (Harmondsworth, Eng.: Penguin Books, 1971), 213–16.

9. Carl J. Friedrich, *Constitutional Government and Democracy*, rev. ed. (Waltham, Mass.: Blaisdell, 1950), 574.

10. Clinton Rossiter, ed., *The Federalist Papers* (New York: New American Library, 1961), No. 70, 423 (Hereafter *The Federalist*.)

11. Clinton Rossiter, *Constitutional Dictatorship* (Princeton, N.J.: Princeton University Press, 1948), 15.

12. Friedrich, *Constitutional Government*, supra n. 9 at 580–84.

13. Rossiter, *Dictatorship*, supra n. 11 at 298–306.

14. Arthur M. Schlesinger, Jr., *The Imperial Presidency* (New York: Popular Library, 1974).

15. Id.

16. Joseph M. Bessette and Jeffrey Tulis, *The Presidency in a Constitutional Order* (Baton Rouge: Louisiana State University Press, 1981), 22. (Hereafter Bessette, *Constitutional Order*.)

17. Edward S. Corwin, *Total War and the Constitution* (New York: Alfred A. Knopf, 1947), 172.

18. John Locke, *Two Treatises of Government* [1690], ed. Peter Laslett (Cambridge: The University Press, 1960). Second Treatise, sections 159–61, 163, 168. See also Francis Wormuth, *The Royal Prerogative 1603–1699* (Ithaca, N.Y.: Cornell University Press, 1939).

19. Locke, *Two Treatises*, *supra* n. 18.

20. Schlesinger, *Imperial Presidency*, *supra* 14 at 309, 450–51.

21. Id.; compare Richard M. Pious, *The American Presidency* (New York: Basic Books, 1979), 84.

22. James Madison, letter to Thomas Jefferson, October 17, 1788, as reprinted in Alpheus T. Mason, ed., *Free Government in the Making: Readings in American Political Thought*, 3rd ed. (New York: Oxford University Press, 1965), 322.

23. Barber, *What the Constitution Means*, *supra* n. 5 at 188.

24. Id. at 188.

25. Bessette, *Constitutional Order*, *supra* n. 16 at 24.

26. Id. at 16–26.

27. Joseph W. Bendersky, *Carl Schmitt: Theorist for the Reich* (Princeton, N.J.: Princeton University Press, 1983), 37.

28. Bessette, *Constitutional Order*, *supra* n. 16 at 16–26.

29. Id. at 25–26.

30. Id. at 22.

31. *The Federalist*, *supra* n. 10 at 152–54 (No. 23).

32. Niccoló Machiavelli, *Discourses*, trans. and ed. Bernard Crick (Harmondsworth, Eng.: Penguin Books, 1970), ch. 34.

33. Ex parte Milligan, 71 U.S. [4 Wall.] 2, 120–21 (1866).

34. Bessette, *Constitutional Order*, *supra* n. 16 at 25.

35. I am aware that this is an argument that some readers will not quickly concede. See, for example, Sandy Levinson, "Law as Literature," 60 Tex. L. Rev. 373 (1982).

36. Barber, *What the Constitution Means*, *supra* n. 5 at 189, 39–62.

37. Id. at 191.

38. See Corwin, *Total War*, *supra* n. 17 at 168–82.

39. Barber, *What the Constitution Means*, *supra* n. 5 at 190.

40. Thomas Jefferson, letter to John V. Colvin, September 10, 1810, *supra* n. 6.

41. Giovanni, Sartori, "Constitutionalism: A Preliminary Discussion," 56 Am. Pol. Sci. Rev. 853 (1962) (emphasis in original).

42. Id. at 855.

43. Id.

44. Id. For a further discussion of the development of this concept and its centrality to modern constitutionalism, see also Charles H. McIlwain, *Constitutionalism: Ancient and Modern*, rev. ed. (Ithaca, N.Y.: Cornell University Press, 1947), 67–122.

45. Sartori, "Constitutionalism," *supra* n. 41 at 853, 861.

46. Karl Loewenstein, *Political Power and the Governmental Process* (Chicago: University of Chicago Press, 1957), 147ff.

47. Herbert J. Spiro, *Government by Constitution* (New York: Random House, 1959), 437.

48. The SouthWest Case, 1 BVerfGE 14 (1951).

49. Lincoln wavered on this point in his First Inaugural Address. The entire speech is reprinted in Roy P. Basler, ed., *The Collected Works of Abraham Lincoln*, 9 vols. (New Brunswick, N.J.: Rutgers University Press, 1953), 4: 262–71.

50. See generally Lon L. Fuller and Melvin A. Eisenberg, *Basic Contract Law*, 3rd ed. (St. Paul, Minn.: West Publishing Co., 1972), 89–102.

51. This approach suggests an answer to a fashionable jurisprudential puzzle: Could a constitutional amendment enacted in conformance with all of the procedural requirements of Article VI nevertheless be "unconstitutional" insofar as it contravenes the fundamental principles of Western constitutionalism? As the West German Federal Constitutional Court argued, "There are constitutional principles that are so fundamental . . . that they also bind the framers." see n. 4, *supra*. If we admit that the framers of constitutional documents, in their attempts to ordain the good society, to construct future political realities, commit themselves to the principles of constitutionalism that give their enterprise meaning, then common sense requires that we also admit that the framers, like the rest of us, are imperfect. They make mistakes, and we must be prepared to admit that their best understanding of the fundamental principles of constitutionalism may have been faulty. Indeed, one of the framers conceded that "I never expect to see a perfect work from imperfect man," language that takes on special significance in light of the founders' efforts to construct "a more perfect union." See *Federalist* 1; also as reprinted in Mason, *Free Government, supra* n. 22 at 252.

52. Georg Henrik von Wright, *Norm and Action: A Logical Enquiry* (London: Routledge and Kegan Paul, 1963), 5 (emphasis in original).

53. See generally Fuller and Eisenberg, *Contract Law, supra* n. 50 at 801–68.

54. Id. at 97–99, 801–68.

55. Krell v. Henry, [1903] 2 K.B. 740.

56. Frederick M. Watkins, "The Problem of Constitutional Dictatorship," in Carl J. Friedrich and Edward S. Mason, eds., *Public Policy* (Cambridge, Mass.: Harvard University Press, 1940), 330–31.

57. The literature on this point is far too voluminous to cite here. Representative pieces include Michael J. Perry, *Morality, Politics, and Law* (New York: Oxford University Press, 1989); Ronald Dworkin, *A Matter of Principle* (Cambridge, Mass.: Harvard University Press, 1985); John Hart Ely, *Democracy and Distrust: A Theory of Judicial Review* (Cambridge, Mass.: Harvard University Press, 1980); Barber, *What the Constitution Means, supra* n. 5; Paul Brest, "The Fundamental Rights Controversy: The Essential Contradictions of Normative Constitutional Scholarship," 90 Yale L. J. 1063 (1981); Walter F. Murphy, "Constitutional Intepretation: The Art of the Historian, Magician, or Statesman?" 87 Yale L. J. 1752 (1978).

58. Emile Durkheim, *The Division of Labor in Society*, trans. W. D. Halls, (New York: The Free Press, 1984), 158–62.

59. Wright, *Norm and Action, supra* n. 52 at 4–6.

60. Frederick Watkins, *The Failure of Constitutional Emergency Powers Under the German Republic* (Cambridge, Mass.: Harvard University Press, 1939), 135.

61. Lord Bolingbroke, *Historical Writings*, ed. Isaac Kremnick, 4 vols. (Chicago: University of Chicago Press, 1972) 2:88.

62. Carl J. Friedrich, *Transcendent Justice: The Religious Dimensions of Constitutionalism* (Durham, N.C.: Duke University Press, 1964), 17.

63. McIlwain, *Constitutionalism, supra* n. 44 at 136.

64. Id. at 139–41.

65. Michael J. Perry, "The Authority of Text, Tradition, and Reason: A Theory of Constitutional 'Interpretation,'" 58 S. Cal. L. Rev. 551, 594 (1985).

66. See, e.g., McIlwain, *Constitutionalism, supra* n. 44 at 21–22.

67. Dante Germino, "Carl Friedrich on Constitutionalism and the 'Great Tradition' of Political Theory," in J. Roland Pennock and John W. Chapman, eds., *Nomos 20: Constitutionalism* (New York: New York University Press, 1979), 22.

68. Wheare, *Modern Constitutions, supra* n. 7 at 138.

69. See generally Noam Chomsky, *Aspects of the Theory of Syntax* (Cambridge, Mass.: MIT Press, 1965); see also James Boyd White, *When Words Lose Their Meaning* (Chicago: University of Chicago Press, 1984).

70. Karl Llewellyn, *Jurisprudence: Realism in Theory and Practice* (Chicago: University of Chicago Press, 1960), 176–77.

71. See generally Barber, *What the Constitution Means, supra* n. 5.

72. William Blackstone, *Commentaries on the Laws of England*, 4 vols. (Chicago: University of Chicago Press, 1979) (reprint of the edition of 1765, printed at the Clarendon Press, Oxford), 1:230, 233–34.

73. McIlwain, *Constitutionalism, supra* n. 44 at 142.

74. Id at 21.

75. Id. at 140.

76. John Locke, *Two Treatises of Government*, ed. Peter Laslett and Thomas P. Peardon (Cambridge: The University Press, 1960), chap. 4, Book II, xi, para. 139.

77. Jean Bodin, as quoted in McIlwain, *Constitutionalism, supra* n. 43 at 167n2.

78. John E. Finn and David Aladjem, "Reasoning About Presidential Prerogative: A Preliminary Account," paper presented to the Northeastern Political Science Association, Boston, Massachusetts, 1986, 21.

79. See White, *Words, supra* n. 69 at 89.

80. For a discussion of the relationship between contingency and constitutionalism, see Barber, *What the Constitution Means, supra* n. 5 at 191.

81. *The Federalist, supra* n. 10 at 303 (No. 47) (emphasis in original).

82. Barber, *What the Constitution Means, supra* n. 80 at 180.

83. Myers v. United States, 272 U.S. 52 (1926).

84. Barber, *What the Constitution Means, supra* n. 5 at 103.

85. Mauro Cappalletti, *Judicial Review in the Contemporary World* (New York: Bobbs-Merrill, 1971), 69–88.

86. McIlwain, *Constitutionalism, supra* n. 44 at 140.

87. For a review, see Walter F. Murphy and Joseph Tanenhaus, eds., *Comparative Constitutional Law Cases and Commentaries* (New York: St. Martin's Press, 1977).

88. Walter F. Murphy, "An Ordering of Constitutional Values," 53 S. Cal. L. Rev. 703, 745–54 (1980).

89. See, e.g., Justice Stewart's dissenting opinion in Moore v. City of East Cleveland, 431 U.S. 494, 535–36 (1971); and Robert H. Bork, "Neutral Principles and Some First Amendment Problems," 47 Ind. L. J. 1, 20 (1971).

90. 431 U.S. 494, 535–36 (1971).

91. Richard Lindley, *Autonomy* (Atlantic Highlands, N.J.: Humanities Press International, 1986), 187.

92. Barber, *What the Constitution Means, supra* n. 5 at 123–26.

93. Arthur Kuflick, "The Inalienability of Autonomy" 13 Phil. & Pub. Aff. 271, 297 (1984).

94. Id.

95. Carl J. Friedrich, *Constitutional Reason of State* (Providence, R.I.: Brown University Press, 1957), 13.

96. Barber, *What the Constitution Means, supra* n. 5 at 128.

97. My argument, in other words, has led not to a single right answer but rather has delineated a set of acceptable reasons and disqualified others. I have therefore hardly succeeded in eliminating controversy, for there remains the problem of choosing among the class of "good" reasons. For a discussion of this issue, see Barber, *What the Constitution Means, supra* n. 5 at 128; White, *Words, supra* n. 69 at 67.

98. White, *Words, supra* n. 69 at 89.

99. Owen Fiss, "Foreword: The Forms of Justice," 93 Harv. L. Rev. 1, 13 (1979).

100. Michael J. Perry, *The Constitution, the Courts, and Human Rights* (New Haven, Conn.: Yale University Press, 1982), 25.

101. Murphy, "Constitutional Values," *supra* n. 88 at 703, 746.

102. Id.; see generally Laurence Tribe, "The Puzzling Persistence of Process-Based Theories of Interpretation," 89 Yale L. J. 1063 (1980).

103. Friedrich, *Reason of State, supra* n. 95 at 10.

104. Carl J. Friedrich, *Transcendent Justice* (Durham, N.C.: Duke University Press, 1964), 3.

105. Kuflick, "The Inalienability of Autonomy," *supra* n. 93.

106. Id.

107. Ely, *Democracy and Distrust, supra* n. 57 at 51; idem, "Discovering Fundamental Values—Supreme Court Forward 1978," 92 Harv. L. Rev. 27–28 (1978).

108. Dworkin, *Principle, supra* n. 57 at 119–45; idem, "Law as Interpretation," 60 Tex. L. Rev. 527 (1982).

109. Murphy, "Constitutional Values," *supra* n. 88 at 703, 706–7 (1980).

110. This is hardly a novel requirement. See, for example, Carl J. Friedrich, *Constitutional Government and Democracy* (Waltham, Mass.: Blaisdell, 1950), 581–83; Rossiter, *Dictatorship, supra* n. 11 at 297–306.

111. Locke, *Two Treatises, supra* n. 18 at sec. 167.

112. See Charles Fairman, *The Law of Martial Rule*, 2nd ed. (Chicago: University of Chicago Press, 1940), 22–25.

113. Id.

114. Watkins, *Constitutional Emergency Powers, supra* n. 60 at 135–36.

115. Bessette, *Constitutional Order, supra* n. 16 at 24–25.

116. For a discussion on this point, see Barber, *What the Constitution Means, supra* n. 5 at 188–90.

117. Friedrich, *Reason of State, supra* n. 95 at 113.

118. See generally Alasdair MacIntyre, *After Virtue*, rev. ed. (Notre Dame, Ind.: University of Notre Dame Press, 1984).

119. McIlwain, *Constitutionalism, supra* n. 44 at 144.

120. For a similar argument in the context of terroristic political violence, see Robert Gerstein, "Do Terrorists Have Rights?" in David C. Rapoport and Yonah Alexander, eds., *The Morality of Terrorism: Religious and Secular Justifications* (New York: Pergamon Press, 1982), 290.

121. Such an argument is, of course, closely related to questions of political obligation. See generally Richard E. Flathman, *Political Obligation* (New York: Atheneum, 1972).

122. I am not foreclosing the possibility that terrorists may, through their use of violence, constructively resign their citizenship. See e.g., Kennedy v. Mendoza-Martinez, 372 U.S. 144 (1963). *Mendoza-Martinez* also held that the burden of proving constructive, voluntary abandonment rests with the government. In other words, the government bears the initial burden of coming forth with *reasons*.

123. Barber, *What the Constitution Means*, supra n. 5 at 126–31, 144–45, 161–63.

124. *The Federalist*, supra n. 10 at 247–55 (No. 40).

125. Id. at 251 (No. 40).

126. Id. at 248 (No. 40).

127. Id.

128. Id. at 249 (No. 40).

129. Id. at 251 (No. 40).

130. The entire speech is reprinted in Basler, *The Collected Works of Abraham Lincoln*, supra n. 49.

131. Id.

132. *The Federalist*, supra n. 10 at 248–49, (No. 40).

133. Friedrich, *Reason of State*, supra n. 95 at 13.

134. Perry, *The Constitution*, supra n. 100. For a discussion of this dispute and its possible implications for public law scholarship more generally, see Sotirios A. Barber, "Normative Theory, the 'New Institutionalism,' and the Future of Public Law," and the reply by Rogers Smith, "The New Institutionalism and Normative Theory: Reply to Professor Barber," and by Martin Shapiro, "Political Jurisprudence, Public Law, and Post-Consequentialist Ethics: Comment on Professors Barber and Smith," in Karen Orren and Stephen Skowronek, eds., *Studies in American Political Development—An Annual*, vol. 3 (New Haven, Conn.: Yale University Press, 1989).

135. Id.

136. Perry, *Morality*, supra n. 57.

137. Id. at 11.

138. Ed. at 44, 53.

139. Michael Moore, "Moral Reality," 1982 Wis. L. Rev. 1061, 1143 (1982).

140. Id. at 1152.

141. Michael Moore, "A Natural Law Theory of Interpretation," 58 S. Cal. L. Rev. 279, 309 (1985).

142. Id. at 301–2.

143. For a discussion of the possibility of universal, or shared interests, see Perry, *Morality*, supra n. 57 at 47; see also Phillipa Foot, "Moral Relativism," in Jack W. Meiland and Michael Krausz, eds., *Relativism: Cognitive and Moral* (Notre Dame, Ind.: University of Notre Dame Press, 1982), 164.

144. For a discussion that doubts the possibility of a noncontextual approach, see Don Herzog, *Without Foundations* (Ithaca, N.Y.: Cornell University Press, 1985).

145. See *The Federalist*, supra n. 10 at 247–55 (No. 40); Marshall utilized a similar form of reasoning in McCulloch v. Maryland, 4 Wheat. 316 (1819).

146. Lon L. Fuller, *The Morality of the Law*, 2nd ed. (New Haven, Conn.: Yale University Press, 1969), 39.

PART II

1. William S. Churchill, *The Aftermath: A Sequel to the World Crisis* (New York: Scribner's, 1929), 319; and as quoted in Richard Rose, *Governing Without Consensus: Conflict in Northern Ireland* (Boston: Beacon Press, 1971), 359.

2. See, e.g., Roger H. Hull, *The Irish Triangle: Conflict in Northern Ireland* (Princeton, N.J.: Princeton University Press, 1976), 267–70.

3. Eamonn McCann, *War and an Irish Town* (London: Penguin Books, 1974), 9.

4. Frank Burton, *The Politics of Legitimacy: Struggles in a Belfast Community* (London: Routledge and Kegan Paul, 1978), 37.

5. William Butler Yeats, "Sixteen Dead Men," in Richard J. Finneran, ed., *W. B. Yeats, The Poems: A New Edition* (New York: Macmillan, 1983), 182.

6. Kevin Boyle, Tom Hadden, and Paddy Hillyard, *Ten Years On in Northern Ireland* (London: The Cobden Trust, 1980), 31–32.

7. Id. at 88–91.

8. Section 31, Northern Ireland (Emergency Provisions) Act (1978).

CHAPTER 2

1. Harry Calvert, *Constitutional Law in Northern Ireland: A Study in Regional Government* (London: Stevens and Sons, 1968), 41–57.

2. Section 2(1), The Government of Ireland Act (1920).

3. Claire Palley, "The Evolution, Disintegration and Possible Reconstruction of the Northern Irish Constitution," 1 Anglo-Am. L. Rev. 368, 389 (1972).

4. Section 75, The Government of Ireland Act (1920).

5. Palley, "Reconstruction," *supra* n. 3 at 383–84.

6. See Calvert, *Constitutional Law*, *supra* n. 1 at 86–110.

7. Id. at 87.

8. Section 5(1), The Government of Ireland Act (1920).

9. See, e.g., Calvert, *Constitutional Law*, *supra* n. 1 at 253, 255–56; W. Don Carroll, "The Search for Justice in Northern Ireland," 6 N.Y.U. J. Int'l. Law & Pol. 28, 50–51 (1973).

10. Id. at 51.

11. Paul Arthur, *Political Realities: The Government and Politics of Northern Ireland* (Burnt Mill, Eng.: Longman Group, 1980), 25–26.

12. As quoted in John Magee, *Northern Ireland: Crisis and Conflict* (London: Routledge and Kegan Paul, 1974), 77.

13. Palley, "Reconstruction," *supra* n. 3 at 400.

14. As quoted in Magee, *Crisis*, *supra* n. 12 at 77.

15. Section 1(1), The Special Powers Act.

16. Section 1(4), The Special Powers Act.

17. Palley, "Reconstruction," *supra* n. 3 at 400.

18. Kevin Boyle, Tom Hadden, and Paddy Hillyard, *Law and State: The Case of Northern Ireland* (London: Martin Robertson & Co., 1975), 8. (Hereafter Boyle, *Law and State*.)

19. *Report of the Commission on Disturbances in Northern Ireland*, Cmnd. 532 (Belfast: HMSO, 1975), paras. 228–30. (Hereafter Cameron Report.)

20. Id.

21. Arthur, *Political Realities*, *supra* n. 11 at 88–92.

22. *Cameron Report*, *supra* n. 19; and as excerpted in Magee, *Crisis*, *supra* n. 12 at 122.

23. As excerpted in Magee, *Crisis*, *supra* n. 12 at 123.

24. See McEldowney v. Forde [1969] W.L.R. 179; Boyle, *Law and State*, *supra* n. 18 at 13–15.

25. See McEdowney v. Forde [1969].

26. See Boyle, *Law and State*, *supra* n. 18 at 14–15.

27. A. T. Q. Stewart, *The Narrow Ground* (London: Faber and Faber, 1977), 16.

28. See e.g., Richard Rose, *Governing Without Consensus: Conflict in Northern Ireland* (Boston: Beacon Press, 1971), 102–3; Arthur, *Political Realities, supra* n. 11 at 103.

29. Arthur, *Political Realities, supra* n. 11 at 103–4; Rose, *Consensus, supra* n. 28 at 103–4.

30. Rose, *Consensus, supra* n. 28 at 103; Arthur, *Political Realities, supra* n. 11 at 103–4.

31. Rose, *Consensus, supra* n. 28 at 102–3; Arthur, *Political Realities, supra* n. 11 at 102–4.

32. Arthur, *Political Realities, supra* n. 11 at 102–3. The sexual imagery associated with the city is no less important in Protestant than in Catholic mythology. For Protestants, Londonderry is "a virtuous Protestant maiden," whose honor they must defend. For Catholics she is "a bedraggled Catholic wench," raped and assaulted by Protestant conquerors. See id. at 100–101.

33. Rose, *Consensus, supra* n. 28 at 103–5; Arthur, *Political Realities, supra* n. 11 at 103–4.

34. Arthur, *Political Realities, supra* n. 11 at 104; Roger H. Hull, *The Irish Triangle: Conflict in Northern Ireland* (Princeton, N.J.: Princeton University Press, 1976), 40–41.

35. Rose, *Consensus, supra* n. 28 at 103; Arthur, *Political Realities, supra* n. 11 at 104.

36. Michael Farrell, *Northern Ireland: The Orange State* (London: Pluto Press, 1980), 247. (Hereafter Farrell, *The Orange State*.)

37. Rose, *Consensus, supra* n. 28 at 103–4; Arthur, *Political Realities, supra* n. 11 at 108–9.

38. Magee, *Crisis, supra* n. 12 at 78.

39. Farrell, *The Orange State, supra* n. 36 at 247; see also Rose, *Consensus, supra* n. 28 at 159–60. Farrell was one of the founding members of the People's Democracy.

40. Rose, *Consensus, supra* n. 28 at 103; Farrell, *The Orange State, supra* n. 36 at 248–49.

41. As quoted in Magee, *Crisis, supra* n. 12 at 118–19.

42. Rose, *Consensus, supra* n. 28 at 104–5.

43. Id.; Farrell, *The Orange State, supra* n. 36 at 249–50.

44. See, e.g., Farrell, *The Orange State, supra* n. 36 at 251; Bernadette Devlin, *The Price of My Soul* (New York: Alfred A. Knopf, 1969), 120; Rose, *Consensus, supra* n. 28 at 104.

45. Cameron Report, *supra* n. 19 at para. 9, p. 73.

46. Arthur, *Political Realities, supra* n. 11 at 109. For an interesting description of Free Derry, see *New York Times*, April 27, 1972.

47. Cameron Report, *supra* n. 19 at para. 9, p. 73.

48. Id. at 24–29.

49. Magee, *Crisis, supra* n. 12 at 119.

50. Farrell, *The Orange State, supra* n. 36 at 252.

51. Id. at 251.

52. Id.

53. Rose, *Consensus, supra* n. 28 at 105; Arthur, *Political Realities, supra* n. 11 at 108–9.

54. Farrell, *The Orange State, supra* n. 36 at 254.

55. Arthur, *Political Realities, supra* n. 11 at 109.

56. Farrell, *The Orange State, supra* n. 36 at 256.

57. Rose, *Consensus, supra* n. 28 at 105–6.

58. Id. at 106; Farrell, *The Orange State, supra* n. 36 at 259.

59. Rose, *Consensus, supra* n. 28 at 106.

60. Id. at 166–69; Hull, *Irish Triangle, supra* n. 34 at 153–54.

61. Hull, *Irish Triangle, supra* n. 34 at 154; Rose, *Consensus, supra* n. 28 at 167–68.

62. Rose, *Consensus, supra* n. 28 at 166–67; Hull, *Irish Triangle, supra* n. 34 at 153–54.

63. Farrell, *The Orange State, supra* n. 36 at 269.

64. Rose, *Consensus, supra* n. 28 at 166–68; Farrell, *The Orange State, supra* n. 36 at 269–70. For an interesting day-by-day account of the trial, see Tom MacIntyre, *Through the Bridewell Gate* (London: Faber and Faber, 1971).

65. Rose, *Consensus, supra* n. 28 at 168–69.

66. Id.

67. Id. at 169; Hull, *Irish Triangle, supra* n. 34 at 153–54.

68. Magee, *Crisis, supra* n. 12 at 120.

69. As quoted in id. at 22.

70. Id. at 259–60; Rose, *Consensus, supra* n. 28 at 107.

71. *Report of Tribunal of Inquiry on Violence and Civil Disturbances in Northern Ireland in 1969*, Cmnd. 566 (Belfast: HMSO, 1972). (Hereafter Scarman Report.)

72. *Report of the Advisory Committee on Police in Northern Ireland*, Cmnd. 535 (London: HMSO, 1969). (Hereafter Hunt Report.)

73. Farrell, *The Orange State, supra* n. 36 at 261–62.

74. As printed in Geoffrey Bell, *The Protestants of Ulster* (London: Pluto Press, 1978), 52.

75. Farrell, *The Orange State, supra* n. 36 at 259–60; Rose, *Consensus, supra* n. 28 at 106–7.

76. Rose, *Consensus, supra* n. 28 at 107; Farrell, *The Orange State, supra* n. 36 at 264.

77. Farrell, *The Orange State, supra* n. 36 at 264; Rose, *Consensus, supra* n. 28 at 107.

78. Rose, *Consensus, supra* n. 28 at 107; Farrell, *The Orange State, supra* n. 36 at 264.

79. Kevin Boyle, Tom Hadden, and Paddy Hillyard, *Ten Years On in Northern Ireland* (London: The Cobden Trust, 1980), 25. (Hereafter Boyle, *Ten Years On.*)

80. Arthur, *Political Realities, supra* n. 11 at 127.

81. For a detailed description, see Boyle, *Law and State, supra* n. 18 at 87–88.

82. Rose, *Consensus, supra* n. 28 at 111.

83. Id.

84. R. (Hume and others) v. Londonderry Justices [1972] N.I. 91; see generally Boyle, *Law and State, supra* n. 18 at 132.

85. Magee, *Crisis, supra* n. 12 at 128; Rose, *Consensus, supra* n. 28 at 96.

86. Conor Cruise O'Brien, *States of Ireland* (London: Hutchinson Press, 1972), 205.

87. Id.

88. Boyle, *Ten Years On, supra* n. 79 at 15–16.

89. *New York Times*, June 4, 1972.

90. Boyle, *Ten Years On, supra* n. 79 at 15–16.

91. O'Brien, *States of Ireland, supra* n. 86 at 205; Magee, *Crisis, supra* n. 12 at

131–32. See also Michael Morgan, "How the British Created the Provos," 275 *Fortnight: An Independent Review for Northern Ireland* 12–13 (1989).

92. Farrell, *The Orange State, supra* n. 36 at 276.

93. Id. at 277.

94. Id. at 279.

95. Id at 280–81; Arthur, *Political Realities, supra* n. 11 at 126–27.

96. Bernard Weinraub, "Inside the Irish Internment Camps," *New York Times Magazine*, April 2, 1972, pp. 39, 44.

97. Id. at 39; see also Magee, *Crisis, supra* n. 12 at 142.

98. Magee, *Crisis, supra* n. 12 at 142.

99. Id.

100. Id.; Boyle, *Law and State, supra* n. 18 at 55–56.

101. David R. Lowry, "Internment: Detention Without Trial in Northern Ireland," 5 Hum. Rts. 261, 274 (1976).

102. *Report of the Commission to Consider Legal Procedures to Deal with Terrorist Activities in Northern Ireland*, Cmnd. 5185 (London: HMSO, 1972) (Hereafter Diplock Report.); as excerpted in Magee, *Crisis, supra* n. 12 at 169.

103. Lowry, "Internment," *supra* n. 101 at 276.

104. Gill H. Boehringer, "Alternative Criminology and Prisoner's Movements: Partnership or Rip-Off?" 1 Alternative Criminology J. 24, 36 (1975).

105. See, e.g., Boyle, *Law and State, supra* n. 18 at 75–76; Arthur, *Political Realities, supra* n. 11 at 112–13; Lowry, "Internment," *supra* n. 101 at 276–77.

106. Bernard Weinraub, "Ulster Rioting Ebbs as Toll Reaches 24," *New York Times*, August 13, 1971, p. 3.

107. *The Sunday Times "Insight Team," Ulster* (London: Penguin Books, 1972); excerpted in Magee, *Crisis, supra* n. 12 at 142.

108. Farrell, *The Orange State, supra* n. 36 at 284.

109. The Debts Act was passed to counter the rent and rates strikes against internment and involves the mandatory deduction at source of social security payments to pay debts to various administrative bodies.

110. Hull, *Irish Triangle, supra* n. 34 at 181.

111. Weinraub, "Irish Internment Camps," *supra* n. 96 at 36.

112. *Report of the Enquiry into Allegations Against the Security Forces of Physical Brutality in Northern Ireland Arising Out of Events on the 9th August*, Cmnd. 4823 (London: HMSO, 1971), paras. 1–3 (Hereafter Compton Report.); see also Boyle, *Law and State, supra* n. 18 at 49; Hull, *Irish Triangle, supra* n. 34 at 188.

113. Compton Report, *supra* n. 112 at para. 105.

114. Id.; Boyle, *Law and State, supra* n. 18 at 49–50.

115. John Wale, "Torture: A Deeper Cause for Despair," *Sunday Times* (London), September 5, 1976, p. 12; quoted in Arthur, *Political Realities, supra* n. 18 at 113.

116. Compton Report, *supra* n. 112 at para. 105.

117. Id.

118. *Report of the Commission of the Privy Councillors Appointed to Consider Authorized Procedures for the Interrogation of Persons Suspected of Terrorism*, Cmnd. 4901 (London: HMSO, 1972), 13–15, 20 (Hereafter Parker Report.); also as quoted in Hull, *Irish Triangle, supra* n. 34 at 183n54.

119. *Times* (London), November 26, 1971.

120. Parker Report, *supra* n. 118; Boyle, *Law and State, supra* n. 18 at 50.

121. Boyle, *Law and State, supra* n. 18 at 50.

122. Parker Report, *supra* n. 118 at 13–15.

123. Application No. 5310/71; see, e.g., Boyle, *Law and State, supra* n. 18 at 155–56.

124. Boyle, *Law and State, supra* n. 18 at 156.

125. See, e.g., id.; Hull, *Irish Triangle, supra* n. 34 at 217–18.

126. Peter Taylor, *Beating the Terrorists? Interrogation at Omagh, Gough, and Castlereagh* (London: Penguin Books, 1980), 23–24; Boyle, *Law and State, supra* n. 18 at 156.

127. Taylor, *Beating the Terrorists, supra* n. 126 at 23–24.

128. Id. at 24.

129. Id.

130. Boyle, *Law and State, supra* n. 18 at 157.

131. European Human Rights Report, p. 81, para. 174 (1979). See generally K. Boyle and H. Hannum, "Ireland in Strasbourg: An Analysis of Northern Irish Proceedings Before the European Commission of Human Rights," 7 Irish Jurist 392 (1976); Kevin Boyle, "Human Rights and Political Resolution in Northern Ireland," 9 Yale J. World Pub. Ord. 165 (1982).

132. See, e.g., Taylor, *Beating the Terrorists, supra* n. 126 at 80–81.

133. *Report of the Committee of Inquiry into Police Interrogation Procedures in Northern Ireland,* Cmnd. 7497 (London: HMSO, 1979), para. 404. (Hereafter Bennett Report.); see also Thomas P. Foley, "Public Security and Individual Freedom: The Dilemma of Northern Ireland," 8 Yale J. World Pub. Ord. 284, 300–301 (1982).

134. Dermot P. J. Walsh, "Arrest and Interrogation," in Anthony Jennings, ed., *Justice Under Fire: The Abuse of Civil Liberties in Northern Ireland* (London: Pluto Press, 1988), 43.

135. Id.

136. Farrell, *The Orange State, supra* n. 36 at 288.

137. Id. at 289.

138. See Arthur, *Political Realities, supra* n. 11 at 129; Boyle, *Law and State, supra* n. 18 at 126–28.

139. Anthony Lewis, "British Inquiry in Ulster Shootings as Emotion Rises," *New York Times,* February 1, 1972, p. 10.

140. Farrell, *The Orange State, supra* n. 36 at 290.

141. Magee, *Crisis, supra* n. 12 at 141.

142. Id.

143. Id.

144. As quoted in Bell, *Protestants of Ulster, supra* n. 74 at 3.

145. *Report of the Tribunal Appointed to Inquire into the Events of Sunday, 30th January 1972, Which Led to Loss of Life in Connection with the Processions in Londonderry on That Day* (H.L. No. 101, H.C. No. 220) (London: HMSO, 1972) (Hereafter Widgery Report.); see also Boyle, *Law and State, supra* n. 18 at 127. Some critics have speculated that Lord Widgery did not actually write the report. See "Did Widgery Write Widgery?" 1 Civ. Rts. 3 (April 28, 1972).

146. See, e.g., Boyle, *Law and State, supra* n. 18 at 126–28; Arthur, *Political Realities, supra* n. 11 at 129.

147. Widgery Report, *supra* n. 145 at 36–38; see also Hull, *Irish Triangle, supra* n. 34 at 191.

148. Widgery Report, *supra* n. 145 at 38.

149. Alvin Shuster, "Londonderry Study Blames Troops," *New York Times,* June 8, 1972, p. 3.

150. Id.; Dash, *Justice Denied: A Challenge to Lord Widgery on Bloody Sunday* (New York: International League for Rights of Men, 1972), 14; Boyle, *Law and State, supra* n. 18 at 130.

234   *Notes*

151. See, e.g., Magee, *Crisis, supra* n. 12 at 150–51; Bell, *Protestants of Ulster, supra* n. 74 at 124–26; Boyle, *Law and State, supra* n. 18 at 32–33.

152. *Belfast Telegraph*, April 12, 1972: reprinted in Bell, *Protestants of Ulster*, n. 74 at 125.

153. Boyle, *Law and State, supra* n. 18 at 32–33. For a general overview of the Ulster Defence Association, see Bell, *Protestants of Ulster, supra* n. 74 at 137–39.

154. As quoted in Magee, *Crisis, supra* n. 12 at 156; see also Farrell, *The Orange State, supra* n. 36 at 304.

155. Magee, *Crisis, supra* n. 12 at 151.

156. Id.; see also Frederick Watkins, *The Failure of Constitutional Emergency Powers Under the German Republic* (Cambridge, Mass.: Harvard University Press, 1939); Arthur M. Schlesinger, Jr., *The Imperial Presidency* (Boston: Houghton Mifflin, 1973).

157. See e.g., Clinton Rossiter, *Constitutional Dictatorship* (Princeton, N.J.: Princeton University Press, 1948).

158. See, e.g., Charles H. McIlwain, *Constitutionalism: Ancient and Modern*, rev. ed. (Ithaca, N.Y.: Cornell University Press, 1947), 1–22.

159. *Northern Ireland Constitutional Proposals*. Cmnd. 5259. (London: HMSO, 1973).

160. For a comprehensive history of the IRA, consult J. Bowyer Bell, *The Secret Army: The IRA 1916–1977*, rev. ed. (Cambridge, Mass.: MIT Press, 1983).

161. Northern Ireland (Emergency Provisions) Act (1978), sec. 31.

162. As quoted in Rosita Sweetman, *On Our Knees* (London: Pan Books, 1972); Magee, *Crisis, supra* n. 12 at 153–54.

163. Magee, *Crisis, supra* n. 12 at 153; Farrell, *The Orange State, supra* n. 36 at 298–99.

164. For a general treatment of Protestant political and social culture in Northern Ireland, see Bell, *Protestants of Ulster, supra* n. 74; Rosemary Harris, *Prejudice and Tolerance in Ulster* (Manchester, Eng.: Manchester University Press, 1972); Ian Adamson, *The Identity of Ulster* (Northern Ireland: W & G. Baird, 1982).

165. Edward Moxon-Browne, "The Water and the Fish: Public Opinion and the Provisional IRA in Northern Ireland," 5 *Terrorism: An International Journal* 41–72 (1981).

166. See "Election '87: And Then There Were Thirteen," 253 *Fortnight: An Independent Review for Northern Ireland* 11–13 (1987).

167. Cynthia Irvin and Edward Moxon-Browne, "Not Many Floating Voters Here," 273 *Fortnight: An Independent Review for Northern Ireland* 7–8 (1989).

168. Id. at 7.

169. Id. at 9.

170. Id. at 9.

CHAPTER 3

1. Tom Hadden, Kevin Boyle, and Colm Campbell, "Emergency Law in Northern Ireland: The Context," in Anthony Jennings, ed., *Justice Under Fire: The Abuse of Civil Liberties in Northern Ireland* (London: Pluto Press, 1988), 8–9. (Hereafter Jennings, *Under Fire*.)

2. Gerard Hogan and Clive Walker, *Political Violence and the Law in Ireland* (Manchester, Eng.: Manchester University Press, 1989), 4–5. (Hereafter Hogan,

Political Violence.) For a judicial interpretation of Section 31, see McKee v. Chief Constable for Northern Ireland, (1984) 1 W.L.R. 1358 (H.L.), (1984) N.Ir. 169.

3. *Report of the Commission to Consider Legal Procedures to Deal with Terrorist Activities in Northern Ireland,* Cmnd. 5185 (London: HMSO, 1972), para. 1. (Hereafter Diplock Report.)

4. My discussion does not, therefore, consider in detail the international legal frameworks and norms that play an important role in shaping British antiterrorism legislation. I shall, however, make brief references to the more important aspects of international and supranational legal obligations, especially when they have led to significant changes in the antiterrorism legislation. For brief but insightful discussions of the role of international law, see Hogan, *Political Violence, supra* n. 2 at 36–38; Jennings, *Under Fire, supra* n. 1 at 17–22; K. Boyle and H. Hannum, "Ireland in Strasbourg: An Analysis of Northern Irish Proceedings Before the European Commission of Human Rights," 7 Irish Jurist 392 (1976); Kevin Boyle, "Human Rights and Political Resolution in Northern Ireland," 9 Yale J. World Pub. Ord. 165 (1982).

5. Kevin Boyle, Tom Hadden, and Paddy Hillyard, *Ten Years On in Northern Ireland* (London: The Cobden Trust, 1980), 57. (Hereafter Boyle, *Ten Years On.*)

6. As quoted in "The Case for Replacement of the EPA by Normal Judicial Process." Unpublished report issued by the Peace People (Belfast, Northern Ireland, 1978), 2.

7. For especially good reviews, see Clive Walker, *The Prevention of Terrorism in British Law* (Manchester, Eng.: Manchester University Press, 1986); Hogan, *Political Violence, supra* n. 2; Jennings, *Under Fire, supra* n. 1; Boyle, *Ten Years On, supra,* n. 5.

8. For a general review of powers of arrest, see Dermot P. J. Walsh, "Arrest and Interrogation," in Jennings, *Under Fire, supra* n. 1 at 27–46.

9. See Hogan, *Political Violence, supra* n. 2 at 116–18.

10. As printed in Richard Harvey, *Diplock and the Assault on Civil Liberties* (London: The Haldane Society, 1981), 35.

11. *The Review of the Operation of the Northern Ireland (Emergency Provisions) Act 1978,* Cmnd. 9222 (London: HMSO, 1984), 95, para. 323. (Hereafter Baker Report.)

12. Hogan, *Political Violence, supra* n. 2 at 4–5.

13. See McKee v. Chief Constable for Northern Ireland, [1984] 1 W.L.R. 1358 (H.L.); see also Clive Walker, "Emergency Arrest Powers," 36 N.I.L.Q. 145 (1985).

14. [1985] 1 All E.R. 1; see also Jennings, *Under Fire, supra* n. 1 at 32–33.

15. Jennings, *Under Fire, supra* n. 1 at 33.

16. *Report of the Committee of Inquiry into Police Interrogation Procedures in Northern Ireland,* Cmnd. 7497 (London: HMSO, 1979), para. 70 (Hereafter Bennett Report.); for a general review, *see* Jennings, *Under Fire, supra* n. 1 at 34–37.

17. Bennett Report, *supra* n. 16 at Appendix I; Boyle, *Ten Years On, supra* n. 5 at 30–31.

18. Baker Report, *supra* n. 11 at para. 276, p. 83.

19. Boyle, *Ten Years On, supra* n. 5 at 30–31.

20. [1971] N.I. 1.

21. Id.

22. Id.

23. Kevin Boyle, Tom Hadden, and Paddy Hillyard, *Law and State: The Case of Northern Ireland* (London: Martin Robertson & Co., 1975), 38–39. (Hereafter Boyle, *Law and State.*)

24. Id.

25. In re McElduff, [1972] N.I. 1.

26. Id.

27. Boyle, *Ten Years On*, *supra* n. 5 at 26–27.

28. *Diplock Report*, *supra* n. 3 at paras. 40–50.

29. Liversidge v. Anderson, [1942] A.C. 206.

30. R. (O'Hanlon) v. Governor of Belfast Prison, ex parte O'Hanlon, [1922] 56 Ir.L.T.R. 170.

31. In re Mackey, [1972] 23 N.I.L.Q. 113.

32. *Report of a Committee to Consider, in the Context of Civil Liberties and Human Rights, Measures to Deal with Terrorism in Northern Ireland*, Cmnd 5847 (London: HMSO, 1975), para. 18. (Hereafter Gardiner Report.)

33. For a general review of the government's internment policy in the early to mid 1970s, see R. J. Spjut, "Internment and Detention Without Trial in Northern Ireland 1971–1975: Ministerial Policy and Practice," 49 Mod. L. Rev. 712 (1986).

34. See Gardiner Report, *supra* n. 32 at para. 148.

35. Standing Advisory Commission on Human Rights, Annual Report for 1979–80, House of Commons Paper, 143, p. 6. The Standing Committee was established by the Northern Ireland Constitution Act (1973), ch. 36, Section 20.

36. Baker Report, *supra* n. 11 at 71, para. 236.

37. For a general description, see Hogan, *Political Violence*, *supra* n. 2 at 86–92; see also Spjut, *supra* n. 33.

38. Boyle, *Law and State*, *supra* n. 23 at 63.

39. Id. at 70; see also Baker Report, *supra* n. 11 at 67–68, paras. 276–78.

40. Boyle, *Law and State*, *supra* n. 23 at 61.

41. See R. v. Officer in Charge of Police Office, Castlereagh, Belfast, ex parte Lynch, [1980] N.I. 126.

42. See n. 30, *supra*, and accompanying text.

43. Boyle, *Law and State*, *supra* n. 23 at 38.

44. Id.; see also Walker, *British Law*, *supra* n. 7 at 123–24.

45. In re Mackey, [1972] 23 N.I.L.Q. 113.

46. Id. (emphasis supplied).

47. R. v. Halliday, ex parte Zadig, [1917] A.C. 260.

48. Liversidge v. Anderson, [1942] A.C. 206.

49. R. v. Halliday, ex parte Zadig, [1917] A.C. 260.

50. Id.

51. Liversidge v. Anderson, [1942] A.C. 206, 270.

52. Id. at 222.

53. Id. at 245.

54. Baker Report, *supra* n. 11 at 84–85, paras. 279, 283.

55. Hogan, *Political Violence*, *supra* n. 2 at 48–49; Dermot P. J. Walsh, "Arrest and Interrogation," in Jennings, *Under Fire*, *supra* n. 1 at 34.

56. Hogan, *Political Violence*, *supra* n. 2 at 122.

57. Boyle, *Ten Years On*, *supra* n. 5 at 65–66.

58. Hogan, *Political Violence*, *supra* n. 2 at 120.

59. Boyle, *Law and State*, *supra* n. 23 at 82.

60. Boyle, *Ten Years On*, *supra* n. 5 at 65–66.

61. Baker Report, *supra* n. 11 at 21, para. 81.

62. Diplock Report, *supra* n. 3 at paras. 35–38 (emphasis supplied).

63. Id.; see also Boyle, *Ten Years On*, *supra*. 5 at 40–41; see also Boyle, *Law and State*, *supra* n. 23 at 97–98.

64. Charles Carleton, "Judging Without Consensus: The Diplock Courts in Northern Ireland" 3 Law & Pol'y. Q. 235, 237 (1981).

65. William E. Hellerstein, Robert B. McKay, and Peter R. Schlam, "Criminal Justice and Human Rights in Northern Ireland: A Report to the Association of the Bar of the City of New York," 43 The Record of the Association of the Bar of the City of New York, No. 2 (1988). (Hereafter Hellerstein, *Bar Report.*)

66. Baker Report, *supra.* 11 at 30, para. 107.

67. Id. at 131–132, paras. 107–8.

68. For a review of some of these proposals, see S. C. Greer and A. White, *Abolishing the Diplock Courts* (London: National Council for Civil Liberties, 1986); Hellerstein, *Bar Report, supra* n. 65 at 65; Jackson, "Three Judge Courts in Northern Ireland, A Paper Prepared for the Standing Advisory Committee on Human Rights," in Annex A to the Standing Advisory Committee on Human Rights Report for 1985–86; Hogan, *Political Violence, supra* n. 2 at 105–9.

69. Boyle, *Law and State, supra* n. 23 at 145.

70. Diplock Report, *Supra* n. 3 at paras. 87, 89.

71. Id.

72. Baker Report, *supra* n. 11 at 54, para. 189 (emphasis in original).

73. Boyle, *Ten Years On, supra.* n. 5 at 47.

74. Bennett Report, *supra* n. 16 at para. 30; Baker Report, *supra* n. 11 at 195; see also Boyle, *Ten Years On, supra* n. 5 at 44–45; see also Hogan, *Political Violence, supra* n. 2 at 115.

75. Bennett Report, *supra* n. 16 at para. 30.

76. Boyle, *Ten Years On, supra* n. 5 at 44.

77. D.P.P. v. Ping Lin, [1976] A.C. 574, 3 All E.R. 175, [1975] 3 W.L.R. 419.

78. In R. v. Corr, [1968] N.I. 147, the court ruled that "[w]hether conduct which does not involve physical force or actual threats amounts to menace is a matter of fact and of degree."

79. R. v. Flynn and Leonard, [1972], May N.I.J.B. 112 (High Court of Justice in Northern Ireland, May 24, 1972); see Boyle, *Law and State, supra* n. 23 at 133.

80. Desmond S. Greer, "The Admissibility of Confessions Under the Northern Ireland (Emergency Provisions) Act," 31 N.I.L.Q. 205, 210n26 (1980).

81. Diplock Report, *supra* n. 3 at para. 91.

82. Id. at para. 89.

83. R. v. Milne, [1978] N.I. 110, 111.

84. R. v. Hetherington, [1975] N.I. 164, 166.

85. Hogan, *Political Violence, supra* n. 2 at 110.

86. Steven Greer and Antony White, "A Return to Trial by Jury," in Jennings, *Under Fire, supra* n. 1 at 52.

87. These include the Bennett Instructions, the Royal Ulster Constabulary Force Orders, and the Home Office Administrative Directions.

88. See Hogan, *Political Violence, supra* n. 2 at 112; cf. R. v. Prager, [1972] 1 All E.R. 1114.

89. R. v. McCaul, unreported, December 1979, Belfast City Commission; see also Boyle, *Ten Years On, supra* n. 5 at 49; Dermot P. J. Walsh, "Arrest and Interrogation," in Jennings, *Under Fire, supra* n. 1 at 41.

90. Diplock Report, *supra* n. 3 at para. 89 (emphasis supplied).

91. Gardiner Report, *supra* n. 32 at paras. 48–50.

92. Id. at para. 49.

93. R. v. Corey, [1979] N.I. 49.

238 Notes

94. Id.
95. Greer, "Confessions," *supra* n. 80 at 220–21.
96. Wong Kam-Ming v. R., [1979] All E.R. 939, 948.
97. R. v. McCormick, [1977] N.I. 105.
98. Id. at 110–11.
99. Id. at 111.
100. Id.
101. R. v. O'Halloran, [1979] N.I.J.B. (C.A.) 45.
102. Baker Report, *supra* n. 11 at 55, para. 193.
103. Greer, "Confessions," *supra* n. 80 at 232–33.
104. Baker Report, *supra* n. 11 at 57, para. 198.
105. Gardiner Report, *supra* n. 32 at 50.
106. Baker Report, *supra* n. 11 at 58, para. 200.
107. Denmark, Norway, Sweden, and the Netherlands v. Greece, Application nos. 3321, 3322, 3223, 3344/67, 12 Y.B. Eur. Con. on Human Rights II (1969). (Hereafter the Greek Case.)
108. Id.
109. Ireland v. United Kingdom, Application No. 5310/71, 2 European Human Rights Reports 25 (1978); see also Baker Report, *supra* n. 7 at 55, para. 192.
110. National Council for Civil Liberties, Briefing on the Northern Ireland (Emergency Provisions) Bill 1986, 4 (December 1986), and as quoted in Hellerstein, *Bar Report*, *supra* n. 65 at 75.
111. See nn. 85 and 86 *supra* and accompanying text. For an overview, see Greer, "Confessions," *supra* n. 80 at 233–36.
112. Leonard Boudin, "Northern Ireland: Freeedom vs. Law and Order," *New York Times*, November 19, 1988, p. A27.
113. As quoted in Craig R. Whitney, "Civil Liberties in Britain: Are They Under Siege?" *New York Times*, October 31, 1988, p. 18. See also Steven Greer, "He May Be Resurrected," in 268 *Fortnight: An Independent Review for Northern Ireland* 10 (December 1988).
114. As quoted in Jamie Dettmer, "IRA Coached for Years in Use of Total Silence," *Times* (London), October 21, 1988.
115. Diplock Report, *supra* n. 3 at para. 71.
116. R.v. Whelan, [1972] N.I. 153 (C.C.A.).
117. Baker Report, *supra* n. 11 at 60, para. 210.
118. Id. at 62, para. 213.
119. See generally Steven C. Greer, "Supergrasses and the Legal System in Great Britain and Northern Ireland," 102 Law Q. Rev. 198 (1986), idem, "The Supergrass System," in Jennings, *Under Fire*, *supra* n. 1 at 73–103.
120. Baker Report, *supra* n. 11 at 47, para. 163.
121. Steven C. Greer, "The Supergrass System," in Jennings, *Under Fire*, *supra* n. 1 at 73.
122. Id. at 74; see also Greer, "Supergrasses," *supra* n. 119 at 230–31.
123. Greer, "Supergrasses," *supra* n. 119 at 201.
124. Id. at 204.
125. Baker Report, *supra* n. 11 at 49, para. 169.
126. Greer, "Supergrasses," *supra* n. 119 at 243; see also Hogan, *Political Violence*, *supra* n. 2 at 123–26.
127. Boyle, *Ten Years On*, *supra* n. 5 at 59.
128. Id. at 60.

129. Id.

130. Id.

131. Id. at 61.

132. Id.

133. Id. at 62.

134. Baker Report, *supra* n. 11 at 37, para. 124.

135. Hogan, *Political Violence*, *supra* n. 2 at 104.

136. Steven Greer and Antony White, "A Return to Trial by Jury," in Jennings, *Under Fire*, *supra* n. 1 at 54.

137. Boyle, *Ten Years On*, *supra* n. 5 at 67–68.

138. Id. at 68; see also Hogan, *Political Violence*, *supra* n. 2 at 120.

139. Carleton, "Consensus," *supra* n. 64 at 225, 235.

140. Id.

141. Boyle, *Ten Years On*, *supra* no. 5 at 83–85.

142. Id. at 83.

143. Id. at 85.

144. Id. at 67–68.

145. Id. at 86.

146. Hogan, *Political Violence*, *supra* n. 2 at 105.

147. Baker Report, *supra* n. 11 at 45, para. 155.

148. See generally Boyle, *Ten Years On*, *supra* n. 5 at 86; Hogan, *Political Violence*, *supra* n. 2 at 102.

149. Peter Taylor, *Beating the Terrorists? Interrogation at Omagh, Gough, and Castlereagh* (London: Penguin Books, 1980), 286–302.

150. Boyle, *Ten Years On*, *supra* n. 5 at 50.

151. Taylor, *Beating the Terrorists*, *supra* n. 149 at 57.

152. Bennett Report, *supra* n. 16 at para. 157. Between 1972 and 1978, nineteen officers were prosecuted. One officer was prosecuted twice. In one case an officer entered a plea of nolle prosequi. In two others, the officers were convicted but won on appeal. In the remaining cases, the officers won at the trial level. Boyle, *Ten Years On*, *supra* n. 5 at 117n34.

153. Hellerstein, *Bar Report*, *supra* n. 65 at 20–21.

154. Boyle, *Ten Years On*, *supra* n. 5 at 78–80.

155. Id. at 78–79.

156. Id. at 79.

157. Attorney General for Northern Ireland's Reference, [1977] A.C. 105 (H.L.), [1975] N.I. 169 (C.A.).

158. Id.; see also Anthony Jennings, "Shoot to Kill: The Final Courts of Justice," in Jennings, *Under Fire*, *supra* n. 1 at 109.

159. Farrell v. Secretary of State for Defence, [1980] 1 All E.R. 166 (H.L.), [1980] N.I. 55 (C.A. and H.L.).

160. Farrell v. United Kingdom, Application No. 9013/80, 5 E.H.R.R. 466 (1983).

161. See Gardiner Report, *supra* n. 32; see also Boyle, *Ten Years On*, *supra* n. 5 at 103–5; Carleton, "Consensus," *supra* n. 139 at 235, 238–39.

162. See generally John E. Finn, "Public Support for Emergency (Antiterrorist) Legislation in Northern Ireland: A Preliminary Analysis," 10 Terrorism: An International Journal 113 (1987)

163. Carleton, "Consensus," *supra* n. 139 at 237.

164. Id.

165. Boyle, *Ten Years On*, *supra* n. 5 at 75.

166. Boyle, *Law and State*, *supra* n. 23 at 144–51.

167. See also Finn "Emergency Legislation," *supra* n. 162.

168. Carleton, "Consensus," *supra* n. 139 at 238–39; see also Finn, "Emergency Legislation," *supra* n. 152,

169. Steven Greer, "The Supergrass System," in Jennings, *Under Fire*, *supra* n. 1 at 91.

170. Overall, the rate is 42 percent. See Jennings, *Under Fire*, *supra* n. at 74; see also Greer, "Supergrasses," *supra* n. 119 at 230–40, 144.

171. "What the People Think About Supergrasses," in 209 *Fortnight: An Independent Review for Northern Ireland* 13 (November 1984); see also Steven Greer, "The Supergrass System," in Jennings, *Under Fire*, *supra* n. 1 at 95.

172. Tony Jennings and Steven Greer, "Final Verdict on the Supergrass System," 232 *Fortnight: An Independent Review for Northern Ireland* 8, 9 (January 1986).

173. Edward P. Moxon-Browne, "Alienation: The Case of Catholics in Northern Ireland," 1 & 2 J. Pol. Sci. 74, 81 (1986).

174. *Review of the Operation of the Prevention of Terrorism (Temporary Provisions) Act 1984*, Cmnd. 264 (London: HMSO, 1987). (Hereafter Colville Report.) The full text of the 1989 Prevention of Terrorism Act was not available when this book went to press.

175. See Brogan, Coyle, McFadden and Tracey v. United Kingdom, 11 E.H.R.R. 117 (1988). The government responded in March 1989 by requesting a temporary derogation from the European Convention.

176. Id.

177. *Review of the Operation of the Prevention of Terrorism (Temporary Provisions) Act 1974–76*, Cmnd. 7324 (London: HMSO, 1978), 135, para. 84. (Hereafter Shackleton Report.)

178. Boyle, *Ten Years On*, *supra* n. 5 at 30.

179. For a discussion of this point in the American context, see John E. Finn, "Statement on CISPES," *CISPES and FBI Counter-Terrorism Investigations*. Hearings before the House Committee on the Judiciary, Subcommittee on Civil and Constitutional Rights, 100th Cong. 2d sess. (June 13, 1988), 84–88.

180. See Peter Hall, "The Prevention of Terrorism Acts," in Jennings, *Under Fire*, *supra* n. 1 at 172.

181. Walker, *British Law*, *supra* n. 7 at 127.

182. Id. at 135.

183. *Review of the Operation of the Prevention of Terrorism (Temporary Provisions) Act 1976*, Cmnd. 8803 (London: HMSO, 1983), para 55. (Hereafter Jellicoe Report.)

184. Peter Hall, "The Prevention of Terrorism Acts," in Jennings, *Under Fire*, *supra* n. 1 at 176; see also Baker Report, *supra* n. 11 at 88–89, paras. 299–304.

185. Baker Report, *supra* n. 11 at 88–89, paras. 303–4.

186. Colville Report, *supra* n. 174 at para. 8.2.6.; Jennings, *Under Fire*, *supra* n. 1 at 176.

187. Divisional Court, October 30, 1980 (unreported); as reported in Walker, *British Law*, *supra* n. 7 at 156.

188. Id.

189. Jellicoe Report, *supra* n. 183 at 16, para. 46.

190. Id. at 16–17, para. 48.

191. Id. at 16, para. 47.

192. Id.

193. David Bonner, "Combating Terrorism: The Jellicoe Approach," 1983 Pub. L. 224, 225 (1983).

194. Walker, *British Law*, *supra* n. 7 at 165.

195. Id. at 166.

196. Id. at 94.

197. Baker Report, *supra* n. 11 at 72, paras. 238–39.

198. Peter Hall, "The Prevention of Terrorism Acts," in Jennings, *Under Fire*, *supra* n. 1 at 157.

199. See id.; Colville Report, *supra* n. 174 at para. 14.1.3.

200. Id.

201. Walker, *British Law*, *supra* n. 7 at 97.

202. Catherine Scorer and Patricia Hewitt, *The Prevention of Terrorism Act*: *The Case for Repeal*. (London: The Cobden Trust, 1981), 56–57 (Hereafter Scorer, *Repeal*.); see also Jellicoe Report, *supra* n. 183 at 83, 84.

203. HM v. Von, [1979] Scots Law Times Notes, 62–64.

204. Walker, *British Law*, *supra* n. 7 at 101.

205. Jellicoe Report, *supra* n. 183 at para. 215.

206. Shackleton Report, *supra* n. 178 at paras. 132–33.

207. Peter Hall, "The Prevention of Terrorism Acts," in Jennings, *Under Fire*, *supra* n. 1 at 162.

208. Id. at 163; see also Hogan, *Political Violence*, *supra* n. 2 at vii.

209. But see n. 175 *supra* and accompanying text.

210. Scorer, *Repeal*, *supra* n. 202 at 59.

211. Id.

212. Walker, *British Law*, *supra* n. 7 at 135; Bennett Report, *supra* n. 16 at 24n6.

213. Walker, *British Law*, *supra* n. 7 at 136.

214. Scorer, *Repeal*, *supra* n. 202 at 59–60; see also Jennings, *Under Fire*, *supra* n. 1 at 39.

215. Baker Report, *supra* n. 11 at para. 299, p. 88.

216. Ex parte Lynch, [1980] N.I. 126 (Q. B. Division).

217. Id.

218. In re McElduff, [1972] N.I. 113, 114.

219. Jellicoe Report, *supra* n. 183 at 76, para. 197.

220. Id. at 65, para. 165.

221. Bonner, "Combating Terrorism," *supra* n. 193 at 230.

222. Jellicoe Report, *supra* n. 183 at 68, para. 177.

223. Shackleton Report, *supra* n. 178 at 41.

224. Jellicoe Report, *supra* n. 183 at 76, paras. 195–97.

225. Scorer, *Repeal*, *supra* n. 202 at 30.

226. Walker, *British Law*, *supra* n. 7 at 62.

227. Scorer, *Repeal*, *supra* n. 202 at 31 (emphasis supplied).

228. Jellicoe Report, *supra* n. 183 at 65, 75, paras. 169, 193.

229. Walker, *British Law*, *supra* n. 7 at 63.

230. Jellicoe Report, *supra* n. 183 at 65, para. 166.

231. Shackleton Report, *supra* n. 178 at para. 41; also as quoted in Scorer, *Repeal*, *supra* n. 202 at 26.

232. Scorer, *Repeal*, *supra* n. 202 at 26.

233. Shackleton Report, *supra* n. 178 at para. 41; see also Jellicoe Report, *supra* n. 183 at 16–17, paras. 47–49.

234. Secretary of State for Education and Science v. Tameside Metropolitan Borough Council, [1977] A.C. 1014.

235. Walker, *British Law*, *supra* n. 7 at 76.

236. Secretary of State for Education and Science v. Tameside Metropolitan Borough Council, [1977] A.C. 1014, 1047.

237. Walker, *British Law*, *supra* n. 181 at 76, 81.

238. (1987) *The Times*, 3 February (Q.B.D.); see Hogan, *Political Violence*, *supra* n. 2 at 96.

239. Walker, *British Law*, *supra* n. 7 at 76–77.

240. Id. at 81.

241. Peter Hall, "The Prevention of Terrorism Acts," in Jennings, *Under Fire*, *supra* n. 1 at 168.

242. Jellicoe Report, *supra* n. 183 at 74, para. 191.

243. Id. at 68, para. 175.

244. Id. at 68, para. 176.

245. Colville Report, *supra* n. 174 at para. 11.6.1; see also Peter Hall, "The Prevention of Terrorism Acts," in Jennings, *Under Fire*, *supra* n. 1 at 169–70.

246. Hogan, *Political Violence*, *supra* n. 2 at 141.

247. Shackleton Report, *supra* no. 178 at para. 28.

248. As quoted in Walker, *British Law*, *supra* n. 7 at 44.

249. Id. at 45.

250. Id. at 51.

251. Jellicoe Report, *supra* n. 183 at para. 212.

252. Walker, *British Law*, *supra* n. 7 at 51.

253. McEldowney v. Forde, [1971] A.C. 632 (H.L.), [1970] N.I. 11 (C.A. and H.L.).

PART III

1. See, e.g., Michael Tanner, "A Total Work of Art," in Peter Burbige and Richard Sutton, eds., *The Wagner Companion* (New York: Cambridge University Press, 1979) passim; Ernest Newman, *Stories of the Great Operas and Their Composers* (Philadelphia: The Blackiston Company, 1945), 36. Translations are from Peter Branscombe's accompaniment to Seraphim Records, Catalogue Number IE 6030 (1967).

2. For a recent but rather different different legal analysis of *Die Meistersinger*, see Lief Carter, "Die Meistersinger von Nürnberg and the United States Supreme Court: Aesthetic Theory in Constitutional Jurisprudence," 18 Polity 272 (1985).

3. Clinton Rossiter, *Constitutional Dictatorship* (Princeton, N.J.: Princeton University Press, 1948), 31.

4. George Schwab, *The Challenge of the Exception* (Berlin: Duncker and Humblot, 1970), 29.

5. Joseph W. Bendersky, *Carl Schmitt: Theorist for the Reich* (Princeton, N.J.: Princeton University Press, 1983), 73; Rossiter, *Dictatorship*, *supra* n. 3 at 33.

6. Frederick M. Watkins, *The Failure of Constitutional Emergency Powers Under the German Republic* (Cambridge, Mass.: Harvard University Press, 1939), 4.

7. Fritz Stern, "Introduction," in *The Path to Dictatorship*, trans. John Conway (New York: Praeger, 1967), xi.

8. Peter Gay, *Weimar Culture: The Outsider as Insider* (New York: Harper and Row, 1968), xiv.

9. Henry Pachter, *Weimar Etudes* (New York: Columbia University Press, 1982), 86.

CHAPTER 4

1. Frederick Watkins, *The Failure of Constitutional Emergency Powers Under the German Republic* (Cambridge, Mass.: Harvard University Press, 1939), 6.

2. William Carr, *A History of Germany 1815-1945*, 2d ed. (New York: St. Martin's Press, 1979), 283. For a general history of Weimar, see Eberhard Kolb, *The Weimar Republic*, trans. P. S. Falla (London: Unwin Hyman, 1988), esp. 129-37.

3. William S. Halperin, *Germany Tried Democracy* (Hamden, Conn.: Archon Books, 1963), v.

4. Ranier M. Lepsius, "From Fragmented Party Democracy to Government by Emergency Decree and the National Socialist Takeover: Germany," in Juan J. Linz and Alfred Stepan, eds., *The Breakdown of Democratic Regimes: Europe* (Baltimore, Md.: Johns Hopkins University Press, 1978), 38.

5. Kurt Sontheimer, "Anti-Democratic Thought in the Weimar Republic," in *The Path to Dictatorship*, trans. John Conway (New York: Praeger, 1967), 36. (Hereafter Conway, *Path*.)

6. Carl J. Schmitt, *The Crisis of Parliamentary Democracy*, trans. Ellen Kennedy, (Cambridge, Mass.: MIT Press, 1985), xxv; see also Lepsius, "National Socialist Takeover," *supra* n. 4 at 35.

7. Peter Gay, *Weimar Culture: The Outsider as Insider* (New York: Harper and Row, 1968), 1.

8. See, e.g., Herbert J. Spiro, *Government by Constitution* (New York: Random House, 1959), 418-21; R. T. Clark, *The Fall of the German Republic* (London: George Allen and Unwin, 1935), chapter 1; Halperin, *Democracy*, *supra* n. 3 passim.

9. Harlow J. Heneman, *The Growth of Executive Power in Germany* (Westport, Conn.: Greenwood Press, 1974), xiii.

10. Gay, *Weimar Culture*, *supra* n. 7 at 1; see also Watkins, *Failure*, *supra* n. 1 at 9.

11. Lepsius, "National Socialist Takeover," *supra* n. 4 at 35.

12. See, e.g., Halperin, *Germany*, *supra* n. 3 at 154-55; Johannes Mattern, *The Constitutional Jurisprudence of the Weimar Republic* (Baltimore, Md.: Johns Hopkins University Press, 1928), 86-96.

13. The Franchise Law of April 1920 exacerbated the effects of proportional representation by establishing the "ticket vote," or the "list system," and divided the country into thirty-five electoral districts.

14. Carl J. Friedrich, "The Development of the Executive Power in Germany," 27 Am. Pol. Sci. Rev. 185 (1933).

15. Id. at 199, 200.

16. See Herbert Krauss, *The Crisis of German Democracy* (Princeton, N.J.: Princeton University Press, 1932), 97-98 (emphasis in original); see also Erich Eyck, *A History of the Weimar Republic*, trans. Harlan P. Hanson and Robert G. L. Waite, 2 vols. (Cambridge, Mass.: Harvard University Press, 1963), 1: 75-77.

17. Ellen Kennedy, "Who Should Defend the Constitution? Schmitt v. Kelsen in Late Weimar" (unpublished paper, 1987), 10, 28n2.

18. Schmitt, *Crisis*, *supra* n. 6 at 22-50; George Schwab, *The Challenge of the Exception* (Berlin: Duncker and Humblot, 1970), 61-62.

19. Alfred Cobban, *Dictatorship: Its History and Theory* (New York: Charles Scribner's Sons, 1939), 137.

20. For a general collection of essays on Weimar's collapse and the reasons behind it, *see* Conway, *Path, supra* n. 5.

21. Here, of course, I reject William Shirer's explanation in *The Rise and Fall of the Third Reich: A History of Nazi Germany* (New York: Simon and Schuster, 1960).

22. Spiro, *Government by Constitution, supra* n. 8 at 421.

23. Arnold Brecht, *Prelude to Silence: The End of the German Republic* (New York: Howard Fertig, 1968), 47.

24. Clark, *German Republic, supra* n. 8 at 81.

25. John E. Rhodes, *The Quest for Unity: Modern Germany 1848-1970* (New York: Holt, Rinehart and Winston, 1971), 205.

26. Brecht, *Prelude, supra* n. 23 at 131; for a contrary opinion squarely placing the blame on Article 22, see Clark, *German Republic, supra* n. 8 at 83, 129.

27. Sydney L. Mellen, "The German People and the Postwar World: A Study Based on Election Statistics, 1871-1933," 37 Am. Pol. Sci. Rev. 601, 611 (1943).

28. Id.

29. James M. Diehl, *Paramilitary Politics in Weimar Germany* (Bloomington: Indiana University Press, 1977), 4, 12-13.

30. Id. at 4. For a general discussion, see John Grumm, "Theories of Electoral Systems," 2 Midwestern J. Pol. Sci. 357-76 (1958).

31. As quoted in Friedrich, "Executive Power," *supra* n. 14 at 197.

32. As quoted in Frederick F. Blachly and Miriam E. Oatman, *The Government and Administration of Germany* (Baltimore, Md.: Johns Hopkins University Press, 1928), 75n54.

33. Heneman, *Executive Power, supra* n. 9 at 168.

34. Watkins, *Failure, supra* n. 1 at 13.

35. Carl J. Friedrich, "Dictatorship in Germany?" 9 Foreign Aff. 118, 128 (1930).

36. Clinton Rossiter, *Constitutional Dictatorship* (Princeton, N.J.: Princeton University Press, 1948), 37.

37. Heneman, *Executive Power, supra* n. 9 at 168.

38. As reprinted in Rossiter, *Dictatorship, supra* n. 36 at 31.

39. Hans Boldt, "Article 48 of the Weimar Constitution: Its Historical and Political Implications," in Anthony Nicholls and Erich Mathias, eds., *German Democracy and the Triumph of Hitler: Essays in Recent German History* (London: George Allen and Unwin, 1971), 79, 88.

40. Friedrich, "Executive Power," *supra* n. 14 at 198; see also Lindsay Rogers, Sanford Schwarz, and Nicholas Kaltschas, "German Political Institutions—Article 48," 47 Pol. Sci. Q. 576 (1932). (Hereafter Rogers, "Political Institutions.")

41. Carl J. Schmitt, *Die Diktatur* (Munich: Duncker and Humblot, 1923); see also Schwab, *Exception, supra* n. 18 at 40-41.

42. Watkins, *Failure, supra* n. 1 at 15.

43. Blachly and Oatman, *Germany, supra* n. 32 at 92.

44. Friedrich, "Executive Power," *supra* n. 14 at 198.

45. Blachly and Oatman, *Germany, supra* n. 32 at 81.

46. Joseph W. Bendersky, *Carl Schmitt: Theorist for the Reich* (Princeton, N.J.: Princeton University Press, 1983), 99-100; see also Carl J. Friedrich, "The Issue of Judicial Review in Germany," 43 Pol. Sci. Q. 188, 193 (1928).

47. November 4, 1925, [RGZ, 111, 320ff]. See Donald P. Kommers, *The Constitutional Jurisprudence of the Federal Republic of Germany* (Durham, N.C.: Duke

University Press, 1989), 7; Frederick F. Blachly, "Judicial Review of Legislative Acts in Germany," 21 Am. Pol. Sci. Rev. 113–16 (1927).

48. As quoted in Friedrich, "Judicial Review," *supra* n. 46 at 188, 197.

49. Rossiter, *Dictatorship, supra* n. 36 at 70.

50. As quoted in id. at 71; RGStr., vol. 59, pp. 185ff.; for a comparison with judicial review of emergency legislation in Northern Ireland, see chapter 3, *supra*.

51. Kennedy, "Schmitt v. Kelsen," *supra* n. 17 at 17.

52. Heneman, *Executive Power, supra* n. 9 at 180ff.

53. Diehl, *Paramilitary Politics, supra* n. 29 at 17.

54. Koppel S. Pinson, "The Communists Drove Ebert to the Military," in *The Creation of the Weimar Republic: Stillborn Democracy*, ed. Richard N. Hunt (Lexington, Mass.: D. C. Heath, 1969), 34; Brecht, *Prelude, supra* n. 23 at 15–17.

55. The wisdom of this arrangement is a perennial source of disagreement in Weimar scholarship. For brief factual accounts, see, e.g., Diehl, *Paramilitary Politics, supra* n. 29 at 18; Rhodes, *Unity, supra* n. 25 at 192–94.

56. Diehl, *Paramilitary Politics, supra* n. 29 at 18–42.

57. Id. at ix.

58. Id. at 83.

59. The right also objected to Articles 228–30 of the Versailles Treaty, which required the new government to surrender German war criminals to the Allied forces. The German government plainly could not extradite given its domestic problems and instead offered to try these individuals in German courts—a compromise the Allies agreed to the following February.

60. Boldt, "Article 48," *supra* n. 39 at 98.

61. Karl Loewenstein, "Law in the Third Reich," 45 Yale L. J. 779, 806–7 (1936).

62. Watkins, *Failure, supra* n. 1 at 34.

63. Rhodes, *Unity, supra* n. 25 at 209.

64. For a comprehensive analysis of the legislation, as well as the dispute between Bavaria and the Reich, see Johannes Mattern, *Bavaria and the Reich: The Conflict over the Law for the Protection of the Republic*, Johns Hopkins University Studies in History and Political Science, vol. 41 (Baltimore, Md.: Johns Hopkins University Press, 1923).

65. Karl Loewenstein, "Legislative Control of Political Extremism in European Democracies," 38 Colum. L. Rev. 591–622, 725–74, 601n31 (1938).

66. For a general discussion, see Modris Eksteins, *The Limits of Reason: The German Democratic Press and the Collapse of Weimar Democracy* (London: Oxford University Press, 1975), 70–74.

67. Karl Loewenstein, "Militant Democracy and Fundamental Rights," 31 Am. Pol. Sci. Rev. 417–32, 638–58, 427 (1937).

68. See nn. 61–65 *supra* and accompanying text.

69. Loewenstein, "Political Extremism," *supra* n. 65 at 759n147.

70. For a complete account, see Mattern, *Bavaria and the Reich, supra* n. 64 at 54–69.

71. Brecht, *Prelude, supra* n. 23 at 134.

72. See Rossiter, *Dictatorship, supra* n. 36 at 41.

73. Id. at 42.

74. Boldt, "Article 48," *supra* n. 39 at 91.

75. Id. at 90–91.

76. As quoted in Rossiter, *Dictatorship, supra* n. 36 at 46.

77. Id. at 47.

78. Id. at 48.
79. Id. at 49.
80. Id. at 38.
81. See, e.g., Boldt, "Article 48," *supra* n. 39 at 90.
82. Blachly and Oatman, *Germany, supra* n. 32 at 102.
83. Friedrich, "Dictatorship," *supra* n. 35 at 118, 132.
84. Spiro, *Government by Constitution, supra* n. 8 at 271.
85. Carr, *Germany, supra* n. 2 at 303; see also Kolb, *Weimar Republic, supra* n. 2 at 51–65.
86. Carr, *Germany, supra* n. 2 at 310.
87. As quoted in Eyck, *Weimar Republic, supra* n. 16 at 268 (emphasis in original).
88. Id. at 258 (emphasis in original).
89. Id. at 269.
90. Boldt, "Article 48," *supra* n. 39 at 94.
91. This is a point of continuing controversy in Weimar studies. See, e.g., Eyck, *Weimar Republic, supra* n. 16 at 270–72; Brecht, *Prelude, supra* n. 23 at 27–28; Boldt, "Article 48," *supra* n. 39 at 93. See also Rogers, "Political Institutions," *supra* n. 40 at 576 and Friedrich's reply in "Executive Power," *supra* n. 14 at 196–97n28.
92. Sallust, *The Conspiracy of Catiline and the War of Jugurtha*, trans. Thomas Heywood (New York: Alfred A. Knopf, 1924); Brecht, *Prelude, supra* n. 23 at 27–28.
93. Watkins, *Failure, supra* n. 1 at 51–61.
94. The strategy is now a common one. Sinn Fein, for example, regularly runs candidates in Northern Ireland while nonetheless refusing to repudiate the IRA's campaign of political violence. For a general, but very dated survey of how European democracies have responded to such tactics, see Loewenstein, "Political Extremism," *supra* n. 65.
95. See Brecht, *Prelude, supra* n. 23 at 14.
96. As quoted in Watkins, *Failure, supra* n. 1 at 53.
97. As quoted in Karl Dietrich Bracher, "The Technique of the National Socialist Seizure of Power," in Conway, *Path, supra* n. 5 at 117.
98. See generally Loewenstein, "Militant Democracy," *supra* n. 67.
99. Loewenstein, "Political Extremism," *supra* n. 65 at 735n36.
100. Carr, *Germany, supra* n. 2 at 312.
101. Id.
102. Watkins, *Failure, supra* n. 1 at 90.
103. Id. at 90–96; Rossiter, *Dictatorship, supra* n. 36 at 51–53.
104. Loewenstein, "Political Extremism," *supra* n. 65 at 745.
105. Id. at 734n36.
106. The literature on this point is voluminous. Concise accounts can be found in Brecht, *Prelude, supra* n. 23 at 56–58, and Eyck, *Weimar Republic, supra* n. 16 at 386–92.
107. Eyck, *Weimar Republic, supra* n. 16 at 420.
108. Watkins, *Failure, supra* n. 1 at 104.
109. Brecht, *Prelude, supra* n. 23 at 65–68, 145–46; Watkins, *Failure, supra* n. 1 at 91; Bendersky, *Schmitt, supra* n. 46 at 154–57.
110. Loewenstein, "Political Extremism," *supra* n. 65 at 745n88; Brecht, *Prelude, supra* n. 23 at 133–37.
111. Bendersky, *Schmitt, supra* n. 46 at 154.
112. Heneman, *Executive Power, supra* n. 9 at 195.
113. Loewenstein, "Militant Democracy," *supra* n. 67 at 424.

114. Karl Dietrich Bracher, "The Technique of the National Socialist Seizure of Power," in Conway, *Path*, *supra* n. 5 at 116. For a contrary opinion, see Anthony Nicholls, "Hitler and the Bavarian Background to National Socialism," in Anthony Nicholls and Erich Mathias, eds., *German Democracy and the Triumph of Hitler: Essays in Recent German History* (London: George Allen and Unwin, 1971), 113–14.

115. See n. 96 *supra* and accompanying text.

116. Karl Loewenstein, "Dictatorship and the German Constitution: 1933–1937," 4 U. Chi. L. Rev. 537, 539 (1936).

117. Watkins, *Failure*, *supra* n. 1 at 117.

118. Loewenstein, "Dictatorship," *supra* n. 116 at 537, 541.

119. Watkins, *Failure*, *supra* n. 1 at 128.

120. Id. at 128; Loewenstein, "Dictatorship," *supra* at 545.

121. Rhodes, *Unity*, *supra* n. 25 at 235; see also Conway, *Path*, *supra* n. 5 at xix.

122. Schwab, *Exception*, *supra* n. 18 at 48.

123. Kennedy, "Schmitt v. Kelsen," *supra* n. 17 at 7.

124. Ellen Kennedy, "Introduction: Carl Schmitt's Parlamentarismus in Its Historical Context," in Carl J. Schmitt, *The Crisis of Parliamentary Democracy*, trans. Ellen Kennedy (Cambridge, Mass.: MIT Press, 1985), xxxvi.

125. Id. at xxxi.

126. Id. at xxxv.

127. Schwab, *Exception*, *supra* n. 18 at 49–50.

128. Id. at 7, 49–50.

129. Bendersky, *Schmitt*, *supra* n. 46 at 37.

130. Schwab, *Exception*, *supra* n. 18 at 49.

131. Carl J. Schmitt, *Political Theology*, trans. George Schwab (Cambridge, Mass.: MIT Press, 1985), 36.

132. George Schwab, "Introduction," in Carl J. Schmitt, *Political Theology*, trans. George Schwab (Cambridge, Mass.: MIT Press, 1985), xvi.

133. Schwab, *Exception*, *supra* n. 18.

134. Bendersky, *Schmitt*, *supra* n. 46 at 37.

135. Schmitt, *Theology*, *supra* n. 131 at 7.

136. See "Introduction," *supra*.

137. For a comprehensive but dated review of the legislative efforts of other European democracies to respond to internal subversion, see Loewenstein, "Political Extremism," *supra* n. 65.

138. Loewenstein, "Militant Democracy," *supra* n. 67 at 427.

139. Carl J. Schmitt, *Legalität und Legitimität* (Munich: Duncker and Humblot, 1932).

140. Schmitt, *Theology*, *supra* n. 131 at xxiii.

141. Bendersky, *Schmitt*, *supra* n. 46 at 147–48.

142. Schwab, *Exception*, *supra* n. 18 at 95.

143. Bendersky, *Schmitt*, *supra* n. 46 at 148.

144. Id.

145. See generally Bendersky, *Schmitt*, *supra* n. 46 at 173–91.

146. Schwab, *Exception*, *supra* n. 18 at 96n21.

147. Bendersky, *Schmitt*, *supra* n. 46 at 151.

148. Kennedy, "Schmitt v. Kelsen," *supra* n. 17 at 7.

149. See part III introduction, *supra*.

150. Bendersky, *Schmitt*, *supra* n. 46 at 107–26; Kennedy, "Schmitt v. Kelsen," *supra* n. 17 at 18–19.

151. Kennedy, "Schmitt v. Kelsen," *supra* n. 17 at 8.

152. For Brecht's account of the trial, see *Prelude, supra* n. 23 at 68–72.

153. Schwab, *Exception, supra* n. 18 at 81.

154. Bendersky, *Schmitt, supra* n. 46 at 97–98, 111; Friedrich, "Judicial Review," *supra* n. 46 at 188, 193.

155. Schwab, *Exception, supra* n. 18 at 81.

156. Id. at 81–86; Bendersky, *Schmitt, supra* n. 46 at 107–26.

157. Schmitt, *Die Diktatur, supra* n. 41.

158. Schwab, *Exception, supra* n. 18 at 82.

159. Id. at 38.

160. Id. at 39.

161. The state's protective legislation, for example, routinely created special courts in apparent violation of Article 105 of the constitutional text. See nn. 61–62 *supra* and accompanying text.

162. Schwab, *Exception, supra* n. 18 at 30–37.

163. Id. at 37–43.

164. Id. at 35.

165. Id.

166. Id. at 30.

167. As quoted in Cobban, *Dictatorship, supra* n. 19 at 336.

168. As quoted in Bendersky, *Schmitt, supra* n. 46 at 153.

169. Id.

170. See generally the following chapter; Bendersky, *Schmitt, supra* n. 46 at 283.

171. Carl J. Friedrich, *Constitutional Government and Democracy: Theory and Practice in Europe and America* (Boston: Blaisdell, 1941), 627.

172. Most important here is Bendersky's book-length treatment, *supra* n. 46, and the translations of Schmitt's work reprinted by the MIT Press and cited throughout; see also George Schwab's earlier but still important work, *The Challenge of the Exception, supra* n. 18.

173. Watkins, *Failure, supra* n. 1.

CHAPTER 5

1. See Introduction, *supra*; Clinton Rossiter, ed., *The Federalist Papers* (New York: New American Library, 1961), No. 1.

2. As quoted in Miklos Radvanyi, *Anti-Terrorist Legislation in the Federal Republic of Germany* (Washington, D.C.: Law Library, Library of Congress, 1979), 4.

3. See John Ford Golay, *The Founding of the Federal Republic of Germany* (Chicago: University of Chicago Press, 1958), 1–6; Peter H. Merkl, *The Origin of the West German Republic* (New York: Oxford University Press, 1963), 7–8; John E. Rhodes, *The Quest for Unity: Modern Germany 1848–1970* (New York: Holt, Rinehart and Winston, 1971), 318–22.

4. Rhodes, *Unity, supra* n. 3 at 339–32; Golay, *Founding, supra* n. 3 at 9–11.

5. As quoted in Radvanyi, *Anti-Terrorist Legislation, supra* n. 2 at 5–6.

6. Preamble, The Basic Law of the Federal Republic of Germany (Bonn: Press and Information Office of the Federal Government, 1987). See also Elmar M. Hucko, ed., *The Democratic Tradition: Four German Constitutions* (Leamington Spa, Eng.: Berg Publishers, 1987).

7. Merkl, *West German Republic, supra* n. 3 at 59–60.

8. Id. at 57–58.

9. Id. at 162.

10. As quoted in Hucko, *Democratic Tradition, supra* n. 6 at 68.

11. Golay, *Founding, supra* n. 3 at 113.

12. Hucko, *Democratic Tradition, supra* n. 6 at 68.

13. See chapter 4, *supra.*

14. Id.

15. Merkl, *West German Republic, supra* n. 3 at 81–82.

16. Donald P. Kommers, *The Constitutional Jurisprudence of the Federal Republic of Germany* (Durham, N.C.: Duke University Press, 1989), 4–5.

17. For a review, see id. at chapter 1; see also Donald P. Kommers, *Judicial Politics in West Germany: A Study of the Federal Constitutional Court* (Beverly Hills, Calif.: Sage Publications, 1976), 100–101.

18. The SouthWest Case, 1 BVerfGE 14 (1951). For a discussion of this point, see Kommers, *Constitutional Jurisprudence, supra* n. 16 at 36–37. All translations, unless otherwise noted, from Walter F. Murphy and Joseph Tanenhaus, eds., *Comparative Constitutional Law: Cases and Commentaries* (New York: St. Martin's Press, 1977).

19. Kommers, *Constitutional Jurisprudence, supra* n. 16 at 37.

20. Id. at 42–43, 54–55, 312, 20–21.

21. Kommers, *Judicial Politics, supra* n. 17 at 44; idem, *Constitutional Jurisprudence, supra* n. 16 at 42–43.

22. Kommers, *Constitutional Jurisprudence, supra* n. 16 at 43.

23. This is an important and often contested point in the Federal Republic's jurisprudence. Kommer's discussion is a useful guide; see id. at 42–43, 312–13.

24. Id. at 37, 312–13, 321–22.

25. Arnold Brecht, *Federalism and Regionalism in Germany: The Division of Prussia* (New York: Oxford University Press, 1945), 138.

26. Donald P. Kommers, "The Basic Law of the Federal Republic of Germany: An Assessment After Forty Years;" in Peter Merkl, ed., *The Federal Republic of Germany at Forty* (New York: New York University Press, 1989), 133–159. See also idem, *Constitutional Jurisprudence, supra* n. 16 at 37–38.

27. As quoted in Hucko, *Democratic Traditions, supra* n. 6 at 70.

28. Article 2(1), the Basic Law.

29. For a discussion of the concept by its originator, see Karl Loewenstein, "Militant Democracy and Fundamental Rights," 31 Am. Pol. Sci. Rev. 417 (1937).

30. As quoted in Hucko, *Democratic Traditions, supra* n. 6 at 75.

31. The Socialist Reich Party Case, 2 BVerfGE 1 (1952); Murphy and Tanenhaus, *Comparative Constitutional Law, supra* n. 18 at 602–3.

32. The SouthWest Case, 1 BVerfGE 14 (1951); Murphy and Tanenhaus, *Comparative Constitutional Law, supra* n. 18 at 208.

33. Murphy and Tanenhaus, *Comparative Constitutional Law, supra* n. 18 at 32; see also Kommers, *Constitutional Jurisprudence, supra* n. 16 at 37, 53–55.

34. See chapter 1, *supra.*

35. Id.

36. In the words of Peter Merkl, "The Court was made a veritable demiurge of West German democracy, of which it would determine both content and form." Merkl, *West German Republic, supra* n. 3 at 172.

37. See, e.g., Anthony Nicholls, "Political Parties and Party Government," in

C. C. Schweitzer et al., eds., *Politics and Government in the Federal Republic of Germany, Basic Documents* (New York: St. Martin's Press, 1984), 193.

38. The Socialist Reich Party Case, 2 BVerfGE 1 (1952); Murphy and Tanenhaus, *Comparative Constitutional Law, supra* n. 18 at 602.

39. 2 BVerfGE 1 (1952).

40. The Communist Party Case, 5 BVerfGE 85 (1956); Murphy and Tanenhaus, *Comparative Constitutional Law, Supra* n. 18 at 621.

41. Murphy and Tanenhaus, *Comparative Constitutional Law, supra* n. 18 at 624.

42. Kommers, *Judicial Politics, supra* n. 17 at 238; idem, *Constitutional Jurisprudence, supra* n. 16 at 227–29.

43. The Socialist Reich Party Case, 2 BVerfGE 1 (1952); Murphy and Tanenhaus, *Comparative Constitutional Law, supra* n. 18 at 603.

44. Murphy and Tanenhaus, *Comparative Constitutional Law, supra* n. 18 at 624; see also Louise W. Holborn et al., eds., *German Constitutional Documents Since 1871* (New York: Praeger, 1970), 41. (Hereafter Holborn, *Constitutional Documents.*)

45. Donald P. Kommers, "The Spiegel Affair: A Case Study in Judicial Politics," in Theodore L. Becker, ed., *Political Trials* (Indianapolis: Bobbs-Merrill, 1971), 15; see also idem, *Constitutional Jurisprudence, supra* n. 16 at 229.

46. Murphy and Tanenhaus, *Comparative Constitutional Law, supra* n. 18 at 626–27.

47. Rhodes, Unity, *supra* n. 3 at 337.

48. Id. at 336; see also Edward H. Litchfield, "Political Objectives and Legal Bases of Occupation Government," in Edward H. Litchfield, *Governing Postwar Germany* (Ithaca, N. Y.: Cornell University Press, 1953), 3–18.

49. As quoted in Golay, *Founding, supra* n. 3 at 23.

50. Article 5(2), Convention on Relations Between the Three Powers and the Federal Republic of Germany, May 26, 1952. As reprinted in Holborn, *Constitutional Documents, supra* n. 44 at 12.

51. Kommers, "Spiegel Affair," *supra* n. 45 at 14.

52. For a discussion of this point and the possible use of such an institution in the United States, see Guenter Lewy, "Does America Need a Verfassungsschutzbericht?" 31 Orbis 275, 286 (1987).

53. For a defense of the office, see "Civil Liberties and the Defense of Democracy against Extremists and Terrorists: A Report on the West German Situation" (pamphlet issued by the Atlantic-Brucke e. V., Hamburg, in cooperation with the American Council on Germany, Inc., New York 1980), 37 (Hereafter "A Report."); compare Gerard Braunthal, *Political Loyalty and Public Service in West Germany: The 1972 Decree Against Radicals and Its Consequences,* (Amherst: University of Massachusetts Press, 1990), 162–64.

54. Ronald F. Bunn, *German Politics and the Spiegel Affair: A Case Study of the Bonn System* (Baton Rouge: Louisiana State University Press, 1968); David Schoenbaum, *The Spiegel Affair* (New York: Doubleday, 1968); see also Kommers, "Spiegel Affair," *supra* n. 45.

55. Kommers, "Spiegel Affair," *supra* n. 45 at 26–27.

56. Id. at 29–30.

57. Murphy and Tanenhaus, *Comparative Constitutional Law, supra* n. 18 at 645; Kommers, "Spiegel Affair," *supra* n. 45 at 27.

58. Kommers, "Spiegel Affair," *supra* n. 45 at 29.

59. As quoted in Lewis Edinger, *Politics in West Germany* (Boston: Little, Brown, 1977), 303.

60. Id. at 304.

61. Id. at 305.

62. C. C. Schweitzer, "Emergency Powers in the Federal Republic of Germany," 22 W. Pol. Q. 112, 118 (1969).

63. Id.

64. R. J. C. Preece, "Federal German Emergency Powers' Legislation," 22 Parliamentary Aff. 216, 220 (1969).

65. Frederick Watkins, *The Failure of Constitutional Emergency Powers Under the German Republic* (Cambridge, Mass.: Harvard University Press, 1939), 135–36.

66. Preece, "Emergency Powers' Legislation," *supra* n. 64.

67. For a comparison with the United States, see James G. Carr, "Wiretapping in West Germany," 29 Am. J. Comp. L.607 (1981).

68. Privacy of Communications Case (the Klass Case), 30 BVerfGE 1 (1970); Murphy and Tanenhaus, *Comparative Constitutional Law, supra* n. 18 at 659; see also Kommers, *Constitutional Jurisprudence, supra* n. 16 at 230–31.

69. Murphy and Tanenhaus, *Comparative Constitutional Law, supra* n. 18 at 662.

70. 2 E.H.R.R. 214 (1978); see "A Report," *supra* n. 53 at 27.

71. The Klass Case, 30 BVerfGE 1 (1970); Murphy and Tanenhaus, *Comparative Constitutional Law, supra* n. 18 at 662–63; see also Kommers, *Constitutional Jurisprudence, supra* n. 16 at 136–37.

72. Murphy and Tanenhaus, *Comparative Constitutional Law, supra* n. 18 at 665.

73. See chapter 1, *supra*.

74. See chapter 3 *supra*.

75. Kenneth H. F. Dyson, "Left-Wing Political Extremism and the Problem of Tolerance in Western Germany," 10 Gov't. & Opposition 306 (1975); Kurt Sontheimer, "Anti-Democratic Tendencies in Contemporary German Thought," 11 Pol. Q. 268 (1969); Robert Burns and Wilfried von der Will, *Protest and Democracy in West Germany: Extraparliamentary Opposition and the Democratic Agenda* (New York: St. Martin's Press, 1988), 99–124; see also Klaus Wasmund, "The Political Socialization of West German Terrorists," in Peter H. Merkl, ed., *Political Violence and Terror: Motifs and Motivations* (Berkeley: University of California Press, 1986), 193–96.

76. Wasmund, "Political Socialization," *supra* n. 75 at 195.

77. Sontheimer, "German Thought," *supra* n. 75 at 270.

78. Mahler was the first German lawyer to file successfully a complaint with the European Commission on Human Rights. Jillian Becker, *Hitler's Children: The Story of the Baader–Meinhof Terrorist Gang* (Philadelphia: J. B. Lippincott Company, 1977), 31.

79. As quoted in Radvanyi, *Anti-Terrorist Legislation, supra* n. 2 at 30.

80. Peter Merkl has termed this the "fire-sale" theory. See Peter H. Merkl, "Rollerball or Neo-Nazi Violence?" in Peter H. Merkl, ed., *Political Violence and Terror: Motifs and Motivations* (Berkeley: University of California Press, 1986), 235–36.

81. For a general review, see Hans Josef Horchem, "Terrorism in West Germany: 1985," in Paul Wilkinson and Alasdair M. Stewart, eds., *Contemporary Research on Terrorism* (Aberdeen, Scotland: University of Aberdeen Press, 1987).

82. Hans Josef Horchem, "Terrorism and Government Response: The German Experience," 4 Jerusalem J. Int'l. Rel. 43 (1980).

83. David Th. Schiller, "The Economic Implications of Terrorism: A Case Study of the Federal Republic of Germany," 7 Terrrorism, Violence, and Insurgency Report 37 (1986); Christopher Hewitt, "The Cost of Terrorism: A Cross-National Study of Six Countries," 11 Terrorism 169 (1988).

84. Braunthal, *Political Loyalty*, *supra* n. 53.

85. Peter Weiss, "Joe McCarthy Is Alive and Well and Living in West Germany: Terror and Counter-Terror in the Federal Republic," 9 N.Y.U. J. Int'l. & Pol. 61, 69 (1976).

86. 1978 Yearbook, European Convention on Human Rights 418, 446; Kevin G. Horbatiuk, "Anti-Terrorism: The West German Approach," 3 Fordham Int'l. L. F. 167, 188 (1980).

87. For an overview, see Becker, *Hitler's Children*, *supra* n. 78 at 257–58.

88. Horchem, "Terrorism," *supra* n. 81 at 141.

89. David Th. Schiller, "Current Terrorist Activities in Germany," 5 Terrorism, Violence, and Insurgency Report 14, 16 (1985).

90. Horchem, "Terrorism," *supra* n. 81 at 147.

91. Merkl, "Rollerball," *supra* n. 80 at 236.

92. Horchem, "Terrorism in West Germany," *supra* n. 81 at 9.

93. Bruce Hoffman, *Right-Wing Terrorism in West Germany* (Santa Monica, Calif.: Rand Corporation, 1986), P-7270, 24.

94. Merkl, "*Rollerball*," *supra* n. 80 at 242.

95. Hoffman, "Right-Wing Terrorism," *supra* n. 93 at 3.

96. Merkl, "*Rollerball*," *supra* n. 80 at 241.

97. Id. at 243.

98. For a study of the controversy surrounding one aspect of internal security policy, *see* Braunthal, *Political Loyalty*, *supra* n. 53.

99. Grant Wardlaw, *Political Terrorism: Theory, Tactics, and Countermeasures* (Cambridge: Cambridge University Press, 1982), 121.

100. Weiss, "Joe McCarthy," *supra* n. 85 at 61–62; see also John Dornberg, *International Herald Tribune*, Supplement, April 1979; Jane Kramer, (20), The New Yorker, 44 (1978).

101. Joseph W. Bishop, Jr., "Can Democracy Defend Itself Against Terrorism?" 65 Commentary 55 (1978).

102. U.S. Congress, House, Committee on the Judiciary, *Report on Domestic and International Terrorism*, Hearings Before the Subcommittee on Civil and Constitutional Rights, 97th Cong. 1st sess., April 1981 (Washington, D..C.: Government Printing Office, 1981), 4.

103. U.S. Congress, Senate, Committee on the Judiciary, *West Germany's Political Response to Terrorism*, Hearings before the Subcommittee on Criminal Laws and Procedures, 95th Cong. 2d sess., April 26, 1978 (Washington, D.C.: Government Printing Office, 1978), 9–10.

104. Id.

105. Id. at 8.

106. See Braunthal, *Political Loyalty*, *supra* n. 53.

107. As quoted in Donald P. Kommers, "Expression and Security in the Federal Republic of Germany: A Constitutional Analysis," paper prepared for the Workshop on German Terrorism, sponsored by the Center for the Study of Civil Rights and Conference Group on German Politics, Center for Continuing Education, University of Notre Dame, February 28–March 2, 1979, 6.

108. Kenneth H. F. Dyson, "Anti-Communism in the Federal Republic of Germany: The Case of the 'Berufsverbot,'" 28 Parliamentary Aff. 51, 54 (1974).

109. Kommers, "Expression and Security," *supra* n. 107 at 7; see also Gerard Braunthal, "Public Order and Civil Liberties," in Gordon Smith, William E. Paterson and Peter H. Merkl, eds., *Developments in West German Politics* (Durham, NC: Duke

University Press, 1989), 312, see also Kommers, *Constitutional Jurisprudence supra* n. 16 at 236.

110. Kommers, "Expression and Security," *supra* n. 107 at 5–6.

111. Braunthal, *Political Loyalty*, *supra* n. 53. Braunthal also notes, however, that the data are unreliable. These figures do not include instances of "banning" in the private sector, also discussed in Braunthal.

112. Peter J. Katzenstein, *Policy and Politics in West Germany: The Growth of a Semi-Sovereign State* (Philadelphia: Temple University Press, 1987), 271.

113. Dyson, "Berufsverbot," *supra* n. 108 at 53.

114. Civil Servant Loyalty Case, 39 BVerfGE 334 (1975). As reprinted in Donald P. Kommers, "Basic Rights and Constitutional Review," in C. C. Schweitzer et al., eds., *Politics and Government in the Federal Republic of Germany, Basic Documents* (New York: St. Martin's Press, 1984), 131–132; see also Kommers, *Constitutional Jurisprudence, supra* n. 16 at 232–35.

115. Kommers, "Expression and Security," *supra* n. 107 at 23–24; Katzenstein, *Policy and Politics, supra* n. 112 at 271; Kommers, *Constitutional Jurisprudence, supra* n. 16 at 238.

116. Radvanyi, *Anti-Terrorist Legislation, supra* n. 2 at 64.

117. As quoted in id. at 50.

118. See, e.g., Weiss, "Joe McCarthy," *supra* n. 85 at 61; Dyson, "Berufsverbot," *supra* n. 108 at 51; Dyson, "Left-Wing Extremism," *supra* n. 75 at 306; Martin Oppenheimer, "The Criminalization of Political Dissent in the Federal Republic of Germany" 2 Contemp. Crises 97 (1978).

119. Oppenheimer, "Criminalization," *supra* n. 118 at 99 (emphasis in original); Katzenstein, *Policy and Politics, supra* n. 112 at 263.

120. See "A Report," *supra* n. 53 at 34.

121. Radvanyi, *Anti-Terrorist Legislation, supra* n. 2 at 66.

122. *See* chapter 1, *supra*; Sontheimer, "German Thought," *supra* n. 75 at 271.

123. See, e.g., Vitarelli v. Seaton, 253 F.2d 338 (1958), *rev'd on other grds*, 359 U.S. 535 (1959).

124. See id. at 341; Cole v. Young, 351 U.S. 536 (1956).

125. Horbatiuk, "West German Approach," *supra* n. 86 at 172.

126. Id. at 173.

127. Wardlaw, *Political Terrorism, supra* n. 99 at 124.

128. Braunthal, *Political Loyalty, supra* n. 53.

129. See Kommers, "Expression and Security," *supra* n. 107 at 27.

130. See *The Penal Code of the Federal Republic of Germany*, trans. Joseph J. Darby (Littleton, Colo.: Fred B. Rothman and Co., 1987), 19.

131. See chapter 3, *supra*. For a similar criticism of the now repealed Section 88a, see Sebastian Cobler, *Law, Order and Politics in West Germany*, trans. Francis McDonagh (Harmondsworth, Eng.: Penguin, 1978), 93.

132. See chapter 3 *supra*.

133. Peter J. Katzenstein, "West Germany's Internal Security Policy: State and Terrorism in the 1970s and 1980s" (unpub. ms.), 50.

134. Id.

135. Radvanyi, *Anti-Terrorist Legislation, supra* n. 2 at 82; Wardlaw, *Political Terrorism, supra* n. 99 at 125.

136. Wardlaw, Political Terrorism, *supra* n. 99.

137. Radvanyi, *Anti-Terrorist Legislation, supra* n. 2 at 77.

138. See Hopt v. Utah, 110 U.S. 574 (1884).

139. See Illinois v. Allen, 397 U.S. 337 (1970).

140. See id.; Snyder v. Massachusetts, 291 U.S. 97 (1934).

141. Contact Ban Case, 49 BVerfGE 24 (1978); Horbatiuk, "West German Approach," *supra* n. 86 at 184 n 109.

142. Weiss, "Joe McCarthy," *supra* n. 85 at 79.

143. Horbatiuk, "West German Approach," *supra* n. 86 at 182.

144. Wardlaw, *Political Terrorism*, *supra* n. 99 at 125.

145. The Federal Constitutional Court, in the Contact Ban Case, 49 BVerfGE 24 (1978), found parts of the original ban lacking in standards to guide officials. In response, the Bundestag enacted changes identifying when exclusion is possible. See Kommers, *Constitutional Jurisprudence*, *supra* n. 16 at 239.

146. Radvanyi, *Anti-Terrorist Legislation*, *supra* n. 2 at 87.

147. Id. at 88.

148. Id.

149. See chapter 3, *supra*.

150. Braunthal, *Public Loyalty*, *supra* n. 53.

151. Dyson, "Left-Wing Extremism," *supra* n. 75 at 321–22.

152. Dyson, "Berufsverbot," *supra* n. 108 at 65.

153. Heinrich Böll, "seven and twenty years later," in "The Poems of Heinrich Böll Since 1972," trans Robert C. Conrad in collaboration with Ralph Ley. 12 University of Dayton Review 5, 6 (1985).

154. Dyson, "Left-Wing Extremism," *supra* n. 75 at 306.

CONCLUSION

1. Nathaniel Ward, "The Simple Cobbler of Aggawam," reprinted in Alpheus T. Mason, Ed., *Free Government in the Making: Readings in American Political Thought*, 3rd ed. (New York: Oxford University Press, 1965), 57, 58.

2. Clinton Rossiter, ed., *The Federalist Papers* (New York: New American Library, 1961), No. 1, 33.

3. Carl J. Friedrich, *Constitutional Reason of State* (Providence, R. I.: Brown University Press, 1957), 13.

4. Niccoló Machiavelli, *Discourses*. trans. Bernard Crick (Harmondsworth, Eng.: Penguin Books, 1970), ch. 34.

5. For a discussion of this point, see chapter 1, *supra*. The term is taken from Herbert J. Spiro, *Government by Constitution* (New York: Random House, 1959), 437.

6. Robert A. Dahl, *A Preface to Democratic Theory* (Chicago: University of Chicago Press, 1956), 143.

7. Alasdair MacIntyre, *The New Statesman*, July 19, 1974. Also as quoted in Paul Arthur, *Political Realities* (Burnt Mill, Eng.: Longman Group, 1980).

Selected References

GENERAL REFERENCES

Anastoplo, George. *The Constitutionalist*. Dallas, Tex.: Southern Methodist University Press, 1971.

Barber, Sotirios. *On What the Constitution Means*. Baltimore, Md.: Johns Hopkins University Press, 1984.

Becker, Carl L. *The Declaration of Independence: A Study in the History of Political Ideas*. New York: Alfred A. Knopf, 1941.

Bessette, Joseph M., and Jeffrey Tulis. *The Presidency in a Constitutional Order*. Baton Rouge: Louisiana State University Press, 1981.

Brest, Paul. "The Fundamental Rights Controversy: The Essential Contradictions of Normative Constitutional Scholarship." 90 Yale L. J. 1063 (1981).

Burton, Anthony. *Urban Terrorism: Theory, Practice and Response*. New York: The Free Press, 1975.

Cappalletti, Mauro. *Judicial Review in the Contemporary World*. New York: Bobbs-Merrill, 1971.

Corwin, Edward S. *A Constitution of Powers in a Secular State*. Charlottesville, Va.: Michie Press, 1951.

———. *The President: Office and Powers*. Rev. ed. New York: New York University Press, 1957.

———. *Total War and the Constitution*. New York: Alfred A. Knopf, 1947.

Crenshaw, Martha. *Terrorism, Legitimacy, and Power: The Consequences of Political Violence*. Middletown, Conn.: Wesleyan University Press, 1983.

Dahl, Robert A. *A Preface to Democratic Theory*. Chicago: University of Chicago Press, 1956.

Dicey, Albert V. *Law of the Constitution* [1885]. 8th ed. Indianapolis, Ind.: Liberty Classics, 1982.

Dworkin, Ronald. *Law's Empire*. Cambridge, Mass.: Harvard University Press, 1986.

———. *A Matter of Principle*. Cambridge, Mass.: Harvard University Press, 1985.

———. *Taking Rights Seriously*. Cambridge, Mass.: Harvard University Press, 1977.

Elster, Jon. *Ulysess and the Sirens: Studies in Rationality and Irrationality*. New York: Cambridge University Press, 1979.

———, ed. *The Multiple Self*. New York: Cambridge University Press, 1986.

Elster, Jon, and Rune Slagstad, eds. *Constitutionalism and Democracy: Studies in Rationality and Social Change*. New York: Cambridge University Press, 1988.

Ely, John Hart. *Democracy and Distrust: A Theory of Judicial Review*. Cambridge, Mass.: Harvard University Press, 1980.

———. "Discovering Fundamental Values—Supreme Court Forward 1978." 92 Harv. L. Rev. 27 (1978).

Evans, Alona E., and John F. Murphy. *The Legal Aspects of International Terrorism*. Lexington, Mass.: Lexington Books, 1980.

Fairman, Charles. *The Law of Martial Rule*. 2nd ed. Chicago: University of Chicago Press, 1940.

Fiss, Owen. "Conventionalism." 58 S. Cal. L. Rev. 177 (1985).

Flathman, Richard E. *Political Obligation*. New York: Atheneum, 1972.

Friedrich, Carl J. *Constitutional Government and Democracy: Theory and Practice in Europe and America*. Rev. ed. Waltham, Mass.: Blaisdell, 1950.

———. *Constitutional Reason of State: The Survival of the Constitutional Order*. Providence, R.I.: Brown University Press, 1957.

———. *Transcendent Justice*. Durham, N.C.: Duke University Press, 1964.

Fuller, Lon L. *The Morality of the Law*. 2nd ed. New Haven, Conn.: Yale University Press, 1969.

Fuller, Lon L., and Melvin A. Eisenberg. *Basic Contract Law*. 3rd ed. St. Paul, Minn.: West Publishing Co., 1972.

Hart, H. L. A. *The Concept of Law*. Oxford: Clarendon Press, 1961.

Kirchheimer, Otto. *Political Justice*. Princeton, N.J.: Princeton University Press, 1961.

Kitson, Frank. *Low Intensity Operations*. London: Faber and Faber, 1971.

Kuflick, Arthur. "The Inalienability of Autonomy." 13 Phil. & Pub. Aff. 271 (1984).

Laqueur, Walter. *The Age of Terrorism*. Boston: Little, Brown, 1987.

Locke, John. *Two Treatises of Government* [1690]. Ed. Peter Laslett. Cambridge: The University Press, 1960.

Loewenstein, Karl. *Political Power and the Governmental Process*. Chicago: University of Chicago Press, 1957.

———. "Reflections on the Value of Constitutions in Our Revolutionary Age." In Harry Eckstein and David E. Apter, eds. *Camparative Politics*. New York: The Free Press, 1963.

MacCormick, Neil. *Legal Reasoning and Legal Theory*. Oxford: Clarendon Press, 1978.

Machiavelli, Niccoló. *Discourses on the First Ten Books of Titus Livius*. Trans. and ed. Bernard Crick. Harmondsworth, Eng.: Penguin, 1970.

MacIntyre, Alasdair. *After Virtue*. Rev. ed. Notre Dame, Ind.: University of Notre Dame Press, 1984.

Madison, James, Alexander Hamilton, and John Jay. *The Federalist Papers*. Ed. Clinton Rossiter. New York: New American Library, 1961.

McIlwain, Charles H. *Constitutionalism: Ancient and Modern*. Rev. ed. Ithaca, N.Y.: Cornell University Press, 1947.

Moore, Michael. "Moral Reality." 1982 Wis. L. Rev. 1062 (1982).

———. "A Natural Law Theory of Interpretation." 58 S. Cal. L. Rev. 288 (1985).

Murphy, John F. *Punishing International Terrorists: the Legal Framework for Policy Initiatives*. Totowa, N.J.: Rowman and Allenheld, 1985.

Murphy, Walter F. "Constitutional Interpretation: The Art of the Historian, Magician, or Statesman?" 87 Yale L. J. 1752 (1978).

———. "An Ordering of Constitutional Values." 53 S. Cal. L. Rev. 744 (1980).

Murphy, Walter F., and Joseph Tanenhaus, eds. *Comparative Constitutional Law: Cases and Commentaries*. New York: St. Martin's Press, 1977.

O'Brien, Conor Cruise. *Herod: Reflections on Political Violence*. London: Hutchinson, 1978.

Parfit, Derek. *Reasons and Persons*. New York: Oxford University Press, 1986.

Perry, Michael J. *The Constitution, the Courts, and Human Rights*. New Haven, Conn.: Yale University Press, 1982.

———. *Morality, Politics, and Law*. New York: Oxford University Press, 1989.

Pious, Richard M. *The American Presidency*. New York: Basic Books, 1979.

Pyle, Christopher, and Richard M. Pious. *The President, Congress, and the Constitution*. New York: The Free Press, 1984.

Rankin, Robert S. *When Civil Law Fails*. Durham, N.C.: Duke University Press, 1939.

Rapoport, David C., and Yonah Alexander, eds. *The Morality of Terrorism: Religious and Secular Justifications*. New York: Pergamon Press, 1982.

Rossiter, Clinton. *Constitutional Dictatorship*. Princeton, N.J.: Princeton University Press, 1948.

Sartori, Giovanni. "Constitutionalism: A Preliminary Discussion." 56 Am. Pol. Sci. Rev. 853 (1962).

Schelling, Thomas C. *Choice and Consequence*. Cambridge, Mass.: Harvard University Press, 1984.

————. "Self-Command in Practice, in Policy, and in a Theory of Rational Choice." 74 Am. Econ. Rev. 1 (1984).

Schlesinger, Arthur M., Jr. *The Imperial Presidency*. New York: Popular Library, 1974.

Schmitt, Carl. *The Crisis of Parliamentary Democracy*. Trans. Ellen Kennedy. Cambridge, Mass.: MIT Press, 1985.

————. *Die Diktatur*. Munich: Duncker and Humblot, 1923.

————. *Legalität und Legitimität*. Munich: Duncker and Humblot, 1932.

————. *Political Romanticism*. Trans. Guy Oakes. Cambridge, Mass.: MIT Press, 1986.

————. *Political Theology*. Trans. George Schwab. Cambridge, Mass.: MIT Press, 1985.

Schwab, George. *The Challenge of the Exception*. Berlin: Duncker and Humblot, 1970.

Smith, Rogers. *Liberalism and American Constitutional Law*. Cambridge, Mass.: Harvard University Press, 1985.

Spiro, Herbert J. *Government by Constitution*. New York: Random House, 1959.

Sutherland, Arthur E. *Constitutionalism in America*. New York: Blaisdell, 1965.

Tribe, Laurence. *Constitutional Choices*. Cambridge, Mass.: Harvard University Press, 1985.

————. "The Puzzling Persistence of Process-Based Theories of Interpretation." 89 Yale L. J. 1063 (1980).

Vile, M. J. C. *Constitutionalism and the Separation of Powers*. London: Oxford University Press, 1967.

Wardlaw, Grant. *Political Terrorism: Theory, Tactics, and Counter-measures*. Cambridge: Cambridge University Press, 1982.

Watkins, Frederick. "The Problem of Constitutional Dictatorship." In Carl J. Friedrich and Edward S. Mason, eds. *Public Policy*. Cambridge, Mass.: Harvard University Press, 1940.

Wheare, Kenneth. *Modern Constitutions*. London: Oxford University Press, 1966.

White, James Boyd. *When Words Lose Their Meaning*. Chicago: University of Chicago Press, 1984.

Wilkinson, Paul. *Political Terrorism*. London: Macmillan, 1974.

————. *Terrorism and the Liberal State*. London: Macmillan, 1977.

————. ed. *British Perspectives on Terrorism*. London: George Allen and Unwin, 1981.

Wood, Gordon S. *The Creation of the American Republic, 1776–1787*. New York: W. W. Norton, 1972.

Wormuth, Francis. *The Origins of Modern Constitutionalism*. New York: Harper, 1949.

————. *The Royal Prerogative 1603–1699*. Ithaca, N.Y.: Cornell University Press, 1939.

IRELAND AND NORTHERN IRELAND

Arthur, Paul. *Political Realities: The Government and Politics of Northern Ireland*. Burnt Mill, Eng.: Longman Group, 1980.

Beckett, J. C. *The Making of Modern Ireland.* New York: Alfred A. Knopf, 1966.

Bell, Geoffrey. *The Protestants of Ulster.* London: Pluto Press, 1978.

Bell, J. Bowyer. *The Secret Army: The IRA 1916–77.* Rev. ed. Cambridge, Mass.: MIT Press, 1983.

———. *A Time of Terror: How Democratic Societies Respond to Revolutionary Violence.* New York: Basic Books, 1978.

Bonner, David. "Combating Terrorism: The Jellicoe Approach." 1983 Pub. L. 224 (1983).

Bowden, Thomas. *The Breakdown of Public Security: The Case of Ireland 1916–21 and Palestine 1936–39.* London: Sage Publications, 1977.

Boyle, Kevin. "Human Rights and Political Resolution in Northern Ireland." 9 Yale J. World Pub. Ord. 165 (1982).

Boyle, Kevin, Tom Hadden, and Paddy Hillyard. *Law and State: The Case of Northern Ireland.* London: Martin Robertson & Co., 1975.

———. *Ten Years On in Northern Ireland.* London: The Cobden Trust, 1980.

Burton, Frank. *The Politics of Legitimacy: Struggles in a Belfast Community.* London: Routledge and Kegan Paul, 1978.

Calvert, Harry. *Constitutional Law in Northern Ireland: A Study in Regional Government.* London: Stevens and Sons, 1968.

Carleton, Charles. "Judging Without Consensus: The Diplock Courts in Northern Ireland." 3 Law & Pol'y. Q. 225 (1981).

Carroll, Don W. "The Search for Justice in Northern Ireland." 6 N.Y.U. J. Int'l. Law & Pol. 28 1973.

Coogan, Timothy. *The IRA.* Rev. ed. London: Fontana Press, 1980.

Devlin, Bernadette. *The Price of My Soul.* New York: Alfred A. Knopf, 1969.

Edwards, O. Dudley. *The Sins of Our Fathers: Roots of Conflict in Northern Ireland.* Dublin: Gill and Macmillan, 1970.

Farrell, Michael. *Northern Ireland: The Orange State.* London: Pluto Press, 1980.

Finn, John E. "Public Support for Emergency (Antiterrorist) Legislation in Northern Ireland: A Preliminary Analysis." 10 Terrorism: An International Journal 113 (1987).

Foley, Thomas P. "Public Security and Individual Freedom: The Dilemma of Northern Ireland." 8 Yale J. World Pub. Ord. 284 (1982).

Greer, Desmond S. "The Admissibility of Confessions Under the Northern Ireland (Emergency Provisions) Act." 31 N.I. L. Q. 205 (1980).

Greer, Steven C. "Supergrasses and the Legal System" 102 Law Q. Rev. 198 (1986).

Harvey, Richard. *Diplock and the Assault on Civil Liberties.* London: The Haldane Society, 1981.

Heskin, Kenneth. *Northern Ireland: A Psychological Analysis.* Dublin: Gill and Macmillan, 1980.

Hogan, Gerard, and Clive Walker. *Political Violence and the Law in Ireland.* Manchester, Eng.: Manchester University Press, 1989.

Holland, Jack. *Too Long a Sacrifice: Life and Death in Northern Ireland Since 1969.* London: Penguin Press, 1982.

Hull, Roger H. *The Irish Triangle: Conflict in Northern Ireland.* Princeton, N.J.: Princeton University Press, 1976.

Jennings, Anthony, ed. *Justice Under Fire: The Abuse of Civil Liberties in Northern Ireland.* London: Pluto Press, 1988.

Johnson, Paul. *Ireland: A Concise History From the Twelfth Century to the Present Day.* London: Granada Press, 1981.

Lowry, David R. "Draconian Powers: The New British Approach to Pretrial Detention of Suspected Terrorists." 5 Col. Hum. Rts. L. Rev. 185 (1976).

———. "Internment: Detention Without Trial in Northern Ireland." 5 Hum. Rts. 261 (1976).

Magee, John. *Northern Ireland: Crisis and Conflict*. London: Routledge and Kegan Paul, 1974.

McCann, Eamonn. *War and an Irish Town*. London: Penguin Books, 1974.

McGuffin, John. *Internment*. Tralee, Ireland: Anvil Press, 1973.

Morgan, Michael. "How the British Created the Provos." 275 Fortnight: An Independent Review for Northern Ireland 12 (1989).

Moxon-Browne, Edward. "Alienation: The Case of Catholics in Northern Ireland." 1 & 2 J. Pol. Sci. 74 (1986).

———. "The Water and the Fish: Public Opinion and the Provisional IRA in Northern Ireland." 5 Terrorism: An International Journal 41 (1981).

O'Brien, Conor Cruise. *States of Ireland*. London: Hutchinson Press, 1972.

Palley, Claire. "The Evolution, Disintegration, and Possible Reconstruction of the Northern Irish Constitution." 1 Anglo-Am. L. Rev. 368 (1972).

Rose, Richard. *Governing Without Consensus: An Irish Perspective*. Boston: Beacon Press, 1971.

Scorer, Catherine, and Patricia Hewitt. *The Prevention of Terrorism Act: The Case for Repeal*. London: The Cobden Trust, 1981.

Spjut, R. J. "Internment and Detention Without Trial in Northern Ireland 1971–1975: Ministerial Policy and Practice." 49 Mod. L. Rev. 712 (1986).

Stewart, A. T. Q. *The Narrow Ground*. London: Faber and Faber, 1977.

Sweetman, Rosita. *On Our Knees*. London: Pan Books, 1972.

Taylor, Peter. *Beating the Terrorists? Interrogation at Omagh, Gough, and Castlereagh*. London: Penguin Books, 1980.

Townshend, Charles. *Political Violence in Ireland: Government and Resistance Since 1848*. Oxford: Clarendon Press, 1983.

Walker, Clive. "Emergency Arrest Powers." 36 N.I. L. Q. 145 (1985).

———. *The Prevention of Terrorism in British Law*. Manchester, Eng.: Manchester University Press, 1986.

Government Publications

The Review of the Operation of the Northern Ireland (Emergency Provisions) Act 1978. Cmnd. 9222. London: HMSO, 1984. (Baker Report)

Report of the Committee of Inquiry into Police Interrogation Procedures in Northern Ireland. Cmnd. 7497. London: HMSO, 1979. (Bennett Report)

Report of the Commission on Disturbances in Northern Ireland. Cmnd. 532. Belfast: HMSO, 1975. (Cameron Report)

Review of the Operation of the Prevention of Terrorism (Temporary Provisions) Act 1984. Cmnd. 264. London: HMSO, 1987. (Colville Report)

Report of the Enquiry into Allegations Against the Security Forces of Physical Brutality in Northern Ireland Arising Out of Events on the 9th August. Cmnd. 4823. London: HMSO, 1971. (Compton Report)

Report of the Commission to Consider Legal Procedures to Deal with Terrorist Activities in Northern Ireland. Cmnd. 5185. London: HMSO, 1972. (Diplock Report)

Report of a Commission to Consider, in the Context of Civil Liberties and Human Rights, Measures to Deal with Terrorism in Northern Ireland. Cmnd. 5847. London: HMSO, 1975. (Gardiner Report)

Report of the Advisory Committee on Police in Northern Ireland. Cmnd. 535. London: HMSO, 1969. (Hunt Report)

Review of the Operation of the Prevention of Terrorism (Temporary Provisions) Act 1976. Cmnd. 8803. London: HMSO, 1983. (Jellicoe Report)

Report of the Commission of the Privy Councillors Appointed to Consider Authorized Procedures for the Interrogation of Persons Suspected of Terrorism. Cmnd. 4901. London: HMSO, 1972. (Parker Report)

Report of Tribunal of Inquiry on Violence and Civil Disturbances in Northern Ireland in 1969. Cmnd. 566. Belfast: HMSO, 1972. (Scarman Report)

Review of the Operation of the Prevention of Terrorism (Temporary Provisions) Act 1974–76. Cmnd. 7324. London: HMSO, 1978. (Shackleton Report)

Report of the Tribunal Appointed to Inquire into the Events of Sunday, 30th January 1972, Which Led to Loss of Life in Connection with the Processions in Londonderry on That Day. H.L. No. 101, H.C. NO. 220. London: HMSO, 1972. (Widgery Report)

WEIMAR GERMANY AND WEST GERMANY

Becker, Jillian. *Hitler's Children: The Story of the Baader–Meinhof Gang.* Philadelphia: J. B. Lippincott Company, 1977.

Bendersky, Joseph W. *Carl Schmitt: Theorist for the Reich.* Princeton, N.J.: Princeton University Press, 1983.

Blachly, Frederick F., and Miriam E. Oatman. *The Government and Administration of Germany.* Baltimore, Md.: Johns Hopkins University Press, 1928.

Braunthal, Gerard. *Political Loyalty and Public Service in West Germany: The 1972 Decree Against Radicals and Its Consequences.* Amherst: University of Massachusetts Press, 1990.

———. "Public Order and Civil Liberties," in Gordon Smith, William E. Paterson, and Peter H. Merkl, eds., *Developments in West German Politics.* Durham, N.C.: Duke University Press, 1989.

Brecht, Arnold. *Federalism and Regionalism in Germany: The Division of Prussia.* New York: Oxford University Press, 1945.

———. *Prelude to Silence: The End of the German Republic.* New York: Howard Fertig, 1968.

Bunn, Ronald F. *German Politics and the Spiegel Affair: A Case Study of the Bonn System.* Baton Rouge: Louisiana State University Press, 1968.

Carr, James G. "Wiretapping in West Germany." 29 Am. J. Comp. L. 607 (1981).

Carr, William. *A History of Germany 1815–1945.* 2nd ed. New York: St. Martin's Press, 1979.

Clark, R. T. *The Fall of the German Republic.* London: George Allen and Unwin, 1935.

Cobler, Sebastian. *Law, Order and Politics in West Germany.* Trans. Francis McDonagh. Harmondsworth, Eng.: Penguin, 1978.

Conway, John, trans. and ed. *The Path to Dictatorship.* New York: Praeger, 1967.

Darby, Joseph J., trans. and ed. *The Penal Code of the Federal Republic of Germany.* Littleton, Colo.: Fred B. Rothman and Co., 1987.

Diehl, James M. *Paramilitary Politics in Weimar Germany*. Bloomington: Indiana University Press, 1977.

Dyson, Kenneth H. F. "Anti-Communism in the Federal Republic of Germany: The Case of the 'Berufsverbot.'" 28 Parliamentary Aff. 51 (1974).

———. "Left-Wing Political Extremism and the Problem of Tolerance in Western Germany." 10 Gov't. & Opposition 306 (1975).

Edinger, Lewis. *Politics in West Germany*. Boston: Little, Brown, 1977.

Eksteins, Modris. *The Limits of Reason: The German Democratic Press and the Collapse of Weimar Democracy*. London: Oxford University Press, 1975.

Eyck, Erich. *A History of the Weimar Republic*. Trans. Harlan P. Hanson and Robert G. L. Waite. 2 vols. Cambridge, Mass.: Harvard University Press, 1963.

Friedrich, Carl J. "The Development of the Executive Power in Germany." 27 Am. Pol. Sci. Rev. 185 (1933).

———. "Dictatorship in Germany?" 9 Foreign Aff. 118 (1930).

———. "The Issue of Judicial Review in Germany." 43 Pol. Sci. Q. 188 (1928).

Gay, Peter. *Weimar Culture: The Outsider as Insider*. New York: Harper and Row, 1968.

Golay, John Ford. *The Founding of the Federal Republic of Germany*. Chicago: University of Chicago Press, 1958.

Halperin, William S. *Germany Tried Democracy*. Hamden, Conn.: Archon Books, 1963.

Heneman, Harlow J. *The Growth of Executive Power in Germany*. Westport, Conn.: Greenwood Press, 1974.

Hoffman, Bruce. *Right-Wing Terrorism in West Germany*. Santa Monica, Calif.: Rand Corporation, 1986, P-7270.

Holborn, Louise W., Gwendolen M. Carter, and John H. Herz, eds. *German Constitutional Documents Since 1871*. New York: Praeger, 1970.

Horbatiuk, Kevin G. "Anti-Terrorism: The West German Approach." 3 Fordham Int'l. L. F. 167 (1980).

Horchem, Hans Josef. "Terrorism and Government Response: The German Experience." 4 Jerusalem J. Int'l. Rel. 43 (1980).

———. "Terrorism in West Germany: 1985." In Paul Wilkinson and Alasdair M. Stewart, eds., *Contemporary Research on Terrorism*. Aberdeen, Scotland: University of Aberdeen Press, 1987.

Hucko, Elmar M., ed. *The Democratic Tradition: Four German Constitutions*. Leamington Spa, Eng.: Berg Publishers, 1987.

Katzenstein, Peter J. *Policy and Politics in West Germany: The Growth of a Semi-Sovereign State*. Philadelphia: Temple University Press, 1987.

Kommers, Donald P. *The Constitutional Jurisprudence of the Federal Republic of Germany*. Durham, N.C.: Duke University Press, 1989.

———. *Judicial Politics in West Germany: A Study of the Federal Constitutional Court*. Beverly Hills, Calif.: Sage Publications, 1976.

Krauss, Herbert. *The Crisis of German Democracy*. Princeton, N.J.: Princeton University Press, 1932.

Lepsius, M. Ranier. "From Fragmented Party Democracy to Government by Emergency Decree and the National Socialist Takeover: Germany." In Juan J. Linz and Alfred Stepan, eds., *The Breakdown of Democratic Regimes: Europe*. Baltimore, Md.: Johns Hopkins University Press, 1978.

Litchfield, Edward H. "Political Objectives and Legal Bases of Occupation Government." In Edward H. Litchfield, ed., *Governing Postwar Germany*. Ithaca, N.Y.: Cornell University Press, 1953.

Loewenstein, Karl. "Dictatorship and the German Constitution: 1933–1937." 4 U. Chi. L. Rev. 537 (1936).

———. "Law in the Third Reich." 45 Yale L. J. 779 (1936).

———. "Legislative Control of Political Extremism in European Democracies." 38 Colum. L. Rev. 591–622, 725–774 (1938).

———. "Militant Democracy and Fundamental Rights." 31 Am. Pol. Sci. Rev. 417–432, 638–658 (1937).

Mattern, Johannes. *Bavaria and the Reich: The Conflict over the Law for the Protection of the Republic.* Johns Hopkins University Studies in History and Political Science. Vol. 41. Baltimore, Md.: Johns Hopkins University Press, 1923.

———. *The Constitutional Jurisprudence of the Weimar Republic.* Baltimore, Md.: Johns Hopkins University Press, 1928.

Merkl, Peter H. *The Origin of the West German Republic.* New York: Oxford University Press, 1963.

———, ed. *Political Violence and Terror: Motifs and Motivations.* Berkeley: University of California Press, 1986.

Nicholls, Anthony, and Erich Mathias, eds. *German Democracy and the Triumph of Hitler: Essays in Recent German History.* London: George Allen and Unwin, 1971.

Oppenheimer, Martin. "The Criminalization of Political Dissent in the Federal Republic of Germany." 2 Contemp. Crises 97 (1978).

Preece, R. J. C. "Federal German Emergency Powers' Legislation." 22 Parliamentary Aff. 216 (1969).

Radvanyi, Miklos. *Anti-Terrorist Legislation in the Federal Republic of Germany.* Washington, D.C.: Law Library, Library of Congress, 1979.

Rogers, Lindsay, Sanford Schwartz, and Nicholas Kaltschas. "German Political Institutions—Article 48." 47 Pol. Sci. Q. 576 (1932).

Schiller, David Th. "The Economic Implications of Terrorism: A Case Study of the Federal Republic of Germany." 7 Terrorism, Violence and Insurgency Report 37 (1986).

Schmitt, Carl J. *The Crisis of Parliamentary Democracy.* Trans. Ellen Kennedy. Cambridge, Mass.: MIT Press, 1985.

———. *Die Diktatur.* Munich: Duncker and Humblot, 1923.

———. *Legalität und Legitimität.* Munich: Duncker and Humblot, 1932.

———. *Political Romanticism.* Trans. Guy Oakes. Cambridge, Mass.: MIT Press, 1986.

———. *Political Theology.* Trans. George Schwab. Cambridge, Mass.: MIT Press, 1985.

Schoenbaum, David. *The Spiegel Affair.* New York: Doubleday, 1968.

Schwab, George. *The Challenge of the Exception.* Berlin: Duncker and Humblot, 1970.

Schweitzer, C. C. "Emergency Powers in the Federal Republic of Germany." 22 W. Pol. Q. 112 (1969).

Schweitzer, C. C., Detlev Kersten, Robert Spencer, R. Taylor Cole, Donald Kommers, Anthony Nicholls, eds. *Politics and Government in the Federal Republic of Germany, Basic Documents.* New York: St. Martin's Press, 1984.

Sontheimer, Kurt. "Anti-Democratic Tendencies in Contemporary German Thought." 11 Pol. Q. 268 (1969).

U.S. Congress, House, Committee on the Judiciary. *Report on Domestic and International Terrorism.* Hearings Before the Subcommittee on Civil and Constitutional Rights, 97th Cong. 1st sess., April 1981. Washington, D.C.: Government Printing Office, 1981.

U.S. Congress, Senate, Committee on the Judiciary. *West Germany's Political Response to Terrorism.* Hearings Before the Subcommittee on Criminal Laws and Procedures, 95th Cong. 2d sess., April 26, 1978. Washington, D.C.: Government Printing Office, 1978.

Watkins, Frederick. *The Failure of Constitutional Emergency Powers Under the German Republic.* Cambridge, Mass.: Harvard University Press, 1939.

Weiss, Peter. "Joe McCarthy Is Alive and Well and Living in West Germany: Terror and Counter-Terror in the Federal Republic," 9 N.Y.U. J. Int'l. L. & Pol. 61 (1976).

Index